PASSIONATE PILGRIMS

English Travelers to the World of the Desert Arabs

ALSO BY JAMES C. SIMMONS

The Novelist as Historian: Essays on the Victorian Historical Novel
Truman Capote: The Story of His Bizarre and Exotic Boyhood
(with Marie Rudisill)
The Secrets Men Keep (with Ken Druck)

PASSIONATE PILGRIMS

English Travelers to the World of the Desert Arabs

James C. Simmons

William Morrow and Company, Inc.
New York

Library of Congress Cataloging-in-Publication Data

Simmons, James C.
Passionate pilgrims.

Bibliography: p.
Includes index.
1. Arabian Peninsula—Description and travel.
2. Travelers—Arabian Peninsula. 3. Travelers—
Great Britain. I. Title.
DS204.5S55   1987   916.2'304   86-28627
ISBN 0-688-06559-7

Printed in the United States of America

First Edition

1   2   3   4   5   6   7   8   9   10

BOOK DESIGN BY BETH TONDREAU

ACKNOWLEDGMENTS

A number of people have made generous contributions of their time and expertise toward the writing of this book.

Howard Morhaim, both the world's best literary agent and a voracious reader on the Middle East, firmly believed in this project from the start. His patience and perseverance were instrumental in bringing this book to a successful conclusion.

The enthusiasm of Pat Golbitz, my editor at William Morrow and Company, was a constant inspiration.

This book profited enormously because a number of people graciously agreed to critique an earlier draft of the manuscript. Special thanks go to Professor William Rodgers of the Department of English at San Diego State University, who generously shared his expertise on Arabian exploration, history, and culture and lent me books from his personal library; Professors John Reardon and Marilyn Throne of the Department of English at Miami University, Oxford, Ohio; and, finally, Michelle Corbin of Gallipolis, Ohio. Pearl Hanig did a splendid job as my copy editor.

A special headache for anyone writing about the Middle East is the transliteration of Arabic words into English. For example, the name of the Libyan leader is variously spelled "Gaddafi" (*Time*), "Kaddafi" (*Newsweek*), "Qadhafi" (*Wall Street Journal*); "el-Qaddafi" (*New York Times*); "Kadafi" (*Los Angeles Times*); "Khadafy" (NBC News); or "Qaddafi" (ABC News).

The fact is that English orthography is not readily adaptable to Arabic phonetics. Written Arabic, like Hebrew, has no vowel signs. For Arabic place-names I relied upon the fifth edition of the *National Geographic Atlas of the World,* but in some cases have preferred the more familiar traditional English spellings of the better-known sites.

CONTENTS

CONTENTS

For Margaret Posey, M.D., and Edna Derrick

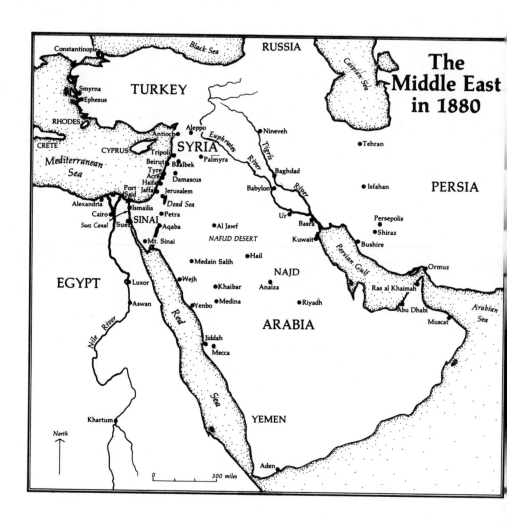

The Middle East in 1880

"Send Us a Lurens!"

On September 18, 1917, under a hot Arabian sun T. E. Lawrence patiently dug a hole beneath two steel ties next to a small bridge on the Damascus–Medina Railway. His white Bedouin robes were mud-stained. He was barefoot. The sand was heavily encrusted, making the digging difficult. Lawrence stripped the paper wrappings off the individual explosive plugs and kneaded them together like bread dough to make a shaking jelly of fifty pounds of explosive gelatin. It took him two hours to bury the charge. Next came the hard job of unrolling the thick wires from the detonator to a ridge fifty yards away, where he attached them to an electric plunger. The stiff wires scarred the wind-rippled surface with long lines "like the belly marks of preposterously narrow and heavy snakes." Lawrence and several Bedouin helpers carefully buried the wires and then with an empty canvas bag and billows swept the sand clean of all marks. The entire job took five hours.

Next Lawrence set up his Lewis machine gun and Stokes mortar, both operated by British soldiers, to obtain the best field of fire. His twenty-five heavily armed Nowasera Bedouins took up their positions some 150 yards from the tracks. And then they waited in the intense heat of the Arabian desert.

Before long a train appeared: two large engines, puffing great clouds of thick smoke and drawing ten coaches jammed with Turkish soldiers, many with rifles at the ready. Dozens of other soldiers rode precariously on the roofs in sandbag nests. Lawrence waited until the second engine was over the charge and then dropped his arm, the signal for his Bedouin helper to press the plunger. "There followed a terrific roar, and the line vanished behind a spouting column of black dust and smoke a hundred feet high and wide," Lawrence recalled later. "Out of the darkness came shattering crashes and long, loud metallic clangings of ripped steel, with many lumps of iron and plate. One entire wheel of a locomotive . . . sailed musically over our heads to fall slowly and heavily into the desert behind."

The machine gunner started methodically raking the roofs of the coaches, the bullets throwing up clouds of yellow chips from the planking. The Turkish soldiers there jerked around and pitched to the ground below. Scores of other soldiers poured out of the coaches, took cover behind the embankment, and opened a heavy fire on the Bedouins twenty yards away. Lawrence shouted to Sergeant W. H. Brook to get the Stokes mortar into action. The stocky Englishman dropped in the first shell, which exploded beyond the train in the desert. He quickly adjusted the elevating screw and slipped in another shell. The second round exploded among the Turks, killing twenty. "The survivors of the group broke out in a panic across the desert, throwing away their rifles and equipment as they ran," Lawrence wrote later. "This was the opportunity of the Lewis gunners. The sergeant grimly traversed drum after drum, till the open sand was littered with bodies."

While the fighting raged around him, Lawrence strolled over to Brook to ask how he was getting on. "The actual ambush of the train was an admirably planned affair carried out with a minimum of loss to us," an admiring Brook remembered later. "Lawrence's bearing made us feel that the whole thing was a picnic."

The Bedouins charged the train, cutting down the handful of Turks who still resisted, and then exuberantly began plundering the coaches. Lawrence wandered along the length of the ruined train, checking the damage. The second engine had taken the full brunt of the mine and was "a blanched pile of smoking iron." The crash had caved in the first coach, a hospital car, and smashed the bodies into a bloody heap near the rear. Most of the other coaches were hopelessly shattered. A group of captured Austrian officers and soldiers appealed to Lawrence for quarter. He told them not to worry, that a Turkish force was already on its way. But a few minutes later an Austrian officer recklessly pulled a hidden revolver and fired at the Bedouins. The enraged Arabs immediately shot them all.

The train had been packed with civilians and the families of officers returning to Damascus. A crowd of thirty women stood to one side, their veils off, shrieking loudly. The ground about the train was littered with dozens of mattresses and carpets, piles of cooking pots, blankets, bags of clothing, and all manner of household effects. The Bedouins were beside themselves in an orgy of looting. "The valley was a weird sight," Lawrence recalled later. "The Arabs, gone raving mad, were rushing about at top speed bareheaded and half-naked, screaming, shooting into the air, clawing at one another nail and fist, while they burst open [the coaches] and staggered back and forward with immense bales, which they ripped [open] by the railside, and tossed through, smashing what they did not want. . . . The Arabs looted to their absolute fill. Camels had become common property. Each man frantically loaded the nearest with what it could carry and shooed it away westward into the void, while he turned to his next fancy."

A fresh contingent of Turkish troops arrived from the nearby garrison at Mudauwra and immediately opened fire on the Arabs. Lawrence's Bedouins and their heavily laden camels galloped into the desert. "Victory always undid an Arab force," Lawrence observed later. "We were no longer a raiding party but a stumbling baggage caravan, loaded to the breaking point with enough household goods to make rich an Arab tribe for years."

Two days later Lawrence and his Bedouins reached the Red Sea port of Aqaba, the center for the Arab Revolt. The sight of their camels loaded almost to the breaking point with valuable plunder excited feverish envy among the other Bedouin tribes. The details of Lawrence's spectacular raid at Mudauwra spread rapidly. The sheik of the Beni Atiyeh Bedouins sent an urgent message to Faisal, the leader of the Arab Revolt: "Send us a lurens and we will blow up trains with it."

The cry went up across western Arabia:

"SEND US A LURENS!"

CHAPTER I

Napoleon in Egypt: Lifting the Islamic Veil

In the early dawn of May 19, 1798, General Napoleon Bonaparte stood on the deck of his flagship, *L'Orient,* in the harbor at Toulon and surveyed his armada of warships. Stretched before him were 13 ships of the line, mounting 1,026 cannons, and 42 brigs, frigates, and other vessels. There were 150 transports carrying 17,000 troops, an equal number of sailors and marines, 1,000 pieces of artillery, 100,000 rounds of ammunition, 700 horses, and almost 600 vehicles. *L'Orient* was a floating fortress mounting 120 cannons in three tiers. The armada slowly made its way out of Toulon's harbor and struggled against the wind toward Corsica. Within a few days three smaller convoys had swelled the ranks of the fleet to 400 ships and 55,000 men.

Only Napoleon and a handful of officers knew their destination: Egypt. The armada arrived off Alexandria on July 1. The Egyptians onshore "looked at the horizon and could not see water, but only sky and ships," one Arab chronicler noted. "They were seized by unimaginable terror." The next day Napoleon landed his troops and embarked upon what a later historian called the "most seminal event in the history of the modern Islamic world."

In May 1798 Napoleon was twenty-eight years old and the idol of all France. He had defeated his foes on every battlefield and recently had won major victories against Austria and Italy. The central European states were safely contained. Spain was helpless. Only England stood against him. Napoleon needed new victories to consolidate his power and extend his fame. Egypt beckoned for two reasons. This Corsican genius intuitively understood that the strategic importance of Egypt lay not in its people or its natural resources but rather in its pivotal position as a land bridge between England and Asia. Throughout the eighteenth century French commercial interests had dominated the Mediterranean region. Beyond, the fabulous markets of British India beckoned. Napoleon knew that England was invulnerable to invasion. But with Egypt safely in his grasp, he could threaten India, the largest and most important of the British colonies, and at the same time revolutionize world trade. "This battle will decide the fate of the world," he grandiosely promised General Joachim Murat.

There was a second reason that brought Napoleon to the Egyptian shores. From the time of St. Louis's Crusade in the thirteenth century France had historically taken a great interest in Egypt. Napoleon saw himself as a modern heir to the Crusaders of the past and was convinced that his destiny lay in the Middle East. "Europe is a molehill," he told his secretary, L.A.F. de Bourrienne, mindful that Alexander the Great had already conquered the East before his twenty-ninth birthday. "Everything wears out. My glory is already past. This tiny Europe does not offer enough of it. We must go to the East. All great glory has always been gained there."

On July 2 the French Army stormed ashore on the beaches west of Alexandria. The city offered little resistance and within forty-eight hours was safely under French control. Napoleon quickly dispatched 18,000 troops to seize the delta towns of Damanhur and Rosetta. For the first time since the Crusades a European country had launched a military invasion against the heartland of the Islamic world and, nearly unopposed, marched in conquest.

Egypt in 1798 was largely unknown to Europe. A handful of Western travelers and merchants had visited its chief cities of Alexandria and Cairo, and fewer still had ventured up the Nile River to explore the lands beyond. Egypt at the time of Napoleon's landing was a thinly populated country of some 2.5 million people (compared with a population of 45 million today), 250,000 of whom lived in Cairo. Virtually no scientific information on Egypt existed in Europe at the time.

The country was nominally under the control of the sultan in Constantinople, who appointed a pasha to rule in his name. In actual fact, the real power lay with the Mameluke beys, or princes, who ruled the twenty-four Egyptian provinces. The term *mameluke* is an Arabic word meaning "bought man." The Mamelukes dated back to 1230, when the sultan Ashraf Moussa bought 12,000 young men in the Caucasus Mountains in southern Russia to form the elite corps of his army. Twenty years later the Mamelukes killed Moussa and took over Egypt. They continued to hold most of the agricultural land, plundered the people through capricious and burdensome taxation, and lived in splendid palaces in Cairo. The Mamelukes rarely had children and replenished their numbers each year through the purchase of several thousand eight- to ten-year-old boys from the Caucasus Mountains, whom they raised as warriors. Egypt in 1798 was racked by vicious political intrigues and grievously oppressed by an arrogant caste that had long ago lost touch with the peoples of the region.

On July 20, 1798, the Egyptian Army of 6,000 Mameluke warriors on horseback and some 10,000 foot soldiers went up against a French force of 25,000 soldiers ten miles from the pyramids. Before the attack Napoleon reportedly addressed a group of his soldiers, pointing to the great bulks of the pyramids on the horizon and saying, "Men, forty centuries look down upon you."

Curious survivors of the Middle Ages, the Mamelukes, like medieval knights, rode richly caparisoned horses and wore elaborate body armor heavily encrusted with precious jewels. Each carried four or five pistols stuck in his belt. The two armies came together. The Mamelukes bravely hurled themselves against the French positions, swinging their razor-sharp sabers and effortlessly cutting off heads. It was a grand but hopeless gesture. The Mamelukes quickly learned the truth of Napoleon's saying "God fights on the side with the most cannons." A French infantry officer, Captain Vertray, later wrote a vivid description of the Battle of the Pyramids.

General Reynier gave the command, "To your ranks!" and in the twinkling of an eye we formed a square six men deep, ready to sustain the shock. This movement had been carried out with really remarkable precision and coolness. . . . The soldiers fired with such coolness that not a single cartridge was wasted, waiting until the very instant when the horsemen were about to break our square. The number of corpses surrounding our square soon was considerable, and the clothes of the dead and wounded Mamelukes were burning like tinder. The blazing wads of our muskets penetrated at the same time as our bullets through their rich uniforms, which were embroidered with gold and silver and floated as lightly as gauze.

Within two hours the Mameluke army was routed. Hundreds, desperate to escape, flung themselves into the Nile, where they drowned. The French soldiers greedily plundered the corpses, sometimes finding as many as 300 gold pieces hidden in the elaborate clothing. "Among the baggage left by the beys and [their soldiers, our men] found abundant stores of comfits and sweets, and quantities of rugs, china, and silverware," Napoleon wrote later in his account of the battle. "All through the night, the minarets of Cairo were silhouetted against the swirling flames of 300 Egyptian vessels. The glow was reflected even by the distant surfaces of the Pyramids."

The Arabs of the desert were not so easily subdued. As the French Army marched through the desert toward Cairo, the Bedouins harassed the invaders with a frustrating persistence. The French quickly learned that the sandy wastes belonged to the Bedouins, who attacked impartially all travelers without regard to politics. "The Bedouin-Arabs, who are ill-armed and can make no resistance, whose ramparts are moving sands, whose lives are space, whose retreat is immensity, by whom can they be vanquished or confined?" complained Dominique Vivant Denon, an artist accompanying the

French. "The Bedouin is the primitive hunter. Indolence and independence are the basis of his character. He keeps himself in continual motion and endures the siege and tyranny of want. We have nothing, therefore, to offer the Bedouin that is the equivalent to the value of robbing us." The French soldiers were amazed at the Bedouin custom of treating all captured soldiers with kindness once they had surrendered their possessions. Their lives were not threatened. Napoleon quickly negotiated a treaty with the Bedouins. "I seated myself among them and we had a long conversation," he wrote in an early dispatch. "This nation is no less than the travelers and writers of accounts have painted it. It is calm, proud, and brave."

Within a few weeks Napoleon, like Caesar before him, had made himself master of Egypt. A French thumb pressed against England's jugular vein. Soon after Napoleon had settled into Cairo, he visited the Great Pyramid and studied its enormous bulk. Then he demanded to know its measurements, quickly computed its cubic content, and calculated that its mass was great enough to build a wall around France ten feet high and one foot thick. Later Napoleon searched out an ancient canal of the pharaohs, unused for more than 1,000 years, which had once connected the Mediterranean and Red seas, and rode for fifteen miles along its dry bed. On Christmas Eve he set out for Suez along the hajj route to Mecca through the desert and returned to Cairo convinced that a new ship canal was possible. Napoleon instructed Jean Baptiste Le Père, his chief engineer, to survey the Isthmus of Suez and report back to him on the feasibility of the project.

Egypt captured Napoleon's imagination. He loved to dress in Arab robes and sleep in tents under a desert sky. Later he confessed: "In Egypt I found myself freed from the obstacles of an irksome civilization. I was full of dreams. I saw myself founding a religion, marching into Asia, riding an elephant, a turban on my head and in my hand a new Koran that I would have composed to suit my needs. In my undertakings I would have combined the experiences of the two worlds, exploiting for my own profit the theater of all history, attacking the power of England in India and, by means of that conquest, renewing contact with the old Europe. The time I spent in

Egypt was the most beautiful in my life because it was the most ideal."

On the other hand, the behavior of the French army of occupation violated the strict morality of Islamic law and deeply offended many local Muslims. "The presence of the French in Cairo was intolerable, especially when the Egyptians saw their wives and daughters walking in the streets unveiled and appearing to be the property of the French, with whom they were seen in public and with whom they cohabited," wrote one disgusted Turkish chronicler of the French occupation. "Before these facts, the Muslims died of shame. It was bad enough for them to see the taverns that had been established in the bazaars of Cairo and even in several mosques. Such a spectacle created an intolerable atmosphere for the Muslims."

Napoleon's problems began to deepen soon after his capture of Cairo. In August 1798 the Royal Navy under the command of Horatio Nelson attacked the French fleet off Alexandria and sank almost every ship, temporarily stranding the French Army in Egypt. "Napoleon's reach had exceeded his grasp," historian Chester Cooper observes. "His grandiose plan and most of his forces were to be the first of many victims of England's sensitivity to any threat to India."

But the worst was yet to come. Soon after the conquest of Egypt had been accomplished, the sultan in Constantinople declared war on France, forcing Napoleon in 1799 to march into the Holy Land with a force of 13,000 men to discourage any Turkish thoughts of an invasion. It was a disastrous campaign, in some ways a forerunner of his war against Russia later. On March 4 Napoleon lay siege to the town of Jaffa, located on the Mediterranean coast some fifty miles from Jerusalem. The Turks managed to hold out for only a few hours. French troops quickly breached the walls and captured the city. More than 3,000 Turkish troops surrendered in good faith after several French officers had agreed to spare their lives. But Napoleon had no use for prisoners. The next day he ordered 2,000 of them shot, largely to impress the pasha Ahmed, who had withdrawn into Acre. It was one of the most savage and inexcusable acts in Napoleon's career. A disgusted assistant paymaster in the French Army wrote later:

The next morning all the Moroccans were taken to the sea shore and two battalions began to shoot them down. They were shot at leisure, and in an instant the sea was red with blood and covered with corpses. . . . The next day 1,200 Turkish artillery-men, who for two days had been kept without food in front of General Bonaparte's tent, were taken to be executed. The soldiers had been carefully instructed not to waste their ammunition, and they were ferocious enough to stab them with their bayonets. Among the victims, we found many children, who in the act of death clung to their fathers. This example will teach our enemies that they cannot count on French good faith. Sooner or later the blood of these 3,000 victims will be upon us.

The East began to exact its revenge almost immediately. Within a few days bubonic plague had broken out in the ranks of Napoleon's army and spread rapidly. Soon afterward the French laid siege to Acre, a historic city where the Crusader castle of Richard Coeur de Lion still stood. By mid-April 3 percent of Napoleon's soldiers had come down with plague, and his army was on the edge of panic. A British blockade of the coast prevented Napoleon from receiving the heavy siege guns he needed to capture Acre. By the time Napoleon ordered a retreat, he had lost 1,200 soldiers dead from enemy action, 1,000 from the plague, and another 2,500 incapacitated because of serious injuries and illness. One-third of his force, the elite of his army, was dead or disabled. Napoleon returned to Egypt and on August 18 sailed from Alexandria for France. In the early spring of 1801 a British army under the command of Sir Hely Hutchison attacked the French forces Napoleon had abandoned in Egypt more than a year before. On June 27 he captured Cairo and took 13,000 soldiers prisoner. The French occupation of Egypt had come to an end.

The French invasion was a momentous event in Middle Eastern history. Napoleon had set into motion forces that eventually under-mined the old order throughout the region. He had clearly demon-strated that the Ottoman Empire was the "Sick Man of Europe," a moribund empire awaiting dissolution. To ensure that future control of Egypt would remain in hands friendly to England, Prime Minister William Pitt concluded a treaty with the Turks agreeing to uphold the integrity of the Ottoman Empire, first against the territorial ambitions of France and later as a counterweight to a reawakened and rejuvenated Russia, which under Catherine the Great had focused obsessively upon Constantinople. This was the beginning of a British preoccupation with the Middle East that lasted for more than 150 years.

The French invasion represented another, more subtle challenge to the Muslim world. "For the first time since its beginnings, Islam faced an ideological and philosophical challenge that threatened the very foundations of Muslim doctrine and society," Bernard Lewis points out in *The Muslim Discovery of Europe*. European secularism expressed through societies that were militarily and economically powerful exerted an enormous appeal to certain elements in the Islamic world. They began to look west for non-Islamic solutions to the problems of the Muslim world. Napoleon's invasion marked the start of the cultural encroachment by Western powers upon traditional Islamic institutions. (The backlash was felt almost 200 years later in the "sacred rage" expressed by such radicals as the Ayatollah Khomeini and the terrorists in Islamic Jihad.) After centuries of isolation the Muslim discovery of Europe would be forced and, for the most part, painful.

In 1902 the American historian A. T. Mahan coined the phrase *Middle East* to distinguish the region of the eastern end of the Mediterranean from the Far East. The area is "middle," too, in the sense that it lies strategically between the richer and more populous continents of Europe and Asia. The people have historically served as middlemen for the goods and ideas that flowed between the East and the West.

But the inhabitants of the region were, of course, far more than mere "middlemen" and certainly not the fanatical, bloodthirsty, xenophobic monsters of the popular Western imagination. Few regions in the world proved such fertile spawning grounds for major ideas and philosophies as the Middle East. It was the birthplace of the world's three great revealed religions: Judaism, Christianity, and Islam. The Arabs were the inheritors of the great scientific, mathematical, medical, and philosophical traditions of late antiquity. They preserved them, elaborated upon them, and finally passed them on to a Europe that had evolved out of the barbarism of the Dark Ages.

"The most important single innovation that the eager, inquisitive, and tolerant Arab scholars brought from afar was in writing numbers," Jacob Bronowski states in *The Ascent of Man.* "The European notation for numbers then was still the clumsy Roman style, in which the number is put together from its parts by simple addition. . . . Islam replaced that by the modern decimal notation that we still call 'Arabic.' " The Arabs also gave the West the concept of zero, algebra, and the foundations of analytical geometry and trigonometry. (In fact, our words *zero, algebra, almanac,* and *zenith* all derive from Arabic words.) European research into astronomy did not surpass that of the Arabs until the late sixteenth century. Sixth-century Arab doctors not only identified smallpox but developed a form of inoculation which virtually eliminated the dreaded disease from much of the Middle East more than 1,000 years before Edward Jenner's cowpox inoculation. The first free public hospital appeared about the same time in Baghdad; by the end of the ninth century the concept had spread to Egypt and soon afterward throughout the Muslim world. To the Arabs we owe our knowledge of the furnace with forced draft in which we smelt our ores and of the wheel on a rotating shaft with which we run our factories and vehicles. Arab traders brought the first orange trees from China to Spain, while Arab farmers gave Europe lemons, melons, apricots, and the cereals with which we make our breads.

The Arab culture was shaped largely by the physical geography and climate of the land. An arid region of baked mountains and scorching desert, the Middle East is the size of the United States but possesses only one-tenth of the arable land. The domestication of the camel some 4,000 years ago made possible human penetration of the vast desert areas of the Middle East. This remarkable animal played a far greater role in the rise of civilization in this region than either the horse or the dog. Without the camel the Arab world would have had a very different history. "Go back once more to the map of the Middle East and think of the Fertile Crescent as a shore with the deserts in the south as a great sandy sea," William Polk and William Mares write in *Passing Brave*. "Before the camel, the 'ship of the desert,' men's ventures were limited to short forays out from the shore. The importance of the camel in the birth of civilization becomes evident when one considers that until roughly 1000 B.C., when the camel became the common property of the peoples of this area, the real Middle East, like an ocean atoll, was nothing more than a thin rim of cultivated land."

The one-hump Arabian camel is a marvel of endurance and adaptation. When the desert is in its winter bloom and the plants have a high water content, camels have gone for as long as two months without drinking. And they will thrive on well water that people have rejected as too salty and foul-tasting. (A popular myth regarding camels, first put forth by Pliny the Elder 2,000 years ago, is that the camel uses its hump to store water for use in dry times. Not so.) So efficient is the camel as a beast of burden—on short hauls, it can carry up to 1,000 pounds, more than an elephant—that the Arab world made no attempt to develop a road system of its own until recently. Indeed, Arabs had abandoned more than 1,500 years ago both the excellent complex of roads inherited from the Romans and the concept of oxcarts.

Westerners have often ridiculed the Islamic concept of paradise as a place where the faithful live for an eternity amid fountains and flowing rivers of the purest water and breathe perfumed air, while beautiful maidens serve them fresh fruit as they sit on luxurious couches. But Muhammad obviously described paradise in terms that would exert the most powerful appeal to the impoverished desert Bedouins, his first followers.

The Islamic strictures against the consumption of pork and wine were also rooted in the harsh realities of life in the desert. Anthropologist Carleton Coon thirty years ago offered the first cogent explanation for the prohibition of pork. (Obviously the early Hebrews and Arabs knew nothing about trichinosis.) Thousands of years ago the people of the Middle East grazed pigs on the forest floor to fatten on acorns and ground cover. But once vast areas had been deforested, the pig became an extravagance in the desert climate of the Middle East. The animal furnished no by-products useful to a nomadic society, while its bare skin could not tolerate the blistering rays of the desert sun. The camel, on the other hand, provided the Bedouin with transportation, meat, milk, wool, and a host of other useful by-products, while evolution had adapted it perfectly for survival in the harsh desert world. Hence, Muhammad prohibited the eating of pork and encouraged the consumption of camel meat. By the same token, he forbade the drinking of wine. No grapes could grow in the arid wastes of the Arabian Peninsula, hence all wine had to be imported on the backs of camels in long caravan marches through the deserts. But bottles of wine are heavy and take up valuable space. Few regions of the world are more unforgiving of mistakes than the Arabian deserts. Survival there has always been tenuous at best. Too much wine clouds the judgment and dramatically increases the likelihood of a terrible death from dehydration.

In 1800 the Middle East was ruled by an Ottoman Empire centered in Constantinople. The name *Ottoman* is a corruption of the name of its first ruler, Osman, who ruled, according to tradition, from 1299 to 1326. The Ottoman Empire reached its zenith in the mid-sixteenth century, when it extended from the gates of Vienna in the north to Yemen and Aden in the south, from Persia in the east to Oran (in present-day Algeria) in the west. No greater threat to Christendom existed than that poised by the Muslim armies and navies. Turkish warships threatened the Portuguese Navy in the Indian Ocean and raided the British Isles. In 1627 a fleet of Barbary corsairs attacked Iceland and returned to Algiers with several hundred captives for the Arab slave markets. The Elizabethan historian Richard Knolles articulated the fears of most Europeans when he called the Ottoman Empire the "present terror of the world." But then Islam had existed from its conception in the seventh century in a state of perpetual conflict with Christendom. (Dante in *The Inferno* put Muhammad in the eighth of the nine circles near the very bottom of hell where Satan himself is found.)

"The Ottoman Empire remained a polity penetrated from its very origins with a sense of mission in the holy war [against the non-Muslim world]," Bernard Lewis writes in *The Muslim Discovery of Europe*. "In this holy war, Europe was a frontier to which the Ottomans, and indeed many other Muslims, looked in much the same way as Europeans were to view the Americas from the sixteenth to the eighteenth century. Beyond the northern and western frontiers lay rich and barbarous lands to which it was their sacred mission to bring religion and civilization, order and peace—while reaping the customary rewards of the pioneer and the frontiersman."

But the "frontier" closed off, as over the centuries the Ottoman Empire suffered a steady series of reverses. In 1492 the armies of Ferdinand of Aragon and Isabella of Castile recaptured Spain from the Moors, while the Portuguese ended the Muslim dominion in Asia. In 1798, when French troops landed at Alexandria, the Ottoman Empire still included most of the Middle East west of Persia; lengthy coastal strips of the Arabian Peninsula; the North African countries of Egypt, Libya, Tunisia, and Algeria; Cyprus; and the Balkan states of Bulgaria, Romania, Albania, and Greece. The Turks were the ruling class. Ninety-five percent of the population throughout the Ottoman Empire was illiterate. Eighty percent belonged to a peasant class tied by centuries of tradition to villages and oases or to nomadic herding through the vast desert regions.

Throughout the Ottoman Empire Islam was the dominant religion. Christians and Jews were prohibited from serving in the army. But generally the followers of all three religious groups lived together more or less peacefully, each under the laws, courts, and customs of its own faith. Institutionalized religious prejudice of the kind that was pervasive in Christendom was rare in the Muslim lands. When the Muslims captured Jerusalem in the seventh century, they left all Jews unmolested. Five hundred years later, when the Crusaders entered the Holy City, they slaughtered all the Jews and Muslims they could find. And soon after Ferdinand and Isabella expelled the last of the Moors from Spain, they issued an edict requiring that all Muslims and Jews still in Spain choose among conversion to Christianity, exile, or execution.

Authority over the empire lay, as noted earlier, with the sultan in Constantinople. But for the daily conduct of local affairs, he relied upon his pashas, who collected his taxes, preserved Ottoman supremacy in their provinces, and safeguarded the major hajj routes to Mecca. Although pashas enjoyed extravagant life-styles, the fruits of extortionate taxes and bribes, their situation was anything but secure. They were not salaried and often subjected to arbitrary recall, confiscation of their properties, and summary executions by sultans unhappy with their performances. The result was an imperial empire in which rule by personal whim replaced rule by law. The Englishman Charles Addison traveled extensively through the region in 1835 and studied at length the system of government within the Ottoman Empire. He wrote later:

> The despotic authority of the Sultan descends to every one of his subordinate officers, who reign absolutely within their jurisdiction, unimpeded by local customs, written laws, or settled opinions. Every office of the state is sold, and in the public registers the value of every important post is recorded. The whole system of the government seems to be built on rapine, pillage, and extortion. The Pasha pays the central government for the administration of his province. . . . The government of his different villages is again sold or farmed out by him, as also are the different taxes. The same system is pursued by these different lessees; their only object in view is to obtain the greatest amount of money that can possibly be extracted during their respective occupations. Thus rapine and robbery descend step by step through every department.

The figure of the pasha became synonymous with arbitrary and cruel abuses of power. One Egyptian pasha, outraged because his horse had lost a shoe, reputedly sent for two horseshoes. The first he ordered put on his horse. He then had the second shoe heated until it was red-hot and ordered it nailed firmly to the foot of his offending groom.

Constantinople was the political, cultural, and economic center of the Ottoman Empire. The Greeks and Romans called the city Byzantium, but that name was changed in A.D. 330, after the emperor Constantine founded a new imperial capital there. The Turkish people always knew it as Istanbul, which finally became the official name only in 1930. Constantinople was still one of the world's most beautiful and exotic cities. It was, in the words of historian Noel Barber, "a hidden world of golden domes and pointed minarets reaching for the sky like manicured fingers; of dark cypress groves hiding kiosks, or villas, their walls of marble, glittering mosaics, or exquisite tiles; of artificial lakes and pleasure gardens, of the mingled scents of herbs and fruit trees and roses, of an imperative silence broken only by the tinkling of scores of fountains."

The nerve center of the vast Ottoman Empire was the Grand Seraglio of the sultan, an impregnable fortress which looked across the Bosporus to the Asian mainland beyond. With a population of 5,000, the Seraglio was a city within a city. Only on rare occasions was a European permitted inside the high walls, and never inside the sultan's harem, which so fired the imagination of Europe. *Harem* is an Arab word meaning "unlawful" and referred to the quarters of a Muslim house or palace where the women dwelled. The only men permitted there were the master and his black eunuchs. Islamic law allowed a man up to four wives and as many concubines and slaves as he could afford. The sultan's harem in the Seraglio was a vast complex of kiosks, villas, and pavilions, set amid terraced gardens and spacious courtyards and ruled over by the queen mother, the most important of the sultan's four wives. Some sultans maintained more than 300 concubines and female slaves, each one trained in the various social and sexual arts to please her lord. Their numbers alone precluded any one woman's spending much time in the sultan's bedchamber. Lesbianism was often rife in the harem.

Dr. Charles Meryon, a British physician who accompanied Lady Hester Stanhope on her Eastern travels, witnessed in 1811 the sultan's weekly procession to his mosque through the streets of Constantinople. He wrote later:

First came some dozens of water-carriers, who bore skins of water across their backs with which they laid the dust as they advanced. Soldiers with knotted whips kept the crowd from pressing on the procession. After these upon a finely caparisoned horse, surrounded by a dozen valets on foot, followed a fierce-looking Turk with a black beard. My companion and I exclaimed, "Here comes the Sultan!" But it was only his coffee-bearer. We made the like remark at a second and a third. But they were his sword and pipe-bearers, who with the emblems of office in their hands passed in succession. Suddenly, the crowd grew hushed. [The sultan appeared.] His person was almost hidden by the lofty plumes of feathers of the attendants who surrounded him, each of whom wore a vest of glittering armour and on his head a crested helmet. The Sultan's horse, a milk-white stallion, was covered with gorgeous robes studded with rubies, emeralds, and other precious stones.

When Napoleon's soldiers landed at Alexandria in 1798, they pierced what had been in effect a cultural veil drawn tightly over the Islamic world and its institutions. As the Ottoman Empire slowly collapsed, it had withdrawn upon itself, restricting all cultural, economic, and diplomatic exchanges with Europe to the minimum. Few Muslims had traveled to Europe. Little information about modern Europe had circulated in the Arab world. Muslim scholars showed little interest or curiosity about events in distant Europe. European universities set up extensive departments of Arabic studies as early as the sixteenth century, and scholars published grammars and dictionaries of Persian and Turkish and translated the principal texts of both languages. But no comparable activity took place in the Muslim world. "We know of no Muslim scholar or man of letters before the eighteenth century who sought to learn a Western language, still less to attempt to produce grammars, dictionaries, or other language tools," Bernard Lewis concludes in *The Muslim Discovery of Europe*. (The first Arab translations of Western books did not appear until the second decade of the nineteenth century. Appropriately, one of the first books printed was an Arabic version of Daniel Defoe's classic novel of isolation *Robinson Crusoe.*) As late as the 1790s the average educated Arab "knew as much of the states and nations of Europe as a nineteenth-century European about the tribes and peoples of Africa—and regarded them with the same slightly amused disdain," Lewis writes.

The Muslim contempt for Europe dated back to the eighth century, when the first contact between the two worlds was established. The Arab world was then a major center of power, wealth, and the arts, while a crude European culture offered only slaves, armaments, and wool for trade. A tenth-century Arab geographer described the peoples of northern Europe as "more like beasts than like men" and lacking in "keenness of understanding and clarity of intelligence." He also noted that a cold climate had made their temperaments "frigid, their humors raw, their bellies gross, their color pale, their hair long and lank." Muslims lumped all Europeans together under the derisive term *Franks* and retained an image of them as barbarians for the next 1,000 years. The Crusades only reinforced the Muslim contempt for all things European. "The city of Acre—may Allah destroy it and return it to Islam—is the chief city of the Franks in Syria," wrote one disgusted twelfth-century Muslim visitor. "It is a land of unbelief and impiety, swarming with pigs and crosses, full of filth and ordure."

The Arab world did little to revise its low estimation of European culture in later centuries. Such major European events as the Renaissance, the Reformation, the scientific revolution, and the Enlightenment passed without notice in the Muslim East. By 1798, when Napoleon finally breached this wall of Muslim provincialism, Europe had long since surpassed the Arab world in power, political stability, standard of living, technology, and the arts.

Provincialism continued to be a major characteristic of the Muslim world throughout the nineteenth century. Most European travelers were quick to comment upon it. "The people of Syria express no curiosity about foreign lands and regions," British traveler Charles Addison noted in 1835. "If you tell them that people in England have ascended into the skies in a balloon or have whirled along at thirty miles an hour over the country without horses, they shake their heads, saying 'Allah is great.' And although they do not dispute your word, yet generally they set you down for a liar."

The early-nineteenth-century European traveler who lifted the veil of the Muslim East often found himself confronting a perplexing cultural labyrinth without apparent solution. Consider, for example, the area of languages. In contrast with Europe, which offered a diversity of languages, both ancient and modern, the Arab world had only one language. Throughout the Ottoman Empire Arabic was the sole language of commerce, religion, and culture. Rare was the individual who spoke a second language. Arabic itself could be utterly baffling, often eluding translation into European tongues. According to the travel writer Jonathan Raban in *Arabia: A Journey Through the Labyrinth*:

> To live in Arabic is to live in a labyrinth of false turns and double meanings. No sentence means quite what it says. Every word is potentially a talisman, conjuring the ghosts of the entire family of words from which it comes. The devious complexity of Arabic grammar is legendary. It is a language which is perfectly constructed for saying nothing with enormous eloquence; a language of pure manners in which there are hardly any literal meanings at all and in which the symbolic gesture is everything. . . . Even to peer through a chink in the wall of the language is enough to glimpse the depth and darkness of that forest of ambiguity. No wonder the Koran is so notoriously untranslatable.

The European multiplicity of languages reflects certain political realities. The great contending forces of Europe have historically been its nation-states. Their activities are inspired and sustained in the name of nationalism. Each state zealously guards its own selfish interests, eager to maintain its independent existence and quick to assert its own preeminence among the larger family of European nations.

The European division of peoples into nation-states was completely unknown in the Muslim world of the early nineteenth century. Such concepts as nationalism and patriotism were foreign to the historical Muslim experience. Many regions lacked even a specific country name. (The modern nation-states in the Middle East are largely the arbitrary creation of European powers after the First World War. The British, for example, carved up the Ottoman province of Syria into Syria, Lebanon, Jordan, and the Palestine mandate.) Instead of defining self-awareness in terms that reflected language, culture, and historical traditions within clearly defined geographical boundaries, the Muslim took his in terms that were sacred rather than secular. Group identity was based on a brotherhood of faith within the framework of Islam. The Muslim worldview divides people into two basic camps: those who accept the teachings of Muhammad and those who do not. In the early nineteenth century the Ottoman Empire was the guardian of the Muslim faith. And the people of that empire—whether Turks, Bedouins, Egyptians, or Damascenes—took their primary identity as Muslims.

(To this day in the Muslim world Western notions of nationalism and patriotism have not entirely superseded the older pattern. A commonly heard Arab proverb insists: "I against my brothers; I and my brothers against my cousins; I and my cousins against the world." Fundamentalist radical leaders such as the Ayatollah Khomeini continue to urge a religious loyalty beyond all nationalistic ties. The Libyan leader Colonel Moammar Khadafy may not enjoy much respect in the Arab world, but when warplanes of the United States bombed his cities, the quickness with which other Arabs rallied to his side reflects the extent to which this deep-rooted sense of an Islamic religious brotherhood is still a potent force in the Muslim world. As far away as Manila a group of 400 Filipino Muslims marched on the United States Embassy, where a pro-Khadafy speaker told the crowd: "Arab blood spilled in the Middle East is the same that bleeds from the Muslims in this country. If America ever hurts a Libyan brother, we shall not forgive any American we chance upon in any street or place in the Philippines.")

Unlike Christendom, which separates church and state, Islam makes no distinction between the religious and the secular life of its people; it distinguishes only between believers and infidels. The community of believers is both a religious community and a political system. "For the believing Muslim, there is no human legislative power," explains Bernard Lewis in *The Muslim Discovery of Europe.* "God is the sole source of law which He promulgates through revelation. The divine law . . . regulates all aspects of human life. Earthly powers have no right to abrogate or even to modify the law. Their duty is to maintain and enforce it, no more. The only latitude left, in principle, is that of interpretation, and this is the task of the qualified interpreters, the doctors of the holy law."

Not only does Islam deny all distinctions between church and state, but it refuses to sanction any religious hierarchy to come between God and the faithful. Islam has no ecclesiastical offices comparable to the popes, bishops, priests, and ministers of Christendom. In Islamic theory every man is his own priest. The humblest Bedouin stands on the same footing before God as the most powerful sultan. (However, the Shi'ite Muslims, a minority, follow mullahs, who mediate between people and Allah.) Nor does Islam have anything corresponding to the liturgy of the Christian Church. And in contrast with many Christian churches, which are in use only Sundays, the Muslim mosque is open day and night, seven days a week, so that the faithful can make their prayers five times a day. It serves, too, as a town meeting hall, a school, a hostel for travelers, and a refuge for the poor.

Because Muhammad held that God's creations—especially people and animals—must not be duplicated by humans, Islamic art in the mosques and elsewhere fell back upon the arabesque, a complex pattern of intertwined geometric and floral figures. Until the late nineteenth century, painting was limited almost entirely to book illustration and miniatures. Portraiture was almost completely unknown in the Arab world of 1800. (When British Pre-Raphaelite artist William Holman Hunt set up a studio in Cairo in 1854 to paint portraits, he was charged by an angry Muslim with seeking "to obtain portraits of true Muslims in great numbers, to return with these to England to call up Satan, and to bargain with him as to the price he would pay for the souls of my victims, and that thus I would become rich beyond conception.") It was not until much later in the century and then only in imitation of European practices that sculpture and the hanging of art on walls penetrated the Islamic world. On the other hand, in the midst of the heat and dust of the Middle East the garden developed into one of the most expressive of the Islamic art forms. (The only garden of classical Islam to survive intact into modern times is the fourteenth-century Court of the Myrtles in the Alhambra at Granada, Spain.)

Because Islam recognizes no law other than the word of God and makes no distinction between sin and crime, lawyers did not exist in the Arab world of the nineteenth century. The ulemas, the doctors of the holy law, fulfilled the functions of both lawyers and priests in Islamic society, interpreting and enforcing the law in all its applications.

The European visitor to the Middle East in 1800 would have found himself in a world largely devoid of roads or wheeled vehicles of any kind. Transportation throughout the Ottoman Empire was by ship or pack animals, chiefly camels, organized in vast commercial caravans sometimes numbering more than 5,000 animals and twice as many attendants. The early-nineteenth-century Middle East was also a world without magazines and newspapers and few printed books, the first printing press not having been imported until the early eighteenth century. (When a disguised John Lewis Burckhardt visited Mecca in 1814, he discovered after a diligent search and much to his regret that no Arabic histories were to be had. He found no libraries or bookshops in the city and saw only one good book for sale, that offered by a visiting Malay Muslim.)

In 1798 the Middle East was still largely unexplored by Europeans, except for a narrow band extending from Constantinople in the north down the Mediterranean coast through Beirut to Cairo in the south. Lady Mary Wortley Montagu, the wife of the British ambassador to Constantinople, complained in 1717 that the Arab world was "seldom visited but by merchants who mind but their own affairs or travellers who make too short a stay to be able to report anything exactly from their own knowledge. They can give no better idea of the ways here than a French refugee, lodging in a garret in Greek Street, could write of the Court of England."

By 1798 fewer than two dozen Europeans since the Crusades had penetrated more than 100 miles from the Mediterranean coast. Only one major expedition of exploration into the Arab world had been mounted by any European government: the Danish expedition of Carsten Niebuhr into Yemen in 1762–63. No European had ever gazed upon the wonders of Petra and Abu Simbel. Virtually nothing was known of the vast Arabian Peninsula with its sacred cities of Mecca and Medina. Even the Christian Holy Land, which had provoked the medieval Crusades, had fallen into obscurity.

That was soon to change, of course. In 1812 John Lewis Burckhardt, a professional Swiss explorer, contracted out to the London-based Association for Promoting the Discovery of Africa. He spent five years dressed in Arab robes methodically exploring Syria, the Holy Land, the Sinai Peninsula, southern Egypt, and the Muslim holy cities of Mecca and Medina. He discovered the ruins at Petra and Abu Simbel. He was a keen scientific observer who took voluminous notes on all aspects of the Middle East. Burckhardt contributed enormously to Europe's knowledge of the region. He had no great adventures and met with no real difficulties, except ill health. He died at the age of thirty-two of dysentery in Cairo.

The European exploration of the Middle East in the nineteenth century was almost entirely a British affair, as it was in that other great arena, East Africa and the search for the headwaters of the Nile River. But the nature of exploration differed radically in the two regions. When Henry Stanley on assignment for the *New York Herald* set off in August 1874 on a search for the headwaters of the Nile, his expedition consisted of three young British assistants, 356 porters, eight tons of supplies, and a forty-foot wooden boat. The unwieldy baggage train stretched for half a mile along the forest paths. The party traveled heavily armed. Stanley's solution to a touchy situation with the local natives was often brute force. He was quite ready to shoot down any tribe that opposed his progress. Stanley always wore Western dress and never learned any of the local African dialects.

But the British explorers into the remoter regions of the Arab world could gain admittance only by denying their European heritage and temporarily assuming the dress, language, customs, and mannerisms of their hosts. In some instances they had to become spies, passing themselves off as Muslims but knowing every waking moment that the slightest slip might expose them as impostors and bring upon them instant execution as infidels. Stealth, not armed force, became the key to a successful expedition into a region ruled over by a Bedouin confederation that could on short notice put 10,000 fierce warriors into the field.

There were profound differences, too, between the European perceptions of black Africans and the Arabs. According to scholar John Dennis Duffy:

> Europeans regarded Africans as nothing more than objects in a landscape which took on meaning and became human only after they had been made over in the white man's image—Christianized, dressed up in shirts and trousers, and fitted into a socioeconomic system similar to what prevailed in Europe. Throughout the century the Arabs, particularly the Bedouins, never lost the fascination they held for Europeans. They perceived them to be a free people, each individual being his own master, living proudly by the skills learned in the harsh desert climes, disdainful of cities, adhering to a code half chivalric, half brigand. For the nineteenth century British Romantic, honor, hospitality, simplicity, and freedom still flowered in the desert Arab. The age's fascination with the Middle East blended subtly into the British nostalgia for the Middle Ages and the lost Camelot.

Travelers to the Middle East faced untold dangers in the early part of the nineteenth century, a time when despotic Turkish pashas, savage bandits, fanatical Muslims, and periodic outbreaks of plague made the region one of the most unsettled and dangerous in the world. A poor preparation, momentary loss of courage, or sudden carelessness often led to a quick death. Comte Joseph Arthur de Gobineau joined a caravan from Baghdad to Persia and later described the fate of one unfortunate young English traveler who failed to complete the journey: "He had fallen in love with the East through reading travel books and he wrote poetry. . . . His hair was long. He had a red silk belt, the kind of sword worn by knights of old, heavy boots with gilt spurs and a feather in his hat. He hadn't much money and to save he ate with the mule drivers and slept on their blankets. He was thin, pale, and weak. He had chest trouble. He died before getting to the Persian frontier."

If the Arab world was poorly known in fact in 1800, it loomed large in myth and legend, exerting an enormous pull, like that of the moon on the ocean tides, on the poets, novelists, dramatists, and painters of Europe. The region's varied riches and bizarre customs absolutely captivated the imaginations of artists and their publics. In the popular mind the Middle East stood for exotic locales, unrestrained passion, sensuous pleasures, and utter freedom from all inhibitions.

A major stimulant was, of course, Napoleon's invasion of Egypt. Although that expedition was a miserable failure militarily, it had the effect of stimulating the interest of Europe in the pharaonic and Muslim civilizations of the East. Napoleon brought with his army nearly 170 scientists, scholars, and artists to study the ancient and modern cultures of Egypt. After his hasty return to France in 1799, they remained in Egypt sketching, measuring, and studying the ruins. Soon Paris was awash in ancient mummies, sarcophagi, jewelry, funereal furniture, tools, statues, and obelisks. (A Frenchman discovered the celebrated Rosetta stone, containing the key to understanding the ancient Egyptian hieroglyphics, but it fell into English hands and ended up in the British Museum.) From 1809 to 1813 the French published the monumental *Description de l'Égypte*, a lavishly illustrated twenty-four-volume encyclopedic survey of ancient and modern Egypt that quickly became the most complete documentation of that nation to appear in the West. All this wealth of antiquities stunned the European imagination.

"There is more interest in the East nowadays than there has ever been," Victor Hugo wrote in 1829 in his preface to *Les Orientales*. "Never before have Eastern studies made such progress. In the age of

Louis XIV everyone was a Hellenist. Now they are all Orientalists. Never have so many intellects explored at one time this great abyss of Asia. . . . The East, either as image or idea, has become a sort of general occupation of the mind as much as of the imagination. There all is big, rich, fruitful. This entire continent is inclining toward the East."

CHAPTER II

Lady Hester Stanhope: The Queen of the Arabs

She stood six feet tall and rode a stallion as skillfully as any officer in the king's cavalry. She was cocky, fiercely independent, and British. Her uncle was the famed Sir William Pitt, the political genius who had entered Parliament at twenty-one and become prime minister at twenty-four. In 1810 she left England, never to return, drawn inexorably to the Middle East, a region that even then loomed large in the popular imagination as a wild, untamed landscape peopled with dark-eyed sheiks charging about their desert kingdoms on superb stallions past the decaying pillars of ancient cities.

Within a few years she had become one of the most famous women of her day, more a creature of myth than history. A century before T. E. Lawrence, she traveled on her own throughout the Arab world, adopting its customs, costumes, and language. She set up a court straight out of the *Arabian Nights* and ruled as an Oriental potentate in her own right. Her reputation and power were so great that not even the Turkish sultan dared defy her. The first English person to identify with the Arabs as "her own people," she found herself in her final years the object of a romantic cult. To many Arabs she seemed to be a goddess, a supernatural being who had come mysteriously among them from another world. To European travelers she was "a marvel of the Middle East," as much to be sought out as the pyramids of Egypt.

She was Lady Hester Stanhope.

After the British writer Alexander Kinglake had visited her in the late autumn of 1835, he wrote in his travel memoir *Eothen:* "Her name was made almost as familiar to me in my childhood as the name of Robinson Crusoe; both were associated with the spirit of adventure. But whilst the imagined life of the castaway mariner never failed to seem glaringly real, the true story of the Englishwoman ruling over Arabs always sounded to me like a fable."

Lady Hester was born on March 12, 1776, at the great house of Chevening, in Kent. Her mother, Lady Hester Pitt, the favorite sister of Sir William Pitt, died when her daughter was four. She was reared by her father, Charles, the third earl of Stanhope, a somewhat eccentric man who combined scientific research with democratic principles and contrived to quarrel with most of his family. He showed little interest in the three daughters from his first marriage and his three sons from a second, leaving their care almost entirely to governesses and tutors.

Lady Hester early showed herself to be headstrong, proud, and domineering. She had boundless self-confidence and honestly believed herself born to command. She was always "playing the empress-queen," in the words of one cousin. "My sister Lucy was prettier than I was, and Griselda more clever," Lady Hester admitted years later. "But I, even when I was only a girl, obtained and exercised, I can't tell how, a sort of command over them. They never came to me, when I was in my room, without sending first to know whether I would see them."

The young Lady Hester showed little interest in the traditional skills expected from women of rank in those days: music, painting, and the other fine arts. In later years she professed a general dislike of women, insisting that in her lifetime she had known but three whom she respected and admired. Her lifelong companion and biographer Dr. Charles Meryon wrote: "She held in contempt the gentler qualities of her own sex, who, in turn, were not slow to resent the masculine characteristics on which she presumed to maintain her assumed position."

A tall, strong, woman with a voice that was deep and resonant, she preferred the company of men to women. She developed into a fine horsewoman, a skill which later contributed greatly to her popularity with the Arabs, and she loved to hunt.

No portrait of Lady Hester exists from this time. But she was always quick to admit that she was never considered attractive. And comments by men who knew her in these years bear this out. "She was neither handsome nor beautiful, for her visage was long, very full and fat about the lower part and quite pale, bearing altogether a strong resemblance to the portraits and busts of Mr. Pitt," insisted one of her acquaintances from this period.

Lady Hester's appeal lay, rather, in an intellect of rare scope and power, a vivid imagination, a quick and brilliant wit, an inexhaustible energy, and a dauntless courage. She was much too challenging intellectually for most men. A close friend of her uncle Sir William Pitt once remarked that he supposed she would marry once she had found a man as clever as herself. Pitt retorted, "Then she will never marry at all," an observation that proved prophetic.

Unhappy at Chevening and restless for a change, Lady Hester in 1800 accepted an invitation from her grandmother to move to Burton Pynsent, a country estate in Somerset. In the fall of 1802 she visited a younger brother in France and crossed the Alps by mule into Italy, where she spent the winter. The next spring the peace between England and France collapsed, as Napoleon prepared to resume his conquest of Europe.

When Lady Hester returned to England, she learned that her grandmother had died and she was without a home. Estranged from the rest of her family, she turned in desperation to Pitt, out of office then but hopeful of returning to power. (He became prime minister again in May 1804.) Her uncle generously invited her into his home at Walmer. Lady Hester, after all, was the daughter of his favorite sister.

"Here I am," Lady Hester wrote to a friend one year later, "happy to a degree, exactly in the sort of society I most like. There are generally three or four men staying in the house; we dine nine or ten almost every other day. Military and naval characters are constantly welcome here; women are not, I suppose, because they do not form any part of our Society. You may guess, then, what a pretty fuss they make of me."

In the three years before his death Pitt became deeply attached to his high-spirited niece. He believed in her sincerity and in her affection for him, admired her courage and cleverness, laughed at her temper, and encouraged her pride. Lady Hester seems to have gained a considerable influence over her uncle and contrived to have a finger in most of the ministerial pies. When reproached for allowing her unreserved liberty of action in state affairs, Pitt was accustomed to reply, "I let her do as she pleases; for if she were resolved to cheat the devil himself, she would do it." She used to add, "And so I would," when she retold the story, always one of her favorites.

During an invasion scare Lady Hester asked Pitt for and received the command of a volunteer regiment, the Berkshire Militia, and she often rode with her illustrious uncle to inspect local coastal defenses erected against Napoleon. On one occasion Pitt told Lady Hester, "I have plenty of good diplomatists, but they are none of them military men; and I have plenty of good officers, but not one of them is worth sixpence in the cabinet. If you were a man, Hester, I would send you to the Continent with 60,000 men and give you *carte blanche*; and I am sure that not one of my plans would fail."

Herein lies the key to understanding the complex person of Lady Hester Stanhope. She possessed the intellect, ambition, education, discipline, and courage that probably would have brought her to greatness as a political leader in England *had she been born a man*. Yet she lived in a time and a society that allowed women no channels whatsoever for the expression of such talents, except in the narrowest of domestic spheres—the supervision of a country house, for example.

Dr. Meryon, who knew her best, perceptively summed up her dilemma: "The dream of Lady Hester's life was sway and dominion—how to obtain the one or the other was the difficulty; for she was born a subject and excluded by her sex from vice-royalties and governments: with the genius of a hero, she could neither take the command of fleets or armies, nor preside in councils of state."

Lady Hester's entire adult life thus became a search, sometimes ludicrous but often heroic, for a means by which she might exercise effectively her innate qualities of leadership. This search gave both meaning and poignancy to her life's adventures. And its intensity and scope made Lady Hester Stanhope unique among the women of her day.

On December 2, 1805, Napoleon defeated the combined armies of the emperors of Russia and Austria in the Battle of Austerlitz, a decisive victory that established him as the undisputed master of Europe. A few days later Pitt took ill. His condition worsened. He died on the afternoon of January 23, 1806, exactly twenty-five years to the day after he had first entered Parliament, a young man of twenty-one.

With Pitt's death, as if by the stroke of a magic wand, all the power, all the glory, and all the grandeur came to a sudden end, and the great minister's favorite niece fell to the level of a private lady, with a moderate income, no influence, and a host of enemies. On his deathbed Pitt had asked that an annuity of £1,500 be granted to Lady Hester, but in the end she was awarded only £1,200, a trifling income for one with such exalted ideas of her own importance. Now, at thirty, with no prospects of wealth, the opportunities she had once enjoyed of making a good match seemed to vanish like a puff of smoke in a winter wind.

Lady Hester took a house on Montagu Square in London, where she entertained her half brothers Charles and James Stanhope, when their military duties allowed them time to spend in town. She led a melancholy life. "She was, in truth, a dethroned princess," her niece the Duchess of Cleveland wrote many years after her death. "Her subjects had fallen off from their allegiance, and the world, that had been at her feet, knew her no more. She had not, perhaps, till then, fully realized the alteration in her position, nor anticipated its inevitable result, and she was bitterly mortified and disappointed. She had been accustomed to queen it in society, to be courted, consulted, and applauded, and she could not endure to find herself now of little or no account."

Lady Hester saw few people in this period. One, General John Moore, she had known from her days at Walmer. Moore was one of only two generals in whom Pitt had put any confidence. He was forty-five years old, fresh from the campaign in Sicily, where he had fought with distinction, and quite fond of Lady Hester. Both her brothers were attached to Moore's staff, and he became a frequent visitor to her house. In later years she insisted that an engagement existed between them. Nothing in Moore's surviving letters suggests this. But it is clear that they had a deep and reverent admiration for each other. She knew him as one of England's greatest generals, and he regarded her as the cleverest and most interesting woman of his acquaintance.

In July 1808 the British Army moved against Napoleon in Spain. After an initial victory the British campaign went badly. In October Sir John Moore took command. Hester's half brother Charles went with him. In late November Hester received a long letter from Moore. He closed it by saying: "Farewell, my dear Lady Hester. If I extricate myself and those with me from our present difficulties, and if I can beat the French, I shall return to you with satisfaction; but if not, it will be better that I should never quit Spain."

Moore proved unable to defeat the French Army in central Spain and fell back on La Coruña (known to the English as Corunna), where ships waited to evacuate his army. James Stanhope arrived from England to join him as his aide-de-camp. One final battle, which the British won, was fought at La Coruña. Sir John Moore fell fatally wounded and died in James Stanhope's arms. His last words were of Lady Hester: "Stanhope, remember me to your sister." Less than an hour later her favorite brother, Charles, was shot through the heart while leading a charge against an enemy position.

The two deaths devastated Lady Hester. The loss of her brother Charles was painful enough. But Moore's death on the same day closed off almost all her options. With him she might have found a life in England worthy of her many talents, a secure haven where she might have spent her remaining years. Without him her future prospects looked bleak indeed.

In near despair Lady Hester retired to an isolated cottage in Wales, where she amused herself by attending to her dairy and taking care of the neighborhood poor. Her health deteriorated. After some months she decided to close down her house in London and go abroad. There was nothing to hold her in England. She had few friends, no power, and no influence. And then there was the question of finances. She had long since come to appreciate the limits imposed by a state pension of £1,200. "A poor gentlewoman is the worst thing in the world," she said.

Her half brother James was soon to join his regiment in Spain. Why not, Lady Hester thought, go with him? The change would do her good. She put together a party, consisting of herself; her maid, Elizabeth Williams; a manservant; her brother James and a friend; and a young medical student from Oxford, Charles Meryon, who was to look after her health and ended up playing Boswell to her Dr. Johnson. On February 10, 1810, they sailed on board the frigate *Jason*. At the time Lady Hester Stanhope only intended to spend two years or so in some pleasant place in the Mediterranean and then return to England.

At Gibraltar she said good-bye to her brother, as it turned out, for the last time. She never saw him again after that or any other member of her family. Lady Hester and her party of three sailed to Malta. They arrived on Easter Day, and there she befriended a young man, eleven years her junior, Michael Bruce. It was an event that was to change momentously her life's direction. Within a matter of weeks the pair had fallen in love, and she had openly taken him as her lover.

Michael Bruce was born in Bombay into a titled Scottish family. At the time of his birth, his father, Craufurd Bruce, worked for the East India Company. Later he returned to London, where he became a senior partner of a bank, a wealthy businessman, and a Member of Parliament. Bruce adored his eldest son, Michael, and spoiled him outrageously. He sent him first to Eton and then to Cambridge. He expected him to take his place in the world and become a great statesman. As part of his education he had decided upon a foreign tour for his son. In June 1807 young Bruce set out for Stockholm. Three years later he was still traveling.

When Lady Hester Stanhope met Michael Bruce on Malta, he was twenty-three years old, a clever, ambitious man, familiar with every kind of travel and adventure, both able and willing to be of the greatest use to her. He was immediately taken by her and wrote his father: "Lady H. Stanhope who is now my Compagnon de voyage is a woman of very extraordinary talent. She inherits all the great and splendid qualities of her illustrious uncle."

She had been in love before, but for him it was the first time. Michael Bruce was dependent upon his father for all his money, and both realized that it would not be long before Craufurd Bruce learned of the liaison. Lady Hester persuaded Michael Bruce that their best course was to write his father directly, inform him of the exact situation, and reassure him that she had only his son's best interests at heart.

Lady Hester's letter was the first to arrive. In amazement Bruce read the following words from a woman he had never met:

> You may have heard that I have become acquainted with your Son; his elevated and Statesmanlike mind, his brilliant talents, to say nothing of his beautiful person, cannot be contemplated by any feeling mind with indifference; to know him is to love & admire him, & *I do both!* Should you hear this in any irregular way, it might give you uneasiness, & you might not only mistake the nature of the sentiments I feel towards him, but my *views* altogether, & imagine that he has fallen into the hands of an artful woman who would take him in, as far as it lay within her power. Sir, you need not be under any of these apprehensions; the affection I feel for him would only prompt me the more to consider his advantage in every point of view, & at this very moment (while loving him to distraction) I look forward to the period when I must resign him to some thrice happy woman really worthy of him. While seeking knowledge & considering plans of future ambition, few persons are perhaps better calculated for his companion than I am, but when he has taken his line, & become a public character, I shall then, like a dethroned Empress, resign to virtue the possession of that perfection which she alone has a right

to, & see whether a sacrifice, demanded by principle & true feeling, cannot be made with as good a grace as one dictated by policy and interest.

We can only guess at Bruce's initial reaction. But he was both worldly and practical. He had long been ambitious for his son to enter Parliament. What better tutor at this critical juncture of his son's life than Lady Hester Stanhope, the talented niece of Sir William Pitt, a woman who had lived for years among the most celebrated and powerful statesmen of the day? She could provide the young Bruce with a unique opportunity to further his education.

In a letter dated August 20, 1810, Craufaud Bruce replied to Lady Hester. He noted candidly that "Our correspondence has certainly commenced on a very extraordinary footing." Then he continued: "I have myself long been of the opinion that at the period when a Man is taking his first station in the operations of the World, he may derive the highest benefit and improvement from the advice and friendly communication with a well informed Female Mind; from them we take advice with more complacency, and other circumstances and feelings lead us to make it form more of a principle for our guidance and conduct;—in *you*, my Son has placed himself under the direction of a Lady who has from Ancestry a Hereditary claim to the most superlative Talents."

To his son Michael, Craufaud Bruce wrote: "You must assuredly derive much improvement to your reasoning powers and to your judgment from communications [with] a Woman possessed of such intellectual powers, and whose ardent wish appears to be to lead forth every latent Talent of your Mind and to inspire you with a greater love of Fame and ambition."

Lady Hester's roll of the dice had paid off handsomely. Openly engaged in a liaison that an increasingly prudish British society would have soundly condemned, she and her lover had admitted it all to a father who held the purse strings. And he, in turn, replied as though he had received the best of news, actually encouraging her to shape his son's mind and habits as she saw fit.

Well might we ask at this point how much of Lady Hester's "love" for Michael Bruce was based on a sincere attraction to his person and how much on the opportunity that he represented for the fulfillment of her "dream for sway and dominion." Did she perceive his future greatness as a statesman, once she had completed his education, as one way that she might have an impact on history and thus achieve for herself at least some measure of completion? Might she not have said to herself, "If I myself cannot be prime minister, then, by God, I will do the next best thing and, like a modern-day Pygmalion, shape a future prime minister from the clay of my own ambitions"?

If those, indeed, were the stakes of the game that Lady Hester was playing, then the risks—the almost certain loss of her place in British society once her affair with Michael Bruce had become general knowledge—would be the price that she would have to pay. But a woman who could write, "I make one rule for my own line of conduct, and one for that of others, and have two separate judgments; I mean one regulated by truth and feeling, and one after the fashion of what is thought right in the world," clearly was a woman who would not lose sleep over society's poor opinion of her.

Lady Hester Stanhope was about to stroll across the stage of nineteenth-century European history like a refugee queen from Greek tragedy.

After four months on Malta Lady Hester became restless to continue her travels. Events had conspired to limit severely her options. She could hardly return to England, not after her public affair with Michael Bruce. Financially she was enjoying a far more affluent life-style in the Mediterrean than was possible back in London on her annual pension, especially with Bruce's contributions. Napoleon's armies controlled most of Europe and the western end of the Mediterranean. As British subjects they would hardly be welcomed in those regions. Only the countries in the eastern part of the Mediterranean remained accessible to them.

Lady Hester decided that they should go to Constantinople. But she was not interested in mere sight-seeing. She had hatched a wild scheme to meet Napoleon. Her physician, Dr. Meryon, wrote home about it in utter disbelief: "You must have heard Lady Hester talk as I have done to believe that she can entertain any such project as what I am going to mention. She intends at Constantinople, to make friends with the French ambassador, and through this means to obtain a passport to travel through France. Protected by this, she will set off from Turkey, proceed through Hungary, Germany, and arrive at Paris. When there, she means to get into Bonaparte's good graces, study his character, and then sail for Britain to plot schemes for the subversion of his plans."

The party set sail on August 2 on the English frigate *Belle Poule* to the Greek island of Zante. From there they made their way to Athens, where they stayed for a month. One of their companions at this time was Lord Byron, who was then better known for his swim across the Hellespont than for the handful of minor poems he had published. Lady Hester did not like him: "I saw nothing in him but a well-bred man, like many others; as for his poetry, it is easy enough to write verses." They quarreled about the rights of women and parted coolly. Byron wrote of her to a friend: "I have seen too little of the lady to form a decisive opinion, but I have discovered nothing different from other she-things, except a great disregard of received notions in her conversation as well as her conduct."

Eager to be off to Turkey, Lady Hester ordered her party onto a Greek ship bound for Constantinople. They sailed on October 16. Their ship almost sank in a violent storm on the Sea of Marmara. They changed ships at the small port of Eregli. The party landed in the middle of the night on November 3 at Topkhana, one of the principal stairs leading to Pera, the Christian district of Constantinople. While the others walked, Lady Hester was carried up the steep hill in a sedan chair, preceded by a Turk lighting the darkness with an enormous lantern. Large dogs poked their heads out of the shadows and barked incessantly as they passed. This was Lady Hester's first experience with the Orient, and it was exotic enough to please her. Already her life in England seemed very far behind.

• • •

In 1810 Great Britain and Turkey were allies in the war against France. British soldiers had fought alongside Turkish forces when Napoleon occupied Egypt. Turkey at this time was convulsed by political unrest. The sultan had recently put down a mutiny among his palace troops. Violent demonstrations occurred frequently in the city. Less than thirty miles from Constantinople two provincial governors waged a petty war. The roads in the countryside were infested with deserters from the army, who plundered and murdered travelers virtually at will. Throughout the empire various factions rose in arms against their Turkish overlords.

Constantinople in 1810 was almost as exotic to the European traveler as was the far side of the moon. Islamic cities differed from their European counterparts in a curious lack of privacy, a condition noticed almost immediately by generations of travelers to the Middle East. Dr. Meryon remarks on it in his memoirs: "In Constantinople, all that one sees is odd and strange, but it is difficult to make another person understand in what that strangeness consists. The mere act of walking on the streets has something in it incompatible with recreation. There are no carriages or vehicles of any kind, and consequently the streets are so silent that people's voices are heard as in a room. All the shops are entirely open to the air; you are, therefore, subjected to the gaze of the shopkeepers; so that the effect is similar to what is felt in walking through a hall, with a row of servants on each side."

The Turkish authorities extended a warm welcome to Lady Hester. She and Bruce settled down to a long series of dinner parties and balls within the European community. She became friends with many prominent Turkish officials, including the brother-in-law of the pasha of Constantinople and the captain of the Turkish fleet. The latter invited her on board one of his ships. She shocked her Turkish host when she showed up wearing men's clothes ("a pair of overalls, a military great-coat, and a cocked hat"), which she considered much more practical for inspecting a ship than the flimsy gowns worn by women of fashion at the beginning of the nineteenth century.

Lady Hester's social success among the Turks was due in no small part to her personal physician. After Dr. Meryon had cured an official at the Danish Embassy, he suddenly enjoyed a great reputation among the Europeans and the Turks and found his services very much in demand. Unfortunately, he was of no assistance when George Canning, the young British minister in Constantinople, learned of Lady Hester's secret visits to the French chargé d'affaires for the purpose of securing a visa to travel in France. The two quarreled violently, and Lady Hester and her party were forbidden entry to the British Embassy. She soon found herself excluded as well from many of the social activities within the European community. To make matters worse, the French refused to issue her a visa. This particular plan to reshape the political destiny of Europe had to be abandoned.

In the fall of 1811 Lady Hester decided to leave Constantinople to winter in Egypt. Accordingly she and her party, which now had grown to thirteen people, set sail on a Greek ship on October 23. Once again they found themselves on the sea in the season of storms. They encountered violent weather almost immediately and had to put in for five days at one of the Greek islands until the winds calmed.

On November 23 their ship was halfway to Alexandria when it suddenly sprang a leak and started to founder. The crew and passengers frantically sought to bail by hand. The captain changed course toward Rhodes. Lady Hester observed the great confusion on board and recognized almost from the first the danger they were in. She ordered her maid to pack a small box with her basic necessities in case they had to abandon ship.

A storm blew up. Enormous waves broke over the deck of the ship, which was so waterlogged that it heeled over. Suddenly, the coast of Rhodes was spotted off the bow. The crew and passengers took to a single longboat and against all odds successfully navigated through the heavy surf to land safely on a small, uninhabited offshore islet. Promising to return with help as quickly as possible, the Greek captain and crew then sailed off, leaving their British passengers on their rocky refuge. Lady Hester and her party endured the next thirty hours without food, water, shelter, or dry clothes. The temperature dropped sharply. At last the Greek crew returned in a larger boat with bread, cheese, and water. Eventually they landed in the middle of a desolate coast in a heavy rain, trudged three miles to a windmill, the only building in sight for miles around, and put up for the night here. The next day in splendid weather the party started toward the town of Rhodes.

Lady Hester's courage in the crisis duly impressed Michael Bruce, who wrote home to his father: "It is impossible for me to do justice to Lady Hester for the coolness and intrepidity displayed by her during the whole of this trying experience. She lost property amounting to two or three thousand pounds. . . . She was very unwell before the shipwreck; and the real hardships which she underwent affected her frame so strongly, that I was under serious apprehension of losing her."

Lady Hester had taken the shipwreck in stride. She wrote to a friend: "Starving, thirty hours on a bare rock, without even fresh water, being half naked and drenched, having traversed an almost trackless country over dreadful rocks and mountains, laid me up at a village for a few days, but I have since crossed the island on an ass, going for six hours a day, which proves I am pretty well now, at least."

As those in the party had lost nearly all their clothes and knew that it would be impossible to buy European clothes in this remote region, they decided to adopt the Turkish costume of a long robe, a turban, yellow slippers, and a pelisse. Dr. Meryon traveled to Smyrna on the Turkish coast to obtain the necessary money and bought sufficient clothes for the entire party. Lady Hester determined to wear the dress of a Turkish gentleman, so that she could travel unveiled. The Oriental dress that she now adopted she never again discarded. "I assure you that if I ever looked well in anything, it is in the Asiatic dress," she wrote home to a friend.

Lady Hester and her friends gladly accepted the offer of a passage on a British frigate from Rhodes to Alexandria. On February 14, 1812, they got their first glimpse of the Egyptian coast and soon arrived in Alexandria, the large harbor of which was congested with ships, certain evidence of its commercial importance. A lively trade in corn between Egypt and England was a major source of revenue to the pasha.

Lady Hester was distinctly unimpressed with Alexandria. "This place I think quite hideous," she wrote to General Hildebrand Oakes, the governor of Malta, "and if all Egypt is like it, I shall wish to quit it as soon as possible." They tarried in Alexandria only long enough to make a few necessary purchases and then started on their way to Cairo, where Lady Hester hoped to meet the pasha, Muhammad Ali.

Cairo at the time was a bustling metropolis of some 250,000 people, the most influential political and economic center in the Middle East after Constantinople. Caravans of camels started there and traveled along well-defined routes to such distant commercial centers as Timbuktu in western Africa and India in the Far East. The bazaars of Cairo prospered on the items of trade that came in by caravan: gold, ivory, salt, spices, slaves, silk, and china. The city was a maze of crowded, narrow streets and dilapidated buildings. The towers and minarets of huge mosques dominated its skyline.

The handful of foreigners in Cairo lived in the European quarter, isolated from the rest of the city by great wooden doors that were closed every evening and during times of plague and civil unrest. Few signs of the French occupation remained to remind the people of Napoleon's stay in the city.

Lady Hester's arrival in Cairo on March 14 caused a great sensation, for she was the first Englishwoman of rank to visit Egypt. And Britain, after all, had decisively deflected Napoleon's thrust into the area. Thus Pasha Muhammad Ali, a man who was soon to play a decisive role in the history of modern Egypt through a skillful courting of the European powers, was eager to meet this niece of Sir William Pitt. He received her with much honor, sending five of his finest horses, splendidly caparisoned, to convey her and her party to his palace. A bevy of officials bearing silver sticks preceded Lady Hester, and she was allowed to ride through the outer courtyards and dismount at the inner gate of the palace itself.

She had prepared herself with due magnificence for the occasion and appeared before the pasha in a splendid Tunisian outfit of purple velvet embroidered with gold, wearing two cashmere shawls for which she had paid £100, one as a turban, the other as a girdle.

Muhammad Ali received Lady Hester and Michael Bruce in the garden of his harem in a small pavilion, so gaily decorated that it appeared to be a fairy palace. They sat on a sofa of scarlet velvet embroidered with gold, ate mint sherbet from cut-crystal glasses, and sipped coffee from fine china cups while they chatted. Afterward the pasha presented Hester with a magnificent charger.

The English party explored the sights of Cairo. The French consul invited them over for the opening of a mummy. After the bandages had been cut away from the body, the right hand was found to hold a papyrus. Dr. Meryon noted with keen interest that the mummy's facial features were poorly preserved.

Some days later Lady Hester's party crossed the Nile and visited the pyramids. Bandits in the surrounding desert made such an expedition a risky venture. However, she engaged a troop of magnificently costumed Mamelukes to escort her and so went there in style without incident.

Throughout these travels Michael Bruce had become even more infatuated with Lady Hester. In his letters back to his father, he talked of himself as "her knight," adding, "I should and would if necessary sacrifice everything for her." He insisted that he had gained more knowledge from his conversations with her than in all his book learning. At one point he even proposed marriage. But she peremptorily cut him off. He wrote in sadness to his father: "It ought to be remembered that this is no common case. There has been no seduction, no binding promises, none of the artifices usually practised by her sex, but it is that of a woman who has refused marriage, the only compensation in my power to offer, and an honor to which I have no right to aspire, and who with a magnanimity almost unparalleled has sacrificed her own reputation in order that she might prove no embarrassment to me."

Lady Hester, however, had things other than marriage on her mind. She had turned her thoughts to the Holy Land, an unsettled and dangerous place for the European traveler. But she had made up her mind. In fewer than two years of travel she had begun to feel a strong spiritual kinship with the Arab world. She was now fluent in Arabic and could read and write the language as well as speak it. Her European heritage was quickly receding behind her.

On May 11, 1812, Lady Hester Stanhope and her party set sail from Alexandria for the Holy Land. She did not know it then, but she had embarked upon an adventure that was finally to allow her to make her mark on history.

On May 16 the party landed at Jaffa. Once the royal harbor of King Solomon, Jaffa was in 1812 the principal port of entry of travelers to the Holy Land, a walled city of some 3,000 inhabitants. Few signs remained of Napoleon's siege there some thirteen years before. Lady Hester landed in Jaffa two years and three months after her departure from Britain. In retrospect, it seems as if a kind of fate had brought her to those shores. As her biographer John Watney has observed, "Never, at any time, had she deliberately aimed herself there; but slowly events, as if taking part in her destiny, had, by denying her other possibilities, driven her to this historic land. Had it not been for the deaths of Sir John Moore and her brother Charles, she might never have left England at all. If Murat had not threatened Sicily, she might have settled there. If Constantinople had been less unfriendly and cold, and Cairo less flea-ridden, she might have stayed in either place. Whether through fate or an inner unacknowledged urge, she was there at last."

Jaffa was crowded with hundreds of Easter season pilgrims who had just returned from Jerusalem. Most were from other parts of the Middle East and in pathetic condition. Except for three Spaniards and one German, there were no other European travelers in Jaffa.

Lady Hester took up residence in the Franciscan monastery. No time was lost in making preparations for the trip to Jerusalem. Eleven camels were hired for the luggage, and thirteen horses for the party.

The governor of Jaffa, Muhammad Aga, at Hester's request, sent two armed horsemen to accompany her.

Lady Hester decided to travel in style. She put on her best Mameluke outfit. It consisted of a hip-length satin vest, with long sleeves, open to the elbow, and fastened at the throat with a single button. Over this she wore a bright red jacket. Her trousers were of the same material with gold-embroidered pockets. Her turban was a cashmere shawl. When on horseback, she wore a white-hooded cloak with silky tassels that, in Dr. Meryon's words, "gave great elegance to her figure." Thus attired, she was frequently mistaken for a beardless boy.

Lady Hester's party set out for Jerusalem. On the way the group encountered an extraordinary sight, a plague of locusts so thick that a house and tree they covered appeared to have been painted green. One evening the English were guests of Sheik Abu Ghosh, a highwayman who extracted large sums from pilgrims for the right to pass through his territory to Jerusalem. Lady Hester's splendid costume so impressed him that he waived all fees, slaughtered a sheep, ordered his four wives to prepare a lavish feast, and conversed with her at length.

The next day the English group continued along a stony track over the last barren mountain and finally saw Jerusalem in the distance. The city lay, somber and imposing, behind its high walls. The party entered by the Gate of Bethlehem.

Lady Hester suddenly remembered an incident from many years before when she had lived with Pitt. A fashionable fortune-teller named Samuel Brothers had been thrown into prison, and he had sent word that he wished to talk with Lady Hester. She'd gone, curious about why he, a stranger, should single her out. Brothers had told her of a prophecy that it was her destiny to fulfill: She would make a pilgrimage to Jerusalem, spend seven years in the desert, be crowned queen of the Jews, and lead forth a chosen people. At the time she had paid no attention to his predictions because she'd had no intention of leaving England. But now, as she rode up to the gates of Jerusalem, she remembered them. She remarked to Dr. Meryon, half-jokingly, half-seriously, that as the first part of Brothers's prophecy had come true, so might the rest.

The group settled in at the Franciscan monastery, the common abode for European travelers to the city for several centuries. Dr. Meryon noted mockingly that their accommodation consisted of "a few rooms bare of everything but fleas." Beggars pestered them wherever they went. The blatant commercialism surrounding the Holy Sepulcher and the Last Walk of Christ was equally disturbing.

The next day Lady Hester's party visited Bethlehem. Dr. Meryon thought that most of the village's men, who carried long knives stuck in their belts, looked more like robbers than shepherds. Hucksters dogged their every step, trying to sell them holy beads and crosses.

Lady Hester left Jerusalem on May 30. She and Bruce hired ten camels and four horses to add to those they already had. Her retinue had now grown to such an impressive size that she was greeted with awe and deference wherever she went. To quote John Watney once more:

> Hester's cavalcade was the continuation of an old tradition. The Kings and Queens of Europe had perambulated through their lands since medieval days, taking with them the whole Court, and conducting their business from whatever site they had chosen. . . . Even when the Court became more settled, wealthy families would make the Grand Tour of Europe in the same style, moving *en bloc* across the European countryside. . . . What was exceptional about Hester's caravanserai was that it was taking place in the Middle East, where there was almost permanent strife between Turkish overlords and their subjected people, particularly the Arabs; and where there were also periodic waves of destructive plagues.

The party made its way slowly toward Acre. The days settled into a recognizable pattern. They camped in the evenings in their large green tents, usually near a stream and a village, where they bought provisions of milk, eggs, chickens, and honey and wood for their fires. The headman supplied guards to watch over the sleeping camp during the hours of darkness. In the cool of the morning they set out once again. During the heat of midday Lady Hester rested in a tent, while Dr. Meryon hurried ahead with the baggage animals to set up the night's camp.

At Acre she dined with a wealthy Jewish banker, Mâlem Haym Shâady. He told her of the unspeakable horrors he had endured years before, when he had worked as the secretary to Pasha el Gezzar, who one day in a pique of temper cut off one of Shâady's ears and his nose and gouged out his left eye. On another occasion the pasha had ordered him baked alive in an oven, only to change his mind after Shâady had been terribly burned over large parts of his body.

At Nazareth Michael Bruce was thunderstruck to find himself suddenly addressed in excellent English by a bare-legged Syrian peasant with a long beard and blue eyes. He proved to be the celebrated Swiss traveler and explorer John Lewis Burckhardt. He wore the usual costume of the Syrian lower classes: a coarse white shirt, a dirty turban, and a pair of shabby slippers. The disguised Burckhardt was slowly working his way south toward Cairo.

In Sidon Lady Hester unexpectedly received an invitation from the emir Bashir II of the Druzes to visit his palace high in the surrounding mountains. The Druzes were a secret religious sect, which had splintered from the main body of Islam centuries before and had sought refuge in the rugged mountainous country around Mount Lebanon. Virtually nothing about them was known at the time, except that they were a warlike people who had successfully maintained their independence for more than 800 years. Wild rumors abounded. Some insisted that the Druzes had originated in Africa; others that they were descended from Crusaders driven into the mountains by the Saracens. Only a handful of European travelers had penetrated the mountain fastness of the Druzes and lived to tell about it. The prospect of a lengthy visit with the Druze leader pleased Lady Hester enormously.

After a full day's ride the party reached Deir el Qamar, the Druze capital, a town of some 8,000 inhabitants that sprawled along the side of a mountain. They lodged at a guesthouse which the emir had prepared for their stay. Its last owner had recently been strangled on orders from Bashir.

While they waited for an official invitation to visit the palace,

Lady Hester investigated the strange cusoms of the Druze people. She was accorded extraordinary liberties. "I understand my ground so well with savage people that I can ask questions no other person dares put to them," she later boasted in a letter to a friend. "Any one who asks a religious question may be murdered without either the Emir Bashir (the Prince of the Mountain) or the Shaykh Bashir (the governor) being able to punish the offender."

The Druze custom of eating raw meat fascinated her. She recounted later: "I purchased of a Druze an immense sheep, the tail weighing eleven pounds, and desired it to be taken to a village, where I ordered the people assembled to eat. When I arrived, the sheep was alive; the moment it was killed it was skinned, and brought in raw upon a sort of dish made of matting, and in less than half an hour it was all devoured. The women ate of it as well as the men: the pieces of raw fat they swallowed were really frightful."

Dr. Meryon conducted his own investigations, in particular of the Druze women with their tall, hornlike headdresses, similar to those worn by medieval European women. He learned that the horns were made of silver, copper, or a kind of cardboard, depending upon the social status of the woman. The women draped black or white veils gracefully over their horns and fastened them to their heads with handkerchiefs tied under their chins. The women slept with their horns on, taking them off only when they bathed or combed their hair. Embroidered trousers and bright yellow slippers completed the costume.

The emir's invitation finally came. With great anticipation the party rode into his palace, which they found to be a rather drab collection of plain rooms, haphazardly thrown together. Lady Hester was the first European traveler ever permitted inside the palace. They stayed two days with the emir Bashir, who proved a gracious host, eager to extend his hospitality to this woman, whom he perceived to be an important representative of a European power that had only recently become a factor in his region's politics. But, as Dr. Meryon observed, he was a dangerous man: "He had mounted his throne in blood, and put out the eyes of his three nephews fearing they would aspire to it, and had reigned as a tyrant and a hypocrite."

The emir presented Lady Hester with a handsome horse, richly adorned. He could never have imagined that this Englishwoman, the first he had ever seen, would in a few years rent a ruined palace on one of his most inaccessible hilltops and set herself up as his rival.

Lady Hester and Michael Bruce were in the midst of a splendid series of adventures unrivaled by any previous travelers to the Middle East. But the enormous costs of the huge caravanserai finally began to weigh upon them. Craufaud Bruce was paying most of the expenses. In one month young Bruce drew bills on his father for £300 and £550. Their travels over the past eight months had cost the elder Bruce £3,700, the equivalent today of almost $100,000. Michael Bruce's bills came due at a time when his father was experiencing financial difficulties as the result of heavy real estate speculation.

Shortly after their month-long visit among the Druze people the two lovers split up temporarily, he to make his way toward the ruins of Aleppo, she to Damascus. The Turkish officials on the coast all urged her not to make the trip, as did the pasha of Damascus. The city, one of the most dangerous for Christians under the best of conditions, was then caught up in a brutal civil war between the newly appointed pasha and his army commander.

Hester was undeterred by the bad news or the warnings that if she tried to enter Damascus unveiled and wearing men's clothing, she would almost certainly be stoned by angry Muslims. On the eve of her departure she wrote to reassure Craufurd Bruce about the impending expedition, full of confidence about her ability to bring it to a successful conclusion: "I hate cowards but I despise rashness. . . . Above 40,000 Arabs are now at war with each other in these parts, therefore you may imagine the state of things in that quarter. But I trust we shall do very well. I have a Turkish Janissary who is the Devil. I have seldom seen a man with finer talents, & more capable for such a journey. My Greek boy also has fine cool courage! As for all the rest, I would not give sixpence for them, tho' I cannot quite do without them. Tents must be pitched & horses fed, as well as their masters."

The journey to Damascus took three days. On September 1 Lady Hester arrived outside the city gates. Once again she was warned not to enter without covering her face behind a veil. The Arabs on the coast had grown used to seeing European women with their faces exposed. Not so in Damascus, where no European woman had ever set foot.

Lady Hester was adamant and refused to yield to local custom. "Lady Hester, therefore, needed no little courage to undergo the trial that awaited her," Dr. Meryon noted. "A woman, unveiled, and in man's attire, she entered in broad daylight one of the most fanatical towns in Turkey. The people gazed at us, and all eyes were turned towards her ladyship. Her feminine looks passed with many, without doubt, for those of a beardless youth. More saw at once that it must be a woman; but before they could recover from their astonishment, we had passed on."

She was enormously pleased and wrote to a friend to boast: "My entry in Damascus, one of the most singular and not one of my least exploits, as it was reckoned so dangerous, from the fanaticism of the Turks in that town, was a triumph."

Damascus, like most of the other cities in the Middle East at this time, was divided into three sections: the Muslim, the Jewish, and the Christian. The Christian quarter was always in the least desirable part of the city. Lady Hester was fully aware of that. Shortly after her arrival she informed the pasha that the house in the Christian quarter was insufficient to her needs and demanded another. The pasha gave in to her demands, and soon the party was settled in a house in the best quarter of Damascus. The entrance opened onto an oblong marble courtyard, in the center of which two lemon trees shaded a fountain in the shape of two serpents spouting cool, clear water. At one end was a salon with a sofa for receiving guests. A wide staircase behind led to a suite of apartments.

Few cities in the world are as old as Damascus, the area having been continuously inhabited for more than 8,000 years. Tradition says that Abraham rested by its waters and Muhammad called it paradise. Later St. Paul was secretly lowered in a basket over the walls to escape the Jews. Its population at the time of Hester's visit was perhaps just under 250,000. Early travelers to Damascus often remarked that it was a city of fountains. Almost every house boasted one, and public fountains spouted in almost every part of the city. Indeed, the abundance of water from mountain-fed streams and rivers was a principal reason why the city flourished as a major caravan stop. Once a year the great religious pilgrimages to Mecca aroused the country to ferment. There were various routes to the Muslim holy city. The western hajj, which started in Damascus and included pilgrims from Constantinople, was one of the most populous, a veritable river of humanity flowing south toward Mecca.

Lady Hester rested for two days. Then she decided upon a ride, determined to test her reception in the city once more. Again she went out unveiled, dressed as a man. A large crowd gathered on the street in front of her house. Lady Hester smiled at them as she mounted her horse. The moment was tense. No one knew what the crowd's response would be. But far from being attacked or insulted, she was cheered. Rumors had circulated through the city that while she had been born in Britain, she was actually of Ottoman descent with Muslim blood in her veins. Others had imagined the possibility of a British occupation of Syria and looked upon Hester has a princess who had come to prepare the way for the expected conquest. Women poured coffee in the roadway ahead of her horse, a rare honor, and saluted her as *meleki,* "queen." All this came at a time when a native Christian who dared leave his quarter on horseback or wearing a conspicuous turban or garment would risk an almost certain savage beating by a mob of zealous Muslim fanatics.

"All I can say about myself sounds like conceit," Lady Hester wrote home, "but others could tell you I am the oracle of the place, and the darling of all the troops, who seem to think I am a deity because I can *ride,* and because I wear arms; and the fanatics all bow before me, because the Dervishes think me a wonder, and have given me a piece of Mahomet's tomb."

The pasha invited her to his palace. She walked through antechambers, lined by rows of silent soldiers and illuminated by flaring candles, to an inner suite, where she found the pasha, a small but dignified man, sitting alone on a crimson sofa. He motioned for Lady Hester to be seated. She presented him with a handsome snuffbox. In return he gave her a beautiful Arab stallion.

In a lengthy account of the experience to Crauford Bruce, Lady Hester wrote enthusiastically: "Of all the things I have seen here, the palace of the Pasha is the finest. It contains above 60 rooms & is magnificent beyond description. Everything in England is a cottage [compared] to it. The fine courts into which the rooms look are all paved with coloured marble full of Fountains & Orange trees & flowers. The rooms have cascades or fountains in them & such a quantity of fine china."

In the meantime, Dr. Meryon visited a hospital for lepers. No medical treatment was provided. Rather, the victims of the disease, living on the alms of the charitable, were brought there to rot. Dr. Meryon created a sensation among his hosts when he clasped the rotting hand of a leper to prove his theory that leprosy was not a contagious disease.

Lady Hester continued her triumphal tour of Damascus. This was a time when her sex worked in her favor. The rich merchants of the city fell over one another for the privilege of inviting her to see their harems, an honor no European had ever before been accorded. Had she been a man, the doors to that most inviolable of Muslim inner sanctums the harem would never have opened to her. Lady Hester wrote proudly to a friend:

I believe I am the only person who can give an account of the manner in which a great Turk is received by his wives and women. The other day I was paying a visit to the wife of a very great Turkish master. Not less than fifty women were assembled in the harem to see me, when in came the lord and master—and all put on their veils, except his wife and his own women. He made a sign and all retired.

We talked for some time and then he proposed dining. He led me into a beautiful court paved with coloured marble, with fountains playing amongst orange trees. In a sort of alcove we found dinner prepared, or rather supper, for it was at sunset. Everything was served in high style by black female slaves and a black gentleman. Immense gilt candlesticks, with candles nearly six feet high, were set on the ground, with a great illumination of small elegant lamps suspended in clusters in different parts of the court.

The proud man talked a great deal and kept me there until ten o'clock, an hour past the time which, if anyone is found on the streets, they are to have their heads cut off. Such is the Pasha's new decree. The Pasha cuts off nearly a head or two every day. All the gates were shut. But all opened for me, and not a word was said.

Lady Hester then accepted an invitation from Mahannah el Fadel, a chief to some 40,000 Bedouins, to travel with his people through the desert. The spectacular sight of thousands of Bedouins and their camels, goats, and horses, moving across the sandy plains in a vast migration, overwhelmed her. For one week she lived among them. They treated her with unfailing respect and courtesy.

Later the Englishwoman gave Dr. Meryon a catalog of the marvels she had experienced in the desert: 12,000 camels coming to water from one tribe alone; the old poets from the banks of the Euphrates River singing the praises and feats of ancient heroes; women with lips dyed light blue and their nails red and their hands tattooed all over with small flowers and other designs.

"I have every reason to be perfectly contented with their conduct towards me, and I am the *Queen* with them all," Lady Hester wrote afterward. Clearly, for the first time since the death of her uncle, she had found a large enough stage on which she might exercise her considerable skills. There, in the desert with her Bedouin hosts, she was a queen. And she acted the part to the hilt: "I have orderly Arabs at my command, and receive dispatches every two or three days, giving me an account of what is going forward in the desert, of what battles have been fought, and with what tribes war has been declared."

Lady Hester had found her element. "To command is to be really great," she proclaimed. "To have talents is to talk sense without a book in one's hands. And to have manners is to be able to accommodate oneself to the customs and tastes of others, and still to make them either fear or love you."

She wrote Craufurd Bruce: "You must not take for granted that I am in robust health because I have so much energy. It is my nature. It is the spirit of my Grandfather, for had I one foot in the grave, I could command an Army, even in Egypt. I am like one of Mahomet's mares, who he ordered to be kept from drinking 48 hours & when carried to a spring, the moment the *battle horn sounded,* they refused the water before them & flew to their master. I have much too much imagination & spirit ever to live again in degraded England."

She now set to work on another grand scheme, one that had obsessed her for some weeks: a trip to the fabled Roman city of Palmyra located in the desert far to the north of Damascus. When she announced her plans, everyone, including the pasha, tried to dissuade her for many reasons: The Bedouins would rape, rob, and murder her; barring that, they would hold her for a queen's ransom; if the Bedouins did not get her, then seventy miles of waterless, trackless desert would. (We may appreciate some indication of the dangers of the region by knowing that as late as 1912 the popular *Baedeker Guide to the Middle East* advised all travelers to Palmyra to take along armed escorts.)

Lady Hester persisted. She would go to Palmyra regardless of the risks. She knew of only three Europeans who had actually visited the site, and they had traveled there disguised as Syrian peddlers. (In fact, there were others she did not know about, but at the most fewer than a dozen in history, and never had a European woman gone there.) Finally the pasha offered her 1,000 of his finest soldiers as an escort.

Her Bedouin friend Nasar, the son of Mahannah el Fadel, visited her one evening and advised her against going into the desert in the company of Turkish troops, enemies to all Bedouins. He told her: "Soldiers of the city know not the tracks and landmarks of the desert; where the wells are; what parts are infested with hostile tribes; who is friendly and who is not. And, when they have led you into difficulties, they will be the first to desert you." Then Nasar suggested that Lady Hester place her trust in him and his Bedouins to escort her safely to Palmyra.

She agreed. After all, she had spent a week with his tribe without any discourtesy being shown her. The prospect of riding at the head of a great column of desert Arabs appealed to her sense of destiny. And Brothers had predicted that she would be queen of the Jews. She was not quite that. But the Bedouins treated her as though she were the queen of the Arabs. "How much more of Brothers' prophecy would come true?" she wondered aloud to Dr. Meryon.

She sent Dr. Meryon ahead to Palmyra to reconnoiter the area and report back to her. Finally all the preparations were completed. On March 29, 1813, Lady Hester wrote enthusiastically to General Oakes on Malta: "Tomorrow, my dear General, I mount my horse with seventy Arabs and am off to Palmyra at last."

Palmyra. The ancient Romans called it "The City of Palms." For the Arabs, it was "The Bride of the Desert."

"A white skeleton of a town, standing knee-deep in the blown sand," was how the English traveler and writer Gertrude Bell described Palmyra when she saw it for the first time in 1900. "And beyond all, the desert, sand, and white stretches of salt, and sand again, with the dust clouds whirling over it, and the Euphrates five days away. Except for Petra, Palmyra is the loveliest thing I have seen in this country."

Remote in its desert fastness, Palmyra is one of the most romantic sites to have come down to us from the ancient world. This ghost city of vast, colonnaded streets, lavishly decorated tombs, ornate stone carvings, and imposing temples combines late Hellenistic, Parthian, and Roman architectural styles on a scale unmatched in the classical era.

Palmyra lies near the narrow strip of land that encloses the Euphrates Valley and that historians have named the Fertile Crescent. This strip of land only fifteen to twenty miles wide begins at a point parallel to the southeastern corner of the Mediterranean, skirts Lebanon and the foothills of the Taurus range, and ends in the Persian Gulf near the site of ancient Ur.

The importance of this slender crescent of fertile land with its abundant water source can hardly be exaggerated. Many historians believe that this area, not Egypt, was the cradle of civilization. Scholars have also traced to the Fertile Crescent the origins of a widespread belief that mankind's first home was in a garden, where the earth produced all it needed to support life bountifully.

From the very dawn of commerce the oasis village of Palmyra—called Tadmor in the Bible—was an important caravan stop. The Sumerian, Babylonian, and Greek civilizations flourished and then passed into decline, while the merchants of Palmyra went about their mundane business of accumulating wealth through trade with far-flung commercial outposts in the Orient and Africa. By the first century B.C. the caravan trade had made Palmyra rich enough to arouse the interest of Rome.

When Roman and Parthian interests clashed in the area, the Palmyrenes did their best to maintain a stance of neutrality between the two competing empires. Although Rome was able to make Syria a Roman province in 64 B.C., Parthia resisted subjugation. In 53 B.C. the Parthians defeated an army of Roman legionnaires. In a gesture of contempt that shocked Rome, the Parthians executed the captured commander, the consul Marcus Licinus Crassus, and used his severed head as a stage prop in a production of Euripides' play *The Bacchae.*

Early in the first century A.D. Palmyra was absorbed into the Roman Empire. From that time onward it played an important role in the frontier between the Roman Empire and Rome's great rival to the east, Parthia. Palmyrene archers enjoyed an excellent reputation within the Roman Army. The Roman naturalist Pliny visited Palmyra and noted its rich soil and pleasant streams but warned his readers that because of the desert surrounding the oasis city, Roman visitors might feel themselves cut off from the rest of the world. In A.D. 129 the emperor Hadrian declared Palmyra a free city, in recognition of its importance to the empire.

Palmyra is closely associated with the name of Queen Zenobia, who was famed for her beauty, masculine energy, and great intellect. After her husband, the Arab king Septimius Odenathus, was murdered about A.D. 267, she proclaimed herself queen of Palmyra and ruled over the tribes of the Syrian desert. Her exploits spread Palmyra's name throughout the Roman Empire, for Zenobia very nearly defeated the might of Rome.

After Zenobia had seized power and declared herself absolute ruler, the emperor Gallienus sent a Roman army against her. But Zenobia smashed them. Had she stopped there, she might well have worked out a truce in her favor with Rome. But she was ambitious for much more, her own empire. In short order, her army conquered the entire province of Syria and seized Bosra, the capital of the Roman province of Arabia. Then, in A.D. 269, Zenobia marched her army into Egypt and within a year had added that country to her rapidly growing empire. In A.D. 271 she proclaimed her son Augustus, a title reserved only for Roman emperors. All Rome was in shock. Never before had the authority of the empire been so successfully contested.

Contemporary accounts of Zenobia are somewhat sketchy and largely Roman, hence biased. But a consistent portrait emerges of a truly remarkable person. The classicist Agnes Vaughan in her biography of Zenobia writes of this third-century queen of the Arabs: "Zenobia was capable of great physical endurance. Though she enjoyed marching on foot with her soldiers, she usually rode a horse or a camel; she detested litters, and used a carriage only on state occasions. In a drinking bout with her generals, she could hold her own. The Roman historian Pollio adds, with a touch of humor, that she drank with Parthians and Armenians only to get 'the better of them.' She was not fond of ostentation, but at her banquets she used 'vessels of gold and jewels, and she even used those that had been Cleopatra's.' "

How different the Roman history of his period might have been had not the reins of power in the empire unexpectedly passed into the capable hands of the youthful cavalry commander Aurelian. In A.D. 270 the legions proclaimed him Caesar. Aurelian personally undertook the reconquest of Asia Minor. He rolled Zenobia's army back to Palmyra and laid siege to her city. That proved no easy task. The walls of Palmyra bristled with javelin throwers, archers, and great catapults that hurled down upon the Romans large boulders and balls of fire. The siege seemed to go on forever. In time the defenders' supply of food and water grew low, and their morale broke. Aurelian's army entered the city and captured Zenobia on the banks of the Euphrates, where she had fled. Aurelian seized the gold of the city, spared the inhabitants, but put to death all of Zenobia's officials and advisers. Zenobia apparently lived out the rest of her days as a Roman matron at Tibur. When Palmyra rebelled once again and massacred the entire Roman garrison stationed there, Aurelian returned, plundered and burned the city, and then put most of its inhabitants to the sword. Palmyra never recovered from this blow. In time it was forgotten and became a ghost city of ruins amid the windswept sands of the Syrian desert.

Lady Hester Stanhope's expedition to Palmyra proved to be her grandest adventure. The ancient city appealed to her love of drama, history, politics, and empire. Two months before her departure, when she wrote Craufurd Bruce at length about what she hoped to accomplish in the desert, she sounded very much like a prime minister plotting the long-range strategy of the British Empire:

My original plan in coming into this country was to procure a very just idea of the Arab character, their customs & their power. The latter I have always considered important to our Indian possessions. I cannot here explain my opinions. Indeed, they more regard the future than the present. But we are always behind with our information. . . . I have most strongly urged [Michael] Bruce to take advantage of an opportunity which may not occur for these fifty years, to visit Palmyra in a way no one else can, & then to proceed to the banks of the Euphrates, where from what I can understand the finest fisheries in the world might be established & where no modern traveller has penetrated except one.

Lady Hester had another reason, of course. Many of the broken columns and temples of Palmyra owed their existence to Queen Zenobia, a figure with whom she felt the most intense spiritual kinship. She sought the remains of Zenobia's greatness as much as she did the remains of Palmyra. In a letter home Michael Bruce speculated on this connection: "If Lady Hester succeeds in this undertaking, she will at least have the merit of being the first European female who has ever visited this once celebrated city. Who knows but she may prove another Zenobia, and be destined to restore it to its ancient splendour?"

When Lady Hester departed Damascus, she rode at the head of an impressive caravan. Twenty-two camels carried tents, baggage, food, and other provisions; another eight, water; and nine, the corn needed for the horses. Lady Hester dressed for the occasion in a magnificent cloak with a leather belt and a horsehair cord around her head, Bedouin-style. She carried a chief's lance and rode on a stallion the pasha had given her.

Directly behind her came her bodyguard—a group of Bedouin chieftains, carrying long lances plumed with ostrich feathers. Their black hair hung in ringlets over their cheeks and necks. Their gaily colored kaffiychs were drawn, like visors, over their mouths.

The atmosphere of the trip was festive. When they were bored, the Bedouins mounted sham fights. They would throw off their headgear, lift high their lances, let out war whoops, select opponents, and then rush furiously at them. Those assailed in turn would pivot sharply to avoid the attacks and then make runs at their assailants. When the Bedouins tired of these games, they would call up the two poets who traveled with them and order them to recite tales in verse of the glorious deeds of past heroes.

When the caravan camped in the evening, an enormous black slave named Guntar, a fearful double-edged battle-ax in hand, stood guard outside Lady Hester's tent.

A constant danger was an assault by the El Faydan Arabs who were the sworn enemies of the tribe of Mohannah. One night, when rumors of an attack were rampant, the English awoke to discover that Nasar and all his Bedouins had fled the camp, leaving them in the middle of the desert with no guide and no idea of where the life-giving wells could be found. The situation was extremely tense. Undismayed, Lady Hester took command and appeared "as cool as if in a ball-room." She gave orders that every man should take up his gun and pistol, and she stationed her little garrison at different points around the camp. Soon Nasar and his Bedouins returned. Lady Hester suspected that it had all been a feint to test her nerve in an effort to frighten her into paying a larger subsidy than the £150 already agreed upon in Damascus.

The next day the caravan rode into the ancient city of Palmyra. The 1,500 Palmyrenes had been warned of the approach of "a great white queen," who rode a stallion worth forty purses and possessed a book that instructed her where to find treasure and a bag of herbs by which she could transmute stones into gold. Lady Hester was met by 200 frenzied horsemen, stripped to the waist, who fired matchlocks into the air and pounded loudly on kettledrums.

The guides led the caravan along down a colonnade nearly a mile long which terminated at a triumphal arch. On the shaft of each of the pillars was a pedestal on which a statue once stood. "What was our surprise," Dr. Meryon wrote, "to see, as we rode up the avenue, that several beautiful girls had been placed on these very pedestals, in the most graceful postures, and with garlands in their hands. While Lady Hester advanced, these living statues remained immoveable on their pedestals. But when she had passed, they leaped on to the ground and joined in a dance by her side."

She was delighted by the reception, especially when a child suspended from the arch held a wreath over her head. Yet another of Brothers's prophecies had come true. "Without joking, I have been crowned Queen of the Desert under the triumphal arch at Palmyra," she boasted later in a letter to a friend. "Nothing ever succeeded better than this journey, dangerous as it was. All pay me homage. If I please, I can now go to Mecca *alone*; I have nothing to fear. I shall soon have as many names as Apollo. I am the sun, the star, the pearl, the lion, the light from Heaven, and the Queen."

The Palmyrenes led Lady Hester to the Temple of the Sun, which became her residence for the next week. She would have stayed longer but for the fact that four Arabs of the El Faydan tribe were found lurking in a nearby spring. Fearing an attack, Nasar insisted she depart the following day.

The return trip was uneventful. On April 13 Lady Hester rode triumphantly into the Syrian city of Hamah. The people thronged the streets, shouting, "*Selmet-ya, meleki, selme, ya syt*" ["Welcome, queen, welcome, madame"]. The Syrians were in a frenzy. "They considered Lady Hester a true heroine, who could perform in triumph what not a pasha in all Turkey durst venture to do with all his troops at his heels," Dr. Meryon noted. Lady Heser's journey to Palmyra had transformed her into a legendary figure.

She herself emerged from the trip with a fresh appreciation of the Bedouins. Henceforth she saw their austere desert life in idealized and transcendental terms, their primitive desert ways embodying for her a purity of motive utterly lacking among the civilized people in Europe. She wrote to a friend, articulating a theme which later travelers to the Middle East voiced time and time again: "When the world becomes still more corrupt, when people—civilized people—become still more brutal and still more incisive, it is a pleasure to reflect that there is a spot of earth inhabited by what we call barbarians, who have at least some sense of honour and feeling, and where one is sure never to be bored with stupidity or gabble, for they are the most brilliant and eloquent people I ever knew."

On May 10, 1813, Lady Hester set out for the coast to spend the summer at the small port of Latakia, a town of some 4,000 people. The year before, a terrible plague, the worst in decades, had broken out in Constantinople. More than 20,000 people had reportedly died. It slowly spread southward and by early 1813 was raging throughout Syria. Lady Hester sought out Latakia because it was reputed to be free of the plague. She and Michael Bruce settled into a large but somewhat dilapidated house; Dr. Meryon, into a smaller one nearby.

By now the good doctor had become almost as famous as a healer as the Englishwoman was as a queen. Great crowds of sick came to him at every stop along the way. He set up a practice in Latakia. Early one morning, while he was hurrying to the house of a sick patient, Dr. Meryon abruptly came upon the body of a man kneeling in an enormous pool of blood, a gory stake protruding from his body just below the sixth rib. Fewer than two hours before, the man—a thief and murderer—had been impaled upon a sharpened stake stuck into the ground, a common form of execution throughout the Turkish Empire.

The plague steadily closed in upon them. In June a ship arrived from Tarsus with the corpses of seven victims on board. The officials in the town turned the ship away. Latakia began to register the first deaths from the dreaded pestilence. Reports that more than 100,000 people had died of plague in Damascus alone reached Latakia.

In October Lady Hester and Bruce separated, he to return to his father in England. Bruce was thoroughly sick of the Middle East and detested the Arabs; unlike Lady Hester or Dr. Meryon, he had never bothered to learn the language. The passions that had once existed between them had long since cooled. Bruce's natural fickleness reasserted itself. And her love of adventure far outweighed her need for physical love. Daily she became more absorbed with her growing power over the Arabs.

More important, she had decided that she had misjudged him. He was not destined for greatness. After their three years together she could now see only his faults. Lady Hester wrote Craufurd Bruce a catalog of them, in the condescending tone of a scolding aunt: "He rides vastly ill for a man with so fine a person, & I have recommended that he go to a riding house. Nothing is so necessary as for an Englishman to ride well. . . . He ought to learn to carve well, & have constant attention for those about him at the table. I hope you will attend very particularly to this, as it is esteemed the most ill bred and vulgar thing among great men not to be attentive at the table. His sisters must watch him also. With a little more care I hope he will lose all his bad habits."

(When Bruce returned to England, he found that his reputation as Lady Hester Stanhope's lover had preceded him and given him added glamour in the eyes of many women. He eventually married, became a Member of Parliament, and took up law.)

Shortly after his departure Lady Hester came down with the plague. A few hours later Dr. Meryon was felled. Lady Hester's maid also became a victim. Lady Hester fought the plague with all the medical means, both European and Arab, at her disposal. They all survived.

There were other adventures. In Lebanon she visited the Monastery of St. Anthony. So great was its antiwoman prejudices that no female had ever penetrated its sacred grounds. Even the chickens were separated, only the roosters being permitted inside the monastery walls. Lady Hester denounced the separations as foolishness and announced that if she were not allowed inside, she would complain to her friend the sultan of Constantinople. The monks finally relented. The Protestant Lady Hester rode triumphantly into the monastery's sacred grounds, conspicuously on the back of a she-ass!

In October 1814 Lady Hester made a modest expedition to Baalbek to visit the collection of Roman temples there. She found the ruins extremely impressive. But a steady rain and the presence of plague in the area persuaded her to return to the coast.

She now turned her attention to her next major project, the excavation of the Roman ruins at Ascalon. Sometime before, she had received a manuscript, reputed to have been copied by a monk from the records of a "Frank" monastery in Syria, which disclosed the hiding places of immense hoards of treasure buried in certain specified spots in the cities of Ascalon and Sidon. Convinced of the authenticity of the document, she wrote the sultan of Constantinople for permission to excavate the treasure. However, Lady Hester had no plans to make herself rich. Rather, she believed that if the treasure were recovered by the efforts of an Englishwoman and presented to the sultan as a token of British esteem, the friendship of the two great nations would be forever cemented. The sultan was convinced and bestowed upon her greater power to carry out the task than had ever before been granted, even to a European ambassador.

In February 1815 Lady Hester arrived at Ascalon and began the excavations. She was greeted with all the honors of a visiting queen. She lived in a tent, splendidly lined with bands of colored satins, which was later assigned to the princess of Wales on a visit. The work of the expedition was begun with much enthusiasm, for it was widely believed that Lady Hester possessed a magic spell that revealed hidden treasure and had come to the East for no other reason but to use it.

The excavations continued for two weeks on the site indicated by the mysterious paper. During the first three days nothing was found except bones, fragments of pillars, and a few vases and bottles. But on the fourth day the workers eighteen feet down unearthed a huge, headless statue of a Roman emperor—the first archaeological artifact ever discovered by an excavation in Palestine. Lady Hester immediately ordered the magnificent statue destroyed. She explained her actions in a letter home: "Knowing how much it would be prized by English travellers, I ordered it to be broken into a thousand pieces, so that malicious persons might not say I came to look for statues for my countrymen, and not for treasure for the Sultan." No treasure was ever found, and soon afterward she abandoned the expedition.

Lady Hester saw herself as the protector of the weak and helpless. Her involvement with a Colonel Boutin illustrates the extent of her authority in this region. Boutin was a soldier and engineer traveling through Syria on official business for the French government. While visiting Lady Hester, he told her of his plans to cross a section of mountains inhabited by dangerous religious fanatics who robbed and murdered all Europeans who entered their territory. He was never again seen alive.

Lady Hester's spies brought her details of Boutin's murder, including the names of the villages involved in the heinous deed. She approached the pasha of Acre, demanding that he send an army to avenge the Frenchman's murder. He refused. She pressed her case. The pasha finally gave ground. She was too powerful a personage to offend. He gave her full command of several garrisons of his crack troops. Lady Hester was beside herself with revenge. She ordered the troops into the mountains, directing their movements from the intimate knowledge of the area she had gleaned from her spies. The soldiers burned the Ansary villages of the murderers, sent their heads as trophies back to Acre, and recovered most of Boutin's property.

But Lady Hester still was not satisfied. In the autumn of 1816 she rode into the Ansary heartland, unarmed and accompanied only by her maid, and visited the villages in the area where her friend had perished some months before. She called the survivors to her and informed them that it was she who had sent the troops who had burned and pillaged their villages. She insisted that henceforth any traveler who entered the Ansary domain must be protected by the laws of hospitality or she would return once more with her troops.

In January 1817 Dr. Meryon departed to England. Lady Hester then decided to quit her travels. She briefly entertained the idea of returning to London. But that was never a serious option. Her love affair with Michael Bruce was general knowledge. In the Middle East she was famous, a queen of the Arabs. Back in London she would merely be an eccentric, a fading spinster with a tarnished reputation, trying to make do on a public pension. And she had lost her faith in England. The English, she wrote to a friend, had ceased to be the "hardy, honest, bold people" she had known in her youth. Instead, she found those qualities now in the "wild Arabs, who will traverse burning sands barefooted, to receive the last breath of some kind relation or friend, who teach their children at the earliest period resignation and fortitude, and who always keep alive a spirit of emulation amongst them! They are the boldest people in the world, yet are imbued with a tenderness quite poetic."

And so Lady Hester resolved to remain in the Middle East, to become a sojourner rather than a traveler. She determined to set up a permanent court suitable for a queen, abandon European customs altogether, and conform entirely to the mode of life of her Arab and Turkish hosts.

In 1817 Lady Hester leased for twenty pounds a year a sprawling, dilapidated country manor located atop an isolated mountain peak near the village of Djoun in the heart of the Druze country. She could not have found a more remote place. She immediately set about restoring the existing buildings and adding many new rooms, terraced gardens, and orchards. A lofty wall surrounded the entire complex, giving it the appearance of a fortress. The principal entrance was through a strong and well-guarded gate. Her own rooms opened upon exquisite private gardens, with arbors, marble fountains, and thickets of roses, where she took her daily walk. The flowers were one of the few luxuries she permitted herself at Djoun, where she adopted an austere life-style.

Lady Hester intended Djoun to be a place of refuge, as indeed, it became, for the homeless, helpless, and persecuted peoples of Lebanon. To them she offered an inviolable asylum, for whoever crossed her threshold had set foot in sanctuary. So powerful was she that no pasha ever succeeded in gaining access to anyone under her protection.

In 1827 the Englishman R. R. Madden visited her hilltop palace and wrote about the experience at length in his book *Travels in Turkey, Egypt, Nubia, and Palestine.* He remembered his arrival: "After the gates were thrown open, I was surprised to observe a thousand little elegancies in the distribution of the walks and the adjustments of the flower pots in the court through which I passed. Everything without was wild and barbarous, but all within confessed the hand of taste. . . . It seemed to me as if I was in some enchanted palace."

A servant brought Madden a note from Lady Hester, stating that she would receive him at sunset. He wrote of his reception:

> The room into which I was ushered was in the Arab style. A long divan was raised at the end. I perceived a tall figure in the male attire of the country, which was no other than Lady Hester herself. She received me in a most gracious manner. In the course of one hour we were on the best of terms. We conversed like people who had been acquainted for years. For the seven hours I had the honor of sitting with her Ladyship, there was never a pause in our conversation. Every subject connected with oriental learning was discussed, and every observation of her Ladyship's evinced a degree of genius that astonished me.

Madden also perceptively guessed the reason behind Lady Hester's move to this isolated mountaintop: the ambition to govern and the need to exercise power. "The situation of her Ladyship is more that of a Bedouin sovereign than of one in a private station," he noted.

He was correct. At Djoun Lady Hester's "search for sway and dominion" had finally ended. The love of rule had come to her almost in the cradle. And now, grown and strengthened with advancing years, it had become an absorbing passion. She dwelt apart, surrounded by dependents and slaves and beyond the reach of social restraints that life in a city would necessarily have imposed upon her. Her temper was more violent at Djoun than before. She punished her servants with great severity, boasting that there was nobody who could give such a hard slap in the face, when required, as she. Once, when she was experiencing a particularly trying time with her servants, she ordered her carpenter to place in a yard two sharpened stakes, similar to those used in executions by impaling. She never mentioned them. But for weeks afterward her servants tiptoed through her palace in a state of sheer terror.

When Dr. Meryon returned for a visit many years later, he reached the same conclusion as Madden:

I found her lying on a sofa in a beautiful alcove, an attendant standing with his hands folded across his breast, in an attitude of respect before her. At these moments, she always wore the air of a Sultaness. In this very alcove how often had she acted the queen, issued her orders, summoned delinquents before her, and enjoyed the semblance of that absolute power, which was the latent ambition of her heart! Hence it was that she at last got rid of all her European servants, because they would not submit to arbitrary punishments but would persist in raising their voices in self-justification. With the Turks it was not so. Accustomed, in the courts of governors and Pashas, to implicit obedience and submission, they resigned themselves to her rule as a matter of course. . . . The love of power made her imperious; but, when her authority was once acknowledged, the tender of unconditional submission was sure to secure her kindness and largesses. All this was royal enough, both in its tyranny and its munificence.

Lady Hester's whims were the law of the day at Djoun. She ruled autocratically, unwilling to tolerate any dissent. She was in all matters queen of her palace and the surrounding countryside. Although the nearby village officially owed allegiance to the emir

Bashir, in fact, it was under her rule. Clearly the emir could not tolerate such an obvious challenge to his own power, and this soon undermined the friendship that dated back to her first visit into the land of the Druzes many years before. She and the emir became bitter enemies.

Lady Hester could not have found a more dangerous foe in all the Turkish Empire than Bashir. He gloried in enough atrocities to make Richard III appear a saint by contrast. In a letter to a friend at home, Lady Hester cataloged his crimes: "I should not be a thoroughbred Pitt, if I could bow low to a monster who could chain together the neck and feet of a venerable, white-bearded, respectable man, who has burnt out eyes, cut out tongues, chopped off the breasts of women, put them on red-hot irons, hung them up by their hair, castrated men alive, and, if a father has escaped from his clutches, has loaded his infant son with his chains!"

The emir Bashir issued orders prohibiting any Muslim, on pain of death, from remaining in her service or carrying food or water into her establishment. Her power was such that none of her servants left her. Still, she found herself a prisoner on her mountaintop. She slept nights with a dagger under her pillow and during the day paraded about carrying a mace with its spike-studded steel head at the end of a short chain. Bands of armed soldiers roamed the neighborhood beyond her walls. Villagers were murdered, and their bodies dumped at her front gate to frighten her.

She refused to be intimidated. She shouted at the emir's messengers: "Tell your master that he is a dog and a monster, and that, if he means to try his strength with me, I am ready."

Lady Hester was in the midst of her troubles with the emir Bashir when Madden visited her. She admitted to him that she would almost welcome a violent death as a grand finale to her life thus far. Madden quoted her as saying:

> I never will return to England. I am encompassed by perils; I am no stranger to them. I have faced them. . . . Here I am destined to remain at war with the Prince of the Mountains. It is true my enemies are capable of assassination. But if I do perish, my fall

shall be a bloody one. I have plenty of arms, good Damascus blades. I use no guns. And while I have an arm to wield a hanger, these barren rocks shall have a banquet of slaughter. And two hundred years hence the Bedouins of the Desert shall talk of the *Sittee Inglis*, how she sat upon her Arab steed, and fell like an Arab chief, when the star of her glory had set forever.

In the end the emir Bashir yielded and left her in peace.

In her later years at Djoun Lady Hester became obsessed with the prophecies pronounced so many decades before by Brothers. He had predicted that she would travel to Jerusalem, spend seven years in the desert, become queen of the Jews, and lead forth a chosen people. At Jaffa she had met a half-crazed Frenchman, who called himself Captain Loustanunau and passed himself off as a prophet. He had shown her passages in the Bible which, he insisted, foretold her coming to the Middle East.

After Lady Hester had moved to Djoun, one of her servants, an old man named Metta, produced an Arabic manuscript from which he read the following prophecy: "A European woman will come and live on Mount Lebanon at a certain epoch. She will build a great house there and obtain power and influence greater than the Sultan's. A boy without a father will join her, and his destiny will be fulfilled under her wing. The coming of the Mahdi will follow, but be preceded by war, pestilence, and other calamities. The Mahdi will ride a horse born saddled; and a woman will come from a far country to partake in the mission." The Duchess of Cleveland, Lady Hester's niece, observed much later:

It was curious that the words of an English fortune-teller should be confirmed by two utter strangers in another quarter of the globe, and the coincidence made a profound impression upon Lady Hester. It seemed to her to place the matter in a new light and held out fascinating possibilities. Part of the prophecy, at least, had been accomplished. She had come to her appointed kingdom, had taken up her abode there, and obtained a degree of power and influence so unprecedented as to be little short of miraculous. Had she not been crowned already as Queen of Palmyra? Might she not be called upon to play a great part in the East?

She thought so. The prophecies obsessed her. She talked at length about the new messiah, or Mahdi, whose arrival had been so confidently predicted. Then there occurred at Djoun an event that electrified her. An Arab chief presented her with a fine bay mare, one of his horses of noble blood, the genealogies of which, preserved with religious care, were said to extend in an unbroken line back to the parent stock in the stables of King Solomon. Some months later the mare gave birth to a foal of great beauty with a curious deformity, shaped like a natural saddle, on its back. Lady Hester was convinced that this was the horse destined to carry the Mahdi into Jerusalem, while she would ride the mare at his side. Each horse had its own groom and received the best of care in her stable. No one was ever permitted to ride them, although she was quick to show them off to her European guests.

Her fame had now spread from London to India. Few travelers visited the Middle East without seeking an audience with the "queen of the Arabs." More and more Lady Hester appeared to the European world as a creature of myth rather than history. The most outrageous stories circulated about her. In Britain it was commonly believed that she had married a handsome Arab sheik and sat on a throne of ivory and gold, robed in brocade and silk, in a splendid palace where cashmere shawls littered the marble floors. She boasted to Dr. Meryon on one of his trips to Djoun: "Why, a Turk told one of my people who was at Constantinople that there is not a Turkish child twenty miles around that place who has not heard of me."

William Bartlett, the British artist, visited Lady Hester at Djoun toward the end of her life. "I, who had expected a crabbed imperious old woman, was most agreeably surprised by the noble but gentle aspect of our strange hostess," Bartlett wrote to a friend. "In youth she must have been most beautiful: her features are remarkably fine, blending dignity and sweetness in a fascinating degree. Her dress was fantastic, but impressive: her turban of pale muslin shadowing her high pale forehead. . . . She conducted us to an arbour in the gardens, quite English in appearance. I made this observation, when she replied, 'Oh, don't say so; I hate everything English!' "

In her final years Lady Hester slid into debt, eccentricity, and poor health. She smoked incessantly, and a terrible cough racked her body. Her eyesight deteriorated to the point where she could no longer read or write. She was in constant pain. Yet her high spirits never failed her. Nor did she ever lose her imperious manner.

When Dr. Meryon came to visit her for the last time, not long before her death, she told him a story. "A young *seyd*, a friend of mine, when riding one day in a solitary part of the mountain, heard the echo of a strange noise in the rocks. He listened, and, hearing it again, got off his horse to see what it was. To his surprise, in a hollow in the rock he saw an old eagle, quite blind and unfledged by age. Perched by the eagle, he saw a carrion-crow feeding him. If the Almighty thus provides for a blind eagle, he will not forsake me."

As Lady Hester's condition weakened, her once-lovely hilltop home fell into ruin. Necessary repairs were neglected. She was no longer able to discipline her servants. They plundered her at will. She took to keeping her few remaining silver spoons in her bed. She sat wrapped in an old blanket. The spout on her teapot was broken. She was down to one cracked cup and saucer. The ceiling in her bedroom was supported by two rough timbers to prevent its collapse.

Little of her former glory remained. She owed her creditors £14,000. They hounded her mercilessly. One of them filed a claim against her with the British government, which stopped her pension to pay it. Back in London Dr. Meryon unsuccessfully sought to raise a fund for her relief.

A few weeks before her death Lady Hester dictated a letter to a friend in England, saying, "Do not be unhappy about my future fate. I have done what I believed to be my duty, the duty of everyone of every religion. I have no reproaches to make." On June 23, 1839, she died "in rags and sordidness among her squalling cats," having foreseen her death the day before.

The Reverend W. M. Thompson, an American missionary, accompanied the British consul from Beirut to Djoun the following day. He left behind an account of her funeral. Her vault was opened, and the skeleton of a man, a houseguest who had died years before, was removed. "Lady Hester Stanhope's body, in a plain box, was carried by her servants to the grave, followed by a mixed company, with torches and lanterns, to enable them to thread their way through the winding alleys of the garden. I took a wrong path, and wandered for some time in the mazes of these labyrinths. When, at length, I entered the arbour, the first thing I saw were the bones in a ghastly heap, with the head on top having a lighted taper stuck in either eye-socket— a hideous, grinning spectacle. It was difficult to proceed with the service, under circumstances so novel and bewildering."

The next morning Thompson and the consul explored the premises and examined thirty-five rooms. "They were full of trash. One had forty or fifty oil jars of French manufacture—old, empty, and dusty. Another was crammed with Arab saddles, moth-eaten, tattered, and torn. They had belonged to her mounted guard. Nothing much of value was found anywhere." The sacred mares, now grown old and worthless, were sold for a small sum at an auction.

Thus ended the life of this most extraordinary woman, who had she been born a man might well have become prime minister. If she had remained in England, Lady Hester Stanhope most likely would have grown old in colorless and soured spinsterhood. Instead, she choose to seek her destiny in the Middle East and found there in a few crowded years the power, glory, and adventure that had eluded her in England.

Hard Times on the Pirate Coast

At noon on October 20, 1808, the British cruiser *Sylph*, an eight-gun schooner, and the frigate *Néréide* with thirty-six guns slowly made their way out of the Persian Gulf, bound for India. They struggled with the winds and beat their way past Musandam Island. Two large dhows, crowded with fierce Qawasim pirates, suddenly appeared from the lee of the island and closed upon the *Sylph*. Lieutenant William Graham, the ship's commander, misjudged the situation and held his fire until it was too late. The dhows crowded alongside the British schooner. Within minutes dozens of pirates had clambered on board the *Sylph*. British resistance was brief. The pirates quickly overpowered the ship and killed most of its crew. The *Néréide* started in pursuit. Late that afternoon it had the dhows within range of its guns and began hammering away. One ball carried away the mast of the lead dhow. The second took a broadside from the *Néréide* and began to sink.

The captain of the *Néréide* reported later:

You will hardly believe that even then, when repeatedly hailed in Arabic, [the pirates] answered by barbarous threats of defiance and straggling musquetry. One dhow was now abandoned and sunk. The other repaired his sail a shot away and continued his course in a very light air, shouting and firing musquetry from loopholes and scuttles. . . . On bearing up to join the [*Sylph*, we] overpowered her with ease. I found they had decapitated almost her whole crew, the second officer and twenty-six men, most sepoys. The Commander's life was saved by being knocked down the hatchway with an immense stone, after having received six spear and sabre wounds.

Today the economic lifeblood of the Persian Gulf is oil. Great flares of burning gas light up the nighttime skies above the oil fields. But 150 years ago piracy was the chief business in the gulf. And then the pillars of black smoke that marked the skies came from burning ships and villages. Hundreds of pirate ships swarmed among the treacherous sandbanks and jagged coral reefs along the remote coastal areas of the Arabian Peninsula, much of which remained uncharted until the twentieth century. "The Pirate Coast has always been a forbidding place, scorching hot in summer, whipped by savage sand storms and swept by sea gales when the *shamal* wind rages down the Gulf from the north in the winter," writes historian Sir Charles Belgrave.

For thousands of years the Persian Gulf has been one of the great highways of Asian trade. It may be the oldest seaway in the world. It was there, some archaeologists believe, that humankind learned the art of marine navigation. Long before Sindbad the Sailor set out in search of trade and found adventure instead, ships from Ur of the Chaldees and Babylon sailed on the gulf, carrying cargoes of teakwood, frankincense, gold, ivory, and copper. Because of its stra-tegic, commercial, and political importance, the Persian Gulf has always been the scene of conflicts involving the great powers of the world. Command of the sea has been the prerequisite of political power in the gulf. Thousands of years before the Russians moved into

Afghanistan to threaten the gulf in fulfillment of a centuries-old dream, pirates plagued its coast and brought about superpower intervention. In 690 B.C. Sennacherib, the Assyrian king, mounted an expedition against them. And the historian Pliny tells us that Roman ships in the gulf carried archers to defend them against attacks by pirates. In A.D. 116 the Roman emperor Trajan ordered a fleet of his ships against the pirate strongholds along the Arabian coast.

In modern times the Portuguese discovered the sea route to India and became the first Europeans since Roman times to venture into the Persian Gulf. In 1508 they captured Muscat at its mouth and built several great forts. Portuguese ships controlled the gulf waters and regulated its trade for more than a century.

The growing British interest in India slowly began to dictate a British presence in the highly strategic Persian Gulf. By the late eighteenth century ships of the British-owned East India Company were calling regularly at Persian ports. Soon there were clashes between British ships and gulf pirates. In 1797 pirates attacked the *Viper*, a ten-cannon cruiser belonging to the East India Company, off the Persian port of Bushire, killing the captain and many of the crew before they were finally repelled. In 1804 Joasmi pirates captured the company ship *Fly* and took the crew to Ras al Khaimah, where they exhibited them as curiosities. ("The Joasmi ladies were so minute in their enquiries that they were not satisfied without determining in what respect an uncircumcised infidel differs from a True Believer," naval officer James Silk Buckingham wrote later.) In 1805 pirates captured two British brigs, slaughtered most of the crew, and chopped off the captain's arm because he had fired a musket at them; he survived only because he quickly immersed his bleeding stump into a large pot of boiling butter.

Such attacks made clear that the pirates held effective control over the Persian Gulf. They were a formidable naval force. Historian J. B. Kelly puts their numbers in the early part of the nineteenth century at 63 large vessels and 810 smaller ships, crewed by 18,000 to 25,000 fighting men. Most were from the Qawasim tribe of Ras al Khaimah on the Arabian coast, extreme Muslim fundamentalists who invested piracy with the aura of a holy war in which an attack upon a Christian ship was a religious duty. "Their occupation is piracy and their delight is murder," insisted one British official posted to Persia. What the pirates lacked in modern armaments, they made up for in ferocity. Their usual strategy was to sail in close to their prey and board. Prisoners were slaughtered.

"I must confess, with a people who are not naturally cruel, I am somewhat surprised they should have adapted the savage and revolting principle of sacrificing their captives," observed James Wellsted, a naval officer with the Bombay Marine, the naval arm of the British East India Company. "They did so with circumstances of horrid solemnity, which gave the deed the appearance of some hellish religious rite. . . . After a ship was taken, she was purified with water and perfumes. The crew were then led forward singly, their heads placed on the gunwale, and their throats cut, with the exclamation used in battle of '*Allah akbar!*'—God is great!"

The most famous of the gulf pirates was Rahmah ibn Jabr, whose exploits are even today a legend in the region. For more than forty years, until his death in 1826, he was a force in the gulf. "No corner of this Gulf was secure from his ravages," wrote an English captain who served in the area. "He swept from shore to shore and passed from isle to isle with the force of a thunderbolt and with the speed of lightning."

As a youth Ibn Jabr saved his money to buy a small boat. With twelve companions he became a pirate. Within a few years he had moved up to a 300-ton ship and a crew of 350 fighting men. By 1816 he commanded a fleet of nine ships and some 2,000 men, many of them black slaves over whom he had absolute authority.

Lieutenant James Buckingham met Ibn Jabr in 1816 and left behind a full description of the notorious pirate: "His figure presented a meagre trunk with four lank members, all of them cut and hacked and pierced with wounds of sabres, spears, and bullets. He had a face naturally ferocious and ugly, now rendered still more so by several scars and the loss of an eye. . . . His usual dress is a shirt which is never taken off from the time it is first put on till it is worn out, no drawers or covering for the legs, a large black goat's skin cloak wrapped over all, and a dirty handkerchief thrown loosely over his head." An enormous cutlass hung at his side. He carried two pistols in his belt.

Ibn Jabr's end came in 1826 in a clash with the ships of Sheik Ahmed of Bahrain. The two fleets came together. Ibn Jabr now completely blind, stood on the high poop of his ship, his eight-year-old son at his side. He issued his commands through Tarrar, a favorite black slave who stood behind him and gave him a detailed description of the battle. Ibn Jabr ordered his dhow alongside that of Sheik Ahmed. As the two ships ground together, soldiers leaped aboard the pirate dhow. Ibn Jabr's men fought fiercely but slowly fell back. The sheik and his soldiers pressed forward toward the poop deck, their cutlasses, spears, and daggers at the ready. Tarrar called off the name of each man as he died. Soon Ibn Jabr was reduced to his bodyguards. "Men," he shouted. "Do we surrender or die?" The pirates roared their defiance. The blind Ibn Jabr leaped into the ship's magazine and thrust a burning match into a powder barrel. He quickly scrambled back on the deck and scooped his young son into his arms. A second later the magazine exploded in a white flash and thunderous roar that tore apart the two ships, killing almost everyone on board, including Sheik Ahmed.

"When the frightful explosion had subsided, nothing was seen but a black cloud on the ocean, enveloping all around like a pall and darkening the very sky," Captain R. Mignan, an English officer at the scene, recalled later. "A few bubbles and the trembling ripple of the sea were the only distinguishable trace of the combatants!"

British authorities soon perceived the necessity of establishing a strong naval presence in the Persian Gulf to ensure the safety of their shipping. Probably no other station involved greater risks and hardships at the time—dust storms at sea; regular visitations of malaria, typhoid, cholera, and plague; and summer temperatures that ranged upwards of 130° F coupled with a high humidity. One officer wrote of it in 1828:

> No one but those who have actually been in the Persian Gulf can imagine the extreme barrenness and sterility of its coasts. Sunburnt and sandy regions lie on all sides. Not even a blade of

grass relieves the aching eye-balls from the intense glare of the sand. The hot season, which continues for five months, is intolerable. Existence then is almost insupportable. The sun is so powerful during the day that it is almost certainly fatal to expose oneself. I have seen men die in the utmost agony and raving mad, from exposure to the sun, after a few hours' illness. . . . Men and officers have alike a miserable life during that season. They merely exist. The extreme hardships and privations they undergo are almost beyond belief. There is no society except among brother officers. The face of a European female is never seen. And it is but seldom that a glimpse is obtained of an Arab or Persian one, they are all so completely veiled and kept so close.

British supremacy in the Persian Gulf was finally established after a series of four successive naval and military expeditions over a fifteen-year period. The chief objective of the British operations was Ras al Khaimah, the heavily fortified town on the Pirate Coast, located on a narrow isthmus some four miles long and one mile wide. Its walls were made of mud and coral blocks and were fifteen feet thick at the base. Strong towers guarded each corner. A massive wooden gate guarded the town's chief entrance. The citadel, a huge building made from stone, faced the gate.

The first two expeditions against Ras al Khaimah in 1809 and 1816 failed to stop the pirate attacks. In late 1819 Britain sent a fighting force of 3,000 soldiers (half Indians, half British) with a company of artillery, and a fleet of a dozen warships and numerous transports against the pirates at Ras al Khaimah. They faced an entrenched force of some 7,000 pirates. The British settled in for a lengthy siege. One night a raiding party of Qawasim pirates crept out on their hands and knees and overran a British battery. With nothing but their spears and cutlasses, they fell upon the surprised British soldiers. Many of the attackers were women. After prolonged bombardment and heavy skirmishing, British forces finally broke through Ras al Khaimah's defenses at dawn on December 9. When the British entered the town, they found it deserted, its inhabitants fled. Only an old woman and three cats were found alive inside. In the fighting

1,000 Qawasim pirates had died. The pirate sheiks sued for peace and agreed to give up their raids on gulf shipping if their people were spared. As a result of this truce, the Pirate Coast became the Trucial States, the designated terrorities of the pirate tribes along the Oman coast. Individual treaties were concluded with each sheik. From 1820 onward the Trucial Coast remained under British domination until 1971.

The Persian Gulf was now a British lake. And Whitehall's attention shifted to the vast Arabian Peninsula. What sort of rule would prevail there? Would its leaders look with favor or hostility upon the British presence in the gulf? Britain quickly acted to secure strategic points along the Arabian coast. In 1839 Aden was annexed to British India. A consulate was established at the Red Sea port of Jiddah near Mecca. It was there that the explorers Richard Burton and Charles Doughty were to find safety and comfort after their dangerous travels through the interior of Arabia.

Today the Portuguese, the British, and the Turks are gone from the Persian Gulf. For the first time since the beginning of the sixteenth century no outside power wields a decisive influence in the gulf.

Meanwhile, Russia bides its time in Afghanistan.

CHAPTER III

The Spell of Far Arabia: A. W. Kinglake and the Grand Tour

In 1585 John Sanderson, an employee of the Levant Company, visited Egypt to survey the commercial opportunities in the region. He stayed in Alexandria, met with various merchants in Cairo about possible trade agreements with England, and paid the obligatory visit to the pyramids. But the famous Memphis mummy pits where hundreds of ancient Egyptians were entombed quickly captured the attention of the ambitious Sanderson. "We were lett downe by ropes as into a well, with waxe candles burning in our hands, and so waulked upon bodies of all sorts and sizes, great and smaule, and some are embaulmed in little earthen pots," he wrote later. "I broke off all parts of the bodies to see how the flesh was turned into drugge and brought home divers heads, hands, arms, and feete for a showe."

Sanderson was not entirely honest with his readers. The enterprising Englishman had, in fact, bribed his way past local officials and carried home more than 600 pounds of mummified flesh, including one entire body. At the time mummy powder sold for eight shillings a pound in London. Sanderson's Egyptian "souvenirs" made him a rich man.

For centuries the European medical community placed a high value on powdered mummy flesh. It was thought to have magical properties highly effective in curing certain illnesses. King Francis I of France always carried a packet of mummy powder on his person in the event of an emergency. And the English writer Sir Thomas Browne marveled in 1635 that "Mummy is become merchandise. Mizraim cures wounds, and Pharaoh is sold for balsam."

A flourishing international trade in mummy flesh soon developed. The Egyptians wondered at a European diet that included both pork and mummified human flesh but rushed to satisfy what appeared to be an insatiable demand. By the seventeenth century European traders were complaining about unscrupulous Egyptian merchants who fraudulently substituted modern corpses for the old. But the use of powdered mummy flesh as a patent medicine continued into the nineteenth century. (As recently as 1975 anthropologist Brian M. Fagan found certain shops of the occult in New York City selling genuine Egyptian mummy for forty dollars an ounce.)

Mummy powder was but one bizarre aspect of a craze for all things Egyptian that swept Europe on the heels of Napoleon's invasion. In Paris a rage for Arab fashions took the city by storm. Men sported red fezzes with silk tassels, while women of means wore turbans. Writer George Sand dressed in Turkish slippers and baggy trousers to seduce the novelist Prosper Mérimée. "Is it living to vegetate like a fungus on a rotten trunk?" the artist Eugène Delacroix complained in his journals about life in Paris. "What can Egypt be like? Everyone is mad for it. Please God! Let the Salon soon bring in enough to allow me to start on my travels."

In 1812 an enterprising British entrepreneur sniffed the winds of cultural change and built in Piccadilly the Egyptian Hall, its façade adorned with sphinxes, hieroglyphics, and statues representing Isis and Osiris. In 1821 it hosted an elaborate exhibit of Egyptian artifacts collected by the Italian Giovanni Belzoni, including a model of Seti's tomb. Nearly 2,000 visitors attended on the first day. A writer to the *Morning Chronicle* complained: "My eldest boy rides on a sphinx instead of a rocking horse, and my youngest has a pap-boat in the shape of a crocodile. My husband has a built-in water-closet in the form of a pyramid and marks his shirts with a lotus. He talks in his sleep of Ibis, Apis, and *Sir* Apis."

The European fascination with the Middle East grew in intensity over the following decades. Writers, painters, and travelers sought easy popularity by catering to a public eager to find confirmations of the fabulous expectations that had been nurtured on the seductive fantasies of the *Arabian Nights*, eighteenth-century Oriental tales, and the popular pornographic novel *The Lustful Turk*. Writers and painters concentrated on depicting what Alexander Kinglake called the "Splendour and Havoc of the East." They conjured up a world of brilliant colors, dramatic turmoil, and exotic characters—a Middle East that was passionate, cruel, hedonistic, and intoxicating. Europe was mesmerized by harems, slave markets, carpet bazaars, whirling dervishes, caravans of caparisoned camels, and dark-skinned Bedouins on Arabian stallions. Delacroix, Eugène Fromentin, Jean León Gérôme, and Horace Vernet filled huge canvases with opulent color and sweeping animated compositions of Middle Eastern scenes, capturing in vivid detail the Arab world of the popular imagination. "An Orientalist picture in a Victorian drawing room was a kind of escape," art historian Philippe Jullian has argued. "To our great-grandparents these canvases were not only a reminder of a different world, of something picturesque and heroic, but they hinted at plea-sures that were often taboo in Europe and titillated a secret taste for cruelty and oppression."

For a nineteenth-century Europe bored with the ease and comfort of a new industrialism, the Arab world fulfilled a role comparable to that of the American West, with the desert Bedouins playing the parts of the Plains Indians. Both were wildernesses of vast expanses of open land and sky that satisfied the cravings of every people for a sense of wonder, adventure, and freedom and testing grounds for those individuals brave enough to venture there. "To Europe—choked by coal smoke, dissected by railways, and shackled by Vic-torian morality—the Middle East promised a paradise: a place where artist-explorers, poet-travelers, and hero-dandies could escape the rigid boundaries of their own culture," writes Jullian. The Middle East was the first culture to attract those discontented Europeans, men and women no longer at ease in their own society, who crossed the cultural frontier while refusing to sever all ties to their homelands and thus learned to see, in T. E. Lawrence's phrase, "through the veils at once of two customs, two educations, two environments."

The enormous appeal of the Arab East throughout much of the nineteenth century lay in large part in its ability to be all things to all visitors, a magical place where one's wildest and fondest fantasies were confirmed. Even so cynical a traveler as Mark Twain could state enthusiastically in 1867 at the start of his Middle Eastern tour: "These [Orientalist] pictures used to seem exaggerations. They seemed too weird and fanciful for reality. But behold, they were not wild enough—they were not fanciful enough—they have not told half the story."

For many visitors to the Arab East, travel became a pilgrimage—an impassioned search for tangible evidence of Christ, the exotic world of the *Arabian Nights,* the noble savage, a perfect horse, romantic love, easy sex, adventure, power, or the glories of ancient civilizations. The myth, not the reality, was what mattered. Few returned from their travels without having their beliefs confirmed or their prejudices agreeably titillated.

England's infatuation with the Middle East came at a time of growing doubts about the new society taking shape at home under the rapid changes wrought by modern technology, industrialism, an expanded commerce, and scientific skepticism. "We live in an age of visible transition—an age of disquietude and doubt—of the removal of time-worn landmarks, and the breaking up of the hereditary elements of society—old opinions, feelings—ancestral customs and institutions are crumbling away, and both the spiritual and temporal worlds are darkened by the shadow of change," a gloomy Edward Bulwer-Lytton grumbled in 1833, articulating a sentiment that was echoed and reechoed by innumerable other Victorians. The nostalgia for the Middle Ages that pervaded the century reflected those doubts.

To a people traumatized by change, there was reassurance in the myth of an "unchanging East," a timeless world miraculously unaffected by the passing millennia, a whole society and culture preserved like some vast insect in amber. Fantasy and nostalgia blurred subtly together. "The unchanged habits of the East render it a kind of living Pompeii," insisted Canon Arthur P. Stanley in 1863. There one could peer through the window of time and view living tableaux from an ancient past. When artist David Wilkie wrote in 1843 that the Arabs "look as if they had never changed since the time of Abraham," he was expressing a commonplace sentiment of the age. So, too, was British traveler Robert Curzon, who visited Egypt in 1833 and imagined himself strolling through illustrations for a deluxe edition of the *Arabian Nights:* "The pilot was an old man with a turban and a long gray beard, who sat cross-legged in the stern of his boat. We looked at him with vast interest, as the first specimen we had seen of an Arab sailor. He was just the sort of man that I imagined Sindbad the Sailor must have been."

But such pleasures were often bittersweet, tinged as they were with a sad awareness that the increased contact with the West would bring momentous changes and overwhelm the picturesque and traditional societies of the Middle East. The Pre-Raphaelite painter William Holman Hunt spent two years traveling through the Holy Land, searching out landscapes and people that would allow for an authentic artistic reconstruction of biblical scenes. "What I saw was for the time studied only to make the records of ancient history clearer," he wrote later. "All traditional manners were threatening to pass away, together with ancient costume and hereditary taste. I saw that in another generation it would be too late to reconstruct the past, save in rural and desert life, if even there."

Until then lovers of the picturesque enjoyed a field day in the Middle East. Even the most outrageous discomforts and inconveniences were often excused and forgotten. "Our vessel was just like the old models in nautical cabinets of ships in the Middle Ages, high tilted at the poop and stern and with masts, spars, and rigging of curious and antique fashion," British artist William Bartlett enthused in the mid-1830s about an Arab ship that took him from Alexandria to Jaffa. "So far so good—to a lover of the picturesque. But this was not all. The craft was perilously crazy. The seams yawned as if the shrunken planks were about to come asunder.

The ropes and sails looked as if the first stiff breeze would snap the one and split the others to shreds and tatters. There was neither chart nor compass on board. It was, in fact, just a sample of the Arab coasting vessels, the wrecks of which so picturesquely bestrew the shores of Syria."

And novelist William Makepeace Thackeray on a visit to Cairo in 1844 exclaimed excitedly: "There is a fortune to be made for painters in Cairo. I never saw such a variety of architecture, of life, of picturesqueness, of brilliant colour, of light and shade. There is a picture in every street, and at every bazaar stall."

Other travelers were drawn by the region's reputation for supposed voluptuousness. Harems, slave markets, and belly dancers titillated the erotic imaginations of many would-be sexual adventurers. Cairo, in particular, had a reputation as a hotbed of all the vices—"that sink of iniquity" one Victorian visitor called it. Pierre Auguste Renoir observed after a visit to Algiers that Arab women were "clever enough to know the value of a mystery. An eye half-seen through a veil becomes really alluring!" Shrouded in the twin veils of exoticism and eroticism, slavery in the Middle East rarely aroused the same abolitionist fervor it did elsewhere. (The German prince Hermann von Pückler-Muskau bought a lovely black slave girl in Egypt in the mid-1830s; when he took her home, she promptly died of tuberculosis in the colder, damp European climate.)

One of the travelers most determined to look upon the Middle East as a place of sexual license was the French novelist Gustave Flaubert, who set out for Egypt in the autumn of 1849. Twenty-eight years old and still unknown as a writer, the youthful Flaubert was tall and muscular with large dark eyes. He was already a sensualist and a devoted patron of prostitutes. "It may be a perverted taste, but I love prostitution," he admitted to a friend. "My heart begins to pound every time I see one of those women in low-cut dresses walking under the lamplight in the rain. . . . The idea of prostitution is a meeting place of so many elements—lust, bitterness, complete absence of human contact, muscular frenzy, the clink of gold—that to peer into it deeply makes one reel." He was also a dedicated Orientalist. "Oh, how willingly I would give up all women in the world to possess the mummy of Cleopatra!" he once exclaimed in a burst of youthful enthusiasm.

Egypt did not disappoint Flaubert. In Cairo he climbed to the top of the citadel and enjoyed the view down on the city. "From here I have Cairo below me: to the right, the desert with camels gliding over it, escorted by their shadows; opposite, beyond the meadows and the Nile, the Pyramids," he wrote home to a friend. "The Nile is dotted with white sails; the two crossed sails spread like two huge wings make the boat look like a swallow in flight. The sky is cloudless blue. The sparrow-hawks are wheeling over our heads. The liquid light seems to flow into the core of things."

But for the most part Flaubert traveled through Egypt as a pilgrim in search of sexual adventures. His tastes ran to the perverse, the grotesque, and the gross. "A week ago I saw a monkey in the street jump on a donkey and try to jack him off," Flaubert wrote home to a friend. "The donkey brayed and kicked, the monkey's owner shouted, the monkey itself squealed—apart from two or three children who laughed and me who found it very funny, no one paid any attention. . . . This is indeed a funny country. Yesterday, for example, we were at a café which is one of the best in Cairo, and where there were, at the same time as ourselves, inside, a donkey shitting and a gentleman who was pissing in a corner. No one finds that odd; no one says anything."

Flaubert quickly fell under the spell of the hazy, magical light conjured by the Nile and the desert. "Smoky film" was how he described it. Dressed in a large white cotton Nubian shirt trimmed with little pom-poms, Flaubert brothel-hopped his way through Egypt from Cairo to Aswan. He bragged in a letter to a friend:

> The day before yesterday we were in the house of a woman who had two others there for us to lay. The place was dilapidated and open to all the winds and lit by a night-light. . . . The two Turkish women wore silk robes embroidered with gold. This is a great place for contrasts: splendid things gleam in the dust. I performed on a mat that a family of cats had to be shooed off—a strange coitus, looking at each other without being able to exchange a

word, and the exchange of looks is all the deeper for the curiosity and the surprise. My brain was too stimulated for me to enjoy it much otherwise. These shaved cunts make a strange effect—the flesh is hard as bronze, and my girl had a splendid ass.

Flaubert never returned to Egypt. But his passion for the Middle East continued through a series of novels such as *The Temptation of Saint Anthony* and *Salammbô*. Always Flaubert associated the East with the escapism of sexual fantasy. (A bored Emma Bovary day-dreams the Oriental clichés of popular fiction.) In 1880, a few days before his death, Flaubert wrote his niece: "For the past two weeks I have been gripped by the longing to see a palm-tree standing out against a blue sky and to hear a stork clacking its beak at the top of a minaret."

For Flaubert, as for so many nineteenth-century travelers, the Middle East was a state of mind as much as a physical fact. Nowhere was that more in evidence than in the common perception of the desert among those Europeans who visited there. "To the Arab the desert is a place of privation, pain, and death," Polk and Mares observe in *Passing Brave*. "For the Westerner the desert is a challenge, a flight into weightlessness, an escape from tedium." From Richard Burton to T. E. Lawrence a certain breed of Englishman craved the desert as a field of self-denial and an arena for personal definition through which he could take a measure of his deepest self.

Many travelers must have sensed the same excitement that Alexandre Dumas felt when he first saw the Egyptian desert in 1837: "My eyes wandered over the vast expanse of sand, the red and glowing horizon, the caravan of long-necked camels, carrying our Arabs in their picturesque costume. All this strange and primitive world, the counterpart of which is found only in the Bible and which seemed to have just come from the hand of God, was before me. And I felt that, after all, the spectacle and the associations were worth the sacrifice of leaving the mud of Paris, crossing the sea, and taking the risk of leaving a few additional bones on the bosom of the Desert."

The deserts of the Middle East, harsh and purgative, soon came to represent for several generations of British travelers a very special escape from the hypocritical and servile aspects of Western civilization. Sir Wilfrid Blunt, a celebrated explorer of the deserts of northern Arabia, spoke in later years of the need "to cast off the slough of Europe, to have done with ugliness and noise, to bathe one's sick Western soul in the pure healing of the East. The mere act of passing from one's graceless London clothes into the white draperies of Arabia is a new birth." And Richard Burton in 1878 exclaimed at the opening of his book *The Gold-Mines of Midian and the Ruined Midianite Cities:* "At last! Once more it is my fate to escape the prison-life of civilized Europe, and to refresh body and mind by studying nature in her noblest and most admirable form. . . . Again I am to enjoy a glimpse of the glorious desert; to inhale the sweet pure breath of translucent skies that show red skies burning upon the very edge and verge of the horizon; and to strengthen myself by a short visit to the Wild Man and his old home."

That "Wild Man" of the desert was, of course, the proud and high-spirited Bedouin, celebrated by countless nineteenth-century travelers to the Middle East. The old perception of the Muslim as the savage, bloodthirsty infidel eager to shed Christian blood gave way to a new myth of the desert Arab as the embodiment of proud independence, old-fashioned chivalry, mystery, and romance. "There is something very romantic in the [Bedouin] mode of life which never seems to lose its zeal," Eliot Warburton wrote after an 1844 visit to the Middle East. "Their love of the desert amounts to a passion, and everyone who has wandered with these wild sons of freedom, where all else are slaves, can understand the feeling."

There was a perception, too, of the Bedouins as natural gentlemen, a native aristocracy embodying an intuitive sense of good breeding. Such upper-class English travelers as Lady Hester Stanhope, Lady Jane Digby, Richard Burton, and the Blunts all felt an immediate sense of affinity with them. Burton compared the town Arabs with the desert Arabs and concluded: "There is degradation, moral and physical, in handiwork compared with the freedom of the Desert.

The loom and the file do not conserve courtesy and chivalry like the sword and the spear."

Such sentiments were more than mere romantic exaggeration. The Bedouins, virtually alone in the Ottoman Empire, had never been conquered and continued to maintain their independence against the arbitrary power of foreign rulers. They had evolved a society free of caste, hence one without any pressures toward conformity. "Their social structures, strong yet flexible, allowed them a great measure of personal liberty, while their traditions offered the widest latitude to their natural ferocity," writes historian Peter Brent. "Their environment assured them security, often at the same time as it destroyed their enemies. They were free people both in fact and in essence, and once that had percolated through the stubborn preconceptions of the Europeans, it was to arouse in the West a lasting—and finally, perhaps, a misleading—respect."

In the latter part of the eighteenth century Dr. Samuel Johnson advised his readers that "the grand object of all travel is to see the shores of the Mediterranean." Within fifty years his countrymen had taken up his advice with a passion. The traditional destinations along the grand tour—Vienna, Paris, the Alps, Rome, the Rhine, among others—were expanded to include Constantinople, the Holy Land, and Cairo. The trickle of tourists to the Middle East in the 1830s became a flood in the 1850s, as the introduction of steamship service between London and Alexandria made the region much more accessible for travelers. A new industry grew up to accommodate them. Hotels and tourist camps blossomed in the deserts. Tour groups began operating in the 1840s. In 1844 officials of the Peninsular and Oriental Company scored a travel first when they gave novelist William Thackeray a free passage on a packaged tour visiting Malta, Athens, Smyrna, Constantinople, Jerusalem, and Cairo in exchange for a series of articles promoting the experience. Two decades later

Thomas Cook revolutionized the Middle Eastern tourist scene. According to historian Sarah Searight:

> In 1869 thirty-two ladies and gentlemen went up the Nile and thirty of them continued on to the Holy Land. By the 1870s the Holy Land tour was a meticulously organised progress that protected its members from the rigours and discomforts of contact with the country as far as possible. It generally lasted thirty days. Visitors slept three to a tent, and there were also two dining tents and three cooking tents to each expedition, all of which had to be taken down and pitched for each halt. Prayers were said morning and evening, on one tour—as an added attraction—"by the famous traveller and Eastern explorer, just escaped from a brigand sheik in the land of Moab, Dr. Tristam."

All this coming and going perplexed and puzzled the Arabs, for whom the ideal of recreational travel was an altogether new concept. Many believed that all those European travelers were actually engaged on secret political missions or furtively seeking buried treasure. This did not prevent local Arabs from capitalizing on the English love of travel. First hundreds, then thousands found work servicing the many needs of the hordes of British travelers. Others hung around the more famous sites, selling little pieces of antiquities, such as small papyruses, coins, figures, and trinkets, or simply demanding *baksheesh.*

Guidebooks and travel memoirs about the Middle East proliferated in the bookstalls of England, leading Robert Curzon to complain in 1849 of a public "overwhelmed with little volumes about palm-trees and camels and reflections on the Pyramids." By then tourism in the region was well advanced and concentrated for the most part in a great crescent extending from Constantinople in the north to Cairo in the south. Travelers doing the full grand tour usually began in Turkey with visits to Constantinople and Smyrna (now Izmir). The more adventuresome traveled overland to the Holy Land. All others took the easier sea route to Jaffa and then made the one-day horseback ride to Jerusalem. For the trip to Egypt the choice once again was between steamer to Alexandria and an overland passage by camel caravan through the Sinai desert along the Exodus route. This second option involved considerable risk, lengthy preparations, and far greater expense, but it took the European traveler through spectacular scenery and immersed him in the fascinating world of the desert Bedouins. "The crowd pressing around the tent came in and, I saw, carried on the shoulders of four men something extraordinary and fabulous," one mid-century traveler wrote in awe later of his experience. "On the gleaming slopes of a mountain of rice, a young camel, undoubtedly a suckling, an innocent victim slaughtered for my welcome, was lying with its legs folded and its neck straight, in the most realistic of attitudes."

One of the best-known Englishman to visit the Middle East was Benjamin Disraeli, who at the age of twenty-six traveled through the region in 1830 and 1831. The trip later helped him win a seat in Parliament after four unsuccessful tries. The Arab world completely captured Disraeli's imperial imagination and turned him into a confirmed Orientalist. "The meanest merchant in the Bazaar looks like a Sultan in an Eastern fairy tale," the future prime minister wrote home. In *Tancred, or The New Crusade,* his 1847 political novel, Disraeli trumpeted such sentiments as "The East is a career"; "Everything comes from Arabia . . . at least, everything that is worth anything"; and "It is Arabia alone that can regenerate the world." In 1875 Prime Minister Disraeli was to buy for Queen Victoria a 44 percent interest in the Suez Canal and plunge England directly into the turbulent politics of the region.

British sufferers from tuberculosis eagerly sought out the drier climate of Egypt. In 1872 the prince of Wales convalesced there after an illness. By the 1860s fashionable British travelers were wintering over in Egypt and then in the spring moving on toward Syria. Most still thought of the Middle East in terms of Egyptian antiquities and the Holy Land. Few traveled farther afield, where Western-style amenities were rare and the personal risks much greater. In 1816, when James Silk Buckingham traveled with a caravan of merchants from Damascus to Baghdad, he assessed himself as only the sixth European in history and the first in more than a century to travel in

Mesopotamia, the country between the Euphrates and Tigris rivers. The situation had not changed that much forty years later, when vast portions of the Arabian Peninsula and Mesopotamia still remained unvisited by Europeans.

Many earlier visitors, those traveling on their own, preferred to don Arab robes. Some, such as Flaubert, wore local garb for the sheer fun of it. Others did so for more practical reasons. "I was advised to abandon the dress of a Christian and assume the costume of the Turk, under the assurance that it would be the means of protecting me from insult and afford greater facility in travelling," one early British visitor wrote. "I accordingly procured such a dress . . . and remained for some time in order to allow my beard to grow, which conveys a kind of authority, and so as to conform in every respect to a Mahomedan figure." And R. R. Madden advised his readers in 1829 against wearing "Frank attire . . . because the Arabs despise us more for our apparel than they even hate us for our creed; our tight clothes appear to them not only ridiculous but indecent; and it is their general impression that our garments make us look like monkeys."

Most independent travelers who did not speak Arabic—and few did—hired the services of dragomans (the Arabic word *tariumān* means "interpreter"). These indispensable agents functioned as guides, guards, and interpreters, usually at a cost of about five dollars per day. They also booked hotel rooms; leased horses, camels, or mules; bought provisions; provided camping equipment when needed; hired Bedouin guides for trips through the desert; and planned the itinerary. In a land conspicuous for the absence of any public transportation, dragomans provided essential services that few travelers could do without. Robert Curzon, who visited numerous Eastern monasteries in 1834 in a search for ancient manuscripts, observed wryly: "The newly arrived European eats and drinks whatever his dragoman chooses to give him; sees through his dragoman's eyes; hears through his ears; and, although he thinks himself master, is, in fact, only a part of the property of this Eastern servant, to be used by him as he thinks fit, and turned to the best account, like any other real or personal estate."

Many travelers to the Middle East often found their favorite fantasies suddenly deflated at the most inopportune time. In the nineteenth century most of the celebrated Egyptian temples lay buried beneath mountains of refuse and sand. A village stood atop the mound of mud and garbage that covered the great temple at Luxor. (Archaeologists did not start clearing the site until 1883.) Flaubert complained that after climbing to the top of the Great Pyramid, he found himself staring at the name and address of a Parisian wallpaper hanger carved in block letters on the summit. And William Howard Russell, the correspondent for the *Times* of London, described a Turkish commission seated upon a divan and observed: "In the height of his delusions respecting Oriental magnificence and splendours, led away by reminiscences of *Tales of the Genii* and the *Arabian Nights*, the reader must not imagine that this divan was covered with cloth of gold or glittering with precious stones. It was clad in a garment of honest Manchester print."

Even in the best of times travel was not easy in the Middle East. "Travelling here is the strangest mixture of fun, danger, inconvenience, good living, and starving," William Bartlett, the British topographical artist, observed after his 1834 journey to the Holy Land. "One night we are entertained in a convent and live in clover; the next finds us in a village khan, sleeping under a shed, and supping on milk and eggs; a third, we are dining and supping out. Sometimes we are kept all night awake by fleas—the next sleeping like a top on good sheets."

Sewers were a rarity throughout the Arab world. "Jerusalem is a walled charnel house," Flaubert complained after a visit to the Holy Land. "It is full of shit and ruins." One British woman traveler in an 1850 handbook on Egypt warned her readers about the ubiquitous flies: "The flies were in such myriads as to defy description. The table, walls, ceiling, and floor literally swarmed with them. I was dreadfully tired and exhausted by the journey and laid myself down immediately in the cleanest looking corner of the divan, but I was not allowed to remain in peace. I had scarcely taken up my position before I was covered with flies from head to foot."

Artists, in particular, often experienced trying times as they ventured into isolated places, paintbrushes and easels in hand, in a search for good picture material. William Holman Hunt rarely went into the countryside without a rifle or revolver handy to ward off curious Bedouins and petty thieves. "No one in looking over my sketches will ever think of the trouble the collection of them has cost me," British artist David Roberts complained in Cairo. He had to shave off his mustaches and promise not to use brushes from pig's hair before local officials would permit him to sketch several of the mosques. But that represented progress in a region where only two decades before, Christians sometimes had been murdered for merely entering an outer courtyard of the Mosque of the Dome of the Rock in Jerusalem.

But most such stories, properly played back in Britain, sent shivers up the spines of eager armchair travelers and contributed further to the exotic appeal of the Middle East. Curzon in *Visits to the Monasteries in Levant* (1849) titillated his readers with numerous horror stories he had collected about the terrible deeds of Turkish pashas and beys. He reported:

A man in Upper Egypt stole a cow from a widow, and, having killed it, he cut it into twenty pieces which he sold for a piastre each in the bazaar. The widow complained to the [bey], who seized the thief and, having without further ceremoney cut him into twenty pieces, forced twenty people who came into the market on that day from the neighbouring villages to buy a piece of the thief for a piastre each. The joints of the robber were thus distributed all over the country. And the story told by the involuntary purchasers of these pounds of flesh had a wholesome effect upon the minds of the cattle-stealers. The twenty piastres were given to the woman, whose cows were not again meddled with during the lifetime of the [bey].

In 1835 Alexander William Kinglake, a youthful London solicitor, made his way by camel across the bleak Sinai desert toward Cairo. His party included two European servants, a dragoman, and four Arab attendants. On the second evening the Arabs announced they had no food and demanded the Englishman share his limited supply. Kinglake quizzed them: Did they not understand the original terms of their agreement that stipulated they were to supply their own food? Yes, they admitted. But now it was too late. They had no food. Kinglake sat beside his tent and quietly ate his dinner. The Arabs pleaded loudly for food. Kinglake refused.

"Then we die!" the Arabs wailed.

"God's will be done," Kinglake told them.

And then he added: "I gave the Arabs to understand that I regretted their perishing by hunger, but I should bear this calmly, like any other misfortune not my own—that in short I was happily resigned to *their* fate."

Kinglake wittily recounted the incident in his highly original book *Eothen* (a Greek word meaning "from the East"), which appeared in 1845. The slim volume took London by storm, quickly ran through six editions, and forever changed the nature of travel memoirs. (Its modern descendants include Evelyn Waugh's *Labels*, Graham Greene's *Journey Without Maps*, and Paul Theroux's *The Great Railway Bazaar*.) "*Eothen* reveals itself as a brilliant acid comedy, a sly masterpiece, as full of tricks as an Egyptian magician," an admiring Jonathan Raban has said. "It is one of the most deliciously nasty books in English literature."

Before *Eothen* British travel books were written to instruct. A heavy burden of tedious research and fact often broke the back of the narrative. But Kinglake decided to amuse rather than teach, trumpeting in his preface that the reader would find *Eothen* completely free from "all details of geographical discovery, or antiquarian research—from all display of 'sound learning and religious knowledge'—from all historical and scientific illustrations—from all useful statistics—from all political disquisitions—and from all good moral reflections."

Eothen is perhaps the first subjective travel memoir. Kinglake had little use for objective description impartially rendered, factual accuracy, and cultural fairness. Instead, he concentrated upon a faithful portrayal of his own emotional responses to the people, situations, and sights encountered in his travels. The subject of *Eothen* is not the

Middle East as much as it is the narrator—his whims, emotions, and prejudices. "As I have felt, so I have written," Kinglake announced. No sentimental traveler, he dismissed Bethlehem in thirteen lines. Ruins bored him, so Kinglake polished off Baalbek in a sentence. As for the desert, he wrote: "I think Childe Harold would have found it a dreadful bore to make 'the desert his dwelling place.' " Always God's young Englishman, Kinglake made no attempt to get to know the Turks and Arabs he met, never bothered to learn Arabic, and always dressed in his hand-tailored British shooting jacket. But he looked at the East with the fresh eyes of youth and wrote about it in a conversational style suffused with a keen sense of wit and irony. "*Eothen* is free as pagan air," Jan Morris once wrote approvingly. "It is travelogue for art's sake."

Kinglake's background reflected a solid middle-class prosperity. His father was a respected banker and lawyer. His mother, the daughter of a doctor, had been as a girl a companion to the young Lady Hester Stanhope when she lived with her grandmother, Lady Chatham, at Burton Pynsent. The eldest of six children, Kinglake was born in Taunton, Somerset, on August 5, 1809. In 1823 he started his studies at Eton, where his classmates included William Gladstone. (Kinglake later remarked of the future prime minister: "He is a good man in the worst sense of the word.") In 1828 Kinglake enrolled in Trinity College, Cambridge, where he became close friends with Alfred Lord Tennyson, Edward FitzGerald, and Thackeray. Kinglake was graduated from Cambridge in 1832 and moved to London to study law. In the autumn of 1834 he decided upon a vacation from his studies and set out for the Ottoman Empire in the company of an Eton schoolmate, John Savile, later Lord Pollington, who had earlier traveled extensively through Russia, Persia, and India.

The pair passed through Berlin, Dresden, Prague, and Vienna before crossing into the Ottoman Empire at Belgrade in present-day Yugoslavia. Because plague was widespread in the Middle East, a strict quarantine barrier separated the two worlds. Kinglake's friends bade them farewell "with nearly as much solemnity as if we had been departing from this life." The two Englishmen climbed into a small boat and slowly made their way across the Sava River to the small town of Semlin (present-day Zemun) on the outskirts of Belgrade. Overhead a solitary black vulture glided on the wind currents above "the Pest-accursed city." They were met at the other side by soldiers wearing "the old Turkish costume—vests and jackets of many and brilliant colours, divided from the loose petticoat-trowsers by heavy volumes of shawl." Each man carried in his belt a pair of pistols, a cutlass, and a dagger, all inlaid with silver and highly burnished.

First, there was an audience with the Turkish pasha, an event recounted later by Kinglake with considerable wit and exaggeration. They met in a great room with a European clock at one end and the pasha at the other. "The fine, old, bearded potentate looked very like Jove—like Jove, too, in the midst of his clouds, for the silvery fumes of the *Narguile* [water pipe] hung lightly circling about him," Kinglake observed. The pasha received his two English guests cordially. He clapped his hands. Several coffee bearers quickly appeared, each carrying a tiny cup in a small metal stand. Other slaves brought water pipes. The three sat together, sipping coffee, smoking contentedly, and conversing through an interpreter. Kinglake's account hilariously captures the absurdity of attempting a dialogue through an interpreter whose eagerness to please both parties overrides any concern for accuracy:

> *Pasha*—The Englishman is welcome; most blessed among hours in this, the hour of his coming.
> *Dragoman* (to the Traveller)—The Pasha pays you compliments.
> *Traveller*—Give him my best compliments in return and say I'm delighted to have the honour of seeing him.
> *Dragoman* (to the Pasha)—His Lordship, this Englishman, Lord of London, Scorner of Ireland, Suppressor of France, has quitted his governments, and left his enemies to breathe for a moment, and has crossed the broad waters in strict disguise with a small but eternally faithful retinue of followers, in order that he might look upon the bright countenance of the Pasha among Pashas—the Pasha of the everlasting Pashlik of Karagho-lookoldour.

Traveller (to his Dragoman)—What on earth have you been saying about London? The Pasha will be taking me for a mere cockney. Have I not told you *always* to say that I am from a branch of the family of Mudcombe Park and that I . . . was a candidate for Goldborough at the last election and that I should have won easily if my committee had not been bought. . . .

Dragoman—[is silent].

Pasha—The end of his honours is more distant than the ends of the earth, and the catalogue of his glorious deeds is brighter than the firmament of Heaven!

Dragoman (to the Traveller)—The Pasha congratulates your Excellency.

Traveller—About Goldborough? The deuce he does!—but I want to get at his views, in relation to the present state of the Ottoman Empire. Tell him the Houses of Parliament have met and that there has been a speech from the throne, pledging England to preserve the integrity of the Sultan's dominions.

Dragoman (to the Pasha)—This branch of Mudcombe . . . informs your Highness that in England talking houses have met and the integrity of the Sultan's dominions has been assured for ever and ever by a speech from the velvet chair.

Pasha—Wonderful chair! Wonderful houses!—whirr! whirr! all by wheels!—whiz! whiz! all by steam!—wonderful chair! wonderful houses! wonderful people!—whirr! whirr! all by wheels!—whiz! whiz! all by steam!

Kinglake and Savile set out on horseback for Constantinople 100 miles away through countryside notorious for bandits. But they traveled without incident, encountering only the corpses of robbers: "The poor fellows had been impaled upon high poles, and so propped up by the transverse spokes beneath them that their skeletons, clothed with some white, wax-like remains of flesh, still sat up lolling in the sunshine and listlessly stared without eyes."

Along the way Savile fell ill from a fever. Kinglake asked about a horse-drawn carriage for his companion and learned that no such thing existed in the Turkish countryside. They finally arrived in

Constantinople in the middle of a nasty ice storm, Savile's uncon-
scious form sprawled across a crude cart.

Constantinople was a grim city at the time. Bubonic plague raged
unchecked. "Its presence lent a mysterious and exciting . . . interest
to my first knowledge of a great Oriental city," Kinglake wrote later.
"It gave tone and colour to all I saw and all I felt." Virtually nothing
was known at the time about the cause of plague. Europeans insisted
that the source of the infection was the touch of a plague victim or
contact with the clothes. They huddled fearfully inside their homes.
Kinglake contrasted the attitudes of the Christian and the Muslim
toward the plague: "The Europeans, during the prevalence of the
Plague, if they are forced to venture into the streets, will carefully
avoid the touch of every human being whom they pass; . . . the
Muslim stalks on serenely, as though he were under the eye of his
God."

The second day Kinglake made his way cautiously through the city
streets. At the water's edge he suddenly found himself compromised
when several men, carrying the corpse of a plague victim, brushed by
him. The incident was a minor one, but it profoundly affected
Kinglake's later travels. He decided to repudiate the European theory
of contagion and go wherever he chose without making any serious
effort to avoid a touch. This attitude of Eastern fatalism delivered
him from undue worry and gave him a freedom of movement few
other Europeans dared enjoy.

Savile recovered from his illness. And the two left Constantinople
for the seaport of Smyrna, the chief commercial connection between
Europe and Turkey, where Savile received a letter urgently request-
ing his return to England. (The following year he was elected to
Parliament.) Kinglake booked passage on the *Amphitrite*, a Greek
brigantine, for Cyprus and from there by another ship to Beirut,
where "the ghostly images of women with their exalted horns stalked
through the streets."

But Kinglake's only interest in Lebanon lay with his mother's old
friend Lady Hester Stanhope. He had been entertained as a boy with
fabulous tales of "the Queen of the Desert, who dwelt in tents and
reigned over wandering Arabs." Kinglake quickly dispatched a letter

to Djoun asking Lady Hester if she would like to see the son of her old Somersetshire acquaintance. A few days later he received an invitation to visit her. After a day's hard ride Kinglake finally reached the manor at Djoun, which looked in the failing light of day like "a neglected fortress."

Late in the evening after he had dined alone, a slave ushered Kinglake into the presence of the English lady. "She rose from her seat very formally, spoke to me few words of welcome, pointed to a chair which was placed exactly opposite to her sofa, at a couple of yards distant, and remained standing up to the full of her majestic height, perfectly still and motionless, until I had taken my appointed place," Kinglake recalled later. "The woman before me had exactly the person of a . . . good businesslike, practical Prophetess, long used to the exercise of her sacred calling. . . . Her face was of the most astonishing whiteness. She wore a large turban." Lady Hester clapped her hands. Two black slave girls suddenly appeared from the shadows with coffee and water pipes.

This was the first of several audiences Kinglake enjoyed with the celebrated "queen of the Arabs." She had a reputation as a great talker, and he sat enthralled through her tales of her earlier adventures in the desert and dozed through her long monologues on the "sacred and profane mysteries of life." She was a brilliant mimic and entertained the young Englishman with an impersonation of Lord Byron's little affectations. "He had picked up a few sentences of the Romaic, with which he affected to give orders to his Greek servant," Kinglake wrote later. "I can't tell whether Lady Hester's mimicry of the bard was at all close, but it was amusing; she attributed to him a curious coxcombical lisp."

Kinglake also learned that the "fierce-looking and ill-clad Albanian soldiers" lounging in the outer courtyard were political refugees who had sought sanctuary at Djoun. When the pasha demanded them, Lady Hester had fired back a short message: "Come and get them." He never did. "Whether it was that [the pasha] was acted upon by any superstitious dread of interfering with the Prophetess . . . or that he feared the ridicule of putting himself in collision with a gentlewoman, he certainly never ventured to attack the sanctuary.

So long as [Hester] breathed a breath of life, there was always this one hillock . . . which stood out and kept its freedom."

Though Kinglake regarded Lady Hester as "a highly eccentric gentlewoman," he never brought his sharp wit to bear upon her curious ways. He understood the East too well and the impact it could have on those Europeans who lived there. He perceived her sympathetically as a great English lady, with all the pride and boldness of her class exaggerated by her seclusion in Djoun and distorted by the mystical influences of the East.

After Djoun, Kinglake traveled through the Holy Land. He added two members to his small party: Dthemetri, a zealous member of the Greek Orthodox Church who became his dragoman, and a young Nazarene guide, who promptly got them lost in the desert beyond the Jordan River, where they wandered for three days and almost perished from thirst.

Kinglake's account of this leg of his journey pays scant attention to the shrines and focuses in typical fashion on the Englishman's highly subjective impressions of what he saw. He recommended the guest rooms in the Franciscan monasteries because the monks there kept the finest wine cellars in the Holy Land. He disdained the Church of the Holy Sepulcher, dismissing it as a "Babel of worshippers—Greek, Roman, and Armenian priests were performing their different rites in various nooks and corners, and crowds of disciples were rushing about in all directions." The year before at the Easter pilgrimage the rivalry among the various Christian churches had led to a riot in the church. More than 200 worshipers had been trampled to death in the melee. Kinglake noted:

> I was amused at hearing of a taunt that was thrown that day upon an English traveller. He had taken his station in a convenient part of the church and was no doubt displaying that peculiar air of serenity and gratification with which the English gentlemen looks on at a row, when one of the Franciscans came by, all reeking from the fight, and was so disgusted at the coolness and placid contentment of the Englishman (who was a guest at the convent) that he forgot his monkish humility, as well as the duties

of hospitality, and plainly said, "You sleep under our roof—you eat our bread—you drink our wine, and then when Easter Saturday comes, you don't fight for us!"

And then there were the fleas. Kinglake later wrote:

No recent census had been taken when I was at Tiberias, but I know that the congregation of fleas which attended at my church alone must have been something enormous. It was a carnal, self-seeking congregation, wholly inattentive to the service which was going on and devoted to the one object of having my blood. The fleas of all nations were there. The smug, steady, importune flea from Holywell Street—the pert, jumping *puce* from hungry France—the wary, watchful *pulce* with his poisoned stiletto—the vengeful *pulga* of Castile with his ugly knife—the German *froh* with his knife and fork—insatiate—not rising from the table—whole swarms from the Russias, and Asiatic hordes unnumbered—all these were there. And all rejoiced in one great international feast.

From Jerusalem Kinglake, a brace of pistols in his belt, made an eight-day journey by camel through the Sinai desert to Cairo. For supplies, Kinglake took along a small tent; two bags of dried bread; two bottles of wine; two goatskins filled with water, tea, sugar; a cold tongue; and a jar of Irish butter. He also insisted upon using his English stirrups, which made riding on the camel much more comfortable. Kinglake quickly reconciled himself to the curious walk of the animal—"an odd, disjointed, and disjoining sort of movement."

In the desert Kinglake met up with his first Bedouins. "Almost every man has large and finely formed features, but his face is so thoroughly stripped of flesh and the white folds from his head-gear fall down by his haggard cheeks . . . that he looks quite sad and ghastly," he noted. He complained about the terrible plainness of Bedouin women and the utter lack of privacy in a Bedouin tent. ("At all events before you finally determine to become an Arab, try a gentle experiment: take one of those small, shabby houses in May

Fair and shut yourself up in it with forty or fifty shrill cousins for a couple of weeks in July.")

The small party traveled across an unchanging terrain of "sand, sand, sand, still sand, and only sand, and sand, and sand again" under the "same circle of flaming sky." The routine never varied. They traveled from sunrise to sunset. Nights were spent at a simple campsite in the desert vastness. After a light supper Kinglake retired to his tent, where "there were heaps of luxuries—libraries, bed rooms, drawing rooms, oratories, all crowded into the space of a hearth rug." The first night, when he lit a candle to read, scores of giant moths rushed into his little tent from the silent desert beyond. In the cold half-light of morning Kinglake feasted on buttered toast and hot tea. As the first rays of sunlight broke over the horizon, the party packed their camels and started again on their journey, leaving behind in the desert only some blackened embers and the heel marks of London boots to mark their sleeping place.

In the early evening of the eighth day Kinglake saw "a dark line upon the edge of the forward horizon, and soon the line deepened into a delicate fringe that sparkled here and there as though it were sewn with diamonds." He had finally reached the outskirts of Cairo. The small party pitched camp as usual. One of the Arabs set out in the darkness toward the distant lights and returned later to hand Kinglake a single stalk of rice, full, fresh, and green, a token of civilization. "The next day I entered upon Egypt," the Englishman wrote later, "and floated along . . . through green, wavy fields of rice and pastures fresh and plentiful and dived into the cold verdure of groves and gardens and quenched my hot eyes in shade, as though in deep, rushing waters."

Egypt was in the midst of one of the most terrible outbreaks of the plague in the nineteenth century. More than half of Alexandria's population of 25,000 had died. The toll in Cairo was much higher, with 1,200 deaths on an average day. (The local people referred to them always as "accidents.") Yet Kinglake found a curious absence of horror. "There was no tumbling of bodies into carts, as in the Plague of Florence and the Plague of London," he noted. "Every man, according to his station, was properly buried, and that in the usual way, except that he went to his grave in a more hurried pace than might have been adopted under ordinary circumstances."

Kinglake arrived in Cairo to find himself the solitary European traveler in the city. All others had stayed away because of the plague. "Most of the people with whom I had anything to do during my stay at Cairo were seized with Plague," he noted grimly. "And all these died." The city's European residents had barricaded themselves into their homes, put guards at their doors, and refused to meet with outsiders.

Kinglake was deeply touched by the courage and kindnesses of his Arab hosts. On an excursion to the pyramids of Sakkara he was the guest of the village elder, a man well aware of the European ideas about contagion. First he assured Kinglake that not one case of plague had occurred in the village. Then he asked the Englishman about the progress of the plague in Cairo. He was given a grim report. "Up to this time my host had carefully refrained from touching me out of respect to the European theory of contagion, but as soon as it was made plain that he, and not I, would be the person endangered by contact, he gently laid his hand upon my arm in order to make me feel sure that the circumstances of my coming from an infected city did not occasion him the least uneasiness," a deeply moved Kinglake wrote later. "In that touch there was true hospitality."

Kinglake rented an apartment from Osman Effendi. This was, in truth, John McLeod, a Scotchman who had been captured at Rosetta by Muslims while a young drummer boy with the Seventy-eighth Highlanders and forced to embrace Islam. He now dressed in Arab robes, spoke fluent Arabic, prayed in a mosque, and kept two wives. "But the strangest feature in Osman's character was his inextinguishable nationality," Kinglake noted. "In vain they had brought him over the seas in early boyhood—in vain had he suffered captivity, conversion, circumcision. . . . They could not cut away or burn out poor Osman's inborn love of all that was Scotch. . . . The joy of his heart lay in this. He had three shelves of books and the books were all thorough-bred Scotch. I recollect he prided himself upon the 'Edinburgh Cabinet Library.' "

Kinglake's biographer Gerald de Gaury has noted that Kinglake left out a turning point in Osman's career. The Arabs had taken him as a slave to Jiddah, Arabia, where he was discovered by John Lewis Burckhardt traveling in disguise to Mecca. Burckhardt bought Osman's freedom, took him back to Cairo, and secured employment for him at the British Consulate. Osman always carried a small pocket Bible with the following inscription on the flyleaf:

> J.M.—it is my name
> And Scotland is my nation
> Perth is my native place
> And Christ is my salvation.

When Burckhardt died in 1817, he left all his property to Osman. The Scotsman himself died from the plague shortly after Kinglake had left Cairo. His body was laid to rest in a Muslim cemetery in the same grave with Burckhardt.

Kinglake made the rounds of the principal sights. One day he visited the slave market, where he saw fifty black girls for sale. A slave trader took the Englishman inside a nearby building and offered to sell him a white Circassian girl. "Her large face was perfectly round and perfectly white," Kinglake noted later. "Though very young, she was nevertheless extremely fat. She gave me the idea of having been got up for sale—of having been fattened and whitened by medicines or by some peculiar diet."

Kinglake hoped to leave Cairo after a few days. But his dragoman fell seriously ill, so he stayed to nurse the man back to health. His party finally left Cairo after nineteen days in the city. "I no sooner breathed the free, wholesome air of the desert than I felt a great burden . . . was lifted away from my mind," he wrote later. "For nearly three weeks I had lived under peril of death. The peril ceased, and not until then did I know how much alarm and anxiety I had really been suffering."

Kinglake's next destination was Suez. He was impatient to get across the desert as quickly as possible and discouraged by the slower pace of the rest of his party. He hurried ahead at a brisk trot before he suddenly realized with horror that he was alone in the vast stretch of desert with no water, no food, and no sense of direction. Nor was there any road or path as such that he could follow to Suez. Instead of his being depressed and frightened, he was thrilled by the turn of events. "Hitherto, in all my wandering I had been under the care of other people—sailors, Tartars, guides, and Dragomans had watched over my welfare, but at last I was here in this . . . desert," he wrote later. *"I myself and no other had charge of my life."* Like Richard Burton, Charles Doughty, the Blunts, and T. E. Lawrence after him, Kinglake exulted in the desert as a testing field on which he could prove his mettle. He pushed ahead in an eastern direction under a blazing sun for several hours. Suddenly two Bedouins, one riding a camel, materialized out of a heat mirage. Desperate for water, Kinglake hurried to them. A large, well-filled waterskin hung from the camel. Kinglake quickly dismounted, rushed over to the water bag, drank long and hard, remounted his camel, and hurried off, all without saying a single word to the two astonished Bedouins. Later he guessed they had probably never before met in the desert a European dressed in a vest and tweed jacket. Late that night he reached the city of Suez. An hour later he was at the British consul's home, sound asleep in the same bed Napoleon had used on his visit there more than three decades earlier.

Kinglake worked his way north through Gaza and from there through the Holy Land to Damascus, the last stop on his grand tour of the Middle East. He had been traveling for almost fifteen months. Damascus had long been infamous for its hostility toward all Christians. "Until about a year or two years before the time of my going there, Damascus had kept up so much of the old bigot zeal against Christians . . . that no one dressed as a Frank could have dared to show himself in the streets," Kinglake observed. He found the city a welcome relief after his long travels through the deserts, an oasis of fountains and gardens.

"This 'Holy' Damascus . . . is a city of hidden palaces, of copses, and gardens, and fountains, and bubbling streams," Kinglake wrote later. "The juice of her life is the gushing and ice-cold torrent that tumbles from the snowy sides of [nearby mountains]. . . . As a man falls flat, face forward on the brook so that he may drink and drink again, so Damascus, thirsting forever, lies down with her lips to the stream and clings to its rushing waters."

Like many European travelers after him, Kinglake fell in love with Damascus. It boasted the most lavish palaces of any city in the Middle East. He was a guest in several of the most splendid, walking across marble floors covered with Persian rugs, simple verses from the Koran emblazoned on the walls. Kinglake's tour through the "Splendour and Havoc of the East" finally came to an end in the bliss of an idyllic Damascus garden near a flowing fountain. He had found his "Earthly Paradise."

A Partridge in a Pear Tree: The Roots of the Lebanese Civil War

The bloody civil war that has ravaged Lebanon since April 1975 had its beginning on the afternoon of September 14, 1841, near the town of Deir el Qamar, when several Christian hunters poached a single partridge on the private shooting preserve of the Druze chief Nasif Bey Abou Nakad.

The present civil war, the latest of several such conflicts, is a legacy of 150 years of religious antagonisms and ineffectual governments that have, in the words of one modern commentator, "made Lebanon what it is today: a country with no unity, a country without a sense of nationhood, a country whose citizens are loyal not to the state but to their religious communities." The earlier quarrels among the various Muslim and Christian elements of the region have been largely forgotten, as journalists concentrate on the war's international aspects. Now, as it was 150 years ago, the behavior of the outside powers has often been unscrupulous and hypocritical, as various foreign governments interfere in the internal affairs of Lebanon to promote their own interests.

"Pity the nation that is full of beliefs and empty of religion," warned the Lebanese poet Kahlil Gibran in *The Garden of the Prophet*. "Pity the nation that acclaims the bully as hero, . . . that raises not its voice save when it walks in a funeral, boasts not except among its ruins. . . . Pity the nation divided into fragments, each fragment deeming itself a nation."

Pity Lebanon.

From 1516 to 1860 Lebanon was largely an autonomous province within Syria. Turkish rule was limited primarily to the coastal plain and the cities of Beirut, Tripoli, Sidon, and Tyre. The region's mountain ranges harbored hardy and clannish mountaineers, a people who mixed religious fanaticism with equal amounts of staunch particularism and a passionate desire for independence.

Throughout its history Lebanon has been a confederacy of different and distinct religious communities, "bound by the mutual understanding that other communities cannot be trusted," as one Lebanese historian so aptly puts it. Of the various Christian and Muslim sects, the Maronites and Druzes were the most successful politically, exhibiting both a tight social organization and the self-confidence of communities long used to self-rule. Although the Maronites favored the northern half of Lebanon, and the Druzes the southern portion, the followers of the two religious sects often intermingled, so that Maronite and Druze villages frequently existed side by side. Both sects suffered from being representatives of a lost cause. The Maronites were remnants of a once-flourishing Christian population in the eastern Mediterranean area, while the Druzes were a heterodox offshoot from the dominant political and cultural body of Islam.

The contemporary Druze leader Kamal Jumblatt once referred perceptively to the Maronites as "that minority obsessed with their sense of being a minority." The sect derives its name from its patron saint, Maron, a fourth-century Syrian hermit. The Maronite Church was born out of the doctrinal schisms that racked the church and threatened the Byzantine Empire in the fifth century. When the heretical Maronites refused to accept the Monothelite doctrine, which affirmed that Christ had both a human and a divine nature but only a divine will, Emperor Justinian II moved against the sect, executing large numbers of its monks, razing their monasteries, and forcing the followers to flee into the remote mountains of northern Lebanon, where many of them have lived ever since.

The Druzes, who so fascinated Lady Hester Stanhope when she visited the emir Bashir, originated as a heretical Islamic sect in Egypt in the eleventh century. Druzes believe in the doctrines of reincarnation and predestination, do not observe the fast of Ramadan, make no pilgrimages to Mecca, and build no mosques for public worship. Because their heretical beliefs put them on the defensive, the Druzes almost from the first espoused a secret faith, hiding in the mountain fastnesses of southern Lebanon, concealing their existence, refusing to proselytize, indeed even refusing to accept new converts or to allow anyone to give up his or her Druze faith. Thus the Druze religion became an hereditary privilege, a sacred deposit, a priceless treasure, to be jealously guarded from profane curiosity. In their religious organization the Druzes make no distinction between clergy and the laity, instead dividing the followers into those who have been initiated into the secret doctrines of the faith and those who have not.

The Maronites and Druzes are the most important of the various Lebanese sects, which include the Greek Orthodox, Greek Catholics, Sunni Muslims, and Shi'ite Muslims. Up to 1830 the two major sects lived together in reasonable harmony. The emir Bashir II, who ruled the country from 1788 to 1840, though closely allied with the Druze community, was secretly of the Maronite faith. In spite of the Druze hegemony in Lebanon, the Maronites were allowed to build churches and convents. But as non-Muslims in a Muslim state, they and other Christian sects in Lebanon had few political rights and were widely discriminated against by the Turkish officials along the coast. By law in the Ottoman Empire, Christians were forced to wear distinctive black turbans and apparel and prohibited from riding on horses or mules, building houses higher than those of their Muslim neighbors, engaging in certain professions, and haggling over prices with Muslim merchants.

In 1831 the Egyptian pasha Muhammad Ali conquered Syria and Lebanon and installed his son, Ibrahim Pasha, as the ruler of the two provinces. Ibrahim initiated various reforms, attacked injustice and corruption, and promoted a political and social equality between Christians and Muslims throughout the region. The last policy, while winning Ibrahim the favor of the Christians, provoked the hostility of the Muslims, who resented the Christians' riding on horseback, dressing as they pleased, and competing with them in such professions as the sale of grains and livestock, which had once been the exclusive preserve of Muslims.

By 1841 the tensions between the Druze and Maronite communities had reached a breaking point. Many of the Druze landholdings had been confiscated and redistributed among the growing class of prosperous Maronite villagers. The Druze chiefs also lost many feudal prerogatives they had enjoyed for centuries. In 1838 Ibrahim armed 4,000 Christians to fight a Druze force that had risen against him. Fearful that Ibrahim's successes might threaten the Turkish Empire, the European powers forced him out of Syria and Lebanon. The Druze leaders sought to reclaim their land and rights, but the Maronites resisted all attempts to limit their new status and prosperity, and their patriarch threatened to exterminate the Druzes if they persisted in their demands.

That was how matters stood on that fateful day of September 14, 1841, in the town of Deir el Qamar. Located some twenty miles southeast of Beirut in the mountains and famous then for its silk manufacture, Deir el Qamar had become an important town with a largely Christian population of some 8,000. Its Christian merchants built spacious houses with marble courts and fountains and furnished them in a style of costly luxury. All the Druze landed property in the region had passed into their hands. The Maronites flaunted their new wealth and influence over their neighbors, inflaming Druze jealousy.

On the afternoon of September 14 a group of Maronite sport hunters trespassed on the private shooting preserve of a Druze chief in the nearby village of Bakleen and shot a partridge. A group of Druzes armed with sticks quickly confronted the Maronites and drove them off the preserve. Instead of apologizing for their error, they sent to Deir el Qamar for heavily armed reinforcements and attacked the

Druze position. By nightfall the Maronites had murdered sixteen Druzes and wounded many more.

The Druze leaders pretended to make a peace but secretly planned their retaliation. It came on October 13, when a large Druze force, banners flying, kettledrums beating, and armed with old rifles, scimitars, daggers, axes, and clubs, laid siege to Deir el Qamar. The fighting raged for several days. Several hundred on both sides were killed or wounded before the town finally fell. The Druze immediately murdered twenty prisoners and were stopped from making a general massacre only by the timely arrival of Colonel H. M. Rose, the British consul general.

But the damage had been done. The war cry had been sounded throughout Lebanon. "When Druze vengeance is once aroused, it is remorseless," commented Colonel Charles Churchill, a British observer on the scene. "They imbrue their hands in blood with a savage joy that is incredibile."

The Christians were no better. A Maronite bishop issued a proclamation, sounding a note that was to be heard with distressing frequency throughout Lebanese history: "Never turn back after a victory, without destroying to the end; spare the females, but as to everything else, such as murdering, plundering, burning, be sure to do all this, and continue your prayers and confessions, for this is a holy war."

A general civil war between Christians and Muslims spread the length and breadth of Lebanon. Although the Maronites far outnumbered their Druze opponents, they invariably lost most of the armed confrontations to the Druzes, who manifested in the field of battle better discipline, stricter obedience to their leaders, and greater adaptability. Thus Maronite attempts to establish a political ascendancy in Lebanon proved an abject failure.

The internal conflict in Lebanon quickly captured the attention of outside powers. The Turkish authorities in Constantinople were, of course, the most directly involved. They had long feared the possibility of the various Lebanese mountain sects coming together into a cohesive body that would be hostile to Turkish interests in the area and so had promoted a policy of fomenting distrust and suspicion among the various factions. When civil war broke out in 1841, the Turks actively supported the Muslims against the Christians, fearing that the latter, if successful in their drive for hegemony, would quickly open Lebanon to one or more European powers and thus undercut Turkish influence in the region. Those fears were not groundless, for the European powers, in particular Britain, France, and Austria, had by common consent assumed the right to superintend the welfare of Christians inside the Ottoman Empire.

This first civil war gradually wound down. A peace agreement was reached in January 1842, but not before some 3,000 people on both sides had perished and dozens of villages had been burned to the ground. The most deplorable legacy of the conflict was the intense feelings of religious hatred that both Druze and Maronite peoples now felt toward each other, ensuring that it would be only a matter of time before another and more vicious civil war would erupt.

Indeed, so dangerous had the situation become that once again it took only the most trivial of incidents to plunge the region into another civil war. On August 30, 1859, in a small mountain village near Beirut, two boys, one Druze and the other Maronite, quarreled. The father of the latter reproached the father of the Druze boy and insisted that the boy be disciplined. The Druze informed his relations, who quickly armed themselves and sent for reinforcements. The next day they demanded an apology for the perceived insult from the Christians. Almost immediately the confrontation flared into violence. The Christians drove the Druze warriors out of their village, killing twenty-eight.

Word of the conflict spread quickly throughout Lebanon, and sectarian violence engulfed the region. Once more the Christian leaders boasted that they would exterminate the Druze communities, having fielded 50,000 armed men to 12,000 or so for the Muslims. But the Maronites again proved woefully unprepared in spite of their larger numbers and quickly suffered major reverses. As the British observer Colonel Churchill noted, "The inferiority of the Christians in military organization to that of the Druzes became apparent from the first collision. The former advanced without the slightest order, dispersed themselves right and left, and seemed each to follow his own inspirations. . . . The Druzes, on the contrary, moved steadily on given points, under the direction of their chiefs, to whom they yielded the most implicit obedience."

The destruction was appalling. Within a few weeks more than sixty villages had been plundered and then torched. Thousands of refugees converged upon Beirut. In the Druze attack on the Maronite center of Jazzin, some 1,200 unarmed men, women, and children were massacred. Other Druze forces looted and burned Christian churches, monasteries, and convents. Monks were hacked to pieces on their altars. Nuns were raped and either turned loose naked into nearby fields or had their throats cut.

"This is a war of religion," one of the Druze leaders declared. "The country is ours or theirs." Indeed, the Druze people saw the war in absolute terms, yielding them either successful and lasting ascendancy in Lebanon or irremediable ruin and humiliation.

Once again outside powers found themselves intimately involved in the struggle. Turkish troops frequently fought alongside the Druze militia. The British Foreign Office also supported the Druzes, while the French and Austrians came in on the side of the Christian forces. The situation became so complicated that there hardly occurred an incident that did not have its impact in the capitals of Europe, especially London and Paris. The Lebanese chief Yusuf Karam complained in a letter to a supporter: "Our affairs have become the concern of Britain and France. If one man hits another, the incident becomes an Anglo-French affair, and there might be trouble between the two countries if a cup of coffee gets spilt on the ground."

Each day brought news of fresh massacres. In their attacks on Muslim strongholds the Christians were just as savage as the Druzes in their assaults on Christians. An American missionary, E. L. Porter, insisted that the Greek Catholic people of Zahlah were "as tyrannical, as unjust and almost as bloodthirsty as the haughty Muslims."

But the Muslims were, as always, far better organized than the Christians and scored more important victories. A force of 1,500

Druze militia attacked the Christian stronghold of Rasheiya in the mountains east of Sidon. The town's inhabitants mounted a spirited defense and repeatedly drove back their assailants until they finally expended their ammunition. Turkish officers inside the town opened the gates to the howling mob outside and then took up positions on balconies above the town's main square, "as if expecting a grand spectacle." Colonel Churchill gave a full account of the slaughter that followed: "The Druzes . . . first fired a general volley, and then sprung on the Christians with swords, hatchets, and bill-hooks. The first victim was Yoosuf Reis, the confidential secretary of the Emir Saad-e-deen. . . . He was seized and cut up piece-meal, beginning with his fingers and toes. The Emir Saad-e-deen was next decapitated. . . . By degrees the moving mass was hewn into. Many had their noses, ears, and lips cut off, and were otherwise horribly mutilated, before the final blow was given." By the end of the day almost 1,000 Christians had been brutally murdered at Rasheiya.

The last major Christian stronghold to fall was Deir el Qamar. The Druze forces met practically no opposition. They entered the town and began looting the houses. They "killed everyone they found in the houses, men and male children indifferently . . . hacking their bodies to pieces with their swords and axes. . . . And whenever they had finished plundering a house, they set fire to it." When the flames finally died down, some 2,000 Christians had perished.

With the slaughter at Deir el Qamar on June 20, 1860, the second major civil war in Lebanon came to an end. Most of the violent action had occurred within a terrifying four-week period. Some 15,000 Christians had died violently, and another 100,000 had become refugees. The Druze losses had been minimal.

Having achieved his principal goal of near eradication of the Christian influence in Lebanon, the Turkish pasha proposed a peace be proclaimed between the two sects on the condition that the past should be forgotten, no plunder be restored, and no indemnification be given. The Maronites had little choice. An uneasy peace settled over Lebanon.

*   *   *

On March 27, 1976, the leftist Druze spokesman Kamal Jumblatt visited Hafez Assad, the president of Syria. The civil war in Lebanon had by then raged for almost a year. Druze forces were advancing into the Maronite heartland north of Beirut. The Maronites were desperate and pleaded for Syrian intervention. Assad had hoped to moderate Jumblatt's extremist stand. He was disappointed.

In a major speech that July Assad remembered his encounter with Druze leader Jumblatt and what he had learned from it: "[Jumblatt] said, 'Let us discipline [the Maronites]. We must have decisive military action. They have been governing us for 140 years and we want to get rid of them.' At this point, I realized that all the masks had fallen. Therefore, the matter was not as we used to describe it. . . . The matter is not between the Right and Left, or between progressives and reactionaries. It is not between Muslim and Christian. The matter is one of vengeance. It is a matter of revenge which goes back 140 years."

CHAPTER IV

Sir Richard Burton and Father William Palgrave, SJ: Travelers into Arabia Deserta

The last phoenix seen alive, according to one Persian writer, was a captive bird in the zoo of the twelfth-century caliphs of Egypt. The rare phoenix (along with the unicorn) was generally thought to inhabit the remote mountain districts deep inside Arabia. The first-century Roman naturalist Pliny the Elder left behind a precise description of this fabled bird, which came to symbolize the human desire for rebirth and immortality.

"The phoenix, that famous bird of Arabia, is the size of an eagle, and has a brilliant golden plumage around the neck, while the rest of the body is of a purple color, except the tail, which is azure with long feathers intermingled of a roseate hue," he wrote. "The throat is adorned with a crest, and the head with a tuft of feathers. It is sacred to the sun. It builds a nest of cinnamon and sprigs of incense, which it fills with perfumes." After a life span of 600 years the phoenix died and was consumed by fire, only to rise newly born from the ashes.

To the ancient world Arabia was a mysterious and fabulous land, a treasure-house of riches and wonders almost beyond imagination. Great camel caravans carried gold, incense, myrrh, frankincense, and cinnamon northward through the deserts to the peoples beyond. The Greek historian Herodotus insisted that the very air over Arabia smelled of perfumes and spices. But these could be had only at great peril. According to Herodotus, cinnamon was found only in the nests of enormous birds stuck high upon inaccessible cliffs, while brilliantly hued snakes with wings guarded the frankincense trees.

Today we can hardly appreciate the enormous importance of incense in an ancient world where a general lack of sanitation required clouds of sweet-smelling smoke to cover noxious odors. Resins, gums, and spices were used routinely in embalming, fumigation, and medicine, but above all, it was the sacred frankincense that the ancient world held as dear as gold. Wendell Phillips, an archaeologist who supervised extensive excavations in Arabia in the 1950s, has written:

> In the twelfth century B.C. Rameses III of Egypt had a special building for storing frankincense for the worship of Amon. The temple in Jerusalem contained a holy chamber for keeping incense under guard. In Persia, Darius received from the Arabs a yearly tribute of a thousand talents, or more than thirty tons, of frankincense. In Babylon, the altar of the god Bel was enveloped in the pleasant vapors of nearly sixty thousand pounds of frankincense each year. Hindus and Buddhists, Greeks and Romans—the gods of all demanded the hardened oozings of a certain kind of tree that grew mainly in one small area of southern Arabia.

The empire builders in Egypt, Assyria, Babylon, Persia, Greece, and Rome hungered after the riches of Arabia and longed to add the vast peninsula to their domains. None ever did. For thousands of years Arabia remained secure and independent—all because of the Arab monopoly on camels. No other people in the Middle East had tamed these remarkable animals, which alone could withstand the terrible heat and dryness of the desert regions. The camel served both as a beast of burden, carrying great loads of incense and spices northward, and as a cavalry steed for the fierce Bedouin warriors who ranged across much of the interior of the Arabian Peninsula. Without camels, no army, no matter how well equipped and disciplined, could venture successfully into the deserts of Arabia. Once, only once, a Roman emperor ordered his soldiers into the burning wastes. Eleven thousand strong, they marched under orders from Augustus deep into the peninsula and fought a victorious battle against a large Bedouin force. Only seven soldiers died in combat, but virtually the entire Roman Army perished from thirst on the forced march back to the Mediterranean.

For more than 1,000 years Arabia prospered. The Romans called the region Arabia Felix, or "Happy Arabia." They traded extensively for frankincense and the wondrous goods of Asia with the wealthy and powerful merchants who lived along its coasts. The Arabian princes of commerce possessed a monopoly on the traffic between the worlds of the Mediterranean and the Far East. One of the most closely guarded secrets of the ancient world was of the reversible trade winds of the Indian Ocean, which blew east toward India in the summer months and west toward Africa in the winter. While Phoenician and Roman ships hugged the coasts and laboriously fought their way into the winds, the Arab dhows sailed effortlessly with the seasonal changes. A Roman sailor finally wrested the secrets of the "trades" from an unwary Arab merchant and soon let loose a flood of oceanic traffic. By the mid–first century A.D. Roman trade with India had boomed. Tigers, rhinoceroses, and elephants appeared in the Roman Circus. Parrots were kept as pets, while ivory, silks, turtle shells, and pearls adorned the very rich. And everyone peppered food.

The Roman fleets bypassing southern Arabia ended its long period of greatness. The camel caravans could never compete with the cheap efficiency of ships. And the spread of Christianity dried up the demand for frankincense. Arabia Felix went into a sharp decline. Its cities became ghost towns. Sand dunes reclaimed a dozen smaller kingdoms, including Sheba, the queen of which once visited the court of King Solomon. Arabia Felix became known as Arabia Deserta.

Roughly the size of the United States east of the Mississippi River and shaped like an enormous playing card tipped on its corner, Arabia is the world's largest peninsula. Starkly primitive, gnarled, and naked, this is a land stripped bare of all lakes, rivers, and forests. Jagged mountains rise grimly from bleak, uplifted plateaus. Great expanses of rolling sand dunes flow to the horizon. A savage sun and scorching winds generate ovenlike temperatures that can kill a person within a few hours. (In 1821 on one day three officers and thirty seamen on the British frigate *Liverpool* died from heat prostration while sailing from Muscat, Oman, to Bushire, Persia.) This was a land remote from the Orientalists' image of the Middle East as a place of extravagant color, voluptuous idleness, and decadent luxury.

Here, in one of the world's harshest environments, lived a wild, nomadic people called Bedouins (from the Arabic *badawi* meaning "desert dwellers"). They alone displayed the endurance and fortitude that allowed them to adapt to this brutal, unforgiving land. Clans of kinsmen grew into tribes. But fundamentally a fierce individualism and an all-embracing distrust of strangers defined their way of life.

"Geographers crowd in the edges of their maps parts of the world which they do not know about, adding notes in the margin to the effect that beyond this lies nothing but the sandy deserts full of wild beasts," the Greek writer Plutarch wrote in his *Lives*. For 1,500 years Arabia was destined to be discovered by Europe, forgotten again, and then discovered once more. As recently as 1918 the British explorer Harry St. John Bridges Philby could call the central desert region of Arabia, known as the Empty Quarter, the "largest blank space on the map outside the polar regions."

Arabia in 1850 was almost entirely unexplored by Europeans except on its coastal fringes. Fewer than a half dozen Europeans had attempted to penetrate inland. One Englishman, G. F. Sadlier, had crossed the interior from east to west in 1818, a feat not to be accomplished again for one full century until Philby made his remarkable explorations of the central portions of Arabia. Much of the peninsula at the midpoint of the nineteenth century was in a violent state of turmoil provoked by the fundamentalist Muslim sect of Wahhabism. Although Arabia was of special interest to Britain, forming as it did the overland link between Egypt and India, the government made no attempt to launch any expeditions of systematic exploration, as it had for the unknown areas of the Pacific Ocean and Antarctica in the previous century. Instead, exploration of the peninsula was left largely to the initiative and courage of a handful of individuals. Two of the most important were Sir Richard Burton and William Gifford Palgrave. In 1853 Burton disguised himself as a Muslim and penetrated the holy cities of Mecca and Medina. In 1862 Palgrave donned Arab robes and traveled extensively through the interior of the Arabian peninsula as a Jesuit spy for the French government.

Dirty Dick. Ruffian Dick. The White Nigger. Burton of Arabia. The nicknames were legion.

Explorer, soldier, diplomat, anthropologist, poet, author, archaeologist, scholar—Richard Burton was a multifaceted genius. One of the greatest European linguists of his century, he spoke fluently twenty-nine languages ("including pornography") and more than forty dialects. He translated into English both the *Arabian Nights* and the *Kama Sutra* and was the greatest authority in his day on the sexual customs of other cultures. His friend Lord Derby said of him, "Before middle age, he had compressed into his life more study, more hardship, and more successful enterprise and adventure than would have sufficed to fill up the existence of a half-dozen ordinary men."

"Discovery is mostly my mania," Burton wrote. He might have added the words of Friedrich Nietzsche: "That which does not kill us makes us stronger." The greatest explorer of his age, Burton first achieved fame in 1853, when, disguised as a Muslim, he penetrated the holy cities of Medina and Mecca and participated in their sacred rites. He then became the first white man to reach Harar, the holy city of Ethiopia and a center of the East African slave trade. There one night on the coast 350 savage Somali warriors attacked his camp, killed one of his companions, and speared Burton through his face. Next he was the first white man to enter East Africa, where he went in search of the source of the Nile River. Later wild Indians chased Burton in North America. And in the west African country of

Dahomey he reviewed an army of women warriors and observed the king's annual sacrifice of 500 victims. In 1863 on the eve of his departure on an expedition into the unexplored regions of Central Africa, Burton wrote home to a friend: "Starting in a hollowed log of wood—some thousand miles up a river, with only an infinitesimal prospect of returning! I ask myself 'Why?' and the only echo is 'damned fool! . . . [T]he Devil drives.' "

A true Renaissance man whose life wedded action to thought, Burton was driven by a compulsion to encompass all man's accumulated knowledge. He shared with David Livingstone, H. M. Stanley, John Speke, and the other explorers of his age an insatiable curiosity about the unvisited regions of the world. But Burton went far beyond them. No subject was too sacred or profane for Burton's researches. (He once researched but never found the time to write "A History of Farting.")

"Burton dared to think and believe what other brave men would have shrunk from contemplating," his biographer Byron Farwell has written. "He was an adventurer in the intellectual and the spiritual as well as the physical world and it was this combination of interests, actively followed, which made him unique, one of the rarest personalities ever seen on earth."

Burton was his age's bad boy. "The adventurer is an outlaw," journalist William Bolitho wisely observed more than fifty years ago. And Burton was just that—a social outlaw, the rebel who with romantic bravado defiantly shattered the social, religious, and political conventions of his day. Horror stories proliferated. Once a society matron asked him at a dinner party if he had brought her a souvenir from his latest adventure, as he had promised. Burton flung an Indian scalp into her lap. At his wedding reception his bride's doctor asked him: "Now, Burton, tell me—how do you feel after you have killed a man?"

"Oh, quite jolly, doctor!" Burton replied. "How do you?"

He once admitted: "Travellers, like poets, are mostly an angry race." Elsewhere he candidly confessed: "Men who go looking for the source of a river are merely looking for the source of something missing in themselves—and never finding it."

Burton was born at Torquay, England, on March 19, 1821. His father, Lieutenant Colonel Joseph Burton, was a man of few achievements but one who took great pride in always conducting himself "as a gentleman." In his youth he had fought a duel with a fellow officer, shot him in the chest, nursed him back to health, and later shot him again in a second duel. In 1820 the Duke of Wellington personally ordered Colonel Burton's dismissal from the service after he had gallantly refused to testify against Queen Caroline in the House of Lords, where she was charged with adultery. In 1818 he married Martha Baker, the daughter of an English squire, largely for the £30,000 she would inherit on her father's death.

Burton's mother is a shadowy figure rarely mentioned in the thousands of pages of his writing. And no wonder, for she had cost him a fortune he later estimated at more than half a million pounds. Old man Baker, Burton's grandfather, loved him, a squalling child with piercing eyes. His own son had bitterly disappointed him, and Baker decided to settle his estate upon his grandson. However, the boy's mother, who was devoted to her brother, protested strongly and delayed the proceedings for as long as possible. After many weeks Baker finally went to his lawyer's office to draw up a new will. As he stepped from his carriage, a heart attack struck him dead on the spot.

Burton's travels began at an early age. Soon after his birth the family moved across the Channel to Tours in central France. Within a few years Martha Burton gave birth to a daughter and a second son. The children's education was left to a lame Scot tutor, John Gilchrist. Burton started Latin at three, Greek at four. But his education was desultory and often unorthodox. One of his favorite stories as an adult concerned the time Gilchrist took his charges to see a woman guillotined in a public square. She had been convicted of poisoning her family. The young Burton clearly relished the quick rattle and heavy fall of the blade, the splash of the blood, and the ghastliness of the exposed head. Afterward he devised a new game called Guillotine, which quickly became a favorite with the children.

Neither parent made any serious attempt to discipline the two boys, whose wild and destructive ways often terrorized the neighborhood. "Like most boys of strong imagination and acute feeling I was a resolute and unblushing liar," Burton confessed in later years. "I used to ridicule the idea of my honour being in any way attached to telling the truth." (The adult Burton, a master of disguises who slipped easily from one identity to another, simply elevated lying to the level of a dramatic art.)

Burton's father was a man of weak character whose response to every crisis was to move. And in the Burton family crises were a common affair. Because of this peripatetic existence, the young Burton at sixteen had a mastery of a half dozen European languages and a range of experiences far wider than most men pick up in a lifetime. In Naples the two Burton boys, aged fifteen and eleven, discovered several brothels near their home. They sent messages to one young prostitute, who invited them over for an afternoon visit. There the two boys had what Burton described in later years as "a tremendous orgy." Passionate letters were exchanged with two of the girls. Some weeks later Martha Burton discovered the correspondence in the boys' bedroom. "A tremendous commotion was the result," Burton remembered years later. "Our father . . . proceeded to condign punishment with the horsewhip; but we climbed up to the tops of the chimneys, where he could not follow us and refused to come down till the crime was condoned."

Burton's father's response to the family crisis was predictable: a move to France. However, before the family could pack, Naples found itself in the grip of a fearful cholera epidemic, with 1,300 people dying each day. One evening the Burton boys borrowed some old clothes from an Italian servant and disguised themselves as undertaker assistants. They slipped out into the streets and spent the night with the carts making the rounds, collecting the corpses. Later Burton recalled the experience, which obviously had made a strong impression upon him:

> Outside Naples was a large plain, pierced with pits, like the silos or underground granaries of Algeria and North Africa. They were lined with stone, and the mouths were covered with one big slab, just large enough to allow a corpse to pass. Into these flesh-pots were thrown the unfortunate bodies of the poor, after being stripped

of the rags which acted as their winding sheets. Black and rigid, they were thrown down the apertures like so much rubbish, into the festering heap below, and the decay caused a kind of lambent blue flame about the sides of the pit, which lit up a mass of human corruption, worthy to be described by Dante.

A reckless bravado, a contempt for social taboos, a high degree of personal risk, an elaborate disguise—all in the pursuit of a forbidden pleasure. In later years these would become the ingredients of the classic Burton adventure.

Burton was completely Europeanized by the age of nineteen. He had received no systematic education and had shown complete disdain toward all the tutors his father had hired. His education had largely been in the ways of the world. He was an excellent fencer and marksman, proficient in several languages, and quite experienced with women—hardly the sorts of accomplishments to impress the authorities of a major university. His whole upbringing had given him a contempt for most authority and a firm conviction that he should be allowed to do whatever Richard Burton wanted to do.

In the early autumn of 1840, about the time Queen Victoria married Prince Albert, Burton's father sent him to Trinity College, Oxford, to study for the ministry. A more unsuitable career for the young Burton could hardly be imagined. He hated England with a passion, calling it the "only country where I never feel at home." After a hilarious start—another student mocked his mustache and Burton immediately challenged him to a duel, a gesture which would have been appreciated at a German university but was completely unsuitable for Oxford—Burton soon carved out a niche for himself as an unruly eccentric. His happiest hours were spent in the college fencing rooms and off campus with his mistress, a young Gypsy girl named Selina. Burton quickly ran afoul of the faculty when he insisted upon speaking his Latin with a Roman accent and giving his classical Greek a modern pronunciation. The masters, unable to appreciate his linguistic ability, failed him.

"Oxford, with notable exceptions, was a hotbed of toadyism and flunkeyism—a place to make rather ignorant gentlemen," Burton decided contemptuously. A school chum, Alfred Bate Richards, said of him later: "Though Burton was brilliant, rather wild, and very popular, none of us foresaw his future greatness, nor knew what a treasure we had amongst us."

Burton finally decided to study Arabic. He was appalled to learn that while England ruled over the largest population of Muslims in the world, Arabic was not offered at Oxford. He set about on his own to learn the language. A friendly Arabist in the Spanish department pointed out his error of writing Arabic characters from left to right instead of right to left. But for the most part Burton mastered the language on his own, creating in the process a system which would in the future allow him to learn a new language in two months. He once described at length his techniques:

> I got a simple grammar and vocabulary, marked out the forms and words which I knew were absolutely necessary, and learnt them by heart by carrying them in my pocket and looking over them at spare moments during the day. I never worked for more than a quarter of an hour at a time, for after that the brain lost its freshness. After learning some three hundred words, easily done in a week, I stumbled through some easy book-work (one of the Gospels is the most come-atable) and underlined every word that I wished to recollect, in order to read over my pencillings at least once a day. Having finished my volume, I then carefully worked up the grammar minutiae, and I then chose some other book whose subject most interested me. The neck of the language was now broken, and progress was rapid. If I came across a new sound like the Arabic *Ghayn*, I trained my tongue to it by repeating it so many thousand times a day. When I read, I invariably read out loud, so that the ear might aid memory. I was delighted with the most difficult characters . . . because I felt that they impressed themselves more strongly upon the eye than the eternal Roman letters. . . . Whenever I conversed with anybody in a language that I was learning, I took the trouble to repeat their [sic] words inaudibly after them [sic], and so to learn the trick of pronunciation and emphasis.

After two terms at Oxford Burton asked his father to withdraw him from the university. The place bored him. And he yearned to seek adventure, glory, and fortune in India, where the East India Company was extending its rule into Sind. His father was utterly unsympathetic. "I went [to Oxford] with no good will, and as my father refused to withdraw me from the University, I resolved to withdraw myself," Burton recalled later. Back at Trinity College, he worked hard to get himself expelled. This done, he arranged to leave in style in a small carriage, tooting loudly on a tin trumpet while driving recklessly over the college's flower beds. Soon afterward his father relented and for £500 purchased his son a commission in the Bombay Infantry.

On June 18, 1842, the twenty-one-year-old Burton sailed from Gravesend on the bark *John Knox* for India, taking with him a Hindustani dictionary and grammar; his guns, swords, and saddles; a dozen white dress jackets; and a wig. In anticipation of the extreme heat and humidity of India, Burton had shaved his head. His bald head together with his high cheekbones and flowing mustache gave his face a Tartarlike sinisterness.

India in 1842 was still a faraway place. The sense of empire that was to be so celebrated in the latter part of the century had not yet taken a firm hold on the English people. There was a growing sense that the colonies were important markets for Britain's industrialism. But colonies meant niggling little wars in remote corners of the globe where native populations seemed curiously slow to appreciate the blessings of British rule. Many in England undoubtedly agreed with Benjamin Disraeli a decade later when he complained of "those wretched colonies, those millstones around our necks."

Burton set sail for the East at a tense time in the evolution of the British Empire. In 1839 the British government had installed a puppet government in Afghanistan to serve as a buffer state against Russian expansionism. British rule there was hopelessly inept and arrogant and quickly aroused the passions of the Afghan people. In January 1842 Afghan irregulars forced the entire British garrison of some 16,000 British and Indian troops, women, and children to depart from Kabul on a fearful midwinter march to Jalalabad ninety miles to the east. Afghan warriors waited for them in the snow-clogged mountain passes. Only one man, a British doctor, survived the ambush and massacre. It was the worst defeat in British military history.

A second crisis had erupted in China, which the East India Company had developed into a major market for Indian-grown opium. In 1839 in an effort to curtail a growing drug problem the Chinese government seized and burned hundreds of tons of opium. Britain denounced the action as a threat to its commercial and political interests in the region and declared war. After two years of fighting, British forces swept through China, taking city after city until Nanking finally fell and the Chinese government sued for peace. The Treaty of Nanking ceded Hong Kong to England and opened five major Chinese ports to British trade, including opium. Soon afterward British missionaries arrived in China to bring Christian enlightenment to the "heathens."

On October 28 Burton finally reached Bombay. He found a city stinking in its own filth with buildings that were "splotched and corroded as if by gangrene." At the British Hotel he saw his first Indian soldier, a sepoy dressed in faded scarlet and blue dungarees with "a dingy face, greasy hair, arms like broomsticks, and a body like a mummy." Deploring the lack of privacy at the hotel, Burton shifted quarters to a sanatorium near the ocean. The place was infested with lizards and rats. And his room smelled of "roast Hindu" whenever the winds blew across the funeral pyres on a nearby beach. But the inmates led "a roystering and rackety life" and introduced him to "all kinds of mischief . . . of which the less said the better." And so he stayed.

Burton quickly settled into a rigorous routine of language study, devoting twelve hours a day to Arabic and Hindustani. For the latter he employed the finest language instructor in Bombay, Dosabhai Sohrabji, who became his close friend and used to say that Burton was the only man he had ever met who could "learn a language running." Burton also moved an Indian mistress into his room. With her he practiced both his Hindustani and the sexual arts of the *Kama Sutra*, taking full advantage of the Orient as a place where the

Victorian gentleman could find a range of sensual pleasures not easily available in Europe.

In April 1843 Burton passed the official examination in Hindustani and then took up in short order Sanskrit, Gujarati, Persian, Sindi, Punjabi, Telugu, Pashto, Multani, Armenian, and Turkish. He was soon made the official regimental translator. "Burton took to languages in India as other men to liquor, intoxicated by the sense of mastery and the exhilaration of unlocking mysteries," states his biographer Fawn Brodie. "Burton was not a pedant with languages but a libertine—mastering, using, and abandoning. Though he spent many hours in these pursuits, they were for him neither an escape nor a substitute for living, for he sampled everything in India with great gusto—the conventional and unconventional, the respectable and the tabooed. Without the language mastery there would have been no easy door to his multiform adventures."

Later in 1846, to the shock of his fellow officers, Burton moved into a bungalow with a collection of forty monkeys of different species and various ages and attempted to learn their language. He kept order with a whip, assigned the animals various ranks and titles, and ordered his servants to wait upon them. He designated one "very pretty, small, silky-looking monkey" as his wife and put pearls in her ears. Burton carefully monitored his monkeys' chattering, took detailed notes, and soon had developed a vocabulary of sixty sounds.

In 1844 Burton's Eighteenth Regiment of the Bombay Indian Infantry was sent to Karachi in Sind. The region was under the command of Sir Charles Napier, who the year before had annexed 500,000 square miles of northern India after killing 10,000 enemy soldiers and capturing 9 princes and more than 400 chiefs in two ferocious battles. "The moral effect of this expedition has been to spread a wholesome respect for our armies among the neighbouring nations," Napier stated in his dispatch to Queen Victoria after the campaign. It was thought that Sind would take a decade to pacify, but within a year Napier had made the region so safe it was said that "if you catch a wasp in your hand, it will not sting."

Eventually Burton found himself attached to Napier as his translator. The gruff sixty-two-year-old Scotsman, who had once been a friend of Lord Byron's took an immediate liking to his young lieutenant. What another general might have objected to as insubordination Napier put down to spunk. Once the two rode together to see a bridge newly constructed across a river. "How many bricks do you think there are in that bridge, Lieutenant Burton?" Napier inquired casually.

Burton quickly snapped to attention, clicked his heels, and shouted out: "Sir, 229,010 bricks, sir!"

Napier soon came to appreciate Burton's remarkable genius for languages and put him to work gathering intelligence. The customary procedure was to rely upon paid native agents. But Burton stained his skin; dressed in a wig, beard, and native costume; and opened a shop in a bazaar as Mirza Abdullah, a wealthy Persian linen merchant. For days at a time he mingled with the native population, asking hundreds of questions and getting to know people from all levels of society. Burton also smoked opium and hashish; attended circumcision feasts, weddings, and funerals; and generally had a free hand to go wherever he chose under his disguise of a wealthy peddler of fine cloth. He enjoyed a view of Indian society that few British officials ever saw. Burton's fellow officers referred to him contemptuously as the "White Nigger," but he looked upon it all as a grand adventure.

Burton reported directly to Napier. On one occasion he told his commander about the brothels flourishing in Karachi to service the British Army. When Burton mentioned that three of the ten brothels catered to homosexual pleasures, Napier was stunned. He demanded a full report. This Burton submitted, describing both kinds of brothel in clinical terms that many in his day would have considered pornographic. He noted, for example, that in the homosexual brothels young boys fetched twice the price of the eunuchs because "the scrotum of the unmutilated boy could be used as a kind of bridle for directing the movements of the animal." (In later years his close friend Frank Harris observed of Burton: "It was the abnormalities and not the divinities of men that fascinated him.") Napier quickly closed the three offending brothels.

In the late summer of 1846 Burton fell ill with cholera and was granted a two-year sick leave. After he had left the hospital, he spent several months recovering in the Portuguese colony of Goa. One day Burton, who had undertaken the study of Portuguese, dropped by the ancient Convent of Santa Monica to examine its library holdings. There he met the school's Latin teacher, "a very pretty white girl, with large blue eyes, a modest smile, and a darling of a figure." Burton immediately set about courting the nun. He quickly sought out the prioress and introduced himself as a wealthy Englishman from a prominent Catholic family on a search for "a good comfortable quiet nunnery" for his pious younger sister. He also hinted that he would provide a large monthly sum for her maintenance. The prioress eagerly gave Burton a tour of the convent grounds and introduced him to the sisters.

Burton's imagination was probably as much stimulated by the formidable challenge of the task at hand and the nature of the "forbidden fruit" as by the thought of any sexual gratifications he might have later. Often using a Goanese servant as a go-between, Burton cleverly courted the young nun, who apparently hated convent life. Finally she agreed to elope. Burton made elaborate plans. He slipped some drugged tobacco to the convent guards, putting them to sleep. Then, late at night, in the company of his Muslim servant, Burton, a dagger in one hand and a key in the other, slipped into the convent garden and made his way through the cloisters toward the cell of the Latin teacher. Unfortunately, in the darkness he made a wrong turn and entered the room of the sleeping sub-prioress, a woman in her sixties. He hastily scooped up the still form and hurried away. Burton to his horror did not discover his mistake until the trio were on the beach outside the convent.

"We have eaten filth," Burton said in disgust, while the old woman screamed in terror. "What are we to do with this she-devil?"

"Cut her throat?" his servant suggested.

"No, that won't do. Pinion her arms, gag her with your handkerchief, and leave her—we must be off instantly."

That was the end of his intrigue. The convent was placed under heavy guard "with all the doors bolted and barred every night as carefully as if a thousand prisoners were behind them."

Burton's stay in India came to an abrupt end in 1848 after someone maliciously forwarded to the government offices in Bombay his confidential report on male brothels. The shock waves destroyed his military career. Rumors abounded to the effect that Burton himself had participated in the activities he had described in such graphic detail. The scandal trailed after him for the rest of his life. Burton sailed for England in May 1849, bitter in defeat.

He settled in Boulogne, France, determined to become a writer. In a burst of feverish activity he produced within two years four books on India. They proved a useful form of therapy and provided him with the opportunity to put his Indian experiences into perspective. They also helped somewhat to rehabilitate his career. In all four books the anthropology overwhelmed the travel narrative. And, as some contemporary critics never tired of pointing out, good taste was often lost in the confusion.

Burton also used the time to indulge another of his major passions—fencing. One of the finest swordsmen in Europe, he was fascinated by the sport. He went up against and beat some of the most celebrated fencers in France. "Fencing was the great solace of my life," Burton wrote years later in his history *The Book of the Sword.* "The sword is a gift of magic, one of the treasures sent down from Heaven." In 1853 he published a 15,000-word manual, *Complete System of Bayonet Exercise.* At the time the British soldier received no training whatsoever on the proper use of his bayonet. Within a few years the British Army had adopted Burton's manual for general use.

He looked about for another major project. There was no longer a future for him in the army. But his imagination seized upon an idea that had come to him in India: a pilgrimage to the forbidden Muslim holy cities of Mecca and Medina. Only one Englishman had been there before. Joseph Pitts, a sailor, had been captured by pirates off the North African coast, sold into slavery in Algeria, and carried to Mecca in 1680. Of the handful of Europeans who had visited the two cities and returned alive, only two had brought out detailed information: the Swiss John Lewis Burckhardt in 1814 and 1815 and a Finnish explorer, George Wallin, in 1845.

Such an expedition obviously involved great personal risk. Burton had probably heard the stories about several disguised Russian and French travelers known to have been discovered in Mecca. All were taken to the nearby desert, swiftly beheaded, and buried in unmarked graves. When Charles Doughty rode with the Damascus hajj part of the way toward Mecca in late 1876, two Turkish troopers with the caravan informed him that scarcely a year passed without the discovery of one or more Christians disguised as Muslim pilgrims. The same soldiers had recently observed two men who had been seized at Muna when they were seen taking notes. Upon examination they were found to be Christians and summarily executed.

In the autumn of 1852 Burton approached the Royal Geographical Society and offered his services "for the purpose of removing that opprobrium to modern adventure, the huge white blot which in our maps still notes the Eastern and the Central regions of Arabia." Roderick Murchison, the society's president, was enthusiastic about the project and agreed to underwrite its cost.

Burton was ecstatic. Arabic had been the first love among his many languages, and he may have sensed that in the Middle East he would find the spiritual home he never had in England. Much later, after his travels had taken him to every continent except Australia and Antarctica, Burton spoke of Arabia as the "land of my predilection." There he found freedom, sexual frankness, a sense of fatalism, violence, and colorful excess, all of which fulfilled certain spiritual needs within him. His *Personal Narrative of a Pilgrimage to Al-Madinah & Meccah* was to go through numerous editions in his lifetime and do as much as any travel book to shape the way Englishmen of the nineteenth century viewed the Arabs. Burton's most ambitious literary project, one destined to consume many years of his life, was a translation of the *Arabian Nights*, edited with copious notes that reflected his immense erudition. His goal was to take the greatest of all Arab literary works and interpret it for the West to give a picture of the Arab world as it really was. Finally, after his death on October 20, 1890, Burton's body was to rest on the outskirts of London in an enormous mausoleum made of Carrara marble and shaped like an Arab tent.

His future wife has given us a vivid word picture of Burton on the eve of his departure for Mecca. "He was five feet eleven inches in height, very broad, thin, and muscular," Isabel Arundell wrote. "He had very dark hair; black, clearly defined, sagacious eyebrows; a brown, weather-beaten complexion; straight Arab features; a determined-looking mouth and chin, nearly covered by an enormous black mustache. . . . But the most remarkable part of his appearance were two large, black, flashing eyes with long lashes, that pierced one through and through and through."

Burton spent five months in London preparing for his journey. He took as his guide the Arab proverb "Conceal thy tenets, thy treasure, and thy traveling." He had himself circumcised, grew a beard, dyed his skin with henna stain, and studied Arab customs. He needed more than simply a fluency in Arabic. He had to know how to sit, eat, drink, walk, gesture, and pray as an Arab did.

Then Richard Burton quietly disappeared. In his place was Mirza Abdullah, an Afghan dervish and doctor. On April 3, 1853, a robe-clad Abdullah and his "English interpretor," Captain Henry Grindlay of the Bengal Lancers, boarded the steamer *Bengal.* Their destination was Alexandria.

Burton stayed for one month in Alexandria, shaping his new identity with a sure touch. "From my youth I have always been a dabbler in medical and mystical study," he admitted. He had carefully selected the roles of dervish and doctor for their obvious advantages. The dervish, whom he labeled a "chartered vagabond," was a kind of religious fanatic often given to wild displays of dancing, whirling, and chanting. It was a perfect disguise in case discovery threatened. "In the hour of imminent danger, [the dervish] has only to become a maniac, and he is safe," Burton wrote. "A madman in the East, like a notably eccentric character in the West, is allowed to say or do whatever the spirit directs."

In his other disguise, as a doctor, Burton possessed a key that would open that most inviolate inner sanctum of the Muslim world, the harem. In fact, no sooner had he settled into his quarters in Cairo than an Arab slave trader across the street asked Burton to tend to the complaints of the black Abyssinian girls who made up his inventory. Burton cured several girls of the "price-lowering habit of snoring," much to the delight of the slave trader. Burton found the girls to be "broad-shouldered, thin-flanked, fine-limbed." He flirted outrageously with them, but his charm went unrewarded.

"How beautiful thou art, O Maryam!" Burton told one girl. "What eyes!"

"Then why," she responded, "don't you buy me?"

"We are of one faith—of one creed—formed to form each other's happiness," he pleaded.

"Then why don't you buy me?" she insisted.

"Conceive, O Maryam, the blessing of two hearts—"

"THEN WHY DON'T YOU BUY ME?"

In his *Personal Narrative of a Pilgrimage* Burton went to great lengths to inform his readers about the benign character of slavery in the Muslim world. "The laws of Mahomet enjoin his followers to treat slaves with the greatest mildness, and the Muslims are in general scrupulous observers of the Apostle's recommendation," he wrote. "Slaves are considered members of the family, and in houses where free servants are also kept, they seldom do any other work than filling the pipes, presenting the coffee, accompanying their master when going out, rubbing his feet when he takes a nap in the afternoon, and driving away the flies from him. When a slave is not satisfied, he can legally compel his master to sell him."

In Egypt Burton discovered the pleasures of *kayf*, the name the Arabs gave to the sensation of voluptuous relaxation one achieved after smoking hashish. He wrote with approval of the "savouring of animal existence; the passive enjoyment of mere sense; the pleasant languor, the dreamy tranquillity, the airy castle-building, which in Asia stand in lieu of the vigorous, intensive, passionate life of Europe." The Arab, he said, possessed "a facility for voluptuousness unknown to northern regions, where happiness is placed in the exertion of mental and physical powers."

While Burton was in Cairo, the Muslim holy season of Ramadan (that "fearful infliction") began with a sixteen-hour fast in which all consumption of food, drink, tobacco, and "even our saliva" was forbidden. "Like the Italian, the Anglo-Catholic, and the Greek fasts, the chief effect of the 'blessed month' upon True Believers is to darken their tempers into positive gloom," Burton observed wryly. "The Mosques are crowded with a sulky, grumbling population, making themselves offensive to one another on earth, whilst working their way to heaven."

As he traveled through Egypt, he observed with contempt the European "author tourists" crowding the country—"that sensible class of men who wish to get over the greatest extent of ground with the least inconvenience to themselves and others." In his disguise as a dark-skinned Muslim visitor to Her Majesty's empire, Burton soon began to rub up against the meddlesome interference of both native and British officials. But at night he could escape all the unpleasantness in an evening stroll through the streets of old Cairo, which Burton called one of life's most memorable experiences. The daytime squalor disappeared, while the moonlight transformed the city into a magical wonderland. "Not a line is straight, the tall dead walls of the Mosques slope over their massy buttresses, and the thin minarets seem about to fall across your path," he wrote. "The whole view is so strange, so fantastic, so ghostly."

Burton found himself "crazed with the spell of Arabia." His travels eventually took him throughout Africa and the Americas, but he never found elsewhere the magic that always awaited him in the Middle East. Burton spent more time in Africa than in Arabia and indeed became his country's foremost authority on that continent. But he was always contemptuous of the Africans and thought that none ever measured up to the Arab slave traders he encountered in the remote regions of central and eastern Africa. "Striking indeed," he remarked, "was the contrast between the open-handed hospitality and hearty goodwill of this truly noble race and the niggardliness of the savage and selfish African—it was heart of flesh after heart of stone."

In spite of his admiration for the Arab, his culture, literature, art, and religion, Burton was always beneath his many disguises an Englishman. His sympathies lay not with England, which he despised, but with the British Empire, where he knew there would always be a home for misfits like him. In *Personal Narrative of a Pilgrimage* Burton urged British rule over Egypt. "Whatever European country secures Egypt will win a treasure," he wrote. "This country in western hands will command India, and by a ship-canal between Pelusium and Suez would open the whole of Eastern Africa."

Burton had inadvertently cast himself in two antagonistic roles, worshiping individualism at the same time he defended the British Empire. In 1853 he was both the rebel against authority, fleeing to the Middle East as a place of freedom after the claustrophobic world of Victorian morality, and the potential agent of that same authority. (In 1869 he returned to serve for two years as the British consul in Damascus.) The creative tension between these two contradictory sides of Burton continued over the years to shape many of his responses to the Middle East.

In Cairo Burton acquired the services of a Meccan, Muhammad el Basyuni, a "beardless youth, of about eighteen, chocolate-brown, with high features, and a bold profile." He also bought supplies for the pilgrimage: tea, coffee, sugar, rice, dates, oil, tobacco, lanterns and cooking pots, a small bell-shaped tent, and three waterskins for the desert. For his doctor's bag he purchased quantities of calomel, bread pills, and cinnamon water. He also bought a *hamail*, a handsome gold-embroidered crimson velvet case for a Koran, slung by red silk cords over the left shoulder. It was the badge of the pilgrim to Mecca. But instead of a Koran, Burton's *hamail* contained his watch, compass, money, penknife, pencils, and slips of paper, which he would hold concealed in the palm of his hand when he wanted to take notes.

Burton hired two camels and two drivers. With a pistol in his belt he settled down on the hard wooden saddle and started for Suez, eighty-four miles away, determined to learn "how much a four years' life of European effeminacy had impaired my powers of endurance." Once he reached the desert, all of Burton's senses sharpened, and he took "a keen enjoyment in mere animal existence." None of his Indian experiences had prepared him for the magnificent, dangerous world of the Arabian desert. He recalled later:

It is strange how the mind can be amused by scenery that presents so few objects to occupy it. Above, through a sky terrible in its stainless beauty, and the splendours of a pitiless blinding glare, the [wind] caresses you like a lion with flaming breath. Around lie drifted sand-heaps, upon which each puff of wind leaves its trace in solid waves, flayed rocks, the very skeletons of mountains, and hard unbroken plains, over which he who rides is spurred by the idea that the bursting of a water-skin or the pricking of a camel's hoof would be a certain death of torture,—a haggard land infested with wild beasts, and wilder men,—a region whose very fountains murmur the warning words, "Drink and away!" What can be more exciting? what more sublime? . . . In the Desert, even more than upon the ocean, there is present Death.

The desert for Burton functioned as both an opportunity for self-denial and an arena for personal testing, shaping his pilgrimage into "a trial of manliness" and heightening his enjoyment of life. Danger for Burton was a kind of drug that made him unfit for a more normal existence. "Believe me, when once your tastes have conformed to the tranquillity of [desert] travel, you will suffer real pain in returning to the turmoil of civilisation," he warned. "The air of the cities will suffocate you, and the care-worn and cadaverous countenances of citizens will haunt you like a vision of judgment."

The dangers were very real. His boy, Muhammad, suspected from the first that he was a heretic or, even worse, an impostor. Each evening, when the group made their prayers, he positioned himself behind Burton and watched his every movement. Once the suspicious boy searched Burton's luggage and discovered his sextant, certain evidence, he insisted, that Mirza Abdullah was a spy. Later at Suez he denounced Burton to the religious authorities as "an Infidel from India." An Islamic scholar questioned Burton at length on the finer points of the faith and afterward pronounced him a true Muslim.

At Suez Burton secured passage on the pilgrim ship the *Golden Wire*, a fifty-ton two-masted dhow which sailed without a compass, log, sounding lines, or charts. Ninety-seven passengers were crammed into a space normally reserved for sixty. Among the pilgrims was a group of Maghrebis from the desert between Tripoli and Tunis, all armed with ten-inch daggers, "their faces full of fierce contempt or insolent familiarity." The Maghrebis started a fearsome brawl. Burton and several companions soon cleared the small poop deck, while the fighting raged on below. When it finally stopped, five men were suffering from severe knife wounds. Then, at 3:00 P.M. on July 6, 1853, the *Golden Wire* shook out its sails and slowly started out of the harbor. Burton cast a wistful glance back at the Union Jack flying over the British Consulate at Suez. Ahead lay Mecca. His hajj had started in earnest.

The voyage on the *Golden Wire* lasted twelve misery-filled days. The ship made its way along the coast by sight during the day and in the evening anchored in a cove. The pilgrims waded ashore to sleep at night on a beach. One evening, as they made their way through the surf, Burton stepped on a sea urchin. At the time he thought nothing about the small piece of black spine embedded in his toe. But the wound soon started festering, and his sore, aching foot almost stopped him from reaching Mecca.

On July 18 the *Golden Wire* finally reached the Arabian port of Yenbo, where the pilgrims disembarked. There Burton hired two camels and a special litter called a *shugduf*, "composed of two corded cots 5 feet long, slung horizontally about half way down and parallel with the camel's sides." Burton used his swollen foot as an excuse, for the *shugduf* with its covered top was used almost exclusively by wealthy women. It allowed him the privacy to take notes without fear of detection.

In the early evening of the eighteenth Burton, several companions, and a dozen camels set out for Medina 130 miles away. Everyone was heavily armed. Omar Effendi, the twenty-eight-year-old Bedouin caravan leader, asked the boy Muhammad, "Where have you picked up that Hindi?"

Burton feigned indignation. "Are we, the Afghans, the Indian-slayers, become Indians?" he demanded of Effendi. "How would you, as an Arab, like to be called an Egyptian?"

There were rampant rumors that Bedouins were raiding pilgrim caravans almost every day. So it was with considerable relief that Burton's party joined a larger caravan of seven Turkish soldiers guarding 200 camels. Days were passed in small tents "in perspiration and semi-lethargy." At night the group traveled through a landscape "fantastic in its desolation—a mass of huge hills, barren plains, and desert vales . . . over broken ground, flanked by huge blocks and boulders piled up as if man's art had aided Nature to disfigure itself."

On July 22 at noon they were joined by a small caravan, bearing two corpses: a Turkish trooper killed in a Bedouin ambush and an Albanian pilgrim who had died from the heat. On the twenty-fourth they arrived in a gorge known as Shuab el Hajj, or Pilgrimage Pass, a fearsome place where Bedouin ambushes were a virtual certainty. No one spoke. As the caravan slowly made its way below the steep sides of the pass, thin blue curls of smoke appeared from the boulders above. Almost immediately the sharp crack of matchlocks echoed off the rocky walls. High above, Burton saw numerous Bedouins "swarming like hornets over the crests of the hill." The pilgrims had the sun in their eyes and could not effectively return the fire. Twelve of them died in the skirmish, and numerous camels were lost. But Burton dismissed the ambush as "a questionable affair" of limited importance.

Burton's success thus far had depended in large part upon his extraordinary ability to assume the identity of a Muslim. Many decades later his widow insisted that Burton did not simply put on a disguise. Rather, when he donned his Arab robes, he ceased to be Richard Burton the Englishman and became Richard Burton the Muslim, so complete was his identification with every aspect of Arab life and culture. He carefully cultivated all the gestures, body language, and customs that identified in a thousand and one little ways a true Arab.

He learned, for example, not to draw attention to himself by sneezing in public, for Arabs regard a sneeze as a bad omen. He also knew that everywhere in the Middle East the left hand was used to wipe clean one's anus. To offer the left hand was a major insult, and no man ever stroked his beard or ate from the communal food dishes using it. And Arabs never urinated standing because the spray made their robes ceremonially impure.

Burton almost lost his life on one occasion when he failed to observe the last custom. One night he left the caravan and went into the desert to urinate. For once he did not squat in the customary Arab position. Suddenly a young Arab happened upon him and immediately understood that Mirza Abdullah was an impostor. In a flash Burton had his knife out and fell upon the hapless youth. In later years, when a friend asked him about the incident, Burton justified himself, saying, "The desert has its own laws, and there— supremely of all the East—to kill is a small offense. In any case what could I do? It had to be his life or mine."

On July 25 the party gingerly made its way across a dark lava field. Suddenly below in the distance sprawled the holy city of Medina. Their journey from Yenbo had taken eight days. The pilgrims dismounted and made their prayers of thanksgiving. "O Allah! this is the Sanctuary of Thy Apostle; make it to us a Protection from Hell Fire, and a Refuge from Eternal Punishment!" they wailed. "O open the Gates of Thy Mercy, and let us pass through them to the Land of Joy!"

Burton was deeply moved and joined in the chorus. "It was impossible not to enter into the spirit of my companions," he wrote later. "And truly I believe that for some minutes my enthusiasm rose as high as theirs." Soon afterward the caravan passed through the gates of the holy city of Medina.

Muhammad first heard the call in A.D. 610 in the season of Ramadan during his fortieth year. He was on a solitary vigil on Mount Hira above Mecca and asleep in a cave when the archangel Gabriel suddenly appeared before him.

"Recite," the angel commanded.

"But what shall I recite?" Muhammad humbly protested.

Then the angel Gabriel told him:

"Recite in the name of thy Lord who created all things, who created man from clots of blood. Recite, for thy Lord is most generous, Who taught by the pen, Who taught man what he did not know."

Muhammad was fearful. "I will go to the top of the mountain and throw myself down that I may kill myself and gain rest," he told himself. As he hurriedly climbed Mount Hira, he heard the voice again, saying: "O Muhammad! Thou art the apostle of God and I am Gabriel." Muhammad looked into the sky and saw there the angel Gabriel in the form of a gigantic man, his legs bestriding the horizon.

The incident is told in the ninety-sixth chapter of the Koran, the holy book containing God's revelations to Muhammad. (*Koran* is an Arabic word meaning "recitation.")

Muhammad returned to Mecca and told his family about his revelations on Mount Hira. "Rejoice and be of good heart," his wife Khadija advised him. "I have hope that thou wilt be the prophet of this people." For a long time Muhammad's only disciples were his family and his closest friend. Three years later, the angel Gabriel appeared once again to Muhammad and commanded him to preach to all mankind.

The pre-Islamic faith of Arabia was a simple one of animism, nurtured by the vast expanses of desert. The Bedouins peopled the flat plains, rugged mountains, and boundless horizons of their world with a host of spirits, some good and some evil, who inhabited the wells, rocks, and trees. A shrine at Mecca held some of the most sacred stones. From the dawn of history it had been a place of pilgrimage. Muhammad eventually incorporated into his new religion the most important relic venerated by these early pagans—the Kaaba at Mecca, a large black meteorite. According to Muslim tradition the stone was originally white when Abraham received it from the angel Gabriel, but the sins of tens of thousands of pilgrims kissing the stone changed its color to a deep black.

Muhammad preached a new faith that was profoundly revolutionary. "In Islam there was to be neither church nor priest, neither orthodoxy nor hierarchy, neither kingship nor aristocracy," wrote historian Bernard Lewis in *Islam in History*. "There were to be no castes or estates to flaw the unity of the believers; no privileges, save the self-evident superiority of those who accept to those who willfully reject the true faith—and, of course, such obvious natural and social facts as the superiority of man to woman and of master to slave. Even these inferiorities were softened by the new dispensation. The slave was no longer a chattel but a human being, with recognized legal and moral rights. Women, though still subject to polygamy and concubinage, acquired property rights not equalled in the West until modern times. And even the non-Muslim enjoyed a tolerance and security in sharp contrast with the lot of non-Christians in medieval—and sometimes modern—Christendom."

Muhammad never claimed to be the founder of a new religion but rather the restorer of an old one, which he called the religion of Abraham—ancient Judaism. (Hence, Allah's affinity with the wrathful Jehovah of the Old Testament.) According to Islamic faith, God sent his prophets Abraham, Moses, and finally Jesus to call his people back to the true faith. Just as the Hebrews had corrupted the original faith of Abraham and Moses, so the Christians had distorted the word of Jesus. Now God called upon his prophet Muhammad to lead his people back to the truth they had deserted centuries before. Henceforth, Jews and Christians were to be regarded as heretics against the one true revealed faith.

Muhammad tried unsuccessfully to convert the Meccans. But they mocked him and persecuted his converts. Ten years after his original revelation, Muhammad's followers numbered fewer than one hundred families. His situation in Mecca had become tenuous. When he learned of plans to murder him and his followers, Muhammad fled across the desert to the town of Medina. There he and his band of true believers built the first mosque, and five times each day they prostrated themselves in prayer. In the next few years Muhammad developed the Islamic commands regarding the family, women, slavery, state, and law.

Those were years of bitter poverty for the small Muslim community. In 624 Muhammad led a ragged band of 314 soldiers on a raid against a caravan destined for Mecca. To their surprise, they encountered a large army of well-armed Meccans. Muhammad's motley band of Muslim believers fought fiercely, convinced that if they died in battle they would enter paradise. They carried the day, the first in a string of military victories that would soon give Muhammad control over much of central Arabia. In time he won the allegiance of the fierce Bedouin nomads.

Islam continued to gain converts. Local officials who opposed Muhammad's teachings were assassinated. In 628 Muhammad decided to return to his birthplace. He announced that he would make a pilgrimage to the Kaaba in the traditional holy month when the Meccan authorities would not dare to harm him. And this he did, accompanied by fifteen hundred followers. He returned again the following year in the company of two thousand believers. And finally, in 630, Muhammad marched once more on Mecca, this time with ten thousand followers. The Meccan authorities finally surrendered and accepted the new faith. Soon afterward most of the tribes in the Arabian peninsula acknowledged Muhammad as their spiritual leader.

It was an extraordinary achievement. In fewer than a dozen years after he had fled Mecca with a price on his head, Muhammad had made himself the undisputed ruler of the entire Arabian Peninsula. He had accomplished all his goals. "O Lord, I have delivered my message and fulfilled my mission," he exclaimed in 632 on his last pilgrimage to Mecca. Later that same year the prophet fell ill, probably from pneumonia, and died at the age of sixty-two.

Islam continued to flourish in the decades following Muhammad's death. Leaders such as Abu Bekr and Khalid Ibn el Walid forged the Muslim people into a nation state. Driven by a religious zeal of an intensity never seen before in the Middle East, an army of highly mobile desert warriors exploded out of the Arabian Peninsula, searching for new enemies to plunder of their riches and new converts for their religion. Heavily fortified city-states and great armies fell before their onslaught. The empires of Persia and Byzantium were overwhelmed. In less than a century after Muhammad's death the new Islamic empire reached across the Middle East and North Africa, from India in the East to the Iberian peninsula in the West. Arab armies even invaded southern Italy. The followers of Muhammad had won the greatest conquest in history.

In 718 Arab armies in Spain crossed the Pyrenees Mountains and began a campaign against the cities of southern France. Carcassone and Narbonne fell. Toulouse was besieged. Muslim cavalry raided throughout Burgundy. In 732 an Arab army laid siege to Bordeaux. In October of that same year the French general, Charles Martel, fought a battle against the Arab army near the city of Tours. The great Arab general Abdul Rahman was killed and his forces decisively defeated. The battle marked the northernmost expansion into Western Europe of the Arab Empire.

In the Arab chronicles of the period the Battle of Tours is remembered chiefly as a minor skirmish against a ragtag band of European barbarians, notable only for the death of Abdul Rahman. But for the West the Battle of Tours marked a turning point in the history of Europe. Had Charles Martel failed, Europe today might well be an integral part of the Muslim world. "The interpretation of the Koran would now be taught in the schools of Oxford, and her pulpits might demonstrate to a circumcised people the sanctity and truth of the Revelation of Mahomet," Edward Gibbon insisted in his *Decline and Fall of the Roman Empire*. "From such calamities was Christendom delivered by the genius and fortune of one man."

Burton spent a month in Medina at the home of Sheik Hamid el Samman, who had been his companion since Suez. He rested for several days, secretly bringing his notes up-to-date. Later Burton, still lame, made the rounds of the sights on a small donkey—"a wretched animal, raw-backed, lame of one leg, and wanting an ear."

Not many years before Burton's arrival Medina's ruler had been a Scotsman. In 1815 Thomas Keith, a private in the Seventy-second Highlanders, was taken prisoner at Rosetta in Egypt and forcibly converted to Islam. He became a Mameluke, rose to the rank of a Turkish general, and then was put in charge of Medina—perhaps the most unusual position ever held by a Scot. Keith administered the holy city for several years and died fighting against the Wahhabis.

The hajj to Mecca was obligatory upon every Muslim, but the visit to Medina was simply a meritorious action known as a visitation. Burton visited the Prophet's Mosque, which tradition insisted had been built over the spot where Muhammad's camel knelt on the Prophet's first arrival into Medina. It had been rebuilt five times, and the present structure dated from the fifteenth century. It became the model for the world of Islam, and all later mosques were constructed on the same pattern as the Prophet's Mosque. Burton thought it looked "mean and tawdry." Afterward he visited Muhammad's tomb, although he doubted that the Prophet's body was actually entombed there.

In his tour of the city Burton visited the slave market. He learned that young black girls regularly sold for £25. A eunuch fetched twice that. He also discovered that on the rare occasion when a white girl came up for sale, she would bring as much as £400, making her a luxury that only the wealthiest princes could afford.

For the trip to Mecca Burton joined the Damascus hajj, the greatest of them all, a river of humanity that stretched several miles across the desert. He was particularly excited to learn that it was to travel along a road where no European had ever gone. The group left Medina early on the morning of August 31, 1853. Burton estimated the number of pilgrims at more than 7,000 with 1,000 irregular Turkish cavalry—"each armed after his own fashion, exceedingly dirty, picturesque-looking, brave, and in such a country of no use whatsoever."

The hajj fascinated Burton. "There is a kind of discipline in these great caravans" he wrote later. "A gun sounds the order to strike the tents, and a second bids you move off with all speed. There are short halts, of half an hour each, at dawn, noon, the afternoon, and sunset, for devotional purposes."

Late in the afternoon on September 9 the hajj traveled along a dry riverbed between steep walls. Burton became aware of a deathly silence that had settled over the caravan. Every pilgrim realized that it was a perfect place for an ambush. Burton scanned the heights. Suddenly the ambush came. "A small curl of smoke, like a lady's ringlet, on the summit of the right-hand precipice, caught my eye," he wrote. "And simultaneous with the echoing crack of the matchlock, a high-trotting dromedary in front of me rolled over upon the sands. A bullet had split its heart, throwing the rider a goodly somersault of five or six yards." The bandits—Burton estimated their number at about 150—continued to pour their fire into the milling mass of humanity. Suddenly a group of Wahhabi Bedouins rode up and after an hour's fight routed the robbers.

Throughout his pilgrimage Burton's inquisitive mind sought information on all aspects of Arab culture. He asked hundreds of questions and poked his nose into all manner of fascinating crannies. Nothing escaped his notice.

On the facial veil worn by Muslim women: "The most coquettish article of woman's attire, it conceals coarse skins, fleshy noses, wide mouths, and vanishing chins, whilst it sets off to best advantage what in these lands is almost always lustrous and liquid—the eye."

On the Muslim custom of having several wives: "The husband must distribute his honours equally, and each wife has a right to her night unless she herself gives it up."

On the making of a eunuch: "A horsehair is tied around the neck of the scrotum and tightened by slow degrees till the circulation of the part stops and the bag drops off without pain."

On Arab superstitions: "The Arabs still retain our medieval superstitions concerning precious stones. The ruby appeases thirst, strengthens cardiac action, and averts plague and thunderbolts. The diamond heals diseases and [prevents] epilepsy and the possession by evil spirits. The emerald cures the stings of scorpions and the bites of venomous reptiles, blinding them if placed before their eyes. The turquoise increases the milk of nursing mothers: hence, the blue beads hung as necklaces on cattle."

On execution by impaling: "A barbarous punishment but highly effective. The stake, commonly called *khazuk,* is a stout pole pointed at one end, and the criminal being thrown upon his belly is held firm whilst the end is passed up his fundament. His legs and body are then lashed to it and it is raised by degrees and planted in a hole already dug, an agonising part of the process. If the operation be performed by an expert who avoids injuring any mortal part, the wretch may live for three days suffering the pangs of thirst."

In the course of several visits to the Middle East Burton developed a strong affection for the desert Arabs, those "knights-errants [who still practice] the wildest form of chivalry." He found the Bedouin "a gentleman in his native wilds. Easy and quiet, courteous and mild-mannered, he expects you to respect him, and upon that condition he respects you—still without a shade of obsequiousness or servility." The object of Bedouin life, Burton insisted, was "to be—to be free, to be brave, to be wise; while the endeavours of other peoples was and is to have—to have wealth, to have knowledge, to have a name."

As a man for whom exploration was a kind of intermittent flirtation with death, Burton was the first European traveler to admire the Bedouins for their predatory character, lauding them for their courage and manliness: "The habit of danger in raids and blood-feuds, the continual uncertainity of existence, the desert, the chase, the hard life . . . habituated them to look death in the face like men." He saw Bedouin society in Darwinian terms, as a life in which only the strongest survived and flourished. The severity of desert existence virtually eliminated physical deformities among the people. The weakly infant almost always died. And the Spartan life kept Bedouins lean. "I never saw a fat man in the desert," he observed.

Burton, who later traveled extensively through the American West, found in the desert Bedouins a kindred people to the North American Indians. "Both have the same wild chivalry, the same fiery sense of honour, and the same boundless hospitality," he noted with approval. "Elopements from tribe to tribe, the blood feud, and the vendetta are common to the two. Both are grave and cautious in demeanour, and formal in manner—princes in rags or paint. The Arabs plunder pilgrims; the Indians, bands of trappers. Both glory in forays, raids, and cattle-lifting; and both rob according to certain rules." But of these "two noble races," he preferred the Bedouin because of "his treatment of women, his superior development of intellect, and the glorious page of history which he has filled."

While Burton the romantic wrote eloquently of the "wild sons of freedom," Burton the imperialist advised the British Foreign Office exactly what repressive measures would most effectively subdue the unruly Bedouins should England annex the Arabian Peninsula into the empire: "By a proper use of the blood feud; by vigorously supporting the weaker against the stronger [tribes]; by regularly defeating every Badawi [Bedouin] who earns a name for himself; and, above all, by the exercise of unsparing, unflinching justice, the few thousands of half-naked bandits, who now make the land a fighting field, would soon sink into utter insignificance."

The exaltation of force was a major theme in Burton's writings. For him the Middle East represented a society in which the strong ruled by strength alone, according to a set of traditional laws. What he admired was what the region offered—a place where anyone tough enough could carve out a kingdom commensurate with his talents without too much worry about compassion and other restraints. He would have understood and approved the needs that drove Lady Hester Stanhope to Djoun. And had he read *The Man Who Would Be King* before his death, he would probably have taken considerable pleasure in Rudyard Kipling's classic novelette.

Dressed in his white pilgrim robes, Burton arrived in Mecca on September 11 shortly after midnight. "Mecca! Mecca!" cried the pilgrims. "The Sanctuary! The Sanctuary!" Burton leaned out from his litter and saw in the dim starlight the outlines of a large city. An hour later he arrived at the house of his boy Muhammad.

Early the next morning an excited Burton visited what only a handful of Europeans in history had ever seen: the sacred Kaaba, what the Muslims called the "navel of the world." Set in the center of a large courtyard inside the Great Mosque, the Kaaba proved to be a square, windowless building covered with black drapery embroidered in gold with inscriptions from the Koran. Set in its southeastern corner was the famous Black Stone, which Islamic tradition insisted had been a gift to Abraham from the angel Gabriel. In the courtyard hundreds of worshipers chanted, "There is no God but Allah alone, Whose Covenant is Truth, and Whose Servant is Victorious."

Burton pushed his way through the sobbing crowd of enthusiasts to the stone. For a full ten minutes he kissed and rubbed the relic. He studied the stone closely and decided it was, in fact, a meteorite. "There at last it lay, the bourn of my long and weary Pilgrimage, realising the plans and hopes of many and many a year," he wrote later. "I may truly say that of all the worshippers who clung weeping to the curtain, or who pressed their beating hearts to the stone, none felt for the moment a deeper emotion than did the Haji from the far north. . . . But, to confess humbling truth, theirs was the high feeling of religious enthusiasm. Mine was the ecstasy of gratified pride."

Burton was determined to visit the inside of the Kaaba and ordered his boy to alert him when the courtyard of the Grand Mosque was empty. Several days later the youth burst in upon him with the news that only a few pilgrims were at the Kaaba. The two hurried there. The entrance was a single door seven feet above the ground. Two stout Meccans raised Burton up while a third helped him inside. In the dim light inside he observed that the floor and walls were made of irregular marble slabs of various colors, many carrying inscriptions from the Koran. A red damask cloth embroidered with gold covered the upper portions of the walls. The heat in the windowless room was intense, and the air foul. Perspiration poured from him. "I thought with horror what it must be like when filled with a mass of furiously jostling and crushing fanatics," Burton noted. Under the very noses of suspicious attendants, he paced off the dimensions of the room and took quick notes on its details. It was the most dangerous moment of his entire pilgrimage. Discovery would have meant instant death at the hands of enraged believers.

Burton also visited Mount Arafat, the Mount of Mercy, where the angel Gabriel was thought to have instructed Adam. The bald 200-foot-high hill was a six-hour camel ride east of Mecca. Burton fought his way along the highway packed with people. He saw five pilgrims die of the heat and wrote: "Each man suddenly staggered, fell as if shot, and after a brief convulsion lay still as marble." He estimated the crowd on the slopes of Mount Arafat at more than 50,000, most encamped in a sprawling tent city. "The main street of tents and booths, huts and shops, was bright with lanterns, and the bazaars were crowded with people and stocked with all manner of Eastern delicacies," he noted. "In one place a half-drunken [Albanian] stalked down the road, elbowing peaceful passengers and frowning fiercely in hopes of a quarrel. In another part, a huge dimly lit tent, reeking hot and garnished with cane seats, contained knots of Egyptians . . . noisily intoxicating themselves with forbidden hemp. There were frequent brawls and great confusion."

The next day Burton attended a sermon on Mount Arafat with several thousand other pilgrims. But his thoughts were on other things than the words of the Prophet of Islam. Nearby sat a lovely eighteen-year-old Meccan girl with pale yellow skin, a graceful figure, and beautiful eyes. A muslin veil covered the rest of her face. Burton flirted cautiously with her. He stared at her until he caught her eye. She replied by slowly drawing back her veil two inches, revealing "a dimpled mouth and rounded chin." And then, almost imperceptibly, she smiled at him. "This pilgrim was in ecstasy," Burton confessed. The sermon ended, and Burton hurried after the girl, only to lose her in the crowd.

His funds almost exhausted, he hired two camels and with Muhammad started for Jiddah on the coast. He welcomed the desert after the crowds and stench of Mecca. "Issuing into the open plain, I felt a thrill of pleasure—such joy as only the captive delivered from his dungeon can experience," he wrote later. "The sunbeams warmed me into renewed life and vigour, the air of the Desert was a perfume, and the homely face of Nature was as the smile of a dear old friend."

After seventeen hours of hard riding, Burton arrived in Jiddah and went straight to the British Vice-consulate. It was still too dangerous to reveal his true identity. "I was left kicking my heels at the Great Man's Gate for a long time, and heard somebody say, 'Let the dirty nigger wait,' " Burton recalled later. "Long inured to patience, however, I did wait, and when the Consul consented to see me I presented him with a bit of paper, as if it were a money order. On it was written, 'Don't recognize me; I am Dick Burton, but I am not safe yet. Give me some money, which will be returned from London, and don't take any notice of me.' "

Burton had a ten-day wait in Jiddah for the British ship *Dwarka*. During that time he relaxed his guard and in some unknown way confirmed his boy's original suspicions. Muhammad suddenly disappeared, telling Burton's other servant, "Now I understand—our master is a Sahib from India; he hath laughed in our beards."

When the *Dwarka* sailed from Jiddah for Suez on September 26, Burton was dressed as an Englishman. Back in Cairo as a joke he donned his Arab robes once more and walked into Shepeard's Hotel, a favorite with British officers. He brushed clumsily past one of them.

"Damn that nigger's impudence!" the officer snapped angrily. "If he does that again, I'll kick him."

Burton suddenly wheeled around. "Well, damn it, Hawkins, that's a nice way to welcome a fellow after a two years' absence."

"By God, it's Ruffian Dick!" a dumbfounded Hawkins blurted out. And the officers, laughing, crowded excitedly around Burton.

In 1865 London booksellers began displaying a two-volume work, its covers embellished in gilt with the design of an Arab and his camel. Entitled *Narrative of a Year's Journey Through Central and Eastern Arabia*, the book recounted an extraordinary crossing of the Arabian Peninsula by William Gifford Palgrave, a somewhat mysterious British adventurer who traveled both as a spy for the emperor Napoleon III and as a Jesuit missionary. He was only the third European to penetrate the interior of Arabia. The most sensational book on Arabia before T. E. Lawrence's *Seven Pillars of Wisdom*, Palgrave's *Narrative* quickly became a best-seller and went through seven editions before 1873. A reviewer for the *Pall Mall Gazette* said of it: "Considering the extent of our previous ignorance, the amount of his achievements, and the importance of his contributions to our knowledge, we cannot say less of him than was said once of a far greater discoverer—Mr. Palgrave has indeed given a new world to Europe." And later travelers such as Sir Wilfrid Blunt, Charles Doughty, and Lawrence himself all paid homage to Palgrave's book as one of the monuments of Arabian travel narratives.

Palgrave's adult life falls roughly into two major stages: from 1848 to 1864, when he converted to Roman Catholicism and became a Jesuit missionary, and from 1865 to 1888, when he worked as a diplomat for the British Foreign Office, serving in a series of remote and unimportant consular posts. He died on September 30, 1888, in Montevideo, Uruguay, where for four years he had been the British minister.

Palgrave's youth was largely uneventful. He was born in London on January 24, 1826. His father was Sir Francis Palgrave, a historian who founded the Public Record Office and served as its keeper of the records. His mother, Elizabeth, was a fellow antiquarian. The young Palgrave enrolled at Trinity College, Oxford, in 1844. But after achieving a distinguished academic record, he stunned his family and friends by suddenly resigning from the university and enlisting in the Bombay Infantry of the East India Company.

On March 2, 1847, Palgrave arrived in Bombay and took up his duties with the Eighth Native Infantry. His career overlapped with Burton's in India. But the responses of the two men to the experiences of the vast subcontinent could not have been more different. The exoticism and paganism of India overwhelmed, appalled, and perplexed Palgrave, who never learned the language or customs of its people. "This is indeed a strange country," he wrote his family. "The very grass and weeds, even the sparrows, are of a different sort from those at home. And the people are indeed a different race. To me, it is a mere riddle; I cannot make anything of it."

Palgrave lasted fewer than the eighteen months. In March 1849 he shocked his family a second time by abruptly resigning his commission, converting to Roman Catholicism, and joining the Society of Jesus to become "a soldier for Christ." His family was at a loss to understand their son's new direction. But Mea Allan, his biographer, has suggested that an early passion for missionary work among the Arabs, aroused by his reading English translations of an old Arabian romance, *Antar,* and the *Arabian Nights,* suddenly returned in force while Palgrave was in India. "As to mission work, the Jesuits were of all the orders the great pioneers," Allan observes. "As yet they had not penetrated Arabia. Here, then, was his work!"

In the spring of 1848 Palgrave enrolled in the Jesuit College in Madras, India, where he spent his next four years. In 1853 he traveled to Rome to complete his theological studies. He eagerly learned Arabic in anticipation of an assignment to a Jesuit mission in Syria. In

September 1855 he was posted to a Jesuit mission at Bikfaya outside Beirut. For the first time in his adult life he was supremely happy. "Imagine my joy," he wrote home, "at finding myself here at last, treading the very Mission ground of Jesus Christ Himself." Palgrave was totally captivated by the Middle East. He mingled with the local Arabs, learned their customs and manners, dressed in their robes, read the masterpieces of Arab poetry, and studied the Koran. He called the Arabs the "Englishmen of the Middle East" and praised them for their "strong love of personal liberty, hatred of minute interference and special regulations, and great respect for authority so long as it is decently exercised." On March 29, 1857, Palgrave was ordained a priest in Beirut, and he celebrated his first mass the next day.

Palgrave's years at the Jesuit missions in Lebanon coincided with the period of rising tensions between Druze and Christian elements. He spent several weeks living in a Druze community in the mountains east of Beirut. "They are the Atheists of the East," he reported back to his superiors. "They give their curse equally to the religion of Moses and the religion of Mahomed, and hold that the happiness of man is in being free from all law and religion. It is [abominable] that such monsters can exist." The tensions finally exploded in the dreadful massacres of entire Christian populations in 1859 and 1860. In Zahlah Druze militiamen murdered four Jesuit priests. Palgrave was in Sidon and barely escaped with his life as angry Druze mobs rampaged through that city, killing scores of Christians. He fled to Europe.

After several months Palgrave proposed to his superiors at the Society of Jesus in Rome that he be allowed to return to the Middle East to mount a major expedition into the heart of the Arabian Peninsula. His professed reason was his desire to enter Arabia in search of converts, "new hearts as yet ignorant of God's mercies which would otherwise be lost." But Palgrave obviously knew from his years in Lebanon that much of Arabia was in the throes of Wahhabism, an extreme fundamentalist Islamic sect, and that opportunities for missionary work would be few and fraught with danger. "The Wahhabee country is to the rest of Arabia as a lion's den, into which few venture and yet fewer return," he wrote later.

A more likely motive was simply that the Middle East had worked its magic on him. His mastery of the Arab language and culture was so complete that he could travel throughout the towns and deserts of Syria as an Arab and not fear detection. Each year he saw the great hajj caravans departing Damascus for Mecca many hundreds of miles to the south. Palgrave knew there were vast expanses of central Arabia where no European had ever penetrated. The temptation to be the first was irresistible. "It was time to fill in the blank in the map of Asia," he admitted later.

His Jesuit superiors quickly approved the expedition and notified the French government, the cooperation of which was regarded as indispensable to the success of the enterprise. Soon Palgrave found himself in a conference with Emperor Napoleon III at the Tuileries palace. The Jesuit's enthusiasm and his knowledge of Arab history and culture impressed the French ruler. Palgrave's scheme for an exploratory expedition into Arabia fitted perfectly into Napolen's own grandiose ambitions for extending French influence throughout the Middle East. A Frenchman, Ferdinand de Lesseps, was even then well along in the construction of the Suez Canal, linking the Mediterranean and Red seas, upon the completion of which, Napoleon hoped, France would rival Britain in the Persian Gulf and the Indian Ocean. In that context, the French emperor reasoned, might not the enormous Arabian Peninsula become an important new market for French goods? An excited Napoleon quickly agreed to advance Palgrave 10,000 francs for his expenses in return for a full intelligence report at the end of his travels.

In the late spring of 1862 Palgrave was back in Lebanon, making his final preparations. His superiors insisted he travel with another priest and assigned him a young Greek seminarian by the name of Geraigeri, who had worked for several years at the mission in Zahlah. The two men carefully assembled disguises. Palgrave decided to travel as an itinerant physician ("a quack, if you will") under the name of Seleem Abou Mahmood-el-'Eys, the "quiet one." Geraigeri was to act as his medical assistant, known as Barakat-esh-Shamee. Like Burton, Palgrave chose the disguise of a doctor for the freedom it would allow him to meet people of all classes. They did not pretend to be Muslims but traveled rather as Syrian Christians. "A Christian and an Englishman may well traverse Arabia . . . without being ever obliged to compromise either his religion or his honour," Palgrave wrote later. "But for this, perfect acquaintance with Eastern customs and with at least one Eastern language, together with much circumspection and guardedness in word and deed, are undeniably required."

On the evening of June 16, 1862, Palgrave, his assistant, Geraigeri, and three Bedouins departed from Ma'an, south of Petra, on their great adventure. Later, at the beginning of his *Narrative,* he wrote:

> The largest stars were already visible in the deep blue depths of a cloudless sky, while the crescent moon, high in the west, promised us assistance for some hours of our night's march. We were soon mounted on our meager long-necked beasts. . . . Behind us lay, in a mass of dark outline, the walls and castle of Ma'an, its houses and gardens. . . . Before and around us extended a wide and level plain, blackened over with countless pebbles of basalt and flint, except where the moonbeams gleamed white on little intervening patches of clear sand, or on yellowish streaks of withered grass, the scanty product of the winter rains and now dried into hay. Over all [hung] a deep silence, which even our Arab companions seemed fearful of breaking. When they spoke, it was in a half whisper and in few words, while the noiseless tread of our camels sped [us] stealthily but rapidly through the gloom without disturbing its stillness.

Palgrave's Bedouin companions were a thoroughly disreputable lot. Their leader, Salim el Atneh, was a close relative to the chiefs of the Howeitat Bedouins from the Dead Sea region. Repeated acts of robbery and pillage plus an occasional murder had led to his expulsion from his tribe and a new life as a desert outlaw. However, Palgrave's previous experience had taught him that "a brave and foresighted man, however unprincipled, may always be trusted to a certain extent." Not as much could be said for the other two Bedouins, members of the Sherarat tribe, "utter barbarians in appearance no less than in character, wild, fickle, reckless." All three wore long, dirty shirts that reached to their ankles, tattered cloaks of striped white and brown cloth, and wide leather belts from which dangled rusty knives. Each Bedouin carried a long-barreled matchlock and a needle-pointed spear.

Palgrave's small party headed west toward the road from Damascus and then turned south toward Al Jawf. It was midsummer, when extreme temperatures kept most travelers out of the bleak desert areas. One morning a strong wind suddenly began blowing, and dark clouds quickly enveloped the clear skies. To their horror the five men found themselves engulfed in a dreaded *simoom*. Only luck saved their lives. They spotted a Bedouin tent in the near distance and arrived there just as the fierce windstorm overtook them. "So dark was the atmosphere and so burning the heat that it seemed hell had risen from the earth," Palgrave wrote later. "At the moment when the worst of the concentrated poison-blast was coming around, we were already prostrate one and all within the tent, with our heads well wrapped up, almost suffocated indeed, but safe while our camels lay without like dead, their long necks stretched out on the sand awaiting the passage of the gale."

The days seemed to stretch out eternally, as the party slowly made its way south toward Arabia. The worst ordeal was the terrible Nafud Desert, a great sand barrier isolating the Arabian Peninsula from the Syrian deserts to the north. "We were now traversing an immense ocean of loose reddish sand, unlimited to the eye, and heaped up in enormous ridges running parallel to each other from north to south, undulation after undulation, each swell two or three hundred feet in average height," Palgrave remembered later with a kind of terror. "In the depths between, the traveller finds himself imprisoned in a suffocating sand-pit, hemmed in by burning walls on every side. At other times while labouring up the slope, he overlooks what seems like a vast sea of fire, swelling under a heavy monsoon wind, and ruffled by a cross-blast into little red-hot waves." So desperate was their situation that in one twenty-four-hour period they took only one hour of rest, driven by the knowledge that certain death from dehydration waited them within a few hours if their meager water supply gave out.

Beyond Nafud lay Hail, a city of some 4,000 inhabitants surrounded by twenty-foot-high mud walls set at regular intervals with square towers and large folding gates. The lofty tower of Emir Tallal ibn Rashid's palace dominated the skyline. Palgrave's party rode into the city and dismounted near the palace. Seyf, the court chamberlain, met them.

"Peace be with you, brothers." He greeted them warmly. "Whence have you come?"

"I am a doctor from Syria," Palgrave answered.

"What do you desire in our town?" Seyf inquired.

"We desire the favour of God most high, and, secondly, that of Tallal."

As the welcoming ceremony continued, Palgrave to his horror suddenly saw approaching a merchant-trader who had known him in Damascus in his capacity as a European priest. The man greeted him and asked what he meant to do in Hail. Palgrave fixed him with "a vacant stare" and said nothing. An exposure now as a European would be a disaster for his travel plans. Another man approached; this sinister-looking Kasim Arab also insisted that he had known Palgrave in Damascus and detailed the exact circumstances of their meeting. Then a third man who came up stated that he, too, knew Palgrave, but in Cairo, "where he lives in a large house . . . and has a very beautiful daughter, who rides an expensive horse." Palgrave easily refuted the third man and made the most of it. He then turned to the other two men. "I do not remember having ever seen you," he told them indignantly. "Many a man besides myself has a reddish beard and straw-coloured mustachios."

Seyf came to Palgrave's rescue and invited his party into the palace to rest. Palgrave and Geraigeri were graciously shown into a reception hall eighty feet long with a great roof supported on six large columns. A black slave served them coffee. The next day they had an audience with Tallal ibn Rashid, the emir of Hail. Palgrave found the emir "short of stature, broad-shouldered, and strongly built, of a very dusky complexion with long black hair, dark and piercing eyes. . . . His step was measured, his demeanour grave and somewhat haughty." Ibn Rashid wore a long cloak of delicately worked camel hair over a white shirt. A large sword, richly inlaid with gold, hung from his side. He was heavily perfumed with musk.

Palgrave remained for several weeks in Hail and in that time became friendly with Ibn Rashid. The emir accepted him as a Syrian doctor but suspected he had another motive for coming to Hail: to buy the celebrated Arabian horses. Word that a Syrian doctor, highly regarded by the emir, was now in Hail quickly spread through the town. Palgrave found himself besieged by people with all varieties of illnesses. He heard their complaints, prescribed bread pills and cinnamon water, and enjoyed several successes with minor disorders.

Many mornings Palgrave and Geraigeri rose from their sleeping carpets and went forth into Hail to watch the town come alive in the early dawn hours. "[Soon all is] life and movement," Palgrave wrote later. "Camels are unloading in the streets, and Bedouins standing by, looking anything but at home in the town. The shoemaker and the blacksmith, those two main props of Arab handicraft, are already at their work, and some gossiping bystanders are gathered around them. At the corner where our cross-street falls into the marketplace, three or four country women are seated, with piles of melons, gourds, egg-plant fruits, and other garden produce before them for sale. My companion falls to haggling with one of these village nymphs."

Palgrave and Geraigeri left Hail on September 8, bearing a passport from Emir ibn Rashid granting them safe passage through his lands. They traveled with a caravan toward Buraydah. Six days later they passed out of Ibn Rashid's territory and descended toward the oasis of El Uyun through a landscape never before seen by any European. Suddenly up ahead loomed a remarkable sight—a desert Stonehenge of enormous uplifted monoliths, a relic from an ancient and pagan era. Great blocks of roughly hewn stones had been tilted on their ends, and other large stones laid across on top and set in an enormous circle. Palgrave rode his camel under one lintel and estimated its height at fifteen feet. His companions advised him that two other such circles existed nearby. "That the object of these strange constructions was in some measure religious seems to me hardly doubtful," an intrigued Palgrave wrote later, speculating they might have served as primitive astronomical platforms similar to his own England's Stonehenge. (The later British explorer Harry Philby vehemently denied the existence of these stone circles, but more recently archaeologists from the University of Riyadh have confirmed the accuracy of Palgrave's account and estimated the age of the monuments at more than 1,500 years.)

From Buraydah Palgrave and Geraigeri started toward Riyadh, the secret city of the fanatical Wahhabis, "who consider everyone save themselves an infidel or a heretic and regard the slaughter of an infidel or a heretic as a duty." Ten days later they approached the gates of Riyadh, "the capital of Nadj and half Arabia, its very heart of hearts." They were the first Europeans ever to penetrate this far into the Arabian Peninsula, "a land infamous as the very mouse-trap of Arabia." Looming above them was Riyadh, "large and square, crowned by high towers and strong walls of defence, a mass of roofs and terraces, where overtopping all frowned the huge but irregular pile of Faisal's royal castle. All around for a full three miles over the surrounding plain waved a sea of palm trees above green fields and well watered gardens; while the singing, droning sound of the water wheels reaches us even where we had halted, at a quarter of a mile or more from the nearest town walls."

Emir Faisal—"old and blind, superstitious and timid, bigoted and tyrannical"—at first refused to permit the Syrian doctor and his entourage entry into Riyadh, offering bribes of money, clothes, and camels to persuade them to continue their journey. Faisal knew that his eldest son, Abdullah, plotted against him and was suspicious of all strangers to his city. But a major goal of Palgrave's expedition had always been the study of Wahhabism, and he was determined to enter Riyadh. His persistence was rewarded. Not only did Faisal relent, but Palgrave spent fifty days in the city.

He devoted much of that time to a thorough gathering of intelligence for the French king on all aspects of Faisal's government. He scouted out the strength of the Wahhabi military forces, investigated the tax system, and culled the census figures.

Nothing about Riyadh suggested the picturesque scenes of the *Arabian Nights* or the Old Testament. Rather, to Palgrave it was as if he had crossed into some mythical kingdom of evil ruled over by a prince of darkness. Even the solitary front gate to Faisal's palace gave off a sinister air. "Deep sunk between the bastions with massive folding doors iron-bound, though thrown open at this hour of the day and giving entrance into a dark passage, one might easily have taken it for the vestibule of a prison," he wrote later. "And the number of guards, some black, some white, but all sword-girt, who almost choked the way, did not seem very inviting to those without, especially to foreigners."

Palgrave was soon permitted to set up practice in Riyadh. He quickly became aware of the Meddeyyi, a religious police that worked to purge the people of all activities thought to be antireligious. These included the playing of musical instruments, singing, children's street games, smoking tobacco, and wearing fine clothes. Armed with long wooden staffs and Korans, the elders of the Meddeyyi had absolute authority to enter houses at whim and inflict summary whippings on all persons they found lacking in religious seriousness.

As the weeks passed, Palgrave's medical practice prospered and proved an invaluable front for gathering additional information on all aspects of Faisal's kingdom. Sitting on a stuffed cushion before a pile of coffeepots ("two for us and ten for show"), Palgrave received everyone from high-ranking court officials to lowly tradesmen. He was surprised to discover that the people on the whole suffered from few serious complaints, a fact he attributed to the region's clean air, dry climate, and moderate temperatures. But he was shocked at the provincialism of the city's inhabitants, who were utterly ignorant of the world beyond. They assumed that the Muslim religion was virtually universal, often asking Palgrave, "Do any Christians or other Infidels still exist in the world?" And most supposed Europe to be merely a town under the rule of the sultan of Constantinople.

Palgrave finally met Faisal himself—"blind, corpulent, decrepit yet imposing with his broad forehead, white beard, and thoughtful air, clad in all the simplicity of a Wahhabi, the gold-hafted sword at his side his only ornament of distinction." But the real power behind the throne was his eldest son, Abdullah, who summoned Palgrave to the palace almost daily. The Englishmen quickly saw the young prince for what he was: a ruthless, dangerous opportunist, who harbored a profound suspicion of all foreigners. By degrees Abdullah tried to draw Palgrave into his court conspiracies. He resisted. And suddenly he found his life threatened by an explosion of royal bad temper.

The crisis erupted soon after Palgrave had treated an ill high-ranking court official with a judicious application of strychnine. He affected a prompt cure and created a sensation in Riyadh. Abdullah invited Palgrave to the palace and, fully understanding its deadly effects when used in larger doses, demanded some of the strychnine. The Englishman immediately realized that Abdullah planned to use the poison against his younger brother, Saud. "Intrigues, treasons, violence itself were hatching beneath the palace walls, and assassination, whether by the dagger or . . . the coffee cup, would have been quite in keeping nor likely to cause the smallest surprise to anyone," Palgrave stated later. He refused the request.

There were other meetings. Each time Abdullah insisted on the strychnine. Then one day, while the two conferred in low tones away from the rest of the court, the prince again demanded the poison. Palgrave leaned over, lifted up the edge of Abdullah's headdress, and whispered in his ear: "Abdullah, I know well what you want the poison for, and I have no mind to be an accomplice to your crimes, nor to answer before God's judgement seat for what you will have to answer for. You shall *never* have it."

Abdullah's face went rigid with rage. He sat there for several minutes in utter silence and then abruptly left the room. The next day the two met again. Abdullah took Palgrave to one side. In a low voice, so that none of the others could hear, he told him: "I know perfectly well what you are. You are no doctors. You are Christians, spies, and revolutionists come hither to ruin our religion and state on behalf of those who sent you. The penalty for such as you is death, that you know, and I am determined to inflict it without delay."

Palgrave remained calm. "Ask pardon of God," he said quickly.

Abdullah was completely taken aback.

"Why so?" he demanded.

"Because you have just uttered a sheer absurdity," Palgrave responded. " 'Christians,' be it so. But 'spies,' 'revolutionists,'—as if we were not known by everybody in your town for quiet doctors, neither more nor less! And then to talk about putting me to death! You cannot, and you dare not."

"But I can and dare," Abdullah replied. "Who shall prevent me? You shall learn that to your cost."

"Neither can nor dare," Palgrave insisted. "We are here as your father's guests and yours for a month and more, known as such, received as such. What have we done to justify a breach of the laws of hospitality in Najd?"

Abdullah in a harsh whisper threatened secret assassins.

Palgrave suddenly stood up and moved away from the prince. In a loud voice that boomed across the royal chambers, he said to the gathered crowd of court officials: "Bear witness, all here present. If any mishap befalls my companions or myself from Riyadh to the shores of the Persian Gulf, it is all Abdullah's doing. And the consequences shall be on his head, worse consequences than he expects or dreams."

A stunned silence settled over the room. Suddenly the prince clapped his hands and ordered coffee. A black slave appeared with a single cup of coffee and presented it to Palgrave. "Is it poisoned?" he asked himself. The Englishman quickly assessed his chances, decided that it was a bluff, and downed the coffee in one swallow.

Palgrave turned quickly back to the slave.

"Pour me out a second," he demanded in a firm voice.

Abdullah slumped in his chair. Palgrave knew he had won.

Late on the evening of November 24 Palgrave and Geraigeri loaded their three camels and slipped out of Riyadh. Within the hour they were back in the desert. "We drew a long breath like men just let out of a dungeon," Palgrave admitted later. They made their way through the desert to Al Qatif, having crossed the entire Arabian Peninsula from the Mediterranean Sea to the Persian Gulf, a truly remarkable journey. The pair sailed for Bahrain, where they parted company, Palgrave for Muscat and Geraigeri (with all the expedition's notes) for Bushire in Persia.

Pelgrave slowly made his way along the Persian Gulf, hopping from ship to ship, each more dilapidated than the one before. Finally he reached the port of Suhar on the Gulf of Oman a mere two days' sail from Muscat. On March 7 Palgrave boarded a large two-masted dhow, roomy and comfortable in contrast with the other ships he had sailed on. It carried a crew of nine and thirteen passengers, including several pilgrims on their way to Mecca. "We hoped for a pleasant and an expeditious voyage," Palgrave recalled later. The ship made its way along the rocky coast under a clear sky. The sails snapped in the wind. In the late afternoon the breeze stiffened, became a gale, and within minutes developed into a major storm. By nightfall the ship was wallowing heavily in the raging seas, its sails in shreds. Two hours later it sprang a leak and settled lower in the water. The captain ordered everyone to abandon ship.

When Palgrave saw the ship was sinking, he climbed the railing and dived into the boiling sea. He turned back and saw in the lightning flashes of the storm the ship disappear below the waves, its mizzenmast making a kind of crazy spiral motion as it sank. "Six men—five passengers and one sailor—had gone down with the vessel," Palgrave wrote later. "A minute later, and boards, mats, and spars were floating here and there amid the breakers, while the heads of the surviving swimmers now showed themselves, now disappeared, in the moongleam and shadow."

He grabbed hold of a piece of timber. Suddenly he spotted in the distance the ship's boat, "dancing like an empty nutshell on the ocean." It was his only hope. He swam to the boat and climbed in. Quickly the others followed. Soon the tiny boat was crowded with seven crew members and five passengers. Three more passengers clung to the sides. The crew urged that all passengers be thrown overboard to lighten the boat. The captain hesitated. At that point Palgrave took command. He lectured the men and set them to work bailing and rowing. He scanned the sky, spotted several clusters of stars, and pointed them south toward the nearest land.

The situation was desperate, and there appeared little chance that any of them would survive the ordeal. "We were in an open, overloaded boat . . . far out at sea, with a howling wind, every moment on the increase, and tearing waves like huge monsters coming on as

though with purpose to swallow us up," Palgrave wrote. "What reasonable chance had we of ever reaching land?"

Palgrave kept them afloat throughout the night. When dawn broke
the next day, they found themselves off the Oman coast, black stone
cliffs rising overhead. He steered them toward a distant beach through
a sea that was "running mountains." At last they arrived opposite the
beach. But between them and safety lay a line of horrendous breakers—"a white yeast of raging waters, evidently ten or twelve feet
deep, through which, weary as we all were, . . . I felt it to be very
doubtful whether we should have strength to struggle." But they had
no choice. Palgrave pointed the tiny boat toward the beach and
steered it into the plunging surf. Within seconds the waves had
engulfed them, and the boat overturned. Palgrave mustered his final
reserves of strength and swam toward the shore. His feet touched
bottom. Finally he dragged himself up onto the sandy beach. He was
soon followed by the others, some stripped naked by the waves.
Miraculously, no one had drowned.

Two days later a feverish Palgrave finally walked into Muscat and
the safety of the British consul's residence. His fever quickly developed into typhoid. But he survived that as well and eventually made
his way back to Rome. He never returned to Arabia.

Years later Palgrave, no longer a Jesuit, wrote a novel, *Hermann
Agha: An Eastern Narrative,* an account of a Saxon boy sold into
slavery in the Middle East. Into that historical romance he poured
his love for all things Arabian. In words that echoed Palgrave's
sentiments, the novel's chief character states: "While I was among
[Europeans], I loved them dearly, but here in the East I have known
truer love, freer breath, a manlier creed, and a wider scope; nor have
I the heart to squeeze myself painfully again into the more regular
and better polished but narrower grooves of European life and
thought."

The Suez Canal: The Highway of Empire

A century ago, as today, the Gordian knot of international diplomacy, that unsolvable puzzle which continued to confound statesmen, diplomats, and military strategists, was centered in the Middle East. For the better part of the nineteenth century the attention of the British Foreign Office was focused on two interlocking problems. At Whitehall they were known simply as the Eastern Question (how to handle Turkey and the increasingly fragile Ottoman Empire) and the Great Game in Asia (how best to secure Britain's interest in India). The two concerns were rarely treated separately, and, indeed, a consideration of one led inevitably to the other. The chief goal of much of the British foreign policy in that period was how best to defend British economic and political interests in India from Russian expansionism. The Foreign Office generally regarded the French threat in the Middle East and Asia as temporary, unlike that posed by Russia, which had become, after the Napoleonic Wars, more powerful and more threatening to Britain than France. From the British perspective the most effective way to limit Russian expansion into the Middle East and Asia was to maintain Turkey and Persia as buffer zones.

Nor was the British concern with India in any way misplaced or exaggerated. With its 75 million people and 1.5 million square miles, British India was the richest prize ever added to any empire. The importance of the trade with India had increased so much in the eighteenth and early nineteenth centuries that to the popular mind in Europe this source of wealth had acquired an almost fabulous character.

The opening of the Suez Canal in 1869 increased Britain's anxiety about the Middle East, dramatically raised the stakes in the Great Game, and enormously complicated the Eastern Question. Probably no other construction project in history has had such widespread repercussions or developed such strategic importance to more major powers than did Ferdinand de Lesseps's "big ditch." The Suez Canal reduced by more than 4,000 miles and two months most voyages between Europe and Asia, while accelerating the geopolitical transformation of the Mediterranean that had begun with the steamship. It changed that body of water from an inland sea to an international highway of commerce in an era of expanding trade and intensive economic and political rivalry. No country benefited more than Britain from the canal's construction. British commerce accounted for two-thirds of its traffic. The Suez Canal soon became, in Otto von Bismarck's words, the "spinal column of the British Empire."

Several years after the completion of the canal Lesseps, its builder, was invited to join the French Academy. On the occasion of his initiation historian Ernest Renan cautioned that the Suez Canal was not merely just another canal. "The Bosphorus by itself had been enough to keep the whole civilized world embarrassed up to the present, but now you have created a second and much more serious embarrassment," Renan advised Lesseps in words that would prove prophetic. "Not merely does the canal connect two inland seas, but it serves as a communicating passage to all the oceans of the globe. In case of a maritime war it will be of supreme importance, and everyone will be striving at top speed to occupy it. You have thus marked out a great battlefield for the future."

The Suez Canal was almost entirely the result of the perseverance and vision of one man, Ferdinand de Lesseps (1805–1894). Few

Frenchmen have been held in higher esteem by their countrymen than he. In 1884, when Lesseps was elected to the prestigious French Academy, the director told the assembled audience, "Next to Lamartine you have, I think, been the most beloved man of our century—a man upon whom the greatest number of legends and dreams have been built."

Lesseps's father was a distinguished member of the French diplomatic service. (Napoleon once praised him as the "government's most devoted and trusted agent.") Lesseps spent his youth at a variety of foreign posts from Aleppo to Lisbon. During his father's service as vice-consul in Alexandria, Ferdinand found himself a favorite at the court of Muhammad Ali. There he became close friends with the pasha's youngest son, Muhammad Said, then a boy of thirteen but already running to fat. His distressed father had imposed upon his flabby son a strict regimen of daily exercise and a diet of lentils and greens. At the Lesseps home the young Muhammad Said found a refuge where he could relax and indulge his weakness for pasta.

The younger Lesseps followed in his father's footsteps, serving as a consul general in Egypt, Spain, and Italy. He resigned from the last post in 1849 largely because of political differences with the new government installed by the French Revolution of 1848. He was forty-four. During five years of quiet retirement in France, Lesseps began to think upon a youthful dream of piercing the Isthmus of Suez with a canal, a dream that soon became an obsession.

On the surface, few men would appear to have been less qualified for the enormous task ahead than Lesseps. He had no specialized qualifications aside from his diplomatic skills. He possessed no background in engineering or international finance and had no connections with any of the great European banking houses. But he was imaginative and supremely self-confident, a man consumed by an idea, who combined the agility and practicality of a career diplomat with the zeal and dedication of a visionary.

Lesseps held two aces in his hand. A Spanish cousin, Eugenia María de Montijo, had married into the French royal family and become empress Eugénie. She proved to be a valuable patron at court when Lesseps needed French diplomatic support for his project. And in Egypt Pasha Muhammad Ali died after a long reign. His son Muhammad Said, the fat boy with a passion for pasta, at thirty-two succeeded his father to the throne.

Lesseps's dream of connecting the Red and Mediterranean seas was as old as the civilizations of Egypt. A canal had existed in that region as far back as 2000 B.C. Known as the Canal of the Pharaohs, it carried shipping between the two seas for more than 1,000 years. Herodotus left the first description of this ancient canal: "The length of this canal is equal to a four days' voyage, and is wide enough to admit two triremes abreast. The water enters it from the Nile a little above the city of Bubastis. It terminates in the Red Sea, not far from Patumos, an Arabian town." The Greek historian also reported that more than 100,000 Egyptians had perished in the construction of the canal.

This early canal gradually fell into disuse and had silted up by the seventh century B.C. The Persian ruler Darius and the Roman emperor Trajan both restored and enlarged the canal. In A.D. 642 the caliph Omar of Egypt reopened the canal, and it rendered useful service until the late eighth century.

When Napolen invaded Egypt in 1798, he was already thinking of a new canal through the Isthmus of Suez as a major objective of his military operation. The instructions signed by the Directorate on April 12, 1798, were explicit on this point: "The Army of the East shall take possession of Egypt. The Commander-in-Chief . . . shall have the Isthmus of Suez cut through, and he shall take the necessary steps to assure the free and exclusive possession of the Red Sea to the French Republic. . . ." Napoleon took a keen personal interest in the project. He spent ten days in the vicinity of Suez, where he retraced the ancient Canal of the Pharaohs. Quick to see the strategic and commercial advantages of such a waterway, Napoleon ordered his chief engineer, Le Père, to make a preliminary survey. Le Père's calculations erroneously showed that the Red Sea was thirty-two feet higher than the Mediterranean and would thus render a canal without locks impossible. Napoleon soon afterward abandoned the project.

Some fifty years later Lesseps set about to realize an ancient dream with nineteenth-century skills and technology. In November 1854 he sailed to Alexandria, where Muhammad Said welcomed his boyhood friend with great pomp and a gift of a fine Arabian stallion. Lesseps joined Said's military entourage on a leisurely journey through the desert to Cairo. On the way the Frenchman instructed the young pasha on the merits of his enterprise. His enthusiasm was infectious, and Said was won over. Soon afterward a royal concession was drawn up. It authorized Lesseps to form an international company under his own direction, the Compagnie Universelle du Canal Maritime de Suez. The concession was to run for ninety-nine years from the day of the opening of the canal. Said, in return, would get 177,000 shares in the new company, 44 percent of the outstanding stock.

The news of the concession stunned the international community in Cairo. A major hurdle had been cleared. But Lesseps understood that other, more difficult obstacles lay ahead. Egypt was part of the Ottoman Empire and owed fealty to Constantinople. The Sublime Porte, the sultan, would have to approve the terms of the concession. But Constantinople would not act contrary to the wishes of its chief ally, Great Britain. And London strongly opposed the project. The French government, on the other hand, was at first indifferent.

Lord Palmerston, the prime minister and an indefatigable protector of British national interests abroad, spearheaded the attack on Lesseps's scheme. In mid-1855 the two had a frank exchange of views. Palmerston, guided by a consideration of what he thought would best secure the safety of British India, defined British interests in terms that were political and strategic rather than economic. He saw clearly that the importance of the Isthmus of Suez was that it was closed and thus provided an excellent natural barrier for the protection of India. He feared that the French government would use a French canal to split Egypt from the Ottoman Empire into the French sphere of influence. Even more important, Palmerston saw the proposed canal "as another lance in the hand of France to pierce the armour of England." In the event of an outbreak of hostilities between the two countries, France, being much closer to the canal, could move easily to capture it, close it to Britain, and send its navy through the canal into the Indian Ocean to capture the British outpost at Aden and threaten India.

Lesseps refused to be discouraged and soon found strong and influential supporters among the tycoons of commerce and shipping in London. Official British objection to the canal was considerably lessened in May 1857 with the outbreak of the Indian Mutiny, the most serious of the indigenous rebellions that spread across Africa and Asia in the years between 1855 and 1860, encouraged by the loss of British prestige in the Crimean War. Additional troops had to be sent to India from Britain around the Cape of Good Hope, a voyage of some 80 days by steamship or 110 days by sail. The Indian Mutiny made dramatically clear to Britain the value of such a canal, which would have allowed the government to send reinforcements to India in half the time.

One by one Lesseps overcame the various obstacles to the start of the construction. In November 1858 he offered for sale some 400,000 shares at 500 francs each. Construction began the following spring. On April 25, 1859, surrounded by a large crowd of laborers, staff, and engineers, Lesseps sank a spade into the sandy soil on the northern edge of the Isthmus of Suez. The occasion marked both the start of the canal and the site of the future town of Port Said, commemorating the name of the Egyptian pasha who had authorized the project.

By October 18, 1862, the first stretch of the canal had been completed, from the Mediterranean to Lake Timsah through some thirty miles of parched desert. Lesseps celebrated the opening of the first stage with an appropriate ceremony. Before a crowd consisting of several hundred distinguished guests in a grandstand hung with colorful bunting and thousands of Egyptian workers lining the banks, he gave the order to cut through the final few feet. As the two waters flowed together, he cried aloud: "In the name of His Highness Muhammad Said, I command the waters of the Mediterranean enter Lake Timsah by the grace of God!"

On January 18, 1863, Muhammad Said died at the age of forty after a long illness. He was succeeded by his nephew Ismail, a man of thirty-three with an all-consuming ambition to make Egypt fully independent of the sultan in Constantinople. He quickly realized that Britain was too firmly committed to its policy of upholding the integrity of the Ottoman Empire to be of any assistance to him in that endeavor. However, Ismail found a ready ally in France.

Construction on the canal continued unabated. Thirty enormous dredges and other sophisticated forms of construction equipment arrived from France. But most of the work was done in the ancient tradition of pyramid building, by hundreds of thousands of forced laborers. The Egyptian work force was supplemented by thousands of European workers, drawn to the Isthmus of Suez by the promise of good money.

A British writer for the *Fortnightly Review* described the scene: "Thousands of men were employed—Dalmatians, Greeks, Croats, Negroes from Nubia, and Egyptian Fellahs, all superintended by French officers. These gangs of men were regularly organized and paid according to the cubic feet of earth they dug out, some earning five or six and others only two or three francs a day. The works were pushed on with great rapidity, steam-traction on railways, asses, mules, men and camels, all contributing towards their completion."

Once Lesseps found himself with a group of convicts who had escaped from a prison on the shores of the Adriatic and run to the isthmus as though it were the Promised Land. The Austrian consul immediately demanded their extradition. But Lesseps negotiated their stay and soon employed them on the canal, sending their money home each month to their families. Lesseps drew from the experience a lesson which he never tired of telling visitors: "I have never had to complain of my workmen, and yet I have employed pirates and convicts. Work has made honest men again of them all; I have never been robbed, even of a pocket handkerchief. The truth is that our men can be got to do anything by showing them esteem and by persuading them that they are engaged upon a work of worldwide interest."

All the evidence does indeed suggest that Lesseps's work force was an inspired one. A French journalist visited the isthmus and interviewed a common French laborer living in a miserable hut in the desert. The man saw himself proudly as "a sentinel placed in an advance post, as a missionary of France and an agent of civilization."

The French brought culture and a lively social life to the remote desert. When W. H. Russell, the correspondent for the *Times* of London, visited the new city of Ismailia on Lake Timsah in 1869, he marveled at the social glitter he found there: "And in an evening you would be tempted, as you hear the click of the billiard-balls and the rattle of the dominoes, and look in through the gauze blinds and see the smoking crowds, to imagine that you were in some country quarters in La Belle France, but for the deep sand, which, rising ankle deep, tells you that the city is built in the heart of the Egyptian Desert."

Construction on the Suez Canal was completed in November 1869, ten years after Lesseps had turned the first spade of sand. When it was over, some 99.4 million cubic yards of earth had been removed to create a narrow ribbon of gray-blue water that stitched with machinelike precision for 98 miles across the pale, sun-scorched sand of the Isthmus of Suez. The average depth of Lesseps's "mighty river" was 24 feet, with a width between 200 and 300 feet. In addition, three new ports had been created at Port Said, Port Ibrahim, and Ismailia. All in all, it was a stupendous achievement.

Lesseps scheduled the inauguration ceremonies for November 16–20, coinciding with his sixty-fourth birthday on November 17. The American correspondent Henry M. Stanley was on hand and called the festivities the "greatest drama ever witnessed or enacted in Egypt."

The pasha Ismail shrewdly saw that the opening of the Suez Canal would give Egypt new status among European nations, so he was determined to exploit the opening ceremonies to add luster and prestige to his name and dynasty. Many of the invited crown heads of Europe declined to attend, chiefly to avoid offending Turkey. But some 1,000, all guests of Ismail, did come. They included such luminaries as the Norwegian playwright Henrik Ibsen, French writers Émile Zola, Théophile Gautier, and Alexandre Dumas, and the British founder of international tourism, Thomas Cook. They arrived in Egypt like "a self-inflicted plague," as Russell of the *Times* put it, and immediately overflowed all the available hotels.

An American observer reported that the harbor of Port Said was crowded on November 16 with "the fleets of nearly every great nation, and the flags of the crescent and the cross floated from every mast-head." He added:

> The Empress of the French, the Emperor Francis Joseph of Austria, the Crown Prince of Prussia, the Princess of Holland, the Khedive of Egypt, and a great number of distinguished men were assembled. A venerable sheik, with flowing beard, took his station in a kiosque and prayed, while the Europeans, in their brilliant uniforms, stood with heads uncovered. Afterwards a procession of Roman Catholic priests ascended a platform prepared for them and conducted their imposing services, while the guns from the ships kept up a salute. The archbishop of Alexandria then delivered a very eloquent sermon, in which he extolled the merits of M. de Lesseps, comparing him to Christopher Columbus, who had, like him, opened the way to a new world.

Early on the morning of November 17 there formed in the harbor at Port Said a procession of dozens of vessels, led by the imperial yacht *Aigle* with Empress Eugénie and Lesseps on board. Bands along the embankment played military music, as one after another the ships entered the canal at fifteen-minute intervals, their order determined by protocol.

The French Orientalist painter Eugène Fromentin described the arrival of the parade of ships at Ismailia:

> A light coil of smoke and the tip of a high mast appear above the high sandbanks of the Northern Canal. From one mast of the ship, still hidden, flies the Imperial flag of France. She is the *Aigle*. She passes beneath us slowly, her wheels barely turning, with a cautious prudence which adds to the solemnity of the moment. Finally, she emerges into the lake. Salvoes of artillery from all the batteries salute her, the immense crowd applauds, it is truly won-

derful. The Empress, from the high poop, waves her handkerchief. She has M. de Lesseps at her side; she forgets to shake his hand before this great multitude, come from all parts of Europe and overcome with emotion.

The crowd on the banks suddenly began cheering frantically, "*Vive la France! Viva l'Impératrice! Viva Lesseps!*" For them the union of the two seas was an achievement of imperial France.

The pasha Ismail had transformed the new city of Ismailia into a fabulous setting for his enormous party. For the occasion he had constructed a palace, triumphal arches, and various buildings to lodge his guests. About 8,000 people were served that night in elaborate banquets at the palace or in vast canopied dining areas. The next day Ismail staged an equestrian spectacle, with galloping Egyptian cavalry and Bedouin horsemen firing their rifles as they rode, plus a six-mile race of camels, "with screaming Arabs on their humps." Arab music of flutes, tambourines, and drums filled the air. That evening the pasha gave a splendid ball for the empress in the palace he had newly built in the Moorish style. Crowding the palace were an estimated 6,000 people, including 2,000 gate-crashers. Little dancing took place, for only 200 women were in attendance.

For the Europeans bold enough to venture beyond the city limits, there were other sights straight out of the *Arabian Nights*. Hundreds of Arab chiefs had come with their tribes and their herds from all over the Islamic world, pitching their tents in the desert beyond Ismailia. An English reporter cataloged the sights to be had at the edge of town where thousands of Arabs had gathered:

> [In some tents were] exhibitions of jugglers; in others, chanting, grunting dervishes; in others, snake charmers, serpent swallowers, glass-eaters; in others, reciters, story-tellers; in some, singing women concealed behind their curtains of gauze. . . . [Everywhere the Arab men sat] packed in rows on their hams—white turbaned, dark robed, grave, fine-looking men. It would take the conceit out of the grand Europeans, who fancy they are the flower of the human race, to walk through a crowd of these splendid children of

the Desert, and measure their stature and breadth of shoulder against those of the men whose drink is water and whose food is millet, maize, and vegetables.

Lesseps had chosen for the motto of his canal the Latin phrase *Aperire terram gentibus* ("to open the earth to all people"). The inaugural festivities seemed to him to support his hope that his canal would bring the peoples of the world closer together. (The same faith later inspired the American poet Walt Whitman; in his "Passage to India" he celebrated the opening of the Suez Canal as the "Year of the marriage of continents, climates, and oceans.")

Shortly after the conclusion of the inaugural ceremonies Lesseps took time out for a much more private celebration. At the age of sixty-four he married for the second time, this time a woman of twenty. The marriage took place in Ismailia. She went on to bear him twelve children before his death at the age of eighty-nine, a few days after the twenty-fifth anniversary of the opening of his canal.

The successful completion of the Suez Canal was a source of national pride for France but a national humiliation for Britain. *The Saturday Review* scoffed, "The Queen of England has opened the Holborn Viaduct, [while] the Empress of the French . . . opens the Suez Canal." The British government, which had for years taken the position that a canal across the Isthmus of Suez was impractical, was finally forced to admit its error. In 1870 Lesseps visited London at the invitation of Queen Victoria, who presented him with the Grand Cross of the Order of the Star of India.

Almost from the start the Suez Canal inspired a rash of other projects for cutting canals through isthmuses, including the Sault Sainte Marie Canals and locks linking Lake Superior to lakes Huron and Michigan. (This worldwide mania for canals probably led the astronomer Giovanni Schiaparelli to announce in 1877 his discovery of "canals" on Mars.)

The Suez Canal exerted a profound impact upon the countries and people of Europe, the Middle East, and Asia. In the words of historian Chester L. Cooper, it "facilitated the international movement of pots and textiles, iron and cotton to and from Asia and thereby conceivably contributed to world harmony. But the shortcut to India and the Orient also intensified the quest for markets and raw materials among the newly industrialized nations of Europe."

The Suez Canal was from the first always much more than merely an artery of commerce shuttling merchant ships from one ocean to another. It was exactly what Lord Palmerston had feared it would be—both a strategic prize of major importance and a lance pointing to the heart of British India at the disposal of whatever country controlled Egypt. The solution was obvious: transform the canal from a French threat to a British imperial asset.

That opportunity came unexpectedly in 1875. A fast-moving Disraeli, back in power as prime minister, snatched the prize in the final act of a long-playing *Rake's Progress* in Cairo. The pasha Ismail went bankrupt. For years he had spent recklessly, indulged without restraint his caprices and fantasies, and run the finances of his government into the ground. "His only notion of economy was underpaying his officials" was how one historian sums it up. By 1875 Ismail owed his creditors £68 million. The annual interest alone was £5 million, more than Egypt's total annual revenue when Ismail came to the throne. His situation was desperate. And the only hard assets remaining for him to sell were the 177,000 shares in the Suez Canal.

When Disraeli learned of Ismail's predicament, he moved swiftly to get those shares for the British government. After a November 18 cabinet meeting on the subject he informed Queen Victoria: "It is vital to Your Majesty's authority and power at this critical moment that the Canal should belong to England." Parliament was in recess. Several ranking cabinet members opposed the purchase. But Disraeli was determined. Acting boldly on his own authority, he sent Montagu Corry, his private secretary, to the office of Baron de Rothschild of the famous banking family.

"The Prime Minister must have £4,000,000," Corry told Rothschild.

"When?" the banker asked, casually eating from a plate of muscatel grapes.

"Tomorrow."

Rothschild popped another grape into his mouth, spit out the skin, and asked: "What is your security?"

"The British Government," Corry replied.

"You shall have it."

Thus the deal was concluded. Money in hand, Disraeli moved swiftly to prevent the French from buying Ismail's shares. With characteristic bravado he wrote his queen: "It is just settled; you have it, Madam. The French government has been outgeneralled."

The transaction made Disraeli a hero in England. "An Englishman feels proud now that he can 'paddle his own canoe' on his own canal," wrote one British newspaper enthusiastically. "No doubt we shall come to possess the whole property and build arsenals on the canal, whence we can supply India in time of need."

The French were infuriated. "The seizure of the Suez Canal by the English Government inaugurates a new type of conquest—conquest by mortgage," a French newspaper editor fumed.

The initial impression of most Britons that Disraeli had bought the Suez Canal lock, stock, and barrel was wrong. Rather, he had made Britain the owner of 44 percent of the Suez Canal Company with ten seats on the company's board of twenty-four directors. "What Disraeli did was to give England a distinctive and important financial footing in a country where everything was geared to the power of the franc," writes A. P. Thornton in *The Imperial Idea and Its Enemies*.

Disraeli's purchase of the canal shares was widely regarded both in Britain and Europe as a prelude to some form of British control over Egypt. However, he continued to insist in his addresses to the House of Commons that the goal of his Middle Eastern policy was to preclude France's occupation of Egypt while maintaining the integrity of the Ottoman Empire.

But major changes were swiftly overtaking the region, making the old policies obsolete. Commercially and strategically this "key to India" was too vital to the British Empire to trust its security to another country. "Britain was switching fleets from the oceans, which she was accustomed to rule, to a narrow channel between lands over which she had no authority," writes Lord Kinross. "Here she needed to ensure a security which the Sick Man of Europe could no longer provide. Inevitably Egypt would come to replace Turkey as the focal point in Britain's Middle Eastern policy. Inexorably, events in Egypt—financial, political, and finally military—marched from now onwards in the direction of British control."

As Ismail's debt debacle unraveled, Britain and France together assumed a much greater role in Egyptian internal affairs. In June 1879 Ismail abdicated and was succeeded by his son, Tewfik, a man easily manipulated by French and British officials. In July 1882 Georges Clemenceau spoke to the French Chamber of Deputies and declared, "Great Britain and France have two essential interests in common— the freedom of the Suez Canal and the proper administration of Egyptian affairs." Egypt's foreign debts were consolidated into a general debt of £91 million. Britain and France took over management of all Egyptian revenues and expenditures in an effort to bring some order to the country's finances. By 1882 Egypt's benefits from the canal seemed few, as one astute American visitor to the area reported: "For Egypt the Suez Canal has proved to have been a commercial as well as a political mistake. It has been the principal cause of her financial ruin, and led to the dethronement of her late viceroy. . . . It was a political mistake because it has placed Egypt upon the highway to India, thus making her an object of jealous solicitude . . . to those nations . . . whose ambitions lie in that direction."

This encroachment by Britain and France upon Egypt's internal affairs came at a time of a budding nationalism coupled with an Islamic religious zeal. In 1882 the hostility to foreign influences came to a head in a mutiny of the Egyptian Army under the leadership of Colonel Ahmed Arabi. Rioting directed largely against French and British interests broke out in Alexandria on June 11. Dozens of Europeans lost their lives in the violence, which quickly escalated to threaten Tewfik's government. Neither Tewfik nor the sultan in Constantinople was able to muster sufficient military forces to stabilize the situation.

Thus, Anglo-French "protective intervention" became imperative, and this required a joint invasion of Egypt. At the last minute the French government backed off, refusing to do anything more than put its fleet off the Egyptian coast as a show of force. British

naval forces shelled Alexandria on July 11, and British troops captured the city on July 20. Tewfik, who had taken refuge on a British
warship, issued orders to the British Army "to occupy all those points
in the Isthmus of Suez which you consider necessary to ensure freedom of traffic through the Canal, and the protection of the population of the Isthmus, and to suppress any forces not recognizing my
authority."

The British moved swiftly to secure complete control of the Suez
Canal by August 24. No French soldiers went with them. The British
then decisively defeated Arabi's forces in the Nile delta and a few
days later occupied Cairo. Dual control was now a thing of the past,
in spite of several unsuccessful attempts by France to resurrect it.
Egypt belonged to Britain alone. The occupation lasted through the
Second World War.

In those years the Suez Canal held a special place in the imaginations of the British people, evoking something much larger and
less tangible than an engineering feat, no matter how brilliant and
audacious it may have been. Within a few years the canal had become an emotionally charged symbol, summing up an empire and its
ethos. The man largely responsible for this was the poet laureate of
the British Empire, Rudyard Kipling, whose poem "Mandalay" appeared in 1890 and took Britain by storm. The poem tells of a British
veteran of the Burma War of 1885, back in England and spiritually
weary, who contrasts his life in a dirty, dreary, rain-soaked London
with the cleaner, greener land of palm trees and rice paddies, sunshine and silence in the Far East. The final stanza is one of the most
famous in modern poetry:

Ship me somewheres east of Suez where the best is like the worst,
Where there aren't no Ten Commandments, an' a man can raise a
 thirst;
For the temple-bells are callin', an' it's there that I would be—
By the old Moulmein Pagoda, lookin' lazy at the sea—
 On the road to Mandalay,
 Where the old Flotilla lay,
 With our sick beneath the awnings when we went to Mandalay!

Oh, the road to Mandalay,
Where the flyin'-fishes play,
An' the dawn comes up like thunder outer China 'crost the Bay!

When Kipling penned his memorable phrase *east of Suez,* we do not know if he meant Suez the isthmus, the canal, or the city. But those three words captured the imagination of an entire people and assumed the power of an incantation. As historian D. A. Farnie has observed, "Within that single sibilant saying Kipling compressed all the mystery of the Orient, the splendour of the gorgeous East and the magic of the Arabian Nights. . . . Kipling endowed Suez and the Canal with an importance which they could never have assumed without him. In particular he rendered the Canal holy in the imagination of a culture which was losing touch with the sacred things of its own past. . . . He made Suez into a new Jerusalem, increasingly sacred to the West as Mecca, Meshed, and Benares were to the East."

"You have marked out a great battlefield for the future," historian Ernest Renan had warned Lesseps. The canal did indeed become the great battlefield that Renan predicted. In both world wars Britain fought to hold control of the canal while Germany and its allies moved to seize the isthmus. Both sides clearly understood that control of the canal was essential to a victory on the Continent.

The Suez Canal was again on the front pages of the world's newspapers in the autumn of 1956, when Britain, France, and Israel mounted a joint invasion of Egypt in a decisive confrontation between the forces of old Europe and the new Middle East. Several months before, on July 26, Egyptian leader Colonel Gamal Abdel Nasser, a militant nationalist, announced his intention to take over the Suez Canal immediately and to nationalize the Suez Canal Company. "This Canal is an Egyptian Canal," he told a wildly cheering audience. "The income of the Suez Canal Company in 1955 reached $100,000,000. [Yet Egypt] received only $3,000,000."

The Suez crisis of 1956 was one of most important events of the mid-twentieth century and forever changed the political landscape of the Middle East. In a coordinated attack the Israeli Army invaded and successfully occupied the Sinai Peninsula, while British and French forces launched a land and air attack on Port Said. For almost three weeks no one could be certain that the Suez conflict would not escalate into a major conventional war, perhaps even a nuclear war. World opinion was almost unanimously opposed to the invasion. The ferocity of the Egyptian resistance stunned Britain and France, and both suffered heavy casualties. The violence was halted only after the United Nations had hurried an international peacekeeping force to the scene.

Few events in the past forty years have had such profound repercussions as this invasion, which the British minister of state for foreign affairs Anthony Nutting called the "last dying convulsion of British imperialism." The operation doomed Anglo-French interests in the Middle East once it was learned that they had a secret military pact with Israel against Egypt's Nasser. Britain's long hegemony in the Arab world abruptly ended, and American influence soared after President Dwight D. Eisenhower assailed the invasion by his closest NATO allies.

Historian Farnie says in *East and West of Suez:*

> The Suez Crisis marked a turning-point in the history of Europe, Asia, Africa, and Egypt if not in that of England or of the Middle East. It stimulated African endeavors to secure full independence from Europe, diverted American attention from the invasion of Cuba by Fidel Castro on December 2, 1956, and so helped bring new centers of world revoluton into existence. In Egypt the Anglo-French-Israeli assault failed to overthrow Nasser but strengthened his position immensely and unexpectedly, making the revolution popular as never before and rallying to his support the richer classes impoverished by his policies. . . . The invasion made Nasser the prisoner of Arab nationalism. . . . In Europe the crisis benefited Germany and Italy at the expense of France and England but destroyed the moral foundations of the

North Atlantic Treaty Organization. France was forced to undertake the devaluation which England avoided but . . . concluded that N.A.T.O. was "the wrong alliance in the wrong place, against the wrong enemy," [and withdrew from that organization to develop its own nuclear capability].

In 1876 a writer in the British magazine *Quarterly Review* predicted: "As in Egypt of old a Pharaoh arose who knew not Joseph, so, ere long, a generation will come which forgets Lesseps."

On Christmas Day 1956 the last of the British and French troops withdrew from Egyptian soil. On Christmas Eve a band of Egyptian soldiers had dynamited the large statue of Ferdinand de Lesseps which had overlooked the canal at Port Said, leaving an empty pedestal. Later the Egyptian Suez Canal Authority published a history of the canal in which no mention was made of Lesseps. The only references were to the hundreds of thousands of Egyptians who had toiled for a decade in the hot sun to construct the canal.

William Gifford Palgrave
Medallion by Woolner

Richard Burton's sketch of Medina

*Emir Bashir II (c. 1760–1851), the
chieftan of the Druzes who became Lady
Hester Stanhope's archenemy at Djoun*

*Lady Hester Stanhope
Drawing by R. J. Hamerton*

A view of Djoun, Lady Hester's home on Mount Lebanon

Dr. Charles L. Meryon,
Lady Hester's physician and
biographer, in Bedouin dress

Lady Hester Stanhope
Drawing by R. J. Hamerton

Jane Digby, Lady Ellenborough
Royal Gallery, Munich

Sir Richard F. Burton, 1876
by Lord Leighton, copyright by
the National Portrait Gallery,
London

Lady Anne Blunt

Lady Anne Blunt's sketch of the plain of Melakh
and the river Euphrates

Lady Anne Blunt's sketch of the ruins of the
palace of El Haddr

Lady Anne Blunt's sketch of her tent, with a view of Mount Hermon

Lady Anne Blunt's sketch of the citadel of Aleppo

Wilfrid Blunt (c. 1860)

*Alexander Kinglake (c. 1863)
by H. M. Haviland, copyright by the
National Portrait Gallery, London*

*Charles Montagu Doughty
(1921) by E. Kennington,
copyright by the National
Portrait Gallery, London*

*Colonel T. E. Lawrence (1919) by Augustus John (1878–1961),
copyright by The Tate Gallery, Millbank, London*

CHAPTER V

Lady Jane Digby el Mesrab: All for Love

In December 1868 John MacGregor, an intrepid Scotsman and the pioneer of British canoeing, arrived in the mountains above Damascus. With him was the *Rob Roy*, a canoe he had constructed to his own specifications for long trips. MacGregor was already a household name in England because of several well-publicized canoe voyages through Western Europe, Russia, and Armenia. Two years before he had founded the Royal Canoe Club with the Prince of Wales as its commodore. In 1868 MacGregor brought his *Rob Roy* to the Middle East to explore the lakes and rivers of Syria and Palestine and to "look upon scenes never opened before to the traveller's gaze which were entirely inaccessible except in a canoe."

MacGregor was the proper British sportsman on a lark, and he never stepped out of that role. He dressed in gray flannel Norfolk jackets, carried a black umbrella as protection against the sun, and wore sunglasses ("spectacles of neutral tint") to ease the eyestrain at midday. He never bothered to learn Arabic.

MacGregor designed the *Rob Roy* to be both transporation and sleeping quarters. Made of seasoned cedarwood and fitted with a small sail, the canoe had an overall length of fourteen feet and a beam of twenty-six inches, yet when it was packed with all its gear, it weighed only seventy-two pounds. Large waterproof pockets on each side of the cockpit held his rifle, pistol, ammunition, brandy flask, books, maps, fishing tackle, money, and food for a week.

MacGregor spent several weeks in Egypt, paddling the *Rob Roy* on the Nile and Suez Canal, before heading north in search of more exciting adventures. In Beirut he hired porters and guides, wrapped his precious canoe in Oriental rugs, and hauled it by wagon over the Lebanon Mountains into Syria. His destination was the source of the Barada River, which spills out of snow-clad mountains at the bottom of a deep canyon through terrain then largely unexplored by Europeans.

After reconnoitering the Barada, MacGregor launched the *Rob Roy* on a remote stretch of the upper river that was "like a Scotch salmon stream." He was instantly caught in a swift current and swept between huge crags and boulders. At times the rapids were so treacherous that he was forced to portage around them. MacGregor found the experience "exhilarating" after the anemic runs on the oily Nile and tranquil Suez Canal. Several days later he emerged from the mountains, fighting one final set of rapids. As he wrote later, "After I had battled with all the difficulties which could be crammed into this time, panting with a tired but wholesome excitement, the sun suddenly appeared, that had been hidden by rocks or trees; the gorge had loosed its hold of us, and the canoe soon floated along the now placid river, while Damascus, old Damascus! gleamed out brilliant before me in the evening light, with its groves of green, and white shining walls, and airy minarets, a glorious scene."

MacGregor's arrival by canoe in Damascus created a sensation. He paddled under bridges, around dripping aqueducts, and past the pasha's palace, while throngs of dumbfounded inhabitants crowded the banks. He stopped beside the gardens of Demetri's Hotel, where he planned to stay. The crowd cheered lustily as he stepped ashore.

MacGregor was clearly the hero of the day in Damascus, and the *Rob Roy*, blue sail hoisted and Union Jack flying from the little mast, the most popular attraction in town. Even the Turkish pasha visited

Demetri's Hotel to introduce himself to the intrepid Scotsman. But of all his hundreds of visitors, one in particular made the greatest impression on MacGregor. "At Damascus I met Mrs. Digby, the English wife of a great Arab chief," he wrote later. "When in English society, her quiet manner as a lady makes one forget that her husband has some thousand spearmen at his beck, and that to get to Palmyra with their aid, the curious traveller must pay a heavy blackmail of yellow gold."

Few women's love affairs so scandalized the polite London society of their day as those of Lady Jane Digby, whose amorous exploits became the stuff of a half dozen best-selling novels. If Lady Hester Stanhope's life was a quest for power, then hers was a quest for love or, more precisely, adventurous loving. She channeled all her life's energies into her romantic attachments and lived "all for love," with complete abandon and almost always with impeccable style. At the age of forty-six she finally found her perfect love in the black tents of the Mesrab tribe of Bedouins in the desert beyond Damascus. In the words of one of her biographers, Lady Jane Digby was "the female counterpart of the Byronic hero—the proud, passionate, moody, often anguished sinner, who defied every rule that confined the human spirit . . . determined to wrest happiness from a gloriously inviting world."

Fluent in nine languages and an accomplished artist with both the watercolor brush and the pencil, Lady Jane was one of the many women, particularly Englishwomen, who found themselves drawn, like the moth to the flame, to the mysterious East and its promise of an emotional fulfillment of a kind that had largely vanished from the West. Lesley Blanch in her book *The Wilder Shores of Love* defines precisely the nature of the appeal in the context of the age:

> It was a time when the West was suddenly aware of the romantic aspects of the East. In the eighteenth century it had been seen as a fabulous backdrop; a stage setting for Mozart's *L'Enlèvement du Serail,* all toppling turbans and giddy goings-ons in key with the elegant salons of Versailles or the Hofburg where it was first applauded. But even such tinkling echoes had died away by the time

the nineteenth century dawned, and Byron's verses were intoxicating an avid public. Now another, more sultry East was seen, although treated with an equal subjectivity. Mock heroics gave place to savage grandeurs. Travelers such as Prince Pückler-Muskau returned with tales of chivalresque Arabs and the splendors of Oriental hospitality. . . . Ingres and Delacroix were covering huge canvases with voluptuous scenes where beneath vast expanses of exoticism and local color, the most disturbing realities of flesh and blood were apparent. And some women . . . instinctively must have sensed the contracting horizons of their age and seen the cold light of reason spreading like a gray streak across the blue. It was to spread over the whole sky. Yet the romantic mirage could still be translated into reality, could still be lived—elsewhere. They turned Eastward trustingly.

Jane Digby was born on April 3, 1807, at Holkham Hall, a Palladian brick mansion in Norfolk, into two of England's important aristocratic families, the Digbys and the Cokes. The family tree included such notables as Sir Edward Coke, the attorney general to both Queen Elizabeth I and King James I and a lord chief justice. Her father, Captain Henry Digby, was a hero of the Battle of Trafalgar. Jane's childhood was typical of that of young girls born in that period into wealthy and noble families. In 1823 her family took up residence in Georgian London. Soon afterward Jane, only weeks out of the classroom, was presented at court, her ticket into fashionable society. Formal dinner parties and balls made up much of her life for the next several months. A strikingly beautiful sixteen-year-old girl "with a most lovely and sweet-turned face," she found herself quite popular with London's eligible bachelors.

Jane was soon engaged to Edward Law, Lord Ellenborough, a man twice her age. He was a widower with no children, wealthy and influential, already a man to be reckoned with in the House of Lords and one whose acid tongue had gained him many enemies. "War and women," he would say, "these are in reality the only fit interests for a man!" As experienced and cynical in affairs of the heart as Jane was innocent, he courted her with romantic verses composed for the occasion. Having convinced herself that she was in love, Jane responded in kind:

> Edward, for thee I alone sigh
> And feel a love unknown before.
> What bliss is mine when thou art nigh!
> O, love me still—I ask no more.

They were married on September 15, 1824. Their relationship soured from the first. During the honeymoon in Brighton the jaded Ellenborough, already bored with his beautiful but inexperienced wife, flirted with a pastry cook's daughter. Back in London, he plunged into his work, ignoring his wife. The situation is neatly summed up by E. M. Oddie, one of Lady Jane's early biographers: "Ambitious, arrogant, and at thirty-four at the height of his intellectual powers, Ellenborough was the wrong age to find immaturity of mind appealing or even interesting. In spite of the Don Juanesque reputation with which society had saddled him, he appears to have been a tepid and indifferent lover. . . . Emotionally, he was cold; she was warm and impulsive."

The marriage soon went the route of William Hogarth's *Marriage à la Mode*. Ignored by her husband, Lady Jane began to move in the London fast set, made friends with older, more experienced women who were utterly unsuitable for someone her age, and surrounded herself with gallants. It was an age and a society in which extramarital liaisons were commonplace and, if managed with proper discretion, carried little social stigma. In view of her impressionable, spontaneous, and emotional nature, it was only a matter of time before she took a lover. She was, after all, a woman who at the age of nineteen could write in her journal, ". . . though righteous Heaven above/ Forbids this rebel heart to love,/ To love is still its fate."

Lady Jane's first lover was Frederic Madden, a handsome and young official of the British Museum who spent several weeks at her ancestral home of Holkham. In the March 13, 1827, entry of his journal, he recorded the arrival of the young Jane without her husband: "Lady Ellenborough . . . arrived to dinner, and will stay a fortnight. She is not yet twenty, and one of the most lovely women I ever saw, quite fair, [with] blue eyes that would move a saint, and lips that would tempt one to forswear Heaven to touch them." Ten days later they became lovers. On March 29, Lady Jane left Holkham, and Madden never saw her again. (He willed his journal to the Bodleian Library at Oxford on the condition that it be kept sealed until 1920, when the details of his brief affair with Lady Jane first became known.)

Later that year Lady Jane started an affair with a cousin, George Anson. Then, on February 15, 1828, she was delivered of a son, Arthur Dudley Law. Local gossips gave George the credit, but her husband accepted the child as his own. Soon afterward the Duke of Wellington appointed Ellenborough to a cabinet position.

His wife continued to be restless. "The misfortune of my nature," she wrote in a journal, "is to consider love as all in all; without this feeling life is a dreary void—no earthly blessing can compensate its loss, and having at first setting out in life sacrificed all without regret to one great absorbing passion, the necessity of loving and being loved is to me as the air I breathe and the sole cause of all I have to reproach myself with."

On the evening of March 10, 1828, she met the man who was to become her first "great absorbing passion," Prince Felix Ludwig Johann von Nepomuk Friedrich zu Schwarzenberg, an attaché to the Austrian ambassador in London. He was twenty-seven and extremely good-looking with hypnotic eyes and an extravagant black mustache. He enjoyed enormous popularity with women. The contrast between the handsome, dashing, stylishly whiskered Schwarzenberg and the pompous Ellenborough could not have been more sharply drawn. Lady Jane and Schwarzenberg met at an embassy ball which she had attended without her husband. She sized him up immediately as the Byronesque lover of her dreams. Schwarzenberg was also smitten. An Austrian Embassy official left behind a description of that first evening:

> Among all these people one lady especially attracted my attention. This was Lady Ellenborough, one of the most beautiful women I have ever seen, blond hair, magnificent complexion, big blue

eyes, young, with the figure of a nymph; in fact, she is everything desirable. It is she whom Schwarzenberg adores, and I did not fail to have myself presented. I was not impressed by her intellect, it's true, but one cannot have everything. The expression of her face is as soft as the sound of her voice, and her whole personality has something of modesty and innocence which enchanted me.

The coldness and formality of a first acquaintance did not last very long between us, and she spoke to me with childish candour about her husband, whom she accuses of being jealous and unkind. She obviously enjoys saying this, but my impression is that Lord Ellenborough is too busy with his political career to give his young wife good counsel.

Within a short time Lady Jane had taken the Austrian prince as her lover. Throughout the summer her green phaeton with its pair of black, long-tailed ponies was parked almost daily outside Schwarzenberg's apartment. The couple made little attempt to hide their affection for each other. They even attended dinners and balls as a couple. Ellenborough never suspected his wife's infidelity, but others gossiped at length about their comings and goings. Lady Jane was deliriously happy and very much in love. A poem in her notebook dated December 22, 1828, and titled "To F. S." reads in part:

> Oh say not that my love will pass
> And all this fondness will be forgot . . .
> My love is not the love of one
> Who feels passion for a day.

A London society long used to discretion in extramarital affairs became increasingly scandalized at the public way in which Lady Ellenborough and Schwarzenberg conducted theirs. In February 1829 the two vacationed together in Brighton. By late spring the situation had deteriorated to a point where it threatened Schwarzenberg's effectiveness at the embassy. The dashing Felix was recalled to Vienna by his patron, Prince Metternich, in a desperate effort to save his protégé's career. When Schwarzenberg broke the bad news to a distressed Jane in early May, she, in turn, informed him that she was three months pregnant with his child. Circumstances had gone beyond her control. She had little choice but to ask Ellenborough for a formal separation. This she did on the evening of May 22. The two never saw each other again after that day. Soon afterward Lady Jane departed for Europe to join her lover.

At that time a divorce was regarded as such a serious matter that it required an act of Parliament. Ellenborough filed for a divorce. When the matter came before Parliament, it was hotly contested. Lady Jane's adultery was never seriously questioned. But Ellenborough's cavalier attitude toward his young wife came in for considerable criticism. "Had he not neglected his proper duties as a husband and put his inexperienced wife into the path of temptation?" many both in and out of Parliament wanted to know. The debate on the divorce was front-page news for days. Lady Jane never contested the divorce and indeed did not seem to give it a second thought. In exchange for the divorce Ellenborough agreed to settle £330 a year on his wife for the rest of her life, a substantial sum in those days. In the midst of the divorce proceedings Lady Jane's young son suddenly died from an illness.

While public sympathy largely rested on her side, divorce was a social damnation from which there could be no redemption. Lady Jane had effectively closed off her options in England. By late summer she had established herself in Paris to await Schwarzenberg's arrival in early November, a few days before she gave birth to a daughter. Lady Jane was still very much in love with her Austrian prince, but all the evidence suggests that his passion for the affair had waned considerably. She had given her all for love, but she soon learned that Schwarzenberg was not prepared to make any major sacrifices that would endanger his career, certainly nothing like a marriage to a woman whose notoriety had already provided material for several sensational *romans à clef*. She continued to live openly with him in Paris as his mistress. By late spring of 1830 she was again pregnant. A son was born in late December but died within a few days.

There had now emerged a pattern that characterized Lady Jane's affairs with a long series of lovers over the coming years. As her biographer Oddie observed over fifty years ago, "It was her tragedy that she took love seriously—so seriously that the man of the moment was always the perfect hero incapable of imperfection, the god for whom no sacrifice was too great. She would love . . . in defiance of the law, glorying in that she had never failed her lover in anything, not even for the sake of virtue. She made love her religion and aspired to heights where few men could hope to follow her, for always her lovers proved themselves men, not gods."

In the spring of 1831 Schwarzenberg finally left Lady Jane and returned to Austria. A stunned Jane fled to Munich to recover herself, leaving her daughter behind in Paris. Munich in 1831 was in the midst of a golden age and one of the most exciting cities, culturally and artistically, in Europe. Much of this renaissance was due to King Ludwig I of Bavaria, a charming, if somewhat eccentric, man, who had reigned for six years. A statesman, poet, scholar, and patron of the arts and literature, he longed to do for Munich what Lorenzo de' Medici had done for Florence. In the words of one historian, "His fetish was beauty in general, and Grecian beauty in particular; beauty in art, beauty in architecture, beauty in women." Hard-of-hearing, with a face marked by smallpox, Ludwig nonetheless enjoyed a reputation as a great lover. (In 1848 his affair with the courtesan Lola Montez scandalized the court and forced him to abdicate his throne.) In 1831 Ludwig was forty-five and in his prime.

Ludwig and Lady Jane met shortly after her arrival in Munich when she took coffee at Tambosi's, a fashionable café. Both were infatuated from the first. "My acquaintance with you seems a dream," she wrote to the king soon afterward. "I can scarce conceive how you have contrived so completely to win my heart and make me thus at ease by setting aside differences of rank and all the barriers that the conventions of the world have raised between us." With an openness that Ludwig found appealing, she told him fully and frankly about her marriage and divorce from Ellenborough and her subsequent love affair with Schwarzenberg. Ludwig replied with a poem in which he proclaimed:

> You who became a victim of love, you will understand me
> As I understand you, dear, whom the world has exiled.
> I will never judge you harshly, even if all the world does!
> I cannot condemn you, because I understand it all.
> You deserve more respect than many who seem guiltless.
> The world judges one way, God another.

Once again gossipers busied themselves about Lady Jane's activities, insisting that she had become the king's mistress. She addressed him as Basily, the Greek version of his name. And he, in turn, called her Ianthe. An English visitor to Munich sent home a story that received considerable play in London society: "Lady E. is received at court and everywhere. . . . Her liaison with the King is never denied. The King is a man of talents. My friend saw in one of his palaces a fine painted ceiling of 'The Triumph of Neptune,' and among the sea-nymphs discovered the portrait of Lady Ellenborough, which the king had given orders to introduce, and which the guide reported readily."

In the meantime, Lady Jane had started an affair with Baron Karl von Venningen, whom she had met while she was out riding. His family had been important in Bavaria since the eleventh century. At the time they met, he was twenty-six and one of the most attractive men in Munich. He fell in love with her at once and started courting her vigorously. Soon afterward they became lovers. Lady Jane immediately informed Ludwig, who accepted the situation without complaint. By July 1832 she was pregnant for the fourth time. Soon afterward she traveled to Italy, where she stayed for the remainder of her pregnancy. Another daughter was born to her on January 27, 1833. Shortly afterward Venningen married her. The couple moved to Weinheim, a small town near Heidelberg.

Tensions developed in the marriage within a few months. Although Venningen was very much in love with his wife, she for her part felt nothing toward him like that great passion she had experienced for Schwarzenberg. She was poorly suited for the life of a *hausfrau*. And she was soon bored with the pastoral tranquillity of Weinheim and longed for the excitement of Munich. In July 1834 she wrote Ludwig: "Munich is the place of all others I love best, but I can say with truth that you, my best and really true friend, are the charm that attaches me to it in so strong and peculiar a manner."

In the spring of 1835 Lady Jane's monotonous routine at Weinheim was broken with the arrival of the French novelist Honoré de Balzac, who was traveling to Vienna. There had been persistent rumors that the two had been lovers during her stay in Paris in 1830 and 1831, but there is no evidence to support that. Balzac already knew her by her reputation and found himself quite taken by her: "This beautiful English lady, so slender, so fragile; this peaches and cream woman, so soft, so mild-mannered, with her refined brow crowned by shining chestnut hair; this creature who glows with a strange phosphorescence, has a constitution of iron."

Lady Jane was Balzac's model for his character Lady Arabella Dudley in *Le Lys dans la vallée,* one of his novels in the series *La Comédie humaine.* The broad outline of this character, an adventurer in love, appears to have been based closely on Lady Jane's person and life. What was of particular interest was Balzac's almost psychic foreshadowing of her actual future, for in his novel he made Lady Arabella Dudley the heir to Lady Hester Stanhope's mantle in the Middle East. Lady Hester sends Lady Arabella a gift of a magnificent Arabian stallion, which she in turn gives to her lover so that he may come swiftly to her in the evenings. Balzac writes of Lady Arabella: "Her passion is quite African; her desires are like a tornado in the desert—the desert whose burning vastness is mirrored in her eyes— the desert, all azure and love, with its unchanging sky and its fresh, starry nights."

Eventually Lady Jane and her husband moved back to Munich. Out of love and vulnerable, she attended in the fall of 1835 a carnival ball where she met the Count Spiridion Theotoky from Corfu, Greece. At twenty-four he was four years her junior. Dark and handsome, he cut a striking figure in his national costume of white fustanella and red velvet vest encrusted with gold. He was immediately attracted to Lady Jane. She, in turn, apparently saw in him a kindred spirit, an invitation to adventure that her stuffy German baron could never match. And most important, Spiro, as she called him, was Greek. Ludwig had first instilled in her a love for all things Greek. Because of his influence, she had taken courses in sculpture and studied classical Greek. For much of the early nineteenth century Greece was a very special place for the British. Byron and other Englishmen had fought and died to liberate it, thus investing the country with an immense emotional and imaginative importance.

By November, when Venningen decided to return to Weinheim, Theotoky had already become his wife's lover. He followed her to Heidelberg, and the two saw each other frequently. According to contemporary reports, Lady Jane was the perfect *hausfrau* during the day, but at night she left the palace and rode her black steed to a rendezvous with her Greek lover. Venningen began to have his suspicions.

One evening the entire business came to a sudden and improbable denouement that would have been more at home in the pages of an implausible romance novel. Theotoky asked Lady Jane to return to Greece with him. She was as much in love with her Greek count as she had been with Schwarzenberg years before. Then, during a ball at Venningen's palace, her husband accused her of an affair with the Greek. There was a violent quarrel. Lady Jane fled the palace and joined her lover. Together they rode away, with her husband in hot pursuit. A heavily armed Venningen overtook the pair near the frontier, hauled an astonished Theotoky out of the postchaise, and demanded a duel on the spot. The Greek vehemently protested his innocence. Venningen insisted upon a duel with pistols. The two men faced one another. Venningen fired a single shot, striking the Greek in the chest above the heart. He collapsed to the ground, bleeding profusely. They all believed he was dying. In a desperate effort to save Lady Jane, he called the baron to his side and insisted that although he had loved his wife to distraction, she had never been his mistress. Venningen, in turn, was devastated, convinced that he had misjudged his wife and slain an innocent man. Theotoky lay in Jane's arms, while the small group waited for the last gasp to come. It never did. Finally, after an hour, Venningen ordered the seemingly mortally wounded man taken back to the palace so that he might die in comfort. However, the Greek rallied the next day and quickly began a rapid recovery, much to the distress of the distraught husband.

After that night's events Lady Jane decided that it was time to ask Venningen for a divorce. He finally agreed. He obviously was still deeply in love with her in spite of her weaknesses. But he no doubt sensed that emotionally she was still an adolescent with an incurable romanticism in affairs of the heart. Although grieved, Venningen was never bitter toward her and remained a faithful friend to the end of his life. They corresponded for forty years. Considering the provocations with which she had presented him, Venningen's treatment of Lady Jane in later years was nothing less than gentle and generous.

Lady Jane's years with Spiro Theotoky were among the happiest of her life. He came closer than any man thus far to fulfilling the romantic fantasy of an ideal lover that she had sought so desperately throughout Europe. In many ways, especially in temperament and sexual predisposition, they were kindred spirits. And it was he who gave her her perfect child, Leonidas, the only one of her children to arouse her maternal feelings.

For much of their marriage the two lived on the small Aegean island of Tinos, where his father served as governor. No greater contrast with Munich, with its social whirl, culture, and grand buildings, could be imagined. In the words of one contemporary visitor, the port of Tinos consisted of "the governor's house, a garrison, a harbor, a town, a rugged landscape, and a goat trail into the country." The couple lived in a whitewashed house with few amenities situated at the end of a narrow, twisted street.

The remoteness of Tinos from the glitter of Munich appears never to have bothered Lady Jane. Instead, the romance of Greece and the rugged picturesque beauty of the island completely captured her imagination. She spent heavily of her own money on the house, importing furniture, art, and silverware from Paris. She and her husband entertained lavishly. Both loved horses and rode together around the island, exploring its every nook. They made excursions to neighboring islands to visit ancient Greek sites, and she developed a passion for archaeology that stayed with her to the end. In short, Lady Jane lived in a grand eighteenth-century manner, while back home England went Victorian with the accession of the queen to the throne in 1837.

Lady Jane's several years of bliss on Tinos came to an end in 1844, when Theotoky was offered an appointment as an *aide-de-camp* to King Otto in Athens. That summer Theotoky introduced his beautiful British wife to the court, where she caused a sensation. Her annual income of £330, which in England would have been a modest fortune at best, was in Greece an enormous sum. Jane built a large mansion outside Athens that was more lavish than even the royal quarters. She soon found herself estranged from Queen Amalie, who grew envious of Jane because the British woman outrode her, outdanced her, and attracted more attention and admiration than she did.

In the summer of 1846 the Theotokys traveled to Italy for an extended vacation in the Tuscan village of Bagni di Lucca. Shortly after their arrival Lady Jane entertained several British women. She had no sooner met her guests when Leonidas, her adored six-year-old son, came out of the nursery onto a balcony three stories above the patio below. He had climbed over the railing, probably to see to whom the strange voices belonged, when suddenly he lost his balance and pitched forward. His little body landed on the pavement just a few feet in front of his horrified mother. Leonidas was killed instantly. The death of her son devastated Lady Jane, who saw the tragedy as a divine retribution for her neglect of her other children. Years later in Syria, when she lived in the black tents of the Mesrab Bedouins as the wife of their sheik, she continued to wear a small gold locket with one of Leonidas's black curls inside. With the death of her son a great void opened in her life. She drifted away from Theotoky.

Lady Jane's response to the untimely death of her son was to plunge headlong into another romantic adventure. In 1851 at the Athens court she met General Cristos Hadji-Petros, who still cut a picturesque figure, although on the far side of sixty. A bandit chief straight out of the pages of Byron's *Don Juan*, Hadji-Petros came from the mountainous part of Greece bordering on Albania. His people called themselves the *Pallikari* ("the brave ones") and earned a good living plundering travelers unfortunate enough to fall into their ambushes. Hadji-Petros and his men had fought fiercely in the Greek War of Independence from Turkey in the 1820s.

The tall and rugged Hadji-Petros was still impressive in spite of his advanced age. As biographer Margaret Schmidt describes him, "The white-haired, mustachioed chieftain . . . made a handsome, imposing figure in his native dress—white cotton shirt with large open collar, white pleated skirt cinched tightly at the waist, white stockings, gold-embroidered vest of red silk, embroidered gaiters buttoned to the knee in the manner of Homer's warriors, red slippers, red cap with blue tassel, and a large leather belt from which hung weapons (two pistols and a yataghan, or scimitar), embroidered handkerchief, money bag, and tobacco pouch."

Hadji-Petros seemed to Lady Jane to be the most romantic man she had ever met. And when she visited him in his mountain retreat at Lamia and saw him surrounded by scores of his picturesque brigands, she was completely swept away. Hadji-Petros was to her a refreshing contrast; next to him the endless social rituals of Otto's court in Athens seemed empty indeed. And just as important, he had a young son, Eirini, whom she immediately adored and thought might fill the void in her life left by the death of her Leonidas. Hadji-Petros, in turn, was overjoyed at finding himself the lover of this beautiful and wealthy British lady, two decades younger than he.

Lady Jane had already had her marriage to Theotoky annulled. She had no ties to keep her in Athens. She sold her house and moved in with Hadji-Petros in his bandit stronghold at Lamia. The Frenchman Edmond About, who visited her there, wrote later: "When she saw Hadji-Petros in his glory, [Lady Jane] imagined that she was born Pallikar; the next day she was reigning over Lamia. All the town was at her feet, and when she came out to go for a walk, the drums were beating in the fields. This delicate woman lived with drunkards, galloped on horseback in the mountains, ate literally standing up on the run, drank retsina, slept in the open air next to a big fire, and found herself in excellent health."

This mountain idyll might have gone on much longer had it not been for the volatile mix of politics back in Athens. When word got about that Lady Jane was living openly with Hadji-Petros as his mistress, an outraged Queen Amalie dismissed the general from his governmental position. He pleaded his case with the queen in a letter, arguing in part: "I can assure you on my word of honor as a soldier that if I am this woman's lover it is not for love's sake but purely for self-interest! She is rich. And I am poor. I have a position to maintain and children to educate. I hope therefore. . . ."

The plea was in vain. Hadji-Petros was not restored to his post in the government. He and Lady Jane, nonetheless, decided to return to Athens. She had agreed to marry him, overlooking the sentiments of the letter as a necessary political ploy on Hadji-Petros's part to recover his position. She was now forty-five years old but looked much younger. Edmond About enthused about her at length after he had visited her in Athens: "[She] is the incarnation of health and physical beauty. She is tall and svelte without being thin. If she were a shade taller, it would be impossible to find a woman more beautifully made. . . . She has large blue eyes, deep blue like the depths of the sea, and beautiful chestnut hair lit with warmer golden tints. . . . Her well preserved skin has the milky whiteness which belongs so essentially to England and which blooms best under thick English fogs."

The preparations for the wedding were well under way when Lady Jane disappeared abruptly from Athens, leaving her lover behind. Their engagement was over. She had discovered to her horror that he had made repeated attempts to seduce her maid, Eugénie. Because of Hadji-Petros's betrayal, she suddenly found herself without goals or direction. In April 1853, shortly after her forty-sixth birthday, Lady Jane with her maid sailed out of Piraeus toward the Middle East, convinced that her life's adventures were finally over. She had no inkling that just over the horizon in the deserts of Syria the grandest adventure of them all awaited her.

In 1853 Syria was unquestionably the most dangerous part of the Ottoman Empire for European travelers. Turkish rule was effective only in the major cities of Damascus, Aleppo, and Homs. A state of anarchy prevailed throughout most of the countryside. Bedouin tribes, driven in the late spring from the desert to find pasture for their flocks, periodically raided villages "like locusts . . . leaving bare, brown desolation where years of toil had made smiling fields and vineyards," as one visitor noted. Heavily armed groups of bandits constantly threatened all travelers and even the caravans. Village fought village in a state of continual bloody warfare.

The Englishman Charles Addison, who traveled extensively through Syria in 1835, bemoaned the chaos he saw everywhere:

Thus, it is that we see the land lie waste, the fertile plains untilled and devoid of inhabitants; a fine country, blessed with all the bounties of nature, and possessing every capability of supporting a numerous population, covered over with the fleeting ruins of modern times, or with the lofty columns and crumbling buildings of antiquity—memorials of wealth that no longer exists, and of a happy and industrious population, now annihilated. In every direction misery and desolation, poverty and wretchedness meet our view. A storm of destruction has swept over the breadth and length of the land.

Conditions were much better in the major cities. The Turkish pasha and his troops provided effective security most of the time. But even in the best of times Turkish rule in Syria was still a perfect example of Richard Burton's definition of government in the Middle East as "despotism tempered by assassination." Even in a region where cruelty was often raised to a virtue, the behavior of the pashas in Damascus sometimes shocked. Some years before, the pasha Suleiman returned from a pilgrimage to Mecca. Eager to ascertain the fidelity of the women in his harem, he sent for a Jewish doctor, who reached a hand through heavy drapes, as was customary then, and took the pulse of one of the women. He found nothing amiss. Suleiman, still suspicious, called in a eunuch and ordered him to disembowel the woman. They discovered a fetus in her womb. The pasha immediately had the doctor tied inside a sack and drowned.

Then he directed a general slaughter of his entire harem and all the palace guards, whom he suspected of impregnating the women.

After her disappointments in Greece, Lady Jane sought solace and escape in the wilds of Syria. She had read Kinglake's *Eothen* with enormous interest. He most likely influenced her choice of an itinerary. Certainly she found in his book much useful information about how best to travel in that region. And his lengthy description of a visit with Lady Hester Stanhope greatly fascinated her. She may even have taken to heart Kinglake's comment on what had brought Lady Hester to Djoun: "I can hardly tell why it should be, but there is a longing for the [Middle] East very commonly felt by proud people when goaded by sorrow." For the first time in her life Lady Jane started keeping a personal journal. (Her early biographer, E. M. Oddie, had access to Jane's notebooks for her book *The Odyssey of a Loving Woman.* They have since been lost.)

Soon after landing in Beirut, Lady Jane determined to follow in Lady Hester Stanhope's footsteps and visit Palmyra. Her later plans were still vague, but she probably expected to return to Europe after that adventure. However, within a month of leaving Athens, while riding along the Jordan River, she had an accidental meeting with a handsome young Bedouin named Saleh. Few details survive of the man. All we know is that she found herself hopelessly infatuated once again. Utterly lacking in the racial prejudice of many of her contemporaries, she saw in Saleh and his Bedouins a people with whom she felt a strong bond of kinship. In 1853 she wrote home to her mother: "My heart warms towards these wild Arabs. They have many qualities we want in civilized life, unbounded hospitality, respect for strangers or guests, good faith and simplicity of dealing among themselves, and a certain high-bred innate politeness, quite unlike the coarse vulgar Fellah."

Lady Jane's new love affair completely revitalized her. "If I had neither a mirror nor memory, I would believe myself fifteen-years-old," she wrote glowingly in her dairy.

Her new romance, however, did not stop her from visiting Palmyra. She expected to return to Saleh, marry him, and settle in the Middle East. It was her love for all things classical Greek that drew her to

Palmyra. She journeyed to Damascus, where she hoped to complete her arrangements for a trip through the desert. The ancient city totally bewitched her, completing the process of separation from Europe that had begun with Saleh. The British consul in Damascus tried to discourage Lady Jane from making the trip to Palmyra, carefully pointing out the dangers such an expedition involved. She refused to be intimidated and opened negotiations on her own with the Mesrab Bedouins, who controlled the desert around Palmyra and who had years before guided Lady Hester Stanhope. Abdul Medjuel el Mesrab, the younger brother to the sheik, agreed for a large sum of money to convey Lady Jane safely to Palmyra and back.

In many ways Medjuel was unique among his Arab brethren, for he exhibited none of their provincialism. He was fluent in several languages, had learned how to read and write, and had made himself an authority on desert history. A small, wiry man with jet black eyes and beard, he was darker than most of his tribe. He was probably in his early forties when he met Lady Jane.

One of the smaller tribes, numbering fewer than 100 tents, the Mesrabs usually traveled for safety with the Ressalin tribe with more than 500 tents. Even then they were dwarfed by such tribes as the Anazeh, which boasted more than 23,000 tents. The Mesrabs, a well-bred and courteous people, who fought only in self-defense and never stooped to looting caravans or holding travelers for ransom, were wealthy in horses and camels.

The negotiations concluded, Lady Jane set out for Palmyra with Medjuel and a band of his Mesrab Bedouins as her escort. As they traveled, she talked at length about her love for Saleh and hopes of settling in Syria. Such an exchange of intimate feelings between a European woman and a Bedouin was virtually unheard of in that day. Medjuel soon found himself increasingly attracted to this bold, self-confident Englishwoman who refused to stand on ceremony and was capable of relating to him as a human being without any of the prejudices of her class. Within a few days he had fallen in love and proposed. But she gently rejected him. He, after all, was already married and the father of several sons. And her heart was still full of Saleh.

The small caravan made its way toward Palmyra through a desert which had little in common with the sandy wastes of the Sahara. Great rifts abruptly scarred the land while spines of rock and shale scoured by the wind and winter rain loomed high above the plains. A sea of dried grasses covered the fine black soil, home to a variety of antelopes, wild asses, and boars.

One day a group of Bedouin raiders fell unexpectedly upon the caravan, howling loudly and shaking vicious-looking spears. Lady Jane's escort fled into the surrounding desert. Only Medjuel remained to defend her. He put up a fierce resistance and completely routed the attacking force. She was thoroughly impressed by his bravery. But it was Saleh whom she loved.

After her trip to Palmyra she still foresaw a future which included Saleh as her husband. She put her business affairs in order. Then she traveled to her lover's desert camp for a reunion. Once there, she was heartbroken to learn that he had never taken her promise to return seriously and had in her absence moved into his tent another woman, a beautiful eighteen-year-old Bedouin girl.

For the next year Lady Jane wandered fitfully around Syria. She joined one of the caravans traveling between Damascus and Baghdad, thinking that she would have one last trip before settling down in Damascus. But her heart was not in the adventure. She recorded in her journal the anniversary of her first meeting with Saleh: "This day last year I rode down to the Jordan and saw Saleh for the first time. Saleh who has had such a terrible, such a fatal effect on my life and may have still."

Her depression continued until her arrival at Hama, an ancient Hittite city that was now a center of Bedouin commerce. Like other Syrian cities, Hama stood with its back to the desert, the din of its bazaars lost in an immense silence beyond. Lady Jane found the desert—"the dear desert I am so fond of"—reassuring. Her thoughts turned increasingly to Medjuel, her companion on her Palmyra adventure. Hama was in the midst of Mesrab territory. Suddenly he appeared, bringing her a gift of a fine Arabian mare. The next day they rode together into the desert. Lady Jane now realized that Medjuel possessed all those qualities in a man for which she had searched for thirty years. She had spent her entire adult life "riding at breakneck speed along the wilder shores of love," in the words of Lesley Blanch, and she had finally reached her destination.

Medjuel was still very much in love. He had followed all her movements through the desert grapevine. And when he had learned that Saleh had taken another woman, Medjuel quickly divorced his own wife in the traditional Muslim manner, sending her home to her own people with all her dowry. He proposed a second time to Lady Jane. Without hesitation she accepted.

She hurried to Damascus to make all the appropriate arrangements. Richard Wood, the British consul there, strongly protested the proposed marriage. The Crimean War raged to the north. And the representative of an England that had opposed Florence Nightingale's nursing of wounded British troops as unseemly for a proper British woman could hardly have been expected to be supportive of a marriage which was without precedent in the Middle East. As far as Wood was concerned, Lady Jane was casting her lot with an uncivilized barbarian, a desert bandit who earned his living raiding caravans.

But she was undeterred. She had thought long and hard about the consequences. Such a marriage would destroy any chance for a reconciliation with her family, while placing her in possible danger—Bedouin life in the desert was full of uncertainties, and Bedouin wives often had to endure considerable abuse—but a willingness to sacrifice for love was as much a part of her nature as her need to love. She had never lost that youthful spirit which had kept her searching the world for an elusive ideal of the perfect lover. Time and time again she had thought she had found him, only to be disappointed. But with Medjuel Lady Jane sensed intuitively that he would not fail her.

On the other hand, he faced strong opposition toward the proposed marriage from his own tribesmen. She was, they argued, a foreigner, an infidel, and a woman beneath his class (Medjuel belonged to one of the four noblest desert families). Lady Jane first realized the intensity of the Mesrab hostility toward her when on a visit to his camp she accidentally dropped a rose and one of his kinsmen ground it into the dust with the heel of his foot, muttering angrily, "Hers."

A Turkish official in Homs married them in a Muslim ceremony. Before the marriage they made a pact. If Lady Jane did not satisfy him sexually, Medjuel would be free to take another wife, as allowed by Muslim tradition. But he was to do so secretly. In the twenty-six years of their marriage he never once took up that option.

For a time the couple lived in Homs, where Medjuel had a house. That first winter together he dispelled any doubts Lady Jane may have harbored that he had married her for her money. He left her for several months to accompany his tribe into the desert to find pasture for their flocks. She noted proudly in her journal: "The wish to send money to his brother, not from my purse, spurs him on."

She took advantage of his long absence in the desert to return to England, her first visit back in more than twenty years, to settle unfinished business matters and seek a reconciliation with her family. She arrived on December 19, 1856, a prodigal daughter finally come home. Throughout her stay she maintained a low profile. Only a handful of family members and close friends knew that she was back. She divided her time between her family in Tunbridge Wells and London, where she transacted business and stocked up on items that were unavailable in Syria. Her family rarely mentioned her marriage to Medjuel. The Indian Mutiny had erupted, and the newspapers were full of horror stories about atrocities committed against British soldiers and civilians. Racial prejudice ran high. Whites were whites. Blacks were blacks. An us-against-them mentality prevailed.

Lady Jane was still in England the following spring when she turned fifty. She wrote in her journal: "All the romance and poetry in life ought to be long since past and over, and here am I still with a beating and burning heart!"

There was little to hold her in England any longer. The changes that had developed upon the ascension of Victoria to the throne had been so profound and far-reaching that there was no longer a place there for a woman such as Lady Jane who lived her life for love. This was an age so squeamish about sex that it bowdlerized Bowdler's edition of Shakespeare and decreed the word *leg* unsuitable for use in polite society. (For fifty years horses broke only *limbs,* never *legs.*) In the Victorian house swarming with children, sex was the great secret, the skeleton in the parental closet. During Lady Jane's visit to England, Dr. William Acton published his textbook *The Function and Disorders of the Reproductive Organs,* in which he argued the medical orthodoxy of the day on women and sex: "I should say that the majority of women (happily for them) are not very much troubled with sexual feeling of any kind. What men are habitually, women are only exceptionally. . . . As a general rule, a modest woman seldom desires any sexual gratification for herself. She submits to her husband, but only to please him; and, but for the desire of maternity, would far rather be relieved from his attentions."

As a survivor from the age of Byron and Shelley, Lady Jane saw clearly that she was too free a spirit to be laced into the corset of Victorian morality. In London, with its cold fogs, smoke-filled skies, and muddy streets, she longed for the clean air and unobscured vistas of her desert world. Most of all, she yearned for Medjuel. She sailed in the spring for Beirut. She never saw England again. When she stepped ashore in Lebanon, Lady Jane felt that she had finally come home. So eager was she for her reunion with Medjuel that she rode through the night rather than lose a day. "With beating heart I arrived at Damascus," she noted in her journal. "He arrived, Medjuel, the dear, the adored one, and in that moment of happiness I forgot all else."

Her mind made up that her future lay in the Middle East and feeling reassured of Medjuel's love for her, she set about defining the perimeters of her new life. She and Medjuel agreed to spend six months of each year in the desert with his Bedouin tribe and the other six months in Damascus.

Probably no other Arab city provoked such a mixed response from nineteenth-century European visitors as Damascus. Unlike Constantinople, Beirut, or Cairo, it offered the foreign visitor a pure Arab experience undiluted by European influences. Its fundamentalist Muslim people were notorious for their intolerance toward all Christians. Their unflinching fanaticism made Damascus the most dangerous city in the Ottoman Empire for the European traveler.

Yet few Arab cities so charmed their European visitors as this ancient metropolis set 2,300 feet up in the mountains on the western margin of the great Syrian desert. Charles Addison called Damascus the "Paris of the East" after his 1835 visit there. "Damascus is a true oriental city and possesses much more character than Constantinople," he stated. "Here everything is eastern: there are no Frank quarters and . . . no fantastic aping of Frank dresses and Frank follies by the command of an innovating Sultan."

Old Testament references suggest that Damascus was regarded as ancient even in the ninth century B.C. Coeval with Ninevah, Ur, and Babylon, it alone survived into modern times. In 1857 the ground plan of Damascus had hardly changed since biblical times despite the ravages of sword and fire. The street called Straight— where Paul of Tarsus received back his sight—still cut through the center of town.

Lady Jane built a large house just beyond the city gates. Her biographer Margaret Schmidt describes it thusly:

> The ground floor of the house was purely Arabic [sic] with three wings enclosing a large courtyard. In the middle of the center wing was a *liwan,* or indoor-outdoor sitting room with one side open to the courtyard, furnished with traditional divans and oriental carpets. The windows of the house were masked with the magnificently carved wooden screens known as *mashrabiyas,* which created fascinating patterns of light and shadow on the walls and floors. Over the center wing were two bedrooms, another *liwan* and, overlooking the English garden behind the house, a very non-Arabic [sic] drawing room furnished in the expensively cluttered style of the great houses of Europe with cornices and ceiling, walls inlaid with mirrors, and windows draped with heavy damask. Into this room went Jane's precious piano, when it arrived from Paris. Here also were her crowded bookshelves, her easel, and her writing desk. . . . One of the most valuable ornaments in Jane's drawing room, however, was Arab—and priceless. This was a lamp from the Great Mosque at Mecca, on a pane of which the sultan

had scratched his seal—the symbol of Allah—as a token of his esteem. The entire house had a fascinating duality reflecting its unusual occupants—half English, half Arab.

Lady Jane's collection of house pets was unique in Damascus: Kurdish hounds, Norfolk turkeys, gazelles, partridges, turtle doves, a tame pelican, an assortment of camels, and more than 100 cats. Because Medjuel, like many Arabs of noble blood, bred Arabian horses, she built large stables in the English design in the rear of the house.

The excitement of the house in Damscus was nicely described by Emily Beaufort, later the Viscountess Strangford, who departed from there to visit Palmyra in the company of Medjuel: "Eleven dromedaries were on their knees, all roaring and growling and groaning, as if they were being killed, after the matter of dromedaries the moment they are requested to kneel and the whole time they are kneeling; all the camel-drivers and armed escort rushing about screaming and shouting—flocks of poultry at one side shrieking, gabbling, and cackling—pet gazelles were hiding in a corner—and a number of beautiful Arab mares were standing transfixed with astonishment at the unwonted crowd and noise."

When she went into the desert for the other six months of the year, Lady Jane left behind her European heritage and traveled with Medjuel as a Bedouin. "Jane Digby was more Bedouin than the Bedawi," Isabel Burton exclaimed in later years. She dyed her lovely chesnut hair jet black, out of respect for a Bedouin superstition that associated fair hair with the evil eye, and wore it in two braids that hung below her waist. She learned to wash her hair in camel urine because it killed lice, refreshed the scalp, stopped any itching, and gave the hair an attractive sheen. She donned the blue cotton gown of the other women in the Mesrab tribe and, like them, went barefoot. In their desert camp she performed all the tasks for Medjuel that any Bedouin woman was expected to do for her husband: setting up and taking down his black goat's hair tents, milking his camels ("dear useful animals" she called them), preparing his food, and washing his feet. She drew a line, however, at the Bedouin woman's habit of tattooing her lips, cheeks, nose, forehead, breasts, and belly.

Such actions quickly overcame the initial hostility of the Mesrab people to her marriage to Medjuel. They called her affectionately *Umm-el-Laban*, "mother of milk," because of the milky whiteness of her skin. She knew that the tribe had finally come to accept her as one of their own when she was delegated the responsibility for handling all the negotiations with the Europeans who wished to pay for Mesrab escorts through the desert to Palmyra.

The Bedouin world that Lady Jane entered was as alien to the European sensibility as a landscape on Mars. For the Bedouins, the moon was their protector, attracting the rain clouds, distilling their moisture into life-giving dew to nurture the plants on which their camels and goats fed, and bringing people comparative safety and refreshing sleep. On the other hand, the sun was the enemy, drying up the life-giving moisture, destroying all life, and making the Bedouins visible to their foes. The sun-moon cycles of the day were what mattered to the Bedouins. The division of time into hours, weeks, and months was largely unknown. For them the year started in autumn, when the moon finally broke the long drought of summer and the first signs of winter rain appeared.

November also marked the start of the Bedouins' annual treks across the desert in search of new pasture for their herds of camels and goats; these vast migrations might cover as many as 2,000 miles and involve thousands of people and tens of thousands of animals. The itinerary that the Mesrabs followed had remained unaltered for centuries. By February they had reached the southern boundary of their territory, a stretch of desert where they could always expect a bountiful crop of succulent plants. They arrived in time for the camels' calving and then, in late March, again moved slowly to the north, following the growth of the new grass. By May the water and grass were largely gone. Then the Mesrabs headed toward the towns. In many ways it was a pleasant pastoral life, and Lady Jane thoroughly enjoyed her winter months in the desert with her husband's tribe.

One aspect of Bedouin life, however, caused her enormous concern at first: the incessant tribal warfare. War was important to the

Bedouin man, giving him an opportunity to display his courage, cunning, and endurance. A Bedouin warrior tested himself in raids against the camps of neighboring tribes, riding in on horseback, firing his rifle, shaking his spear, and stealing as many camels and horses as possible. But the booty itself was never of much importance, for the Bedouin would often give it away without a second thought, sometimes to the wife of the very man he had just robbed. The policy of the Turkish officials was divide and conquer—that is, to keep the Bedouin tribes "wholesomely engaged in internecine war," as Lady Anne Blunt so aptly put it, so that they would never unite against their Turkish overlords.

In those early years Lady Jane fretted constantly about her husband's safety when he was away in the desert. (The Mesrab Bedouins had by then made Medjuel their sheik.) But as time passed and she began to think more like a Bedouin, she finally accepted, too, this aspect of her desert world. She provided the Mesrabs with the finest modern rifles and the fastest horses and camels her money could buy. (Her annual income was now £1,500, a sizable fortune.) In 1868 she noted with gusto in her journal: "A day never to be forgotten! Cannon and musketry was heard in the morning, and about [noon a] dozen Arab horsemen rushed into town with the too true news that Hassaim Bey had indeed attacked our camp with Ibn Merschid, and after pouring a volley of balls into our tents, had carried off all our camels, but, thank God, had killed none of our men."

(Much later, in 1873, when Jane was sixty-five, she rode into battle alongside her husband in a major conflict between the Saba and Rowalla Bedouins. The Rowalla Bedouins had usurped the traditional grazing lands of the Saba Bedouins. As allies by blood to the Saba people, the Mesrab Arabs were expected to help out. Shortly after the fighting erupted, Turkish troops suddenly and unexpectedly intervened on the side of the Rowalla Bedouins. Both the Saba and Mesrab forces were routed and suffered heavy casualties. An erroneous report circulated that Lady Jane Digby, the *Umm-el-Laban* of the Mesrab Bedouins, was one of the slain. Word was quickly flashed to Beirut and thence to London, Paris, and other European capitals. Lengthy obituaries, most unfriendly, became the order of the day.)

A major crisis developed in 1860, when the sectarian violence that had wreaked such havoc in Lebanon finally reached Damascus. The city had long been notorious for its hostility toward non-Muslims. Damascus was the last major city in the Ottoman Empire to accept foreign consuls, largely because of its sacred importance as the annual assembly point for tens of thousands of pilgrims for the northern hajj to Mecca.

The traditional hostility toward Christians was further inflamed by the reforms introduced by Ibrahim Pasha, much as it had been in Lebanon. Anti-Christian feelings swelled as a result of the reluctance of the Muslims to give up their traditional superiority and to accept the Christians as their equals. Under Egyptian rule Christians for the first time enjoyed such privileges as building churches wherever they wanted, carrying arms, and riding on horses through the streets. The Christians in Damascus quickly flaunted their new liberties, carrying crosses in public processions, hanging and ringing church bells, celebrating religious feasts in public, and even insulting and attacking Muslims on occasion.

On July 9, 1860, anti-Christian violence erupted in Damascus in an extension of the warfare that had racked Lebanon the month before. In one day some 5,500 Christian men, women, and children were murdered, and most of the Christian houses, churches, and convents sacked and burned. Local authorities under the leadership of the Turkish pasha Ahmed took few measures to check the fanatical spirit or to prevent anti-Christian demonstrations. Large numbers of heavily armed Lebanese Druze militia were permitted to enter Damascus. When the first outbreaks of anti-Christian violence occurred, Ahmed sent as guards for the Christian quarter of the city a regiment of Muslim soldiers who had earlier been involved in anti-Christian riots. There was probably collusion between Ahmed and a number of local Muslim leaders to punish the Christians.

The incident that triggered the massacre involved three Muslim youths who were arrested for trampling upon crosses and made to go in chains and sweep the Christian quarter. On their way an angry mob formed, protesting the punishment and demanding the freedom of the trio. Within minutes the cry went up to kill the Christians.

Shops closed. Hundreds of Muslims returned to their homes for guns, swords, axes, spears, knives, and weapons of every description. The Turkish soldiers stationed at the gates to the Christian quarter opened them wide and urged the mob inside. Those without arms were turned away and told they could not enter and loot until they had weapons. The mob surged into the Christian quarter, routing the terrified inhabitants from their houses and shops. Christian women were raped in the streets, the men forcibly circumcised. Those not slaughtered on the spot were often locked into churches and then burned alive.

Colonel Charles Churchill, a British officer in the area at the time, left a vivid description of the horrors of that day: "By sunset the whole Christian quarter was in a blaze, the flames waving and mounting, in huge billowy surges, like a sea of fire; while in the midst were seen distracted crowds of women, some carrying infants in their arms, shrieking and rushing along the flat roofs, and springing from house to house. Many lost their footing and fell, breaking their arms or legs, or perishing miserably. . . . In whatever direction the affrighted fugitives turned, they were met by steel and fire. Nothing short of a complete and overwhelming destruction seemed to await them."

The violence was not just directed toward the native Christian population. All the foreign consulates, except the British, were burned. The Dutch consul was murdered in the streets, and the American consul severely wounded. Few Christians, foreign or Syrian, made a resistance. One exception was the Greek consul, an excellent marksman, who survived by retreating to the roof of his house with a rifle, a trunk filled with cartridges, and a bottle of raki. He spent the afternoon drinking, singing, and banging away happily at every Muslim he saw, until the streets about were littered with the bodies of dozens of aba-clad figures.

The hero of the day was Abd el Kader, a celebrated emir of Algeria whose exploits were legendary. From 1832 to 1847 he had led a holy war against the French, holding at bay a half dozen of their best generals before he finally surrendered. The French took him as a prisoner of war to Paris, where they treated him with chivalrous generosity. After 1852 they allowed Abd el Kader to go into exile in Damascus. When the old warrior learned of the slaughter taking place, he provided hundreds of fleeing Christians with a sanctuary on the grounds of his heavily fortified house. (Later that year the French government awarded Abd el Kader the Legion of Honor for his heroic efforts that day.)

Lady Jane's house was situated in the Muslim section of town. She was keenly aware of the anti-Christian violence ravaging other parts of Syria but fervently prayed that Damascus would be spared. "The Druzes and Christians are fighting dreadfully," she wrote in early July. "Should war really break out in Damascus, may strength and faith be given to us who trust in the Lord who is stronger than all evil-doers."

Medjuel, however, placed his faith in his Mesrab warriors and stationed several dozen heavily armed Bedouins at strategic points inside their compound in case the violence should threaten them. Lady Jane's position as the Christian wife of a devout Muslim was, of course, well known throughout Damascus. But such was the respect in which she was held by the Muslim community that the mobs, as they passed by her house on the way to the Christian quarter, merely stopped to ask Medjuel if he needed additional help in protecting his wife and household. Nor was she harmed when she entered the city to save as many Christians as she could find.

On July 16 news of the terrible massacre reached Paris. The French government immediately ordered 7,000 troops to Lebanon. The other European powers were equally outraged. Britain dispatched several warships. Fearing European intervention on behalf of the Christians, the Turkish authorities moved quickly to quell the riots. By mid-August 111 Turkish officers and soldiers, who had been implicated in the massacres, had been shot, while the pasha Ahmed and 56 other public officials were hanged. As a final punishment the entire male population of Damascus that was eligible for conscription was forcibly recruited into the Turkish Army.

The 1860 upheaval in Damascus was never repeated, and the city slowly recovered. In the meantime, Lady Jane's marriage prospered. On her birthday in 1869 she confessed in her journal: "Sixty-two years of age, and an impetuous romantic girl of seventeen cannot exceed me in ardent, passionate feelings!" She never ceased to dread separations from her husband, those times when he was in the desert without her, attending to the business of his tribe. Once Sheik Faris el Maziad led a raid on the stables at their house in Homs, stole the pick of her horses, and rode them through the streets, defying the Mesrabs to get them back. Medjuel went after El Maziad. For more than a week she had no word from him. Suddenly he reappeared in Damascus, and she wrote in her journal: "Medjuel returns! Ah, such are the moments when one forgets all the sorrows and enemies and past months of anxiety, in the great bliss of meeting him again."

On another occasion Lady Jane received word that Medjuel was stricken with a terrible fever. She hurried to the Mesrab camp and found her husband nearly dead from what appeared to be cholera. She nursed him carefully and treated him with European medicines. Yet his condition worsened. When all seemed hopeless, she yielded to the pleas of his kin to let them try traditional Bedouin medicine. Two tribesmen held the feverish Medjuel down, while another applied a red-hot iron rod four times to his skull. His flesh hissed when the brand touched his skin, and his hair flamed. Sweat poured from Medjuel's body. His fever broke the following day, and he began a rapid recovery.

One day Medjuel sent Lady Jane an urgent message to come to Homs. His favorite son, Schebibb, was seriously ill. Within an hour she was on her way. This time not even the Bedouin medicine could help. The boy died soon afterward, plunging Medjuel into despair. She was helpless to comfort him. She attended the Muslim funeral ritual. "Afterwards a sheep was sacrificed and given to the poor; the old sheiks chanted to his memory for the last time—and all is over!" she wrote later.

Throughout these years Lady Jane received a steady stream of distinguished guests at her Damascus home. In 1871 she entertained Lord Redesdale. Although he was quite taken with her, Medjuel disappointed him, not conforming to his preconceptions of what a great Bedouin chief should look like. "As a matter of fact, he was

233

quite an ordinary and common-looking little man," Lord Redesdale wrote later. "Nevertheless, she seemed very fond and proud of him, and evidently in this wild nomad life between the desert and Damascus, she had found a happy haven of rest after the adventures of her stormy youth."

Such condescension was, unfortunately, all too common on the part of English visitors to Damascus. Once Lady Jane entertained the wife of a local British missionary. She had just redecorated her house and took her guest on a tour through the rooms. The woman applauded Lady Jane's exquisite taste in furniture and art and then blurted out: "All this for a barbarian!"

"But he really isn't a barbarian," Lady Jane replied in mock astonishment. "Why, he has already learned how to use a knife and fork!"

Of all her European visitors, the one with whom she felt the closest spiritual kinship was Richard Burton. He arrived in Damascus on December 31, 1869, with his wife, Isabel, to be the new British consul. It was appropriate that he and Lady Jane Digby should meet and become friends. Had she been born a man, her career might well have resembled Burton's.

Burton was at a delicate phase in his career. He was probably the leading authority in Britain on Africa and one of Europe's top linguists. In late 1864 the Foreign Office, not quite knowing what to do with him, had buried him in Santos, Brazil, a village in a mangrove swamp some 230 miles south of Rio de Janeiro. The place was a pesthole, fever-ridden and infested with insects and snakes. Burton remained in Santos for eighteen months and then resigned the consulship, citing boredom as his reason. Afterward there was a 1,500-mile trip down the São Francisco, portions of which had never been explored, on a raft made of two enormous canoes lashed together. In 1868 Burton had traveled to Paraguay to visit the battlefields of a war that country had waged against its neighbors for four years with catastrophic results. (By 1870 when the war finally ended, more than 1 million were dead out of a population of 1.3 million.) In February 1869 he learned that he had been appointed to the consulship in Damascus.

For Burton the appointment was a fulfillment of an old dream. He was eager to return to the desert, the scene of his triumph seventeen years before, when he reached Mecca. The scholar in Burton was impatient to be back at work researching a new translation with scholarly notes of the *Arabian Nights* with particular attention to Arab sexual life and customs. And he was heartily sick of South America. "The New World, which had been my latest scene of action, wearies with its want of history, of association, and consequently of romance," Burton wrote in *Unexplored Syria*, the book that grew out of his experiences in Damascus. "The Old world of Palestine is as oppressively old as the New is uncomfortably new; it is over-ripe, while its rival is yet raw. . . . And if the present of the New World is bald and tame, that of the Syrian Old World is, to those who know it well, perhaps a little too fiery and exciting."

This time, unlike his trip to Mecca in 1853, Burton was not traveling alone. He had taken a wife. Isabel Arundell Burton was every bit an Orientalist as her husband. When she was an impressionable young girl, she had confessed in her diary to a craving for "Gypsies, Bedouin Arabs, and everything Eastern and mystic; and especially a wild and lawless life."

Few women in Victorian England were as obsessed as Isabel Burton. She knew from an early age that she must have two things in her life or she would never be happy: Richard Burton and the East. The two blurred together, so that in her mind they stood interchangeable, the one representing the other. She knew only that she must have them both. So with the single-mindedness of a runaway locomotive, she set out to marry her Richard.

Isabel Arundell first met Burton in Boulogne in September 1850, when she was a tall, blue-eyed girl of nineteen. She and her sister were out walking when Burton approached from the opposite direction. Isabel noted the moment in her diary: "He looked at me as though he read me through and through in a moment, and started a little. I was completely magnetized, and when he had got a little distance away I turned to my sister, and whispered to her, 'That man will marry me.' "

The next day the two sisters went for another walk along the same route. Burton was waiting for them. He asked Isabel if he might see her. Flustered, she refused, insisting that her mother would never permit it, and then hurried away. But she was already in love. As she remembered the moment later in her biography of her husband, "I could think of no more at the moment. But I stole a look at him, and met his gypsy eyes. . . . [After that day] I never lost an opportunity of seeing him, when I could not be seen; and I used to turn red and pale, hot and cold, dizzy and faint, sick and trembling, and my knees used nearly to give way under me."

Burton seemed to her a fulfillment of her life's destiny. Years before she had visited a Gypsy camp near her home in Essex. The tribe had adopted the name of Burton. A Gypsy woman named Hagar had predicted her future: "You will cross the sea, and be in the same town with your Destiny and know it not. Every obstacle will rise up against you, and such a combination of circumstances, that it will require all your courage, energy, and intelligence to meet them. . . . You will bear the name of our tribe, and be right proud of it. You will be as we are, but far greater than we. Your life is all wandering, change, and adventure. One soul in two bodies in life or death, never long apart."

While still a young girl, Isabel described in her diary her perfect husband:

> My ideal is about six feet in height; he has not an ounce of fat on him; he has broad and muscular shoulders, a powerful, deep chest; he is a Hercules of manly strength. He has black hair, a brown complexion, a clever forehead, sagacious eyebrows, large, black wondrous eyes—those strange eyes you dare not take yours from off them—with long lashes. He is a soldier and a *man*; he is accustomed to command and be obeyed. . . . He is a gentleman in every sense of the word . . . and of course he is an English-

man. . . . Such a man only will I wed. I love this myth of my girlhood—for myth it is—next to God; and I look to the star that Hagar the gypsy said was the star of my destiny.

Burton with his "questing panther eyes" obsessed Isabel from their first meeting. She pursued him with the fierce determination of a cheetah chasing down its prey on the Serengeti Plains. Sometime after her meeting with Burton, Isabel wrote to her mother: "I wish I were a man. If I were, I would be Richard Burton; but, being only a woman, I would be Richard Burton's wife." He would become her proxy; through Burton, she would live out her life's destiny.

Isabel was an incurable romantic. Burton's biographer Fawn Brodie writes of her that "she lived by myth, knowing it to be myth, and used the myth as a weapon to keep herself inviolable. But having designed an ideal as a bulwark to keep herself from being pushed into a tawdry marriage, she stumbled upon her ideal—this tall, dark, well-muscled stranger, this soldier-adventurer who seemed the very essence of masculinity, and who miraculously bore the name the very stars had foretold would one day be her own."

Like Lady Hester Stanhope before her and T. E. Lawrence after her, Isabel Burton was driven by an inner compulsion coupled with a firm belief in destiny that conspired with outer events to propel her onto the stage of the Middle East, where she knew her most important life's drama would be acted out. Her life, like theirs, possessed the inevitability of ancient Greek drama.

Marriage to Burton, however, still lay in the distant future. There was a four-year separation while he went off to Mecca, India, and Somaliland. Then they were engaged and apart once more for his important expeditions into East Africa in search of the headwaters of the Nile River. They were finally married on January 22, 1861, in London.

Now, nine years later, the Burtons were in Damascus, and the second of her life's dreams was about to be fulfilled. Always the Orientalist, she enthused on the eve of their departure: "My destination was Damascus, the dream of my childhood. I should follow the footsteps of Lady Mary Wortley Montagu, Lady Hester Stanhope, and the Princess de la Tour d'Auvergne, that trio of famous European women who lived of their own choice a thoroughly Eastern life, and of whom I looked to make a fourth. I am to live among Bedouin Arab chiefs; I shall smell the desert air; I shall have tents, horses, weapons, and be free."

The Burtons settled into a house beyond the city walls next to a mosque, joining a small European community, which consisted largely of consular, missionary, and medical people. His duties as consul required that he keep a watchful eye over the thirty or so people under British protection, gather intelligence on Turkish intrigues, assist whatever British travelers passed through the area, and arrange trade agreements.

Within a fairly short time Burton was friendly with every Arab chief in the city and had made himself privy to a variety of political intrigues. On several occasions he dressed in his old disguise and passed as an Arab in the bazaars. Isabel Burton noted with pride: "He was the sole example of one not born a Muslim, who have performed the Hajj, could live with Muslims in perfect friendship after. They considered him *persona grata*—something more civilized than the common run of Franks—they called him Hadji Abdullah, and treated him as one of themselves."

Burton was ecstatic to be back in the Middle East once again and "face to face with the difficulties of Arabic; of strange weights and measures; of new ideas; of outlandish manners and customs, which took me back half-a-dozen centuries." More important, he had come home to adventure. The constant challenge and excitement of exploring the less accessible parts of Syria during that first year in Damascus revitalized him. Recalling those times in late November 1871, when he was back in London at a meeting of the Anthropological Institute, Burton boasted: "My post was one of great difficulty and of greater dangers. I [was] shot at by some forty men, who, fortunately, could not shoot straight; I [was] wounded on another occasion; and lastly . . . I [was] pursued by a party of about three hundred Bedawin assassins, placed upon our track by [the] Governor-general of Syria."

On April 5, 1870, Burton made a "holiday excursion" to Palmyra, every bit as dangerous as when Lady Hester Stanhope had traveled there some sixty years before. He cataloged the dangers—the desert heat, the lack of water, the risk of attack by Bedouins, and forced marches at night—and complained about the enormous expense of hiring a large Mesrab escort. He spent five days at Palmyra, where he undertook archaeological excavations in an ancient cemetery and unearthed several skeletons, fragments of statuary, and other artifacts. Burton was distinctly unimpressed with most of the Bedouin warriors he encountered: "Thirty Englishmen, mounted on good horses and armed with breechloaders and revolvers, could, I believe, sweep the whole desert from end to end."

Isabel Burton, for her part, slipped comfortably into the role of the wife of Richard Burton. "Our lives [in Damascus] were wild, romantic, and solemn," she wrote later. Fancying herself a reincarnation of Lady Hester Stanhope, she dressed in Arab costumes whenever she ventured into Damascus. On occasion she was taken as Burton's son. "It all *sounds* indecent, but all Arab clothes are so baggy and draping that it matters little whether or not you are dressed as a man or woman," she insisted. She spent long hours lounging in the Turkish baths or visiting the harems, entertaining the women there with anecdotes about her social life back in Britain.

Generally, however, Isabel Burton never went beyond being a mere poseur. When she was about Damascus, no one ever took her for anything but what she was: a middle-aged British woman dressed in Arab clothes. She played the part without ever grasping the subtleties and never managed to shed the prejudices of her class and age. On occasion she displayed extraordinary insensitivity. Once she took Lord Redesdale on a tour of a mosque and, upon finding a Muslim at prayer, interrupted his devotions and demanded that he move out of her way.

Professing a deep interest in the local Arabs, she nonetheless always saw them as social inferiors no matter how highly ranked in their own culture they may have been. Her snobbishness was nowhere more apparent than in her attitude toward Lady Jane Digby's husband, Medjuel. Even though she regarded Lady Jane as her closest friend in Damascus, she could still write later:

When I first saw her, she was a most beautiful woman. . . . She blackened her eyes with kohl, and lived in a curiously untidy manner. But otherwise she was not in the least extraordinary at Damascus. But what was incomprehensible to me was how she could have given up all she had in England to live with that dirty little black—or nearly so—husband. . . . I could understand her running away with Schwarzenberg; but the contact with that black skin I could not understand. Her *Shaykh* was very dark—darker than a Persian, and much darker than an Arab usually is. All the same, he was a very intelligent and charming man in any light but as a husband. That made me shudder.

Lady Jane, however, left Isabel Burton awestruck. She wrote later:

There was nothing Lady Ellenborough could not do. She spoke nine languages perfectly, and could read and write in them. Her letters were splendid; if on business there was never a word too much, nor a word too little. . . . She was honored and respected as queen of her tribe, wearing one blue garment, her beautiful hair in two long plaits down to the ground, milking the camels, serving her husband, preparing his food, giving him water to wash his hands and face, sitting on the floor and washing his feet, giving him his coffee, his sherbet. . . . She looked splendid in Oriental dress, and if you saw her in the bazaar you would have said she was not more than thirty-four years of age.

Burton, too, was often at the house of Lady Jane Digby. He thought her, "out and out the cleverest woman [I] ever met." She proved an invaluable source of information on the sexual customs of Arab women in the harems, which Burton included in the notes to his translation of the *Arabian Nights*.

Burton's arrival in Damascus in late 1869 coincided with the opening of the Suez Canal. His two years there brought forcefully home to him the realization that British diplomatic and political interest had shifted abruptly from Asia Minor to Egypt. (After he left Damascus, the consulate was downgraded to a vice-consulate.)

Burton's stay in Damascus came to a sorry end because he was recalled to London in disgrace. He had meddled constantly in local politics, provoking the wrath of Turkish officials in Constantinople, who complained to London. Further, he was none too discreet about expressing his preference for local Muslims over the Jews and Christians. Matters came to a bitter head when Burton attacked Jewish bankers under British protection for charging usurious rates of 60 percent on their loans and then pressuring him to collect their money from the ruined Arabs. The Foreign Office told him flatly that interference in the projects of Jewish financiers was not part of a consul's business. In the meantime, Isabel Burton, an ardent Roman Catholic, had been busy proselytizing within the Muslim community. The local Turkish authorities also complained to London that there had been a disquieting number of converts to Catholicism since the Burtons had arrived in Damascus.

On August 16, 1871, Burton received a letter from the London Foreign Office. It read in part: "I regret to have now to inform you that the complaints which I have received from the Turkish Government in regard to your recent conduct and proceedings render it impossible that I should allow you to continue to perform any consular functions in Syria."

The recall was totally unexpected and a severe blow to Burton. He set off by horseback immediately for Beirut, leaving behind a note for his wife: "I am recalled. Pay, pack, and follow at convenience."

Isabel Burton, too, was crushed. "O! how shall I tear the East out of my heart?" she cried desperately in her journal. As she packed their belongings, scores of people from the Muslim, Jewish, and Christian communities dropped in to offer their regrets. On her last evening in Damascus she went for a final ride into the desert to visit a Bedouin camp. There she attended to a boy dying of a fever.

"Do you wish to be with Allah?" she inquired.

"Yes," he told her. "But how can I?"

"Are you sorry for all the times you have been naughty and said bad words?" she asked him.

"Yes," he replied. "If I get well, I will do better, and be kinder to grandmother."

"I thought that was enough," Isabel Burton remembered later. "I parted his thick matted hair, and, kneeling, I baptized him from the flask of water I always carried at my side." The next day she set out for Beirut to join her husband.

The final years of Lady Jane Digby's life passed quietly. In 1877 she turned seventy. She no longer had the stamina to go with her husband's people on their long winter migrations through the desert. That year the worst Bedouin war in recent history broke out between the Shammar and Anazeh peoples. All the smaller tribes, including the Mesrabs, were involved. For the first time in years Lady Jane was unable to ride at her husband's side when he went into combat.

Even after she had stopped going into the desert, she continued to be Damascus's most famous resident. European travelers to the city eagerly sought an audience with her. Sir Edwin Pears, who spent almost half a century in the Middle East, visited her in 1876. He wrote later in his book *Forty Years in Constantinople:*

I found her a close observer, an excellent talker, with keen flashes of insight and wit, and, what interested me most of all, with an experience of harem life of which she spoke frankly, of quite exceptional character. She told me many stories of her Eastern experience. On one occasion, by a mistake, the whole of her husband's trible flocked into Damascus and took possession of her house, sleeping on the stairs, the landings, and anywhere they could lie down. She was the only woman in the house. . . . I intimated that she must have been alarmed with the crowd of these wild fellows. She immediately retorted that she was greatly alarmed, but not . . . at anything which her husband's tribe would do. Her fear was that some of the many Turkish soldiers near her house would make some remark derogatory to her, in which case, she said, not a Turk in the neighborhood would have been left alive. On mentioning this story to my friend, he said that he entirely believed it because the attachment of the Bedouins to their chieftain's wife was passionate, and each would have been ready to die for her.

Soon after her seventy-third birthday Medjuel brought her a present of the most beautiful horse she had ever seen. "If he does not suit me, I shall never get a horse that does," she told him. Her passion for her husband continued unabated until the end. "It is now a month and twenty days since Medjuel last slept with me!" she fretted in her journal after more than twenty-five years of marriage. "What can be the reason?" Apparently she never considered that her husband, too, had grown old and perhaps grown beyond physical passion.

In July 1881 she fell ill with dysentery. Medjuel watched helplessly as his wife grew weaker each day. None of the doctors could help her. On August 11 she died quietly in her sleep.

Lady Jane's body was buried in the Protestant cemetery in Damascus. Her minister explained to Medjuel that as her chief mourner he must ride in a carriage behind the hearse. He had never before attended a Christian burial service, and the ritual struck him as bizarre. But because she had been with him to so many Muslim funerals, Medjuel felt strongly that he owed his wife's memory this.

The funeral procession slowly made its way through the streets of Damascus. The walls of the carriage closed in upon Medjuel, suffocating him. Finally he could take it no more. He leaped from the carriage and fled, much to the embarrassment of the European mourners. Riding his wife's favorite horse, he returned just as Lady Jane's coffin was being lowered into the open grave. Afterward he rode silently out of Damascus into the desert to sacrifice a favorite camel, as was the Bedouin custom when a wife died.

Perhaps the most fitting epitaph for Jane came from her friend Richard Burton. "Lady Jane Digby el Mesrab," he once said, "was a woman whose life's poetry never sank to prose."

Divine Wind:
The Horse of the Desert

In 1844 the British traveler Eliot Warburton was much impressed by the Arabian horses he saw on his visit to the Middle East. He called them all "noble animals, . . . no less remarkable for their chivalrous dispositions than their strength and endurance: gallant, yet docile; fiery, yet gentle; full of mettle, yet patient as a camel." In Damascus Warburton was deeply moved by a story he heard about a French officer, a horse fancier, who once met a Bedouin riding a beautiful horse. The Frenchman decided that he absolutely had to have the animal and so made "its poor proprietor" a generous offer. To his surprise, it was immediately refused. When the Turkish pasha learned of this, he ordered the Bedouin to yield up his horse to the French friend. "With tears in his eyes, the poor man dismounted from his loved companion and kissed him on the forehead," Warburton wrote in *The Crescent and the Cross.* "Then, suddenly exclaiming, 'Thou has been the friend of the free, thou shalt never be the servant of the slave!' he shot the animal dead."

The oldest breed of horse in the world and famous for its strength, beauty, endurance, and long life, the Arabian has long been a universal choice among horse breeders eager to improve their herds. In the popular imagination the legendary horse is as much a part of the romantic fantasy of Arabia as its Bedouin owner, the perfect warrior united with his perfect steed riding at full gallop through a landscape of rolling dunes and ruins of ancient cities. For more than a century many in Europe firmly believed that somewhere in the vast wilderness of Arabia existed the ideal horse, fine-boned and swift, a horse of such excellence that its Arab masters refused even to show it to an infidel.

The horse occupied an almost mystical position in Bedouin society. "Love for the horse flows in Arabic blood," observed General Melchior Josèph Eugène Daumas, a major nineteenth-century French scholar on the Arabian horse. "The noble animal is a comrade-in-arms and the friend of the chieftain; . . . he is praised in verses, he is eulogized in conversation. . . . Among the Arabic people everything is directed toward cultivating love for the horse; religion makes it a duty, as the unquiet life, the ceaseless struggles, and the immense distance to be covered in a country where there are absolutely no means of rapid transportation, make the horse an absolute necessity."

In Bedouin society the possession of a thoroughbred mare always conferred upon its owner enormous prestige as an indisputable symbol of power. The horse served as inspiration for some of the greatest Arab poetry. One sage insisted:

> Paradise on earth is found on the back
> Of a good horse;
> In the study of good books, or
> Between the breasts of a woman.

Scores of Arab proverbs center on the horse:

Happiness in this world, rich booty, and eternal reward are attached to the horse's forelock.

An evil spirit cannot enter a tent where a purebred horse is kept.

He who forgets the beauty of horses for that of women will not prosper.

Horses are birds without wings.

When someone cannot comply with all his religious duties, let him keep a purebred horse for God's sake and all his sins will be absolved.

Money spent on horses is, in the eyes of God, like giving alms.

The martyrs of the Holy War shall find in Paradise horses made of rubies, and they shall fly at their master's whim.

The high status accorded the horse in Arab society reflected the critical role it played in the lives of the Arabs of the desert. A man's choice of a horse often meant the difference between a great warrior and a good one, between a free man and a captive. The harsh conditions of the desert environment required toughness and endurance in a horse. The Bedouins bred their horses to endure long rides across hot deserts, to go entire days without water, and to eat whatever was available, not just grass and grain. Arabian horses have been known to cross more than 100 miles of desert in a single day. And in the eighth century the horses carried the Muslim armies out of the Arabian Peninsula and allowed them to conquer an empire that reached from India in the east to Spain in the west.

The Arabian horse in the desert was never the beautifully groomed and well-fed animal we find in today's stables. In the Bedouin camps the horses were uncombed, dirty, long-haired, gaunt, and miserable-looking creatures. Grooming was unknown in the desert. Only the trained eye could detect the bone and muscle structure that denoted a truly superior breed. Lady Anne Blunt, who ran the Crabbet Arabian Stud in Sussex, understood this when in 1879 she and her husband visited the celebrated stables of the emir Muhammad ibn Rashid in northern Arabia. "As [the horses] stand there in the yard, slovenly and unkempt, they have little of that air of high breeding one would expect," she wrote. "It requires considerable imagination to look upon them as indeed the *ne plus ultra* of breeding in Arabia. We made the mistake, too, of judging horses by condition, for, mounted and in motion, these at once became transfigured."

The Arabian horse has long enjoyed a reputation for thriving on human companionship. "The Bedouin horse is extremely good-tempered, without any viciousness, and more the friend than the slave of his rider," John Lewis Burckhardt observed in *Notes on the Bedouins and Wahabys*. One reason for this tameness, he thought, was that the Bedouins never allowed a horse at birth to fall upon the ground. Instead, "they receive it in their arms and so cherish it for several hours, occupied in washing and stretching its tender limbs and caressing it as they would a baby."

In the West the horse is either a luxury or a work animal. But for the Bedouin the horse was a family friend. He treated a young foal much as he did his sons, assigning it a place in his tent to sleep and feeding it camel's milk. The Bedouin welcomed even his adult horses into his tent to escape the fierce sun at midday or the cold at night.

A host of superstitions grew up around the markings on a horse. Two lines of hair growing together on its chest acted as a lucky charm for the rider, so that he would never come to harm. The Bedouins believed that any horse with a star on its right neck was destined to die in combat. A star on the shank, on the other hand, meant that the owner's wife would prove unfaithful. Evil markings could cut a horse's value by two-thirds.

The horse was the favorite animal of God, whom He had created before people. "God created the horse from the wind, as He created Adam from clay," wrote Abd el Kader, the great nineteenth-century Arab general and scholar. "He said to the South Wind: 'I want to make a creature out of you. Condense.' And the wind condensed. . . . [Then God said:] 'You shall be lord of all the other animals. Men shall follow you wherever you go; you shall be as good for pursuit as for flight; you shall fly without wings; riches shall be on your back and fortune shall come through your mediation.' Then He put on the horse the mark of glory and happiness—a white mark in the middle of the forehead."

Understanding that the horse would play a major role in future religious wars, the Prophet Muhammad made its care a special obligation of Muslims. "Who feeds and looks after a horse for the triumph of religion is making a magnificent loan to God," he told his followers. Muhammad shrewdly mixed religion with the difficult art of the breeding and training of horses and thus caused the Arabian horse to multiply and be perfected. Thus, from Muhammad's time forward the breeding of horses became an obsession with the Arabs, who sought, in the name of Allah, to improve their stock. Bloodlines were carefully chronicled in oral tradition, sometimes extending back hundreds of years.

God said: "The horse shall be cherished by all my [followers]; he shall be the despair of those who do not obey my laws, and I will not place upon his back any but men who adore me." Muhammad thus prohibited the sale of horses to all infidels under penalty of death and damnation. The emir Abd el Kader summarily executed all Arabs convicted of selling horses to Christians.

In September 1863 Carlo Guarmani received a summons to travel to Paris from the director general of the Imperial Stud of Napoleon III. For twenty years the Italian had served as a consul in Jerusalem. Fluent in Arabic, he had journeyed extensively in disguise among the Bedouin tribes of western Syria, buying horses, which he then sold for a high profit to eager breeders in Europe. A contemporary, who had observed with astonishment Guarmani's activities in Syria, enthusiastically recommended his services to his European superiors:

> Guarmani is gifted with an adventurous spirit, high courage, and a thorough knowledge of the Arab tongue. He frequently lives a nomadic life. Inured to fatigue and hardships, thoroughly conversant with local usages, dressed as a Bedawin and mounted on horseback, he penetrates far into the desert. There he spends long days living in a tent, studying the Arab horse, and becoming so well acquainted with the various tribes that I fully believe him to be the only European able to scour the desert without risk. He is as fully acquainted with the cunning as with the ingenuity of the

Bedawin. He selects with great knowledge and buys shrewdly splendid stallions. Even I was amazed on beholding some of his horses, and still more amazed on learning the price. I feel I can assert without fear of being mistaken that any government which succeeds in making its own the truly exceptional gifts and knowledge which this young man has been shown to possess would be rendering a signal service to its country.

The result of this praise was Guarmani's meeting with the director general of the Imperial Stud. But the French emperor did not want Syrian horses. For some years enormous interest among European breeders had been building in the Najd in central Arabia, a legendary region celebrated for centuries as the home of the finest Arabian horses. The director general made Guarmani an offer. In exchange for a large sum of money, would he do what no European had ever done before—penetrate the Najd in disguise and buy horses for His Majesty's Imperial Stud? The Italian accepted. Soon afterward he received a similar offer from King Victor Emmanuel II in Italy.

In late January 1864 a heavily armed Guarmani, dressed as an Arab, set out from Jerusalem on his mission for the two European kings. In his new identity he was Khalid Agha—a Turk, a Muslim, and the master of the horse to the pasha in Damascus on a mission to buy horses. "I estimated my journey as a distinctly dangerous undertaking," Guarmani wrote later. "Indeed, it was judged an impossible one by all those who had lived for years in the East."

Guarmani traveled southward from Jerusalem through territory that was largely unvisited by Europeans. He was welcomed with typical Bedouin hospitality by the various tribes he met along the way. In a camp of Beni Sakhr Bedouins he joined a group of hunters in pursuit of a leopard. They tracked the beast to its den. The big cat tried desperately to escape. But one of the Bedouins impaled it through the neck with a lance. The wounded leopard was brought back to camp, where it served "as a plaything for the children and a subject of curiosity to the women" until it finally died.

Guarmani and a Beni Sakhr guide set out on camels for Taima,

350 miles to the south, and arrived there just eight days later. He learned that the entire Najd was in a state of severe turmoil. Faisal ibn Saud, its ruler, had declared war on the Ataiba Bedouins, a powerful tribe inhabiting the northwestern desert. To make matters worse, the emir Tallal ibn Rashid of Hail was involved in a war against Rowalla Bedouins to the north. The situation looked bleak, and Guarmani soon found himself entangled in the feuds and intrigues of rival tribes. Sheik Rajiia of the Walad Ali Bedouins received him warily, believing him to be a Turkish spy, and refused to allow the Italian to see his fine herd of horses.

On February 29 Guarmani arrived in the oasis village of Khaibar, located on the edge of a lava field in one of the most inhospitable parts of the Arabian Peninsula. The town's entire population was black, descendants of slaves once owned by local Bedouins who had themselves died from smallpox.

Guarmani next spent three days at Jabal Alam in an Ataiba Bedouin encampment numbering more than 1,000 tents. They were preparing for combat with Abdullah ibn Saud of Riyadh. Guarmani calculated that his chances were better with the Ataiba forces than alone, so he petitioned their chief, Maflak ibn Sfuk, for permission to accompany them. Early one morning the Ataiba Bedouins broke camp and marched eastward. It was a vast procession headed by 200 horsemen, while behind came the women, children, flocks, and at the rear rode 700 riflemen on camels. They made a forced march for four days. Constant skirmishing with the Saudi forces soon took their toll; the Ataibas lost all their flocks plus 60 dead and 200 wounded. They retreated quickly back to Jabal Alam.

Maflak ordered his people to take up defensive positions in a rocky gorge, and there they made a stand against the vastly superior Saudi forces. The first major attack came on March 14 and was repelled. The next day the Saudis attacked again. Guarmani estimated their numbers at more than 10,000 men. Fierce fighting raged throughout the day. The Saudis finally retired shortly before sunset "without having either dislodged us from our eagles' nest or having broken our brave cavalry."

Guarmani took advantage of the heavy fighting to make a careful

examination of the Ataiba horses tethered in the gorge. He wrote
later:

My post was in the safest hiding-place in the gorge, with the
wounded, the women, and the baggage. At the most I was permitted from time to time to wander round amongst the horses
tethered to the bushes by their fetlocks; and was thus enabled to
study them at leisure, not minding the spent bullets which whizzed
over my head or fell harmlessly at my feet. My observations were
most interesting, for the Ataiba horses are by far the strongest in
the desert. At times I was distracted by the groans of the wounded
who were brought in to be dressed and by the cries of the women
who received them with joy, and encouraged them to return to
the fight as soon as possible, as soon, that is, as the dust and
charcoal had staunched the blood streaming from their wounds, or
as their cuts had been bound up.

That night Sheik Sultan ibn Rubayan, the foremost chief of the
Ataiba Bedouins, arrived with reinforcements of 400 horsemen and
5,000 camel-borne riflemen. They moved immediately against the
Saudi encampment, which they took completely by surprise, and
slaughtered hundreds of sleeping and exhausted warriors. The Saudi
forces were completely routed.

The next day Guarmani opened negotiations with a joyful Sheik
ibn Rubayan for the purchase of several horses. He quickly concluded
a fine bargain: four stallions "in their prime" in exchange for one
hundred camels. Afterward Guarmani joined in the Ataiba victory
celebrations. Fifty camels were slaughtered and roasted. The Italian
sat in the company of the sheiks before a camel roasted whole and
served up on an enormous platter of savory rice.

The Ataibas broke camp shortly after sunset. "I nearly wept when
Maflak embraced me in the [Bedouin] manner, and I was left alone
with my guides on that vast and bloody plain," Guarmani recalled
later. "Jackals, ravens, wolves, and vultures were devouring the
corpses. My horses trembled with fear. All night I watched and

caressed them, leaving them to the care of my companions at daybreak while I went in search of grass."

Two days later Guarmani's small group joined the defeated Saudi forces and rode with them toward Anaiza to the west. The Italian was particularly excited at the prospect of a visit to Anaiza, one of the largest towns in the Najd, whose "principal commerce consists in rearing horses bought by the merchants as colts from the Badawin; they export them to Kuwait on the Persian Gulf, whence they are sent to Persia or India."

Guarmani found Anaiza to be a city of approximately 10,000 inhabitants, located in the desert at the midpoint between the Persian Gulf and the Red Sea. He quickly sought out the horse market, only to learn that most of the horses had been sent to Kuwait a few days before.

A few days later Guarmani arrived in Hail, the largest city of northern Arabia, which had impressed Palgrave the year before. As he passed through the medieval gate, he saw hanging to one side a rotting corpse. In response to his questions, Guarmani was told that the dead man had been a Persian Jew, who had disguised himself as a Muslim and journeyed into the Najd to buy horses for the shah. He had been uncovered in a mosque when he failed to recite the proper prayers. Muslim worshipers murdered him on the spot.

The Italian had no sympathy for the dead man, who obviously had journeyed into Arabia poorly prepared. "If his fate was a sad one, it must be owned he had deserved it," he wrote later, a sentiment that both Burton and Palgrave would unquestionably have endorsed. "When a man decides to risk himself in a great adventure, he must use every means in his power and be prepared to suffer all the consequences of his enterprise."

Later Guarmani learned that news of the Jew's death had reached Jerusalem, where the dead man's identity had been confused with his own. Word of his supposed death was quickly sent back to his family in Italy. "My family mourned me in earnest," he noted, "whilst all the time I was in excellent health, eating *pilaff* or *temmen*, and making my *rikat* to God in my heart, but to Mohammed with my lips, in all due reverence; and remembering Christ's Sermon on the Mount, not to mention the stench of that Jew's rotting corpse, I was determined not to be amongst the poor in spirit and enter Paradise with the fools."

Guarmani spent three days in Hail. He had an audience with the emir Tallal ibn Rashid, who "welcomed me with embraces and kept me talking about five hours. From time to time he had my beard perfumed and offered me both black and white coffee." He agreed to provide Guarmani with twenty horsemen to escort him to Mustajidda, where his horses were.

Each day Guarmani went to the large square near Hail's main mosque to watch Tallal ibn Rashid dispense a traditional form of Bedouin justice. "He ordered death for assassins, cut off the hand of those who wounded another," he wrote later. "For liars and false witnesses he ordered their beards to be burned over a fire, which often ended in their eyes being burned as well; imprisonment was the punishment for thieves; rebels had their goods confiscated. . . . His sentences were just and his generosity [was] excessive."

The women of the central Najd, with their "bronze complexions, large almond-shaped eyes, and flashing black pupils," particularly impressed Guarmani. They oiled their long, glossy black hair with a scentless pomade made from finely powdered palm bark and clarified fat obtained from sheep's tails. The girls of the villages of Wusaita and Aqda were notorious prostitutes. "They sell grass in the mosque square at Hail, covered by a black *sciambar* so transparent as to be scarcely a veil at all," Guarmani wrote later. "This they always contrive to let fall as if by chance when a customer, 'sent by the Prophet,' pleases them. . . . 'Bargain for me,' she says; and it is an act of prostitution and not of marriage when it is settled. . . . The bride's price amounts to a few talers; after a month a divorce is pronounced and fresh loves are sought." Because many of their lovers were young men from the branches of the Ibn Rashid family, the emir Tallal was always "ready to shut his eyes and accept an accomplished fact."

On April 5 Guarmani and his armed escort departed Hail, and they reached Mustajidda on the afternoon of the next day. He lingered there for thirteen days and then traveled with his small party back to Hail. On May 4 they joined a large raiding party Tallal ibn Rashid was leading against the Sherarat Bedouins. The Italian rode with the column for two days, before splitting away to head north. At the last moment he persuaded an Ataiba Bedouin to sell him a young gray stallion.

Guarmani's party moved swiftly north without incident to Al Jawf, where they joined a caravan of several hundred people. On the fifth day they were attacked by a raiding party of 200 Sherarat riflemen. "Suddenly the Bedawin put their dromedaries at a trot and swept around to our left flank, which we promptly defended," Guarmani recollected later. "Then they wheeled round to the front, firing about a hundred shots and accompanying their attack with their war-cry."

The caravan sustained two dead and another ten wounded and then quickly surrendered. Guarmani knew that if he were captured, he would lose his horses as spoils of war. He ordered the loads on his camels lightened. Then he and his three men, riding the horses, broke out of the melee and charged at full gallop across the desert. Guarmani's horse was shot from under him, but he quickly mounted the fifth animal and continued on his way, thirty Sherarat Bedouins hot on his heels. At every opportunity, the four turned on their pursuers and fiercely counterattacked. Finally the Sherarat Bedouins quit the chase and returned to loot the caravan.

That night Guarmani and one companion made their way back to the dismal scene of the ambushed caravan. "Our companions were still in there," he wrote later, "the men quite naked and the women in nothing but their long gowns, with their hair loose, for they had been robbed of even their veils. Finding that we could be of no help to them, we left at ten o'clock at night."

A few days later, after four months of travel through one of the most dangerous regions of the world, Guarmani with his four horses arrived safely back in Jerusalem, his mission accomplished.

CHAPTER VI

Sir Wilfrid Scawen Blunt
and Lady Anne Blunt:
Pilgrims to Najd

*I*n the autumn of 1867 Wilfrid Scawen Blunt, a young attaché on his way to an assignment at the British Embassy in Buenos Aires, broke his journey for a time in Rio de Janeiro. There he met Richard Burton. The banality of the consulship at Santos had turned the great explorer into a near alcoholic and plunged him into the depths of a constant depression. The proper Blunt, always the impeccable gentleman, was shocked at Burton's wretched state and loss of control. "His dress and appearance were those suggesting a released convict, rather than anything of more repute," he recalled in 1906. "He wore, habitually, a rusty black coat with a crumpled black silk stock, his throat destitute of a collar, a costume which his muscular frame and immense chest made singularly and incongruously hideous, above it a countenance the most sinister I have ever seen, dark, cruel, treacherous with eyes like a wild beast's." Burton reminded Blunt of "a black leopard, caged, but unforgiving."

Only twenty-eight years old and a budding Orientalist, the younger Blunt was eager to pump Burton, no matter how degenerate he may have become, for information about the Middle East. The two spent many evenings together, Blunt listening, while Burton talked for hours on end about religion, philosophy, politics, and travel, "till he grew dangerous in his cups, and revolver in hand would stagger home to bed."

In short order, Blunt fell under the magic of the man whom Frank Harris once described as "a magnificent story teller, with intermingled appeals of pathos and rollicking fun, campfire effects, jets of flame against the night." Blunt listened, enthralled, and, through the drunken tales of an inspired genius, felt himself snared by the spell of faraway Arabia.

Years later Blunt recalled with a kind of horror Burton's extraordinary capacity for exerting his will over another person. He saw the effect Burton had upon his wife, Isabel. "She was indeed entirely under his domination, an hypnotic domination Burton used to boast of," Blunt observed. "I have heard him say that at the distance of many hundred miles he could will her to do anything he chose as completely as if he were with her in the same room."

One evening Burton tried to impose his will on the younger Blunt, an episode he recalled later with extreme discomfort: "I remember once his insisting that I should allow him to try his mesmeric power on me, and his expression as he gazed into my eyes was nothing less than atrocious. If I had submitted to his gaze for any length of time— and he held me by my thumbs—I have no doubt that he would have succeeded in dominating me. But my will also is strong, and when I had met his eyes of a wild beast for a couple of minutes, I broke away and would no more."

Blunt never saw Burton again. But the encounter in Rio de Janeiro had changed his life. Henceforth Blunt was destined to be a pilgrim in the Arabian desert on a flight from what he perceived as the corruption, ease, and decadence of an England grown fat and lazy on the riches of a new industrialism. With him would be his wife, Lady Anne—a consummate horsewoman, a linguist with a scholar's command of classical Arabic, and the granddaughter of Lord Byron.

Country gentleman, poet, diplomat, explorer, sportsman, breeder of Arabian horses, and insatiable womanizer, Wilfrid Scawen Blunt was born into a supremely powerful and self-confident class, free from doubt or pressure. Yet in spite of his background—or perhaps because of it—he achieved an extraordinary empathy with the desert Bedouins and became the first British champion of Arab nationalism.

T. E. Lawrence referred to Blunt in reverent tones as a "prophet." George Bernard Shaw put him at the center of his play *Heartbreak House*, dividing his personality between two characters, Captain Shotover and Hector Hushabye. And a young Ezra Pound thought so highly of Blunt's poetry that he traveled in the company of William Butler Yeats to his home in Sussex to ask for some of his "stuff" for the American magazine *Poetry* because of the "glory of his name."

Blunt was born on August 17, 1840, the second son of Francis Blunt, the scion of an old Sussex family. (His father had served with the army in the Spanish campaign of 1808 during the retreat from La Coruña and had been with Sir John Moore, Lady Hester Stanhope's friend, when he was killed in battle.) "I was born under circumstances peculiarly fortunate as I think for happiness," he remembered at the beginning of his memoirs. "Those of an English country gentleman of the XIXth Century—my father a Sussex squire of fair estate, owning some four thousand acres of land mostly poor but very beautiful in the most beautiful of Southern counties—my mother of the same social rank, respectable both and locally respected. Such a position at such a date, 1840, was perhaps as good a starting point for a happy life as could well have been afforded me."

Unfortunately, Blunt's father died two years later, and he never knew the safety of a stable childhood. His mother leased the family estate, Crabbet Park, and wandered with her three young children in a desultory fashion throughout England and Europe. In his memoirs Blunt looked back on his youth as "a considerable misfortune" and thought that the "ideal life ought to begin and end under the same roof."

After his mother's sudden conversion to Roman Catholicism in 1851, Blunt attended Catholic schools, where, as the smallest boy in his class, he was constantly bullied. The experience affected him profoundly and left him with a lifelong empathy for the underdog. As a boy, Blunt exhibited the extraordinary capacity for sympathy that was characteristic of him as a man. A boyhood friend once recalled how the young Blunt liked to keep caterpillars in paper boxes. He "had insisted upon pricking holes in the lids in the forms of constellations, so that the caterpillars inside might think they were still out of doors and could see the stars."

At the age of eighteen Blunt passed the examination for the diplomatic service, and for twelve years he served as a attaché to British embassies and legations in Athens, Constantinople, Lisbon, Madrid, Paris, and Frankfurt. He always treated lightly this period of his life. "I learned a little of my profession, amused myself, and made friends" was how he summed it up in later years. "We attachés and junior secretaries were very clearly given to understand . . . that it was not our business to meddle with the politics of the Courts to which we were accredited, only to make ourselves agreeable socially and amuse ourselves, decorously if possible."

The 1860s in Europe were quiet years with no major diplomatic crisis to muddy the waters. The handsome Blunt had much time to devote to other matters, in particular the pursuit of his favorite pastime, the seduction of women. Photographs from this period show a young man of romantic good looks tinged with melancholy in poses of studied elegance. "No life is perfect that has not been lived— youth in feeling—manhood in battle—old age in meditation," Blunt wrote years later in the preface to *The Love Sonnets of Proteus*, and the sentiment stands as an accurate summary of his life. Spending his youth in feeling, Blunt engaged in a series of sexual intrigues with beautiful, often married, aristocratic women. Many of them had connections with William Morris, the Pre-Raphaelite artist. The most passionate of his attachments was to Catherine Walters, a famous courtesan, whose Mayfair parties often included the prime minister William Gladstone among the crowds of wealthy young gentlemen. Blunt met Walters in Paris in 1863 and soon fell hopelessly in love. She became both the greatest passion of his life and his inspiration for a series of love sonnets.

But Blunt was to marry a very different sort of woman. Lady Anne King Noel, twenty-nine years old when he met her for the first time in Florence, Italy, was rich, chaste, and attractive in an unassuming way, quite a contrast with the kind of women who had previously appealed to Blunt. He recalled in later years:

> She thought herself plainer than she was, and had none of the ways of a pretty woman, though in truth she had the prettiness that a bird has, a redbreast or a nightingale, agreeable to the eye if not aggressively attractive. She had beautiful white teeth and a complexion [that was] rather brown than fair. . . . In stature [she was] less than tall, well poised and active, with a trim light figure set on a pair of small high-instepped feet. It is thus I see her in recollection, an unobtrusive quiet figure, . . . dressed in pale russet with a single crimson rose for ornament, rather behind the fashion of the day, but dignified and bright.

She came with a remarkable family history. She was the child of Lord Byron's daughter, Augusta Ada, and had been brought up largely by her grandmother, Lady Byron. She had spent most of her youth in Europe. By the time Blunt met her, Lady Anne already boasted several impressive achievements: fluency in French, German, Italian, and Spanish; a considerable artistic talent (she had studied drawing under John Ruskin); and some musical skills (she owned two Stradivarius violins and practiced on them five hours a day).

Blunt was attracted to her almost from the first. A marriage to the heir of the Bryonic tradition appealed very strongly as a major first step in his own poetic progress. Nor was he indifferent to the obvious advantages of her annual income of some £3,000 when his own, as a second son, had dwindled to £700. Later Blunt discovered that he had in her a perfect companion for his Arabian travels. She was a woman courageous, tough, resourceful, cool-headed in life-threatening crises, self-reliant, and adaptable, who shared his major interests in Orientalism and horses.

The two were married on June 8, 1869, in London. In December Blunt resigned from the Foreign Office, and they set off on a series of *Don Juan*-style adventures in the more accessible regions of the Muslim world. In the summer of 1873 the couple visited Constantinople. There they bought a half dozen packhorses, donned the clothes of the region, and spent six halcyon weeks "wandering in the hills and through the poppy fields of Asia Minor, away from the beaten tracks and seeing as much of the Turkish peasant life as our entire ignorance of their language allowed." The Blunts made a perfectly matched couple for this sort of an excursion. He noted in his journal at the time: "What I thought, she thought, what I did she did, what I felt she felt. These times were our true times of marriage, more than in Europe, and they were happy times." But the trip also impressed upon him "the honest goodness of these people and the badness of their Government" and thus served as an important first step in his political education.

The Blunts wintered over in Algeria. There his political education was carried one step farther when they observed "an Eastern people in violent subjection to a Western"—namely the French. The recent Franco-Prussian War had been followed by an uprising in Algiers, which the French repressed violently, confiscating native property and handing it to French settlers. Blunt's sympathies were entirely with the Arabs. The couple left Algiers and journeyed into the Sahara, where they had their first contact with Bedouin tribes. "We caught glimpses of these nomads in the Jebel Amour and of their vigorous way of life, and what we saw delighted us," Blunt wrote later in his *Secret History of the English Occupation of Egypt.* "The contrast between their noble pastoral life on the one hand, with their camel herds and horses, a life of high tradition filled with the memory of heroic deeds, and on the other hand the ignoble squalor of the Frank settlers, with their wineshops and their swine, was one which could not escape us. . . . It was a new political lesson which I took to heart, though still regarding it as in no sense my personal affair."

In the winter of 1875–76 the Blunts visited Egypt. The trip began as nothing "more serious than that of another pleasant travelling adventure in Eastern lands." At Suez they decided to go to Cairo "in a less conventional way than that of ordinary tourists." They hired camels and several Bedouin attendants and traveled to the Egyptian capital along the old caravan route. During their weeks in Egypt Blunt found himself favorably impressed with the fellahin, a people "cheerful, industrious, obedient to law, and pre-eminently sober," and was appalled at the clumsy corruption of the pasha Ismael's government. While the Blunts were in Egypt, Disraeli bought the pasha's shares in the Suez Canal Company for England. "An evil augury for Egypt" Blunt called it. After leaving Egypt, the Blunts once again hired Bedouins and camels and made a leisurely trip through the desert of the Sinai Peninsula to Jerusalem. The trip was not without its hazards. While crossing the desert, the small group exhausted its supply of water and almost perished from thirst. But the Blunts emerged from the experience with a rudimentary knowledge of the Arabic language, an insatiable desire to learn more about Muslim culture, and a determination to mount a major expedition of exploration into the central desert of Arabia.

These were years of pain as well as pleasure. Lady Anne suffered one miscarriage after another. The first occurred just two months after their wedding and proved to be the start of a depressing pattern. A year later she delivered a son, who died after four days. In 1872 she delivered twin girls. One died immediately. Lady Anne took the other in her arms. "Oh, it was so lovely to me, it had feet and hands like its father, and its voice went to my heart," she wrote. The baby died a few days later. And so it went through one terrible pregnancy after another. Both were keenly aware that their families were among only sixty-eight in England that had come over from Normandy with William the Conqueror in 1066. Blunt, especially, was desperate for a son to carry on the family line. Each failure devastated him.

Then, in the spring of 1872, Blunt's older brother unexpectedly died, and he inherited the ancestral estate at Crabbet Park. Suddenly, the couple found themselves with a country house, 4,000 acres, fifteen servants, and an annual income of £21,000. Blunt immediately set about restoring the dilapidated Tudor manor house at a cost of £5,000. He settled comfortably, indeed ecstatically, into his new role as a country squire. And on February 6, 1873, Lady Anne gave birth to a daughter. She lived, and they named her Judith Anne Dorothea. She was to grow up an only child.

In late November 1877 the Blunts sailed from England. Their plans were vague. They only knew they wanted to visit the legendary city of Baghdad and spend the winter in the less frequented parts of

Mesopotamia. The Euphrates River valley appealed to their sense of adventure and history. The area had recently been very much in the news as the "future high-road to India." Plans were afoot to construct a British railroad along the valley to the Persian Gulf. Yet few Europeans had traveled through the area with any thoroughness. The last Englishman known to have done so was a Colonel Charles Chesney in 1835. While not exactly a blank space on the map, "the Euphrates is more of a mystery to the general public than any river of equal importance in the Old World," Blunt wrote in the preface of Lady Anne's book *Bedouin Tribes of the Euphrates*. Furthermore, the region was rich in history. The flotsam of ancient empires littered the nearby deserts.

The late 1870s were a time of momentous change in the Middle East. The Ottoman Empire was coming unglued—"like some vast, mud-walled palace at last collapsing under its own weight," as one historian puts it. In 1875 Turkey's foreign debt amounted to £200 million; the annual interest alone was £12 million, out of an annual revenue of £22 million. Popular dissatisfaction with the regime ran high. Entire regions had slipped away from effective Turkish control. In 1876 the Christian provinces of European Turkey, aided by Russian agents, revolted against the sultan, only to meet with savage repression. In 1877 a revolution in Constantinople toppled Sultan Abdul Aziz. Russia declared war on Turkey. In the spring of 1878 a Russian army reached the gates of Constantinople. Disraeli ordered the British fleet through the Dardanelles just in time to stop Russian soldiers from entering the city. Under British pressure, the Turks and Russians made peace and signed the Treaty of San Stefano. Two months later the British signed a secret agreement with the new sultan, Abdul Hamid II, guaranteeing the integrity of the Asian portions of the Ottoman Empire. In return, Turkey granted Britain full control over the island of Cyprus.

It was against this backdrop of political turmoil that the Blunts arrived in Aleppo, Syria, in December 1877. Turkish control throughout Mesopotamia was lax, and they enjoyed a freedom of movement unknown to previous European travelers. Heavy storms kept them in Aleppo for a month. They passed much of the time in pleasant conversation with the British consul, James Skene, a distant cousin of Lady Anne's through a Scottish princess. A veteran of thirty years' service in the Middle East, the elderly Skene was an authority on the desert. He excited the Blunts' imaginations with vividly narrated tales of Bedouin life and encouraged them to expand their original plan of a journey to Baghdad into a systematic progress through the various Bedouin tribes of the Euphrates and Tigris River valleys.

Extensive preparations were made for the expedition. The Blunts ordered three Jewish tailors to make them a large tent, bought horses and mules, and hired a cook and other helpers. On January 9, 1878, their small caravan, accompanied by Skene, departed from Aleppo. They made their way across desolate hills under a leaden-colored sky. A cold wind blew in their faces. After an uncomfortable night in the wretched squalor of an Arab village, the Blunts entered the desert. By late morning they had come upon their first Bedouin encampment, a small collection of tents with flocks of sheep nearby. "Shabby as they were, they had a look of neatness after the houses we had left," Lady Anne noted in her journal.

Soon afterward the party reached the edge of the plain and looked down on the Euphrates River. "Often as I have tried to imagine the scene since we first decided on our journey, the reality surpasses all," Lady Anne wrote enthusiastically. Blunt estimated the width of the valley at perhaps five miles. Chalky cliffs rose 150 feet on both sides. The valley floor was a long, level meadow, "green as emerald," and covered with Bedouin camps and flocks of sheep. The valley teemed with various kinds of wildlife. Great flocks of ducks, geese, plovers, and coots hugged the riverbanks. Magpies, pheasants, and partridges filled the nearby woods. When the Blunts camped that night, local Arabs warned them that maneless Babylonian lions, rare in other parts of Mesopotamia, were common in the valley. The Britons learned that not long before a lion had killed and eaten a man from a nearby encampment.

The party was heavily armed. Both the Blunts were excellent shots. He carried a twelve-shot Winchester rifle and always kept a double-barreled shotgun close at hand. She wore a revolver on her hip. On January 15 their party passed a grim reminder of the hazards of travel in that part of the world: the graves of two Germans, murdered for their horses four years earlier. "I suppose they made some resistance," Lady Anne noted laconically in her journal, "but here by the wayside their journey ended, and their lives."

Two days later the Blunts entered the town of Deyr. Fifty Turkish soldiers on horseback welcomed them in the name of His Excellency the pasha Husayn, who politely extended the hospitality of his house to the small party. And they, just as politely, accepted, knowing they really had little choice in the matter. Blunt understood at once that the pasha had mistaken them for British spies, sent to scout the Euphrates river valley and the state of the Turkish garrisons there. And so they were installed in "honorable captivity" and watched carefully whenever they ventured into the town.

On January 27 the Blunts finally received permission to leave Deyr. Their friend Skene returned to Aleppo, while they joined a small caravan the mules of which carried bales of Manchester cotton destined for the bazaars of Baghdad. They made good time. Near the village of Hitt they suddenly noticed a strange smell, "like that one perceives in London when a street is being laid down in asphalt." Local Arabs told them of numerous wells of "black water" in the vicinity. The next night a heavy snow fell. Their tent froze until it was "hard as iron." Icicles hung from Blunt's beard. The snow turned to a cold drizzle that never seemed to stop. They were miserable. "We thought bitterly of the tracts of burning sand in which Baghdad is popularly supposed to stand," Lady Anne recorded in her journal. Then with great relief they reached Baghdad on the banks of the Tigris River. "At last the City of the Caliphs loomed through the driving rain, a grimy and squalid line of mud houses rising out of a sea of mud. Even the palm-groves looked draggled, and the Tigris had that hopeless look a river puts on during the rain."

Within a few hours the Blunts were at the residence of the British consul and settled happily into familiar English surroundings. "Here all our troubles are over for the present," Lady Anne wrote in her journal, "and we are sitting, clothed and in our right minds, close to a table spread with a table-cloth and decked with knives and forks.

There are flowers on it and fruit, and on the sideboard I can see a ham. Servants of the Indian type and clothed in white are running in and out." The Blunts heard the first international news in six weeks: "The Russians are at the gates of Constantinople. An armistice is already signed, and nearly the whole of European Turkey has been ceded to Russia."

Celebrated as the city of the *Arabian Nights*, Baghdad 1,000 years before had been one of the great cities of Asia, a center of art, literature, and learning. Richard Burton called it "a Paris of the ninth century." Great caravans bearing the silks and spices of India and China had passed through Baghdad on their way to the Western world. Then Europe had discovered the sea route to India by way of the Cape of Good Hope, and the caravans from the East had become fewer and had finally stopped altogether. Terrible plagues ravaged the city. In 1774 virtually the province's entire population of 2 million had perished. In 1831 the plague had struck again and killed more than 100,000 people. By 1878 Baghdad's population had fallen to 80,000.

Baghdad disappointed the Blunts, as it has virtually all modern travelers. Freya Stark called it "a city of wicked dust." And Robert Casey, who visited Baghdad in 1930, dismissed it as "a dust heap—odorous, unattractive, and hot. Its monuments are few, its atmosphere that of squalor and poverty." Lady Anne Blunt noted that Baghdad was "a city long past its prime, a lean and slippered pantaloon, its hose a world too wide for its shrunk shanks. The houses are low and mean, and built of mud, and the streets narrow and unpaved as those of any Mesopotamian village. . . . Baghdad, stripped of its [former] wealth, is uninteresting, a colorless Eastern town, and nothing more."

With nothing to keep them in Baghdad, the Blunts were eager to be on their way. They bought all their supplies and four young camels in the bazaars. The Blunts had hoped to learn something about the conditions in the Tigris River valley. But they met no one who had ever visited the area. "In all respects we are starting, rather like babes in the wood, on an adventure whose importance we are unable to rate," Lady Anne noted in her journal. "It may be perfectly easy, as

Wilfrid thinks, and it may be as dangerous as others would have us believe." Their goal continued to be a visit with one of the great Bedouin sheiks.

On February 24 the Blunts departed Baghdad and were once more enjoying the "freedom" of desert life. "One of the charms of tent life is the feeling of absolute ownership one has in each spot of ground one camps in—the right to do precisely all one likes with it," she wrote. "Liberty . . . is the greatest of all blessings, and in its perfect form is not to be found in Europe."

For this leg of their journey the Blunts traveled without escorts, interpreters, or guides, a fact that Blunt thought would predispose the Bedouins in their favor. They exchanged their horses for camels, which soon proved their superiority to horses on the long marches across the desert. Lady Anne called them "docile, affectionate beasts" and found herself growing quite fond of them.

These were happy times for the Blunts. The weather improved dramatically. They traveled across a desert in its winter bloom, a vast undulating plain of grass and flowers littered with the ruins of ancient civilizations. ("Arabic," Blunt liked to say in later years, "is a language to be shouted across great spaces—a language of the open air and the desert.") An excellent hunter, Blunt kept their small party supplied with fresh meat. Nights were spent in camps with minor sheiks. They were often the first Europeans these Bedouins had ever seen.

The Blunts wore Arab clothes for convenience rather than disguise. Whenever the Bedouins inquired of their identity, they described themselves as "English persons of distinction." They brought their British manners with them into the desert and judged their Bedouin hosts accordingly. "Good breeding and good birth are nearly always found together in the desert," Blunt observed. And his wife was in complete agreement. Her journal is full of comments about the manners of individual Arabs. One minor sheik is criticized as a "*parvenu*" who displayed "poor breeding." Another is faulted for his "petty meanness" and "a great want of dignity." A third, while "very poorly dressed," nonetheless displayed in his demeanor the signs of good breeding—"quiet, frank, unobtrusive, and full of kind attentions"—which typed him at once as a man of high rank and birth.

In mid-March the Blunts arrived at a large Bedouin encampment set in a meadow white as snow with camomile blossoms. Newborn camels, "creatures all legs and neck," peeped out of the bushes. Suddenly, the Britons came upon a large tent with seven peaks, surrounded by a dozen others, and they knew it had to belong to an important sheik. Out strolled the man they had sought for weeks, Faris, one of the two great sheiks of the Shammar tribe. He greeted them "with a smile that had so much honesty in it and good-will that we felt at once that we were safe in his hands." The Blunts were immediately won over. "I think we have found at last that thing we have been looking for, but hardly hoped to get sight of, a *gentleman* of the desert," she noted approvingly in her journal.

The twenty-seven-year-old sheik enjoyed enormous popularity among his people and a reputation as one of his tribe's greatest warriors. "In person Faris is small, as a true Bedouin should be, but he is a model of grace and strength and activity," Lady Anne wrote enthusiastically about her host. "On horseback there is no one in the tribe who can come near him; and it is a fine sight to see him put his mare to her full speed, and make his lance quiver over his head till it almost bends double. . . . He is, besides, very good looking, with features typically Arabian, a clear olive complexion not darker than that of a Spaniard, an aquiline nose, black eyebrows meeting almost across his forehead, and eyes fringed all round with long black lashes."

Faris immediately recognized the Blunts as his social equals and took them into his confidence, explaining in great detail the complicated politics of the Shammar tribe and its relationship with the Turkish government. One afternoon Blunt and Faris went alone into the desert for a demonstration of the Englishman's shotgun, a type of gun the Bedouin had never seen before. They acted like boys on an adventure. When one of Blunt's shot birds dropped into a nearby river, Faris excitedly stripped off his clothes and leaped into the water to retrieve it.

That evening Faris announced that he wished to make Blunt his blood brother. It was obviously a great honor and one rarely bestowed on outsiders. In front of witnesses, the two men took hold of each other's girdles with their left hands, raised their right hands, and solemnly repeated in Arabic the oath "O God! O, my God! Brothers today, tomorrow, and hereafter." So impressive was the ceremony that the three of them sat in silence for many minutes afterward. Then Faris spoke up. "You must stay with us. Our people shall make you tents like their own, and I will give you camels, and you shall live with us instead of going away to your own country."

Faris's act of swearing brotherhood with Blunt dramatically changed their footing within the Shammar tribe. Before they had been treated with courtesy; now they were shown true affection. Faris's mother sent for Lady Anne and greeted her as her "daughter," insisting that if she ever were in trouble, she must send for her sons. Faris, who had earlier refused all the Blunts' invitations to dine with them because they were his guests, sent word that he would take dinner with them. Lady Anne served up a banquet of sweetmeats, curry, and coffee with sugar—all luxuries lacking in the Bedouin camp.

A week after arriving in Faris's camp, the Blunts took their leave. The sheik and some of his men accompanied them for several miles. When they finally parted, Faris told them with great feeling, "Our tribe is your tribe, our tents are your tents. Come back to us soon."

A few days later the Blunts arrived again in Deyr, where they stayed only briefly, eager as they were to be back in the desert, where they felt more at home than in the towns. They pointed their small caravan toward the ruins of Palmyra. With them was Muhammad ibn Aruk, the young son of the sheik of a village near Palmyra, whom they had added to their group in Deyr. He cut a splendid figure on his gray Arabian horse, a fifteen-foot-long lance cradled over one arm.

At Palmyra the Blunts decided to head south when they learned that the Anazeh Bedouins were camped in the desert. Muhammad quickly agreed to show them the way. After a ride of several days they arrived at a vast gathering of Bedouins. An hour of riding was required just to pass through the herds of camels and the hundreds of tents to reach Jedaan, the great sheik of the Anazeh tribe. He failed to measure up to the high standards set by Faris earlier. "I do not like him," Lady Anne wrote. "He seems a selfish man, entirely occupied with his own schemes and ambitions, and lets one see many a little meanness, which better breeding would have concealed." The Blunts passed much of their time looking at Arabian horses.

After a few days the Blunts left Jedaan and rode in search of the camp of the Rowalla Bedouins. On April 14 they crossed a low ridge and suddenly came upon "the most wonderful spectacle the desert has to show—the Rowalla camp." The Blunts estimated the number of tents at 20,000 and the camels at more than 150,000. "At the first sight I felt an emotion of almost awe, as when one first sees the sea," Lady Anne wrote in her journal. "Nothing that we have seen hitherto in the way of multitude approaches to this." After a ride of two hours through the camp they reached an enormous tent, perhaps 100 feet from end to end. As they dismounted, a short man with a face much pitted from smallpox greeted them. This was the powerful sheik Sotamm ibn Shaalan, who could field 5,000 fierce warriors on short notice.

Several days later the Blunts departed the Rowalla camp and finally, after almost four months of travel among the various Bedouin tribes, headed toward Damascus. On their last night in the desert Blunt offered the young Muhammad the money they had agreed back in Deyr to pay him for his services. Much to their surprise the Bedouin youth emphatically declined, exclaiming: "If the Beg were to fill my *kaffiya* with silver pieces, yet I would hold it as nothing to the honor of being his brother." That evening the two men took the sacred blood oath, forever linking them as brothers. When they parted the next day, Blunt gave his new brother his Winchester rifle as a farewell gift.

By noon the next day the Blunts were in Damascus and soon afterward journeyed on to Beirut. There they experienced their first rude shock with European life in the Middle East. Only then did they appreciate the profound changes in their tastes, prejudices, and opinions that their long sojourn among the Bedouins had produced in them. They sat in the dining room of their inn on a divan, drinking coffee, still dressed in their Bedouin robes. Suddenly the door to the dining room burst open. In came a throng of a dozen men and women "clad in trousers and coats, or in scanty skirts and jackets, according to their sex, but all with heads uncovered and looking strangely naked. . . . The dresses, voices, gestures, and attitudes of these men and women struck us not only as the most grotesque, but the most indecorous we had ever seen." To their horror, the Blunts learned that the visitors were all British "lords and ladies of distinction," just arrived on a yacht from Malta.

The Blunts sailed home to England with six Arabian mares that were to form the heart of the famous Crabbet Arabian Stud farm. The idea had been the brainchild of their Aleppo friend James Skene, who also joined as a general partner. Blunt believed that the Arabian was the finest horse in the world and that in order to develop its full potential, it must be bred in England. Within a few years the Crabbet Stud's reputation had spread throughout England.

Lady Anne started immediately writing an account of the trip, *Bedouin Tribes of the Euphrates.* Her husband wrote the preface and added several chapters at the end on the politics and history of the area. No longer the detached observer, Blunt had become an impassioned advocate of the Bedouin cause: "I felt that these wild people were wiser than ourselves. They had solved the riddle of life by refusing to consider it, even understand that there was a riddle at all. Thus I came back to England strengthened and consoled."

Blunt found in the Bedouin society answers to the perplexing religious and philosophical questions that plagued many Victorian thinkers. The Bedouins, he believed, embodied a superior sense of morality to the Europeans'. The aristocratic Blunt sensed that beneath the wildness of Bedouin manners lay a respect for traditional moral authority. But, he insisted, the laws they obeyed were Bedouin, not Turkish or European, and they had to be judged by their own standards. In his experience, once the Bedouins had given their trust, they proved absolutely trustworthy. "Acts of petty larceny are unknown among the Anazeh and Shammar," Blunt wrote. "During the whole of our travels we never lost so much as the value of a shilling. Highway robbery, on the other hand, is not only permitted but held to be a right. . . . By desert law, the act of passing through

the desert entails forfeiture of goods to whoever can seize them."
(And, he might have added, even the Prophet Muhammad had
personally led raiding parties against the rich caravans traveling to
Mecca.)

The continual warfare that raged among all the Bedouin tribes
was, for Blunt, further proof of the moral superiority of their culture.
He observed:

> War, however, is not there the terrible scourge it is among
> civilized nations. The idea of civilized war is to kill, burn, and
> utterly destroy your enemy until he submits, but a milder rule is
> observed in the desert. There the property of the enemy, and not
> his person, is the object of the fighting. It is not wished that he
> should be destroyed, only ruined, the extreme penalty of defeat
> being the loss of herds, of tents, tent-furniture, and mares. Beyond
> this Bedouin warfare does not go. The person of the enemy is
> sacred when disarmed or dismounted. . . . No man is killed ex-
> cept by accident. Indeed, it is held to be a clumsy act to kill
> outright; for the object of battle is sufficiently obtained by merely
> dismounting or wounding the enemy.

Blunt wrote about a Bedouin code of ethics as it existed in its
purest, most idealized form. He understood that rogue Bedouins
roamed the desert, forming "small tribes apart from the rest," and
that Bedouins who had moved to the towns often exhibited corrupted moral characters. Other European travelers to the region
sometimes felt differently about the Bedouins. But the aristocratic
Blunts found in the pure Bedouin society a code of conduct stressing
a commitment to high standards of behavior similar to the chivalric
ideal that had motivated their own ancestors several centuries earlier.

In late 1878 the Blunts decided to return to the Middle East, this
time to penetrate northern Arabia and visit Najd, the highlands
sacred to all the Syrian Bedouins as their ancestral homeland and the
birthplace of the Arabian horse. Isolated by rugged mountains and
fierce deserts, few regions in the world were more inaccessible. Only

three European men had preceded them. Lady Anne would be the first European woman to visit the Arabian Peninsula.

For such confirmed Orientalists as the Blunts, the Najd was utterly irresistible, and their proposed trip quickly took on the intensity of a religious pilgrimage. "To us, imbued as we were with the fancies of the Desert, Nejd [*sic*] had long assumed the romantic colouring of a holy land," Blunt wrote in the preface to Lady Anne's next book, *A Pilgrimage to Nejd.*

Once again the Middle East provided the Blunts with an escape from the Western world. "It is strange how gloomy thoughts vanish [when] one sets foot in Asia," Lady Anne wrote upon their arrival in Damascus. "Only yesterday we were still tossing on the sea of European thought, with its political anxieties, its social miseries, and its restless aspirations . . . and now we seem to have ridden into still water, where we can rest and forget and be thankful."

In Damascus their expedition took on an important new twist. Blunt's Bedouin blood brother Muhammad ibn Aruk wanted to seek a wife among distant relations in Najd. Eight generations before, his ancestors had migrated to the Mesopotamian plains. No one in his tribe had ever returned. It was fitting for the Blunts to help him in this effort. Few acts conferred greater honor in Bedouin society than that of one brother assisting another in the selection of a wife. And traveling with him offered important benefits. Everywhere the Blunts were accepted as members of an Arabian family, no small advantage when passing through a part of the world where men were often murdered merely because they were Christians.

In Damascus Blunt carefully put together a small party that included Muhammad, his cousin Abdullah, Hanna, who had served as their cook on their previous expedition, his kinsman Ibrahim, two helpers, two horses, four camels, and two greyhounds. Once again the Blunts were determined to travel light and share in the lives of the Arabs along the way.

First there were people to see in Damascus before their departure. They paid a visit to Lady Jane Digby and her husband, Medjuel, the latter providing them with much useful information about the Najd. He impressed them as "a very well bred and agreeable man . . . with all the characteristics of good Bedouin blood." (Few visitors to the Medjuel household displayed Lady Anne's excellent sense of priorities. Nowhere in her lengthy narrative of their meeting does she mention Lady Jane's earlier history. For the Blunts, it was simply irrelevant.)

Next they sought out Abd el Kader, the Algerian savior of the Christians during the terrible uprising of 1860. Blunt was eager to meet him because of his reputation as a leading scholar on the Arabian horse. The old warrior received them graciously, and they conferred at length about the place of the horse in Arab culture.

Then the Blunts visited the pasha Midhat, newly arrived in Damascus to be the governor-general of Syria. Midhat represented a new kind of administrator for the Ottoman Empire, a reformer. He confided in the Blunts his grandiose plans for bringing "civilization" to Damascus. "Tramways are the first step in civilization," he told them excitedly. "I shall make a tramway around Damascus. Everyone will ride. It will pay five per cent."

On December 13, at the first streak of dawn, the small party loaded their camels, skirted the gate through which St. Paul was supposed to have entered, and departed Damascus, heading south on the hajj road to Mecca, an appropriate beginning for their pilgrimage to Najd. For several days they followed an ancient Roman road through small farming communities, which gradually thinned out. In a week they reached the desert. There they were at greatest risk. "The edges of the desert are always unsafe, whereas, once clear of the shore, so to speak, there is comparatively little risk of meeting anybody, friend or foe," Lady Anne wrote in her journal.

On Christmas Day the party feasted on roast camel. ("When young it resembles mutton," Lady Anne noted approvingly.) As they traveled farther south, fresh food of any sort became scarce. One day an enormous pinkish cloud passed overhead. Millions of fat red locusts whirred past and then settled down, covering the ground with a crawling red carpet. The Blunts quickly learned that in the desert a plague of locusts was a great blessing for all its creatures. Larks, bustards, ravens, hawks, buzzards, and other birds gorged on the insects. Camels and horses munched them. For the Bedouins they were a welcomed addition to a limited diet and often the only source of protein for weeks at a time.

"Locusts are now a regular portion of the day's provision with us and are really an excellent article of diet," Lady Anne wrote enthusiastically. "After trying them in several ways, we have come to the conclusion that they are best plain boiled. The long hopping legs must be pulled off, and the locust held by the wings, dipped into salt and eaten. . . . Wilfrid considers that [the red locust] would hold its own among the *hors d'ouevre* at a Paris restaurant." She thought they had a vegetable taste, "not unlike green wheat in England." Early morning was the best time to gather them, she observed, for then they were still sluggish from the cold and hundreds could be quickly collected with little effort.

The journey southward progressed uneventfully. By now the group was deep into the desert. Signs of people were rare. They had met no other Arabs for several days. That changed abruptly on January 3. The Blunts had ridden ahead of their small party through a landscape of pure white sand dunes. They stopped for a rest. The greyhounds chased one another playfully in the sand. The Blunts munched on dates. Suddenly from behind they heard an ominous thud, thud, thud on the sand. They spun around to confront to their horror a troop of a dozen horsemen bearing down on them at full gallop, lances at the ready. Blunt leaped to his feet. "Get on your mare," he shouted to his wife. "This is a raid." It was one of those rare occasions when they were unarmed. Within seconds the Bedouins had surrounded them. Blunt frantically tried to protect himself from the thrusting lances. Lady Anne shouted to the nearest horseman, "*Ana dahilak*—I am under your protection," the usual form of surrender among the Bedouins. Blunt threw himself off his mare, another Bedouin sign of surrender. The attack stopped abruptly. The Bedouins seized their horses and other possessions, which, according to the law of the desert, now belonged to them.

The Bedouins escorted the Blunts under guard back to their camp, where the others had taken up defensive positions behind their kneeling camels, rifles at the ready. Muhammad stepped forward and addressed the chief.

"*Min entum?*—Who are you?"

"*Roala min Ibn Debaa,*" the Bedouin answered.

"*Wallah?*—Will you swear by God?"

"*Wallah!* We swear," the chief replied. "And you?"

"Muhammad ibn Aruk of Tudmur."

"*Wallah?*"

"*Wallah!*"

"And these Franks are traveling with you?" the Bedouin chief asked in amazement.

"*Wallah!* These Franks are friends of Ibn Shaalan."

The danger had passed. They had fallen into the hands of friends. Ibn Shaalan, the Rowalla sheik whom the Blunts had visited the previous spring, was bound by the code of desert hospitality to protect his guests even in this faraway place, and none of his people dared threaten them. Furthermore, Muhammad was a Tudmuri Bedouin and as such could not be molested by the Rowalla because his tribe paid a tribute to Ibn Shaalan for protection.

As soon as the relationships were sorted out, the Bedouins returned the horses and other possessions, even Blunt's tobacco pouch. Nothing was held back. Some of the younger men lamented the loss of the beautiful mares. "But Arabs are always good-humoured, whatever else their faults," Lady Anne commented in her journal, "and presently we were all on very good terms, sitting in a circle on the sand, eating dates and passing round the pipe of peace. They were now our guests."

For the Blunts the experience provided additional insight into the traditional moral code of the Bedouins and the sense of honor that prevailed even among those who seemed the wildest. True, the party had been fiercely attacked. But the purpose of the raid was to seize their property, not take their lives. Once they had surrendered, the violence ceased. And after everyone had been properly identified, the Bedouins made their apologies and restored the goods. For Blunt, it was one more example of the moral superiority of the Bedouins.

"What struck us as strange in all this was the ready good faith with which they believed every word we said," Lady Anne noted with amazement. "We had spoken the truth, but why did they trust us?

They knew neither us nor Mohammed; yet they had taken our word that we were friends, when they might so easily have ridden off with our property. Nobody would ever have heard of it, or known who they were."

She added an afterthought: "We liked the looks of these young Rowalla. In spite of their rough behaviour, we could see that they were gentlemen. They were very much ashamed of having used their spears against me and made profuse apologies; they only saw a person wearing a cloak and never suspected that it belonged to a woman."

On January 5 the Blunts reached Al Jawf, 400 miles south of Damascus, a walled village of some 600 houses, "square boxes of mud," clustered near a medieval stone castle. The Blunts pitched their tents alongside the residence of the acting governor. Al Jawf was, in effect, a conquered town, occupied by soldiers of the great emir Muhammad ibn Rashid from Hail to the south. In the evening a special sword dance was performed in the Blunts' honor. One performer beat out a rhythm on a drum made from palmwood and horsehide, while six soldiers held their swords high, chanted solemnly, and slowly danced in a circle.

The Blunts left Al Jawf and traveled twenty miles to another oasis village, Meskakeh, to a small farm set in a square plot of barley surrounded by a hedge of wattled palm branches. There Nassr ibn Aruk, a distant relation of Muhammad's, lived with his sons and his sons' wives and their children. Nassr received Muhammad and his friends, "as if they had been expecting us every day for the last hundred years." The Blunts settled in at the Nassr farm for three days, welcoming both the rest and the opportunity to learn more about Arab domestic life. Blunt thought Nassr resembled "some small Scottish laird, poor and penurious, but aware of having better blood in his veins than his neighbors."

The first order of business was to find a wife for Muhammad. Soon he was talking excitedly about Muttra, a fifteen-year-old granddaughter of Nassr. "I could see that already he was terribly in love, for with the Arabs a very little goes a long way," Lady Anne wrote in her journal. "Never being allowed to see young ladies, they fall in love merely through talking about them."

She quickly set up an interview with the girl. "I liked Muttra's face at once," she wrote. "She has a particularly open, honest look, staring straight at one with her great dark eyes like a fawn. . . . I was pleased with the intelligence Muttra showed in this conversation and decide that Mohammed would be most fortunate if he obtained her in marriage."

That evening Blunt presided over the negotiations for marriage. Muhammad was "all in a flutter" and very pale. Blunt pleaded the youth's case with the Meskakeh branch of the Ibn Aruks. At last it was settled. Nassr agreed to send Muttra with an escort of thirty horsemen to Palmyra the next year. Blunt announced that as Muhammad's brother he would pay the negotiated dowry of fifty Turkish pounds. ("It was not very dignified, this chaffering about the price," Lady Anne complained. "People do better in England leaving such things to be settled by their lawyers.") Finally a marriage contract was formally drawn up and signed by all parties. Afterward they celebrated. A kid was killed and eaten, songs were sung, and stories told.

On January 12 the Blunt departed from Meskakeh with a local guide for the next—and most dangerous—stage of their journey, the lengthy crossing of the terrible Nafud. Blunt estimated the greatest breadth of the desert area at 150 miles, it greatest length at 400 miles. In the late afternoon their party came across a ridge, and there, in the near distance, was the Nafud. "The thing that strikes one first about the Nefud [sic] is its colour," Lady Anne wrote. "It is not white like the sand dunes we passed yesterday, nor yellow as the sand is in parts of the Egyptian desert, but a really bright red, almost crimson in the morning when it is wet with dew." She filled a bottle with the red sand to take home to make an hourglass.

The Nafud's other remarkable phenomenon was the long lines of horse-hoof-shaped hollows of red sand, called *fuljes,* which pitted its surface in great numbers. Blunt measured some of the larger *fuljes* at almost 300 feet deep and 1,500 feet across. Progress was slow. One day blurred into the next. Their routine never varied. After several days the Blunts began to see signs of the terrible toll the Nafud had extracted from other travelers. Virtually every hollow had its collection of bones, usually of pack animals. In one *fulje* they saw the remains of forty Suelmat Bedouins and their camels, who ten years before had lost their way and perished from thirst. Dried skin still clung to many of the sun-bleached skeletons. "People who die in the Nefud seldom have anyone to bury them," Lady Anne observed matter-of-factly in her journal.

One of the Nafud's few "luxuries" was the entire absence of the insect pests that make life a torment in other regions of the Middle East. "Even the fleas on our greyhounds died as soon as they entered the enchanted circle of red sand," Lady Anne noted. One day, while resting near a pile of loose stones, Blunt suddenly spotted a painted lady butterfly sunning itself in a sheltered spot. He calculated that since there was no vegetation suitable for the caterpillar of the butterfly nearer than Hebron, it had to have flown at least 400 miles. "Here it seemed happy in the sun," he observed.

After a week the Nafud began to take its toll. The camels broke down and often refused to carry their loads. Their situation quickly became desperate. On January 19 Lady Anne wrote in her journal: "A terrible day for the camels and men. . . . The pace of the caravan has been a little over a mile an hour. At one moment it seemed as if we should remain altogether in the Nefud. The sand to tired camels is like a prison, and in the sand we should have remained." In late afternoon they finally broke free of the Nafud and reached the safety of the oasis of Jubbah. Beyond lay Najd.

On January 24 the Blunts' party arrived at Hail, the capital city of Najd and the home of the emir Muhammad ibn Rashid, the most powerful of all Bedouin sheiks and the richest prince in Arabia. They had sent ahead from Jubbah letters of introduction. The emir's chamberlain, a tall man with a snow-white beard, welcomed them with great solemnity in the courtyard of the emir's medieval castle. He guided them to a great reception hall seventy feet long with a stone roof supported by enormous columns. Slaves served them coffee as they sat on pillows.

Suddenly, the Emir ibn Rashid arrived. He was magnificently attired in several robes of purple linen and embroidered Indian silk worn under a black aba stitched in gold. In his waistband he carried several golden-hilted daggers and a handsome golden-hilted sword, ornamented with rubies and turquoise. He greeted the Blunts and Muhammad warmly. "He looked every inch a king," Lady Anne noted. "His eyes were deep sunk and piercing, like the eyes of a hawk, but ever turning restlessly from one of our faces to the other, and then to those beside him."

After an hour's discussion the emir invited them to his *mejlis,* the daily court where he dispensed justice according to the Bedouin code. The Blunts were not prepared for the magnificent spectacle of the ceremony. In a large courtyard 800 soldiers, silver-hilted swords at their sides, stood guard. The emir sat on a raised seat, flanked by his favorite slave, whose duty it was to guard him constantly from assassins. In front waited a half dozen supplicants, who presented him with petitions for grievances and had their cases summarily decided.

An official of the emir showed the Blunts to a guesthouse near the castle. That afternoon they had another meeting with Ibn Rashid and presented him with gifts of a cloak, a revolver, a telescope, and a Winchester rifle. Afterward he took them on a tour of his gardens and his kitchen. In the latter he proudly showed them seven monstrous pots and declared that three entire camels could be boiled in each. (The Blunts soon learned that this was no exaggeration. The emir slaughtered forty sheep or seven camels each day to feed some 200 guests.)

On the following day Lady Anne asked Ibn Rashid's permission to visit his harem. This was graciously granted. A black slave woman led her back to the women's quarters, where the emir's three wives, elegantly dressed and surrounded by a host of slaves, entertained her. After a long discussion with the women Lady Anne decided that life in the emir's harem was tedium of the worst kind.

"What do you all day long?" she asked a younger wife.

"We live in the castle," the woman replied.

"Don't you go out at all?"

"No, we always stay in the castle."

"What a pity! Don't you ever go outside Hail into the desert?"

"Oh, no, of course not."

"But to pass the time, what do you do?"

"We do nothing."

"I should die if I did nothing," Lady Anne replied. "How do you manage to spend your lives?"

"We sit."

Lady Anne was dumbfounded. "Thus, supreme contentment in the harem here is to sit in absolute idleness," she wrote that evening in her journal. "It seems odd, where men are so active and adventurous, that women should be satisfied to be so bored; but such, I suppose, is the tyranny of fashion."

Hardly a day passed during the Blunts' stay in Hail that did not bring some surprise. One evening at a banquet the emir suddenly produced a telephone (invented by Alexander Graham Bell fewer than three years before!) and ordered a demonstration. One slave remained inside the banquet hall; the other went to an outer courtyard. The emir gave a message to the nearby slave, who then repeated it into the mouthpiece. "O, Abdullah, where are you? The emir wants you." After a brief pause the second slave with the receiver in the distant courtyard successfully shouted back the message. "We expressed surprise," an amazed Lady Anne noted in her journal. "Indeed, it was the first time we had ever seen the toy, and it is singular to find so very modern an invention already at Hail."

Blunt, in the meantime, busied himself with an investigation into the political arrangements of Ibn Rashid's court, a traditional form of government which, he believed, dated back virtually unchanged to the days of the Old Testament. (Turkish rule did not extend into the Arabian Peninsula.) He later eulogized the Bedouin form of government as the "purest example of democracy in the world," one that had been shaped by the dictates of desert existence to accommodate the Bedouin's commitment to individual freedom. "Each man's tent, to paraphrase the English boast, is his castle, where he is free to do as he likes," Blunt wrote. "In it he is free of all control, whether from tax-gatherer or policeman, and he is obliged to contribute nothing, not even his services in time of war, to his neighbors."

For purely practical reasons, of course, it was in the individual Bedouin's interest to relinquish some of his absolute independence for the sake of protection. One man alone could not have survived for long in the desert, for other Bedouins would soon have plundered him of his animals and personal belongings. The Bedouin thus lived with his tribe and took part with them in the common defense of their community. This required that he yield up some of his personal freedom and accept the general laws and regulations of the group. But—and this was important to Blunt—his participation was always voluntary. He could at any time withdraw his support from the group and go his own way without fear of retribution.

Two other things impressed Blunt about the Bedouin system of government: its simplicity and its safeguards against tyranny. As for the first, each tribe was under the nominal rule of an elected sheik, an honor entrusted by tradition to one or two families. The position carried many duties and few advantages. The sheik's responsibilities included extending the hospitality of the tribe to guests, deciding disputes about the ownership of a camel or a sheep, settling domestic quarrels, and transacting all the political business of the tribe. In return, he was accorded the privilege of leading the tribe from camp to camp and awarded extra shares in all booty taken on raids.

In fact, a sheik had virtually no absolute power, even though he might field 5,000 warriors. "He represents only the united will of the tribe," Blunt observed. "And in political matters he has to follow rather than lead public opinion." The lowest shepherd in the tribe could always address the sheik by his first name, and sheiks were discouraged from affecting any style of dress or manner that might set them apart from their tribe. Wealth counted for little in the judging of the importance of a man in Bedouin society; but high birth, descent from families of traditional good breeding, conferred immense prestige.

The system thus had built-in protections against arbitrary and dictatorial rule. Popular feeling invested a sheik with power. That same popular will could withdraw it. Even as wealthy and powerful a sheik as Mohammed Ibn Rashid understood this. "The Emir knows well that he cannot transgress the traditional unwritten law of Arabia with impunity," Blunt wrote. "An unpopular sheykh would cease, *ipso facto*, to be sheykh, for, though dethroned by no public ceremony and subjected to no personal ill-treatment, he would find himself abandoned in favour of a more acceptable member of his family. The citizen soldiers would not support a recognized tyrant in the town, nor would the Bedouins outside. Princes in Arabia have, therefore, to consider public opinion before all else."

Blunt found in Ibn Rashid's benevolent rule a form of government that seemed to have realized the noblest political dreams of the Westerner. "Here was a community living as our idealists have dreamed, without taxes, without police, without conscription, without compulsion of any kind, whose only law was public opinion, and whose only order a principle of honour," he wrote. "Here, too, was a people poor yet contented, and, according to their few wants, living in abundance, who to all questions I asked of them . . . had answered me invariably, 'Thank God we are not as other nations are. Here we have our own government. Here we are satisfied.' "

Nor was Blunt's enthusiasm misplaced. Historian Albert Hourani states in *Europe and the Middle East:* "As European romantics, [the Blunts] were perhaps already inclined to find perfection in what was simple, unspoiled, and spontaneous. . . . The dynasty of Ibn Rashid . . . was not perhaps as virtuous as Blunt thought it; its annals were stained like those of other dynasties, but what Blunt admired in its rule did really exist—the unforced ease in the relationship of ruler and subjects, the existence of a code of justice preserved by the public conscience and which the ruler could not ignore."

Blunt's own background unquestionably conditioned him to an enthusiastic acceptance of a Bedouin society ruled with a light but confident hand, and in accordance with traditional values, by a rural aristocracy whose claim to power was based on birth rather than wealth. His own England, after all, was that of the Sussex countryside, of the squire living like a little king on his 4,000 acres among his tenants, looking after them, and enjoying the fruits of his position because he fulfilled certain hereditary obligations.

As the first European horse breeders to visit Arabia the Blunts had one other major objective: a visit to Ibn Rashid's stud farm, the most famous in all Arabia. They spent many hours with the emir in his stables, examining his horses and discussing their finer points and genealogies. The climax of their stay in Hail was an invitation from Ibn Rashid to join him and his advisers for a ride through the desert. "It was a fortunate day for us," an excited Lady Anne wrote later, "because we saw what we would have come the whole journey to see—all the best of the emir's horses out and galloping about."

On February 2 the Blunts departed Hail, relieved to be again in the desert. They joined a large caravan of Persians returning from a pilgrimage to Mecca, a vast spectacle of 4,000 camels and hundreds of men that spread out for three miles across the desert. A mounted troop on caparisoned camels led the procession, carrying Emir ibn Rashid's standard, a great purple flag with a green border and a white inscription in the middle. That evening Lady Anne wrote in her journal: "Our tents are a couple of hundred yards away from the Hajj camp. The pilgrim [muezzins] have just chanted the evening call to prayers, and the people are at their devotions. Our mares are munching their barley, and our hawk (a trained bird we bought yesterday in Hail) is sitting looking very wise on his perch in front of us. It is a cold evening, but oh how clean and comfortable in the tent!"

The Blunts generally snubbed the Persians, finding them "without a sense of propriety . . . and in comparison with the Arabs coarse and boorish." A Persian riding a camel was, Lady Anne thought, "the most ridiculous sight in the world; he insists on sitting astride and seems absolutely unable to learn the ways and habits of the creature he rides." The Arab escorts, too, treated the Persians with contempt, making them the butt of jokes from dawn to dusk.

The march northward was long and tedious but largely uneventful until the end. After two weeks most of the pilgrims ran out of food. The Blunts' supply lasted longer, but within another week theirs, too, was exhausted. Conditions quickly became desperate. On February 24 Lady Anne wrote in her journal that "everybody is at the starvation point." The toll on the camels was dreadful, as dozens simply lay down and died. They finally reached the village of Qasr Ruheym, having marched 170 miles in six days on empty stomachs. On March 6, in heavy rains, the Blunts arrived back in Baghdad. That night for the first time in almost three months they slept in beds.

Lady Anne wanted to end their travels there. But Blunt insisted upon pushing on through the lower Euphrates River valley to the Persian Gulf. She thought the plan of "doubtful wisdom." And her instincts proved correct. The trip was a disaster from the start. The attendants they hired in Baghdad proved to be rogues of the worst sort. The travel was more exhausting than on any of their other trips. Blunt took ill with a severe case of dysentery and almost died. "Our trip was fit only to be damned with six Ds—not only disagreeable, difficult, dangerous and all but disastrous, but disappointing and disheartening," Lady Anne wrote her brother afterward. "Wilfrid will *never* want to go on any hard journey again, I will swear to that!"

Finally, on April 25, the Blunts reached the Persian port of Bushire, having completed a trek of some 2,000 miles. They were probably the first Europeans in modern times to travel overland the complete distance between the Mediterranean Sea and the Persian Gulf. At Bushire the Blunts wearily sought out the British consul. "When we arrived at the door of the Residency, the well-dressed Sepoys in their smart European uniforms barred us from the door with their muskets," Lady Anne wrote later. "They refused to believe that such vagabonds, blackened with the sun and grimed with long sleeping on the ground, were English gentlefolks or honest people of any sort."

Blunt's experiences in northern Arabia represented the final and most important stage in his political education. He came out of the Najd firmly convinced that for the Arabs to develop their full potential, they had to break free of Turkish rule. He resolved to dedicate his life to that end. "If I can introduce a pure Arabian breed of horses into England and help to see Arabia free of the Turks, I shall not have lived in vain," he wrote. The Arabs became his life's passion. By temperament a romantic, Blunt now channeled all his Byronic craving for action and adventure into politics and became the first British crusader for Arab nationalism. For the next twenty-five years the Middle East provided his life with direction and meaning.

Blunt's stay in Ibn Rashid's court in Hail had convinced him that Muslim society contained the seeds of its own renewal. He wrote a series of magazine articles, later collected in book form as *The Future of Islam,* in which he proposed an Arabian caliphate under British protection as an alternative to the Ottoman Empire. He urged that the caliphate be centered in Mecca and patterned after the Vatican state, which functions as the temporal domain of a European pope. Such a political arrangement, Blunt hoped, would restore the Arab genius to its former glory and at the same time bring concrete benefits to England. "Christendom has pretty well abandoned her hopeless task of converting Islam, as Islam has abandoned hers of conquering Europe," he wrote. "It is surely time that moral sympathy should unite the two great bodies of men who believe in and worship the same God." Blunt tied his scheme to the future of British India with its large Muslim population. Such an allegiance, he argued, would go a long way toward securing the loyalty of the Muslims there.

In the 1880s no one took Blunt's ideas seriously. "An English Don Quixote," one of his unsympathetic contemporaries scoffed contemptuously. But thirty years later the British Foreign Office in Cairo struck an agreement with the sherif of Mecca to support his plans for an Arabian caliphate, the independence of which would be guaranteed by Britain, in exchange for his support in the war against Turkey. However, by then Blunt was a forgotten man, a mere footnote in the histories of the region.

Blunt's political education soon led him to lose faith in the benevolence of British imperialism. An 1879 trip to India convinced him of the shortcomings of British rule there. He was shocked at the way the poverty-stricken Indian peasants were taxed to support a bloated British administration. "I am disappointed with India, which seems just as ill-governed as the rest of Asia, only with good intentions instead of bad ones or none at all," he wrote later.

The events in Egypt in 1881 and 1882, when a mutiny of Egyptian troops led to a British occupation of that country, turned Blunt into an outspoken anti-imperialist. He took up the cause of Egyptian nationalism and campaigned vigorously on behalf of Colonel Ahmed Arabi, who had led the uprising against foreign influences. Blunt stood virtually alone in Britain. His letters, articles, and personal appearances on behalf of Egyptian interests brought him a "storm of abuse." Many of his lifelong friends cut him cold.

Blunt's bitterness increased when he realized that the British occupation of Egypt would continue indefinitely. His disenchantment with the policies of the British Empire became complete. Soon he was writing: "We were better off and more respected in Queen Elizabeth's time when we had not a stick of territory outside the British Islands."

Vast changes were sweeping the Muslim world in the last two decades of the nineteenth century. The changes horrified Blunt, convinced as he was that regeneration depended upon a return to traditional Muslim values. Under European domination the Arab world in the name of reform began to adopt policies of Westernization. Western concepts of law and education were introduced. The ulemas, the doctors of Muslim religion and law, found themselves reduced in power and influence in a state increasingly ruled by Arabs who spoke English and had been educated in Western ways. New books, often translations from the West, replaced the sacred and classical texts as reading material for the new bureaucratic elites.

By 1900 throughout much of the Muslim world the traditional Islamic concepts were in retreat before the wave of new and disruptive ideas imported from Europe. "In this new world, theology was seen as old-fashioned and irrelevant," the Middle Eastern scholar Bernard Lewis writes in *Islam in History*. "The only hope of salvation was economic, social, and above all political reform, conceived and, as it were, applied in accordance with a succession of imported European ideologies."

Almost alone in England, Blunt was appalled at this erosion of Muslim values, but he was powerless to do anything about it. He likened the cultural pollution of the Islamic world to the physical pollution he had observed along the banks of the Suez Canal, "garnished by a continuous jetsam of empty brandy and rum bottles cast up by the waves and marking the unholy track of Western civilization."

(A century later this conflict between traditional Muslim and Western values has taken on an increased urgency with the appearance of Muslim fundamentalists in Libya, Iran, and other parts of the Middle East determined to wage a jihad, or holy war, against Western powers. What unites the Ayatollah Khomeini, the Shi'ite mullahs, and the true believers of Islamic Jihad is a sense that for 150 years the West has totally overwhelmed the Islamic world culturally and in the process made its traditional institutions and values seem second-rate. In this century the European powers, primarily Britain and France, broke up the Ottoman Empire into different secular states and installed dynasties that were often hostile to a way of life based on a strict reading of the Koran. In the fundamentalist credo the shah of Iran and the reigning family of Saudi Arabia are classic examples of Muslim leaders who sold their souls to the infidels for the sake of temporal power and wealth. After the Suez debacle of 1956 the United States replaced Britain as the great power in the Middle East and today takes the blame from Islamic fundamentalists rebelling against historic developments that largely predate its active role in the region.

(Because Islam represents a wedding of religion and politics, the sense of religious betrayal always leads in time to political action to restore the purity of an Islam thought to have been corrupted. "If *imitatio Christi* meant renouncing worldly ambition and seeking salvation by deeds of private virtue, *imitatio Mohammadi* meant sooner or later taking up arms against those forces which seemed to threaten Islam from within or without," Malise Ruthven observes in *Islam in the World.*)

"Blunt had a great deal of both sheykh and squire deeply ingrained in him," his grandson, the earl of Lytton, wrote years later. After 1880 Blunt took to wearing Bedouin dress around his Sussex estate. And in 1882 he and Anne purchased Sheykh Obeyd, a thirty-seven acre house and walled garden on the outskirts of Cairo in the desert near the pyramids. At the time it was Blunt's gesture of support for nationalist Egypt. But after his political disillusionment the romance continued to hold him. Sheykh Obeyd became Blunt's refuge, where he went for spiritual recovery after the bruising political fights in England.

A family friend, Frederic Harrison, visited Sheykh Obeyd in 1895 and wrote home a full description of Blunt's life in the Arab paradise he had crafted for himself:

> The garden, which covers about forty acres, is full of oranges, olives, apricots in blossom and roses in bloom—so that, although it is in the Desert, it is a wilderness of water and greenery. . . . The house is a genuine, roomy, and airy Egyptian villa in two storeys, with a large flat roof on which we spend early morning and evening, take afternoon tea and coffee, and lounge. . . . Under the palm grove, in front of the gate and outer court, the Arabian brood mares and their foals are tethered and are feeding down the clover. There are about twenty-five of them . . . tended by a small tribe of Bedouin lads in burnouses, who live in tents under the palms. The sight is like a bit from Genesis in real life. The camel encampment is some distance off, in the actual Desert, where there is another tribe of Bedouins who never come under a roof.

Blunt allowed few Western influences to intrude upon the paradise he had carved out of the desert. "The ladies adopt the Arab dress and go about in long flowing white burnouses and oriental headdresses, worn over embroidered satin," Harrison noted. "Everything is carried on in Arab style—no European servants except Lady A's maid. Nothing but Arabic is spoken. And the house from top to bottom is local Egyptian in form, ornament, and furniture. This morning we mounted Arabs—Wilfrid looking very grand in his burnous and turban on a fine bay."

Blunt continued to celebrate the Bedouin culture in his poetry, long after he had given up his political actions as futile. In his sonnet "To the Bedouin Arabs" he says:

> Children of Shem! Firstborn of Noah's race,
> But still forever children; at the door
> Of Eden found, unconscious of disgrace,

And loitering on while all are gone before;
Too proud to dig; too careless to be poor;
Taking the gifts of God in thanklessness,
Not rendering aught, nor supplicating more,
Nor arguing with Him when He hides His face.
Yours is the rain and sunshine, and the way
Of an old wisdom by our world forgot,
The courage of a day which knew not death.
Well may we sons of Japhet in dismay
Pause in our vain mad fight for life and breath,
Beholding you. I bow and reason not.

The Blunts slowly drifted apart. She lived a reclusive life at Sheykh Obeyd, now her chief home, rarely returning in later years to Crabbet Park in Sussex. Arabic, not English, became her first language and, she insisted, the language of her dreams and thoughts. Blunt often sought the companionship of other women. In 1895, when he was fifty-five, he had a passionate affair in the Egyptian desert with the daughter of an earlier mistress. In 1900 he started an affair with a young woman, Dororthy Carleton, whose pet name for him was Merlin. In 1906 she moved in with him at Crabbet Park. This precipitated a separation with Lady Anne. "I think of happy days alone with you in desert places," she wrote him. "Would that we had never come back from them." They continued to correspond on friendly terms and attempted, unsuccessfully, a reconciliation in 1915.

On December 15, 1917, Lady Anne Blunt died in Cairo. Her body was buried in a small cemetery on the edge of her beloved desert. Blunt observed that she was "of the salt of the earth. Nobody was ever so entirely and naturally good as she was."

He died on September 10, 1922. By his own orders there was no ceremony, only a simple Bedouin-style funeral. His body was wrapped in an Oriental carpet and carried by six of his workmen to a grave several hundred yards from Crabbet Park.

T. E. Lawrence visited Blunt on each return from the Middle East to pay homage to him as one of two surviving veterans of Arabian exploration. (The other was Charles Doughty.) After Blunt's death, he wrote a short account of his last visit to Crabbet Park: "An Arab mare drew Blunt's visitors deep within a Sussex wood to his quarried house, stone-flagged and hung with Morris tapestries. There in a great chair he sat, prepared for me like a careless work of art in well-worn Arab robes, his chiselled face framed in silvered, curling hair. . . . Blunt was a fire yet flickering over the ashes of old fury."

CHAPTER VII
....

Charles M. Doughty:
A Saint in Arabia Deserta

....

Of all the explorers of Arabia, Charles M. Doughty may well have been the most improbable—a Cambridge student of early English literature, who joined the thousands of pilgrims in the great hajj at Damascus and traveled south toward Mecca with a copy of Chaucer's *Canterbury Tales* in his saddlebags. A cross between a medieval itinerant scholar and a 1960s-style hippie wanderer, Doughty was the first European to venture openly as a Christian Englishman into the northern Arabian Peninsula. He traveled on his own without the benefits of financial backing by a society or a government that Burton and Guarmani enjoyed or of the triple shield of class, wealth, and Arab "blood brothers" that protected the Blunts. For two years he lived in the remote wilderness areas of the Arabian Peninsula, where few Europeans had ever before penetrated, his survival dependent entirely upon the hospitality of local Arabs. Probably no other explorer of his age suffered more hardships and constant abuse than Doughty, who wrote at the end of his wandering: "I passed one good day in Arabia; and all the rest were evil because of the people's fanaticism."

Doughty's massive account of that journey, *Travels in Arabia Deserta*, still stands as the most complete portrait of Bedouin life ever attempted. T. E. Lawrence called it "a book not like other books, but something particular, a bible of its kind . . . the first and indispensable work upon the Arabs of the desert" and insisted that Doughty "took all Arabia for his province and has left to his successors only the poor part of specialists." Doughty's *Travels* proved the major inspiration for Lawrence's *Seven Pillars of Wisdom*.

Doughty was born on August 19, 1843, at Theberton Hall in Suffolk. His father was an Anglican minister; his mother, the daughter of a cleric. He was a sickly infant at birth, and his desperate father baptized him immediately. Within a few months his mother died, and six years later his father. A kindly uncle reared the young Doughty. His ambition from early youth was a career in the British Navy to fulfill a family tradition. But in 1856 a slight speech impediment caused Doughty to fail the navy medical examination. He carried the disappointment with him for the rest of his life. In October 1861 Doughty enrolled as a student of geology at Caius College, Cambridge. One of his fellow students remembered him years later as "shy, nervous, and very polite, [without] a sense of humour."

"I am a private man," Doughty at seventy told his biographer David G. Hogarth. This aloof, solitary, self-contained nature stayed with him to the end. The fact is that we know next to nothing about Doughty's inner life. He rarely wrote or spoke about his feelings, had few friends, and left only a handful of letters and an impersonal journal. The outer facts of his life are well established, but the motives for many of his actions remain obscure.

In 1865 Doughty traveled to Norway to study glaciers and glaciation. There he lodged in farms and the houses of gamekeepers and accompanied his hosts on hunting expeditions, sleeping at night in log huts on the high mountain slopes. With a guide, Doughty crossed the Nigaard Glacier and later explored two northern glaciers which he insisted "had never been visited by travellers." The following year he published a long paper on the Jostedalsbreen glaciers.

In 1868 Doughty appeared at the Bodleian Library in Oxford, determined to study on his own early English literature and imbued with the idea of writing "a patriotic work" about the origins of England. "By setting forth the noble simplicity of the Nation's beginnings, he would recall his countrymen to a strong-minded patriotism, from which he felt they had fallen away," states his biographer Hogarth. "He, their *vates sacer*, must speak in verse, and this, to be appropriate, must be couched in that English pure and undefiled which was spoken before national degeneracy began—the English which Spenser last used in a day which was already declining from its noon."

In the late summer of 1870 Doughty left England for a period of extended travel through Europe and North Africa. On August 31, 1872, he climbed Mount Vesuvius near Naples to witness an eruption. "I waded ankle-deep in flour of sulphur upon a burning holly soil of lava," Doughty recalled years later in *Travels in Arabia Deserta.* "I approached the dreadful ferment, and watched that fiery pool heaving in the sides and welling over, and swimming in the midst of a fount of metal. . . . The eruption seen in the night, from the saddle of the mountain, a mile-great sheaf-like blast of purple-glowing and red flames belching fearfully and uprolling black smoke from the volcanic gulf, now half a mile wide."

While in Greece in 1874, Doughty suddenly decided to plunge into the Middle East, perhaps, as one early critic speculated, "to follow methodically our civilization back to its source and explore the pit out of which we were digged." He traveled leisurely down the Mediterranean coast from Turkey to Egypt. In 1875 Doughty embarked with a Bedouin guide upon a three-month journey by camel through the Sinai Peninsula. In that remote wilderness where the bare bones of the planet's creation stood naked and revealed, the major intellectual interests of his life—geology, philology, archaeology, and Christianity—seemed to have coalesced into a unifying pattern.

In early May Doughty left Sinai and headed toward the tightly guarded, glowing façades of Petra. "I had then no other intention

than to see Petra," he recalled. "I could speak very little Arabic."
Traveling from Bedouin camp to camp, he finally reached Petra.
Later, in his meditative epic, *Mansoul*, Doughty remembered the
splendor of the ancient scene:

> Then under Midian's Cliffs,
> Behold a Valley of Tombs, hewn in sand-rock.
> Were those the eternal sumptuous sepulchres;
> Of old forgotten tradeful merchant-wights;
> That gold and frank-incense fetched, from far South parts:
> Dwellers themselves, in villages of clay walls;
> Which sliding Time now utterly hath dissolved.

That evening Doughty learned from his Bedouin hosts of another
city, Medain Salih, lying many miles to the south, its origins lost in
time. Two days later he was back in Maan. There in a coffeehouse
he heard further talk of the ruins of Medain Salih with their
magnificent inscriptions and sculptures of birds. Local Arabs told
him the dead city lay ten days' march to the south of Petra along the
hajj road from Damascus. They suggested he join the pilgrim
caravan and travel in its safety to Medain Salih, something a
Christian could do if he made clear his intent from the first not to
seek Medina or Mecca.

Suddenly Doughty discovered a purpose to his travels. He would
become the first European to visit Medain Salih and the half dozen
fabulous stone cities reputed to be clustered nearby in the desert. He
returned to Vienna in September 1875 and wrote the Royal Geographical Society to plead for financial assistance: "Central Africa
has been explored [but not northern Arabia] for the danger and
difficulty of the way and the natural malice of Arabs. My desire is to
return immediately to go with the pilgrims to the discovery of those
unknown cities and inscriptions." His letter was never answered.

Doughty decided to mount his own expedition into northern
Arabia. His six-month experience with the Bedouins had convinced
him that while he could manage their life-style, he would first need
to become fluent in Arabic. He arrived in Damascus, where he lived

for a year in preparation for his grand adventure. He took as his tutor in Arabic a Lebanese Christian and refused to mix with the small European community in the city.

Doughty's preparation intensified as the summer of 1876 approached. He took the Arab name of Khalil, which he thought phonetically close to "Charles." (However, the Bedouins of Arabia generally called him *Engleysy* ["Englishman"] or *Nasrany* ["Christian"].) Although he wore Arab robes, Doughty refused to hide his Christian religion or British heritage. His motive here is obscure. Certainly his refusal to travel as a Muslim made his journey much more difficult and dangerous. It may have been nothing more than a stubborn pride in his identity as a Christian Englishman coupled with a contempt for the Muslim faith—"the dreadful-faced harpy of their religion."

Intending to pass as a hakim, or doctor, Doughty brought a medical handbook and a supply of simple medicines. He also collected a cavalry rifle, a pistol, two scientific German books on Arabia, an edition of *The Canterbury Tales* (in the original Middle English dialect), an aneroid barometer, a thermometer, and a small sextant. In his pockets Doughty carried two small notebooks and a meager sum of Turkish money. Both the British and Turkish authorities refused him all assistance.

The immediate goal of Doughty's travels was exploratory. "Of the Peninsula of the Arabs, large nearly as India, we have been in ignorance more than any considerable country in the world which remains to be visited," he wrote in his *Travels*. But in the preface to the third edition he made clear that his travels in Arabia had assumed for him a transcendental dimension as a pilgrimage to "the prehistoric Nest wherein were nourished and brought up and from whence have issued and dispersed themselves those several human swarms which became widespread, [those] powerful Semitic Peoples, [who] since History began have left an indelible impress upon the three Continents of the Old World and especially on the religious sentiment of so chief a portion of mankind."

On the night of November 12, 1876, Doughty on his mule joined the great pilgrim caravan, already some 6,000 strong with more than

10,000 camels. The next morning they departed on the forty-day journey to Mecca. Doughty later wrote:

> We waited to hear the cannon shot which should open that year's pilgrimage. It was near ten o'clock when we heard the signal gun fired; and then, without any disorder, litters were suddenly heaved and braced upon the bearing beasts, their charges laid upon the kneeling camels, and the thousands of riders, all born in the caravan counties, mounted in silence. . . . At the second gun, fired a few moments after, the Pasha's litter advances and after him goes the head of the caravan column. [After] fifteen or twenty minutes we, who have places in the rear, must half, that is until the long train is unfolded before us. Then we strike our camels and the great pilgrimage is moving. There go commonly three or four camels abreast and seldom five. The length of the slow-footed multitude is near two miles, and the width some hundred yards in the open plains.

Doughty had embarked upon his greatest adventure.

Today during the month of the hajj two million Muslims from more than sixty countries converge on the holy cities of Mecca and Medina. The plane has replaced the camel as the preferred means of travel for most of the pilgrims. Built at a cost of $5 billion, the King Abdul Aziz International Airport near Jiddah covers thirty-five square miles and is larger than the airports of Paris, Chicago, and New York. Fifty years ago only 30,000, or about one Muslim in 10,000, made the pilgrimage to Mecca each year. Today the hajj attracts two in 1,000 Muslims, a result of both improved transportation facilities and a rise in Islamic consciousness. Malise Ruthven writes in *Islam in the World*:

> In the past the hazards of travelling restricted observance to a very small number. The trip to the Holy Land took many months

and sometimes lasted years; it was not unknown for a man to spend the better part of a lifetime on it, setting out as a youth from one of the distant fringes of the Muslim world and arriving back half a century later, having worked his passage as an itinerant craftsman or labourer. Returning pilgrims have long borne the honoured title *Hajji,* and are accorded the reverence normally given to religious dignitaries—a factor which may partly account for the pilgrimage's continued and growing popularity.

The *hajj* (the Arabic word means "a journey towards God") refers to the third of the religious duties of Muslims. (The others are the recitation of the creed, prayers, fasting, and charity to the poor.) It is obligatory upon every adult man and woman to journey once to Mecca to submerge the individual self with the will of God. (However, Muhammad specifically exempted those Muslims who lack the money.) The hajj takes place in the twelfth month of the lunar calendar. The pilgrimage existed long before the birth of Muhammad. The objects adored were the idols within the Kaabah. Ancient Mecca, in fact, owed its prosperity to the celebration held during the annual religious ceremonies.

The yearly pilgrimage to Mecca is the great unifying force of a diverse Islamic world, allowing Muslims of all ages, classes, professions, and nationalities to come together. The hajj has always been a religious event with pronounced political overtones, embodying the political ideals of Islam: universal justice and equality, regardless of tribe, race, or material wealth. Throughout the history of Islam many of the most revolutionary movements have originated in Mecca during the pilgrimage.

(Malise Ruthven states that the Ayatollah Khomeini, for whom there can be no distinction between religious and political activity, has long insisted that attempts to make the hajj into a purely spiritual event have corrupted the original intent of Muhammad. "Revive the great divine political tradition of the *Hajj,*" he has urged his followers. "Acquaint Muslims with what is taking place in dear Lebanon, in crusading Iran, and oppressed Afghanistan. Inform them of their great duties in confronting aggressors and international plunderers."

Other Islamic radicals agree. One of their political tracts states: "*Hajj* is the antithesis of aimlessness. It is the rebellion against [accepting] a damned fate guided by evil forces. The fulfillment of the *Hajj* will enable you to escape from the complex network of puzzles.")

Until the mid-nineteenth century there were three main caravan routes to Mecca. The Cairo hajj included pilgrims from North Africa. Its route lay across the Sinai Peninsula and along the coastal fringes of Arabia to Mecca. The other great caravans started from Damascus and Baghdad. Some of the early Muslim emirs and pashas mounted lavish caravans. In 1324 Mansa Musa, the king of Mali, traveled across the Sahara with 500 servants, each bearing a 6-pound staff made of pure gold. Each of his 100 camels carried 300 pounds of gold. During a lengthy stay in Cairo Mansa Musa was so generous giving away his gold to the poor that it took years for the price of the metal to recover. He distributed the rest of his wealth at Mecca and Medina and returned to Mali a pauper.

Historian Paul Lunde writes:

> The caravans were highly organized. An official, called the *Emir el Hajj*, was responsible for the safety of the pilgrims. He had a troop of soldiers under his command, as well as a phalanx of officials. The caravan was organized like a moving city, with the emir, a judge, two notaries, a secretary, and an official charged with the care of the animals, another in charge of provisions, a saddler, a chef with a staff of cooks, and even an inspector of weights and measures. The caravans usually marched at night in order to avoid the heat of the sun and pitched camp near wells when they could, posting sentries to guard against attack by bandits. Each watering place along the route was provided with a small fortress and a rest house. The pilgrims were grouped in the caravan according to their point of origin—all pilgrims from the same town traveled together—and maintained the same position in the line of march. From the thirteenth century on, the Egyptian and Syrian caravans were each accompanied by a *Mahmal*, a kind of wooden litter, sumptuously decorated, that contained a copy of the Koran. The *Mahmal* itself was a symbol of political

sovereignty over the holy places of Islam, the Koran inside sym-
bolizing the unity of the religious and secular authorities of Islam.

For all but the very wealthy who could afford to travel with private
armies, the hajj was an enterprise fraught with great dangers. The
enormous crowds of pilgrims suffered appalling casualties from heat,
bandits, and plague. In 1826 12,000 pilgrims on the Damascus hajj
perished in the scorching blasts of a single *simoom*. Along certain
stretches of desert the skeletons of hundreds of camels, donkeys, and
horses, along with numerous rough graves of pilgrims, dotted the
landscape. Bandits ruthlessly attacked the caravans, picking off strag-
glers and infiltrating in the night to murder and loot in the confusion. "If discovered, they draw their daggers and cut their way
through; for, if taken, they can expect no mercy," John Lewis
Burckhardt reported in the early part of the nineteenth century.
"The usual mode of punishment on such occasions is to impale them
at the moment the caravan starts from the next station, leaving them
to perish on the stake or be devoured by wild beasts."
Even worse were the devastating effects of plague on the caravans.
Very often the pilgrims carried cholera to Mecca, infecting other
believers, who in turn took the disease back to their cities with
appalling effects. In 1865—twelve years after Burton's hajj—returning pilgrims took cholera to Egypt, where 60,000 people died. Other
pilgrims carried the disease as far away as New York City and
Guadeloupe before the plague was finally checked in 1874. It returned with force in 1893, when pilgrims to Mecca found the streets
choked with stacks of corpses.
Lodovico Varthema, almost certainly the first European to reach
Mecca, traveled there in the company of the Damascus hajj. We
know next to nothing about his life except for a series of extraordinary journeys he made in the early sixteenth century. He was Italian,
probably from Rome. In 1503 he arrived in the Middle East, "longing
for novelty as a thirsty man longs for fresh water," and made his way
to Damascus. Varthema shrewdly befriended the Mameluke captain
in charge of the pilgrim caravan. The officer, a "Christian renegade,"
agreed for a steep price to get the Italian to Mecca. Varthema dressed

in a Mameluke's uniform, bought a horse, and took the Arab name of Yunis. On April 8 the hajj departed from Damascus. Varthema estimated the number of pilgrims at 40,000.

On the fourth day Varthema encountered his first Bedouins. He wrote later in his travel narrative:

> They ride for the most part without saddles and in their shirts. Their arms consist of a lance of Indian cane ten or twelve cubics in length with a piece of iron at the end, and when they go on any expedition they keep as close together as starlings. These Arabs are very small men and of a dark tawny colour. They have a feminine voice and long, stiff, black hair. And truly these Arabs are in such vast numbers that they cannot be counted, and they are constantly fighting amongst themselves. They [come down to the hajj road] when the caravan passes through to go to Mecca, in order to lie in wait at the passes for the purpose of robbing the caravan. They carry their wives, children, and all their furniture and also their houses upon camels. Their houses are like the tents of soldiers and are of black wool and of a sad appearance."

Varthema reported several skirmishes with the Bedouins, but the Mameluke escort kept casualties to a minimum. The Italian learned to sleep in the saddle on the twenty-hour marches that lasted until the Mameluke captain ordered a halt during the noonday heat. The camels were unloaded and fed "five loaves of barley-meal, uncooked, and each about the size of a pomegranate." They traveled hard for eight-day stretches and then rested for two days at wells. During the final leg, between Medina and Mecca, hundreds of pilgrims died from thirst. On May 18, 1503, Varthema reached Mecca.

The overland caravans continued in importance until the opening of the Suez Canal in 1869. After 1873 a majority of pilgrims made their hajj by ship. The Damascus caravan still flowed south, but with drastically reduced numbers, until 1908, when the Hejaz Railway was completed. A project of Sultan Abdul Hamid II, the railroad ran 800 miles from Damascus to Medina. The Turkish engineer who surveyed the route simply followed the caravan route. The railway provided inexpensive, fast travel to the holy cities of Islam. But it also became a strategic artery of major importance to the crumbling Ottoman Empire. With his new railway the sultan now had the means to pour an uninterrupted stream of troops into Arabia.

The Bedouins watched with fascination as the first trains—they called them the "Iron Camels"—chugged through their desert realm. For a people accustomed to centuries of lucrative raiding against the hajj caravans, the trains marked the end of an era, too. Ten years later under the leadership of T. E. Lawrence, they took their revenge in some of the most daring ambushes of the great desert war.

Doughty's caravan marched a short distance the first day to allow the pilgrims and their animals an opportunity to adjust to the new routine. That evening the vast procession set up camp in the desert. Sentries were posted. A paper lantern hung outside each tent. Crickets chirped in the darkness. The sounds of flutes, drumbeating, and Persian prayer chants carried over the camp. Doughty lay in his tent, enjoying the "Arcadian sweetness" of the moment before falling asleep.

At four o'clock in the morning the signal gun boomed. "That shot is eloquent in the desert night, the great caravan rising at the instant, with sudden untimely hubbub of the pilgrim thousands," Doughty wrote later. "There is a short struggle of making ready, a calling and running with lanterns, confused roaring and ruckling of camels, and the tents are taken up over heads. [Within minutes] the pilgrim army is remounted. The gun fired at four hours after midnight startled many wayworn bodies; and often there are some so weary, usually those come on foot from very great distances, that they may not waken, and the caravan moving on they are left behind in the darkness."

The huge procession traveled over no road as such, merely over a series of parallel paths worn into the hard-packed clay and gravel surface by hundreds of previous hajj caravans. After a twenty-mile march it reached the first well, guarded by a stone watchtower and manned with Turkish soldiers. The pilgrims refreshed their supplies of water and then moved on. The ruins of past civilizations—"cyclopean ground walls, laid without mortar, and street lines of basalt pavement, a colonnade and some small temple"—dotted the landscape as the caravan slowly made its way southward.

On the seventh day of the march the pilgrims saw their first Bedouins, four young, long-haired warriors who rode up to beg ("insolently") a handful of tobacco. "In their camps they would be kind hosts," Doughty observed, "but had we fallen into their hands in the desert we should have found them fiends." Long lances balanced on their shoulders, the four warriors rode bareback upon their horses. Arrogantly they put on a display of their riding prowess, galloping hard, wheeling about abruptly, and thrusting their spears at imaginary enemies. "Under the most ragged of these riders was a perfect young and startling chestnut mare," Doughty noted. "Never combed by her rude master, but all shining beautiful and gentle of herself, she seemed a darling life upon that savage soil not worthy of her gracious pasterns."

Doughty was fascinated by the details of daily life within the great hajj, which suggested to him on a smaller scale what life must have been like in that other great hajj of the Old Testament when Moses led the Jews out of Egypt toward the Promised Land. Nothing missed Doughty's alert eye. He observed the caravan's dogs, which walked the entire 2,000 miles from Damascus to Mecca and back, and the slaves who carried the burning coals for the pipe smokers in litters. He estimated the caravan's rate of march at two and a half miles per hour and counted the number of steps a camel takes in one minute (fifty). A camel driver, he learned, earned the English equivalent of eight pounds for his forty-day march to Mecca. With his thermometer Doughty measured the average temperature of well water (66° F.) and insisted that he never found water in Arabia that was not lukewarm.

Doughty tells us that when a wealthy Persian woman died en route, her servant sewed the body into the bloody hide of a freshly slaughtered camel and carried it, stinking and swelling, to Mecca. He heard stories about the terrible hajj of 1872, which returned from Mecca with cholera in its ranks, leaving scores of dead and dying behind at each stop. One man, buried prematurely by his family in a shallow desert grave, revived later in the warmth of the noonday sun to find himself without water or food in the middle of an empty desert. He managed to walk alone several hundred miles, going from Bedouin camp to Bedouin camp, until he finally reached his home in Damascus. But his family refused to accept him, insisting that he was merely an impostor. "Had they not but a few weeks before laid their kinsman in his grave, stark dead, in Arabia?"

Early on December 4 the caravan approached the "mountains of fantastic rock," which guarded the low basin of Medain Salih. Several Arabs had promised Doughty, "You will see wonders—horses in the rock and all overturned and standing above downwards." At the end of that "misty warm Sunday morning" the caravan pitched camp in the plain, deep inside the Arabian Peninsula. There Doughty left the hajj, the first part of his journey completed, and took up residence with the Turkish soldiers in a nearby fort guarding the well.

Medain Salih, famous in Muslim mythology as one of seven great cities cut from rock, owed its prosperity to the commerce in frankincense, cinnamon, and gold from Arabia Felix. The prophet Salih appeared to the inhabitants, a pagan people, and demanded they convert to the ways of Islam. But the people scoffed and demanded a sign. This he gave them. A camel, ten months pregnant, stepped out of the mountainside. Some months later the people slew the cow. The rocks opened to swallow the calf, whose cries Doughty was told could still be heard deep within the earth. Soon afterward Salih visited upon the impious city a great whirlwind, killing the people and turning their houses upside down.

When Doughty visited Medain Salih, it was a major watering place along the hajj route to Mecca, a village of about 1,300 people located 550 miles south of Damascus. He was eager to visit the ruins, but the Turkish officer refused his permission. In the meantime, Doughty befriended a man who was to change his life radically: Zeyd el-Sbeychan, a minor sheik of the Fukara tribe. He described the Bedouin as "swarthy, nearly black—of mid-stature and middle age with a hunger-bitten stern visage . . . and a high and liberal understanding. Nothing in Zeyd was barbarous and uncivil. His carriage was that haughty grace of the wild creatures. In him I have not seen any spark of fanatical ill-humour."

Zeyd became Doughty's companion when the Englishman finally received permission to explore the nearby ruins, sketch the buildings, and transcribe the inscriptions. He learned that the "cities" were actually clusters of ancient tombs cut from sandstone rock. Each had a width of twenty-two feet and was flanked by sculptured cornices and Corinthian columns with enormous stone eagles set over yawning doors. Inside, the two men found many open graves, filled with human bones. Doughty examined piles of rags littering a sandy floor and then hastily dropped them when he discovered they were "those dry bones' grave-clothes!" A "loathsome mummy odour" clung to his own robes long after he had left the tombs.

Doughty visited 100 such tombs, all once belonging to families that had grown wealthy on the caravan trade. Amid mounds of broken pottery he found shattered foundations of clay houses, which had long since crumbled into dust. Only the tombs, mute reminders of the fabulous incense trade that once flowed northward from Arabia Felix, survived.

Doughty, "a lonely Christian in the midst of a stirring multitude of Muslims," waited two months for the return of the hajj from Mecca. Then, on February 5, he saw the pilgrims stream into the plains south of Medain Salih, their numbers heavily depleted by a smallpox epidemic. "This terrible disease and cholera fever are the destruction of nomad Arabia," he observed sadly. "The pilgrimage caravans . . . are as torrents of the cities' infection flowing every year through the peninsula."

Doughty had originally planned to return with the hajj to Damascus after Medain Salih. Now he elected to remain in Arabia with his friend Zeyd to study the Bedouin way of life. He made arrangements to have his detailed notes on the ruins of Medain Salih delivered to the British consul in Damascus. Doughty's friends in the hajj all sought to persuade him to return with them. "If one goes into Arabia, he should carry his shroud under his arm," one warned him.

Another insisted, "Why cast your life away? You know them not. But we know them. The Bedouins are fiends."

Doughty began his year of wandering among the Bedouins with few resources. His money amounted to less than twenty pounds. He had his supply of medicines and a hope that he could sell his medical services for small sums. But chiefly he planned to rely upon the traditional Bedouin code of hospitality for his survival in the desert.

On the morning of February 15, as the hajj wound northward from Medain Salih, Doughty and Zeyd rode eastward into a "wasteland of gravel and sand, full of sandstone crags." Zeyd suddenly stopped his camel. "This is the land of the Bedouin," he told Doughty, making a great sweep of his arm. Then the Arab studied the Englishman's face closely to see his reaction to the empty desert beyond. Finally he said, "Hear, O Khalil, you will live here with us, and we will give you a maiden to wife. If any children be born to you, when you do go hence from here, they shall be as my own and remain with me."

That evening they arrived in Zeyd's camp. Doughty found none of the prosperity there that he had seen among the Syrian Bedouins. But his welcome was a warm one, these Arabs having no suspicions of the *Nasrany*, or Christian. Zeyd immediately invited Doughty into his tent ("poor and low") and introduced him to his young wife, Hirfa, saying, "Khalil, here is thy new 'aunt,' and, Hirfa, this is Khalil; take good care of him."

The next day the small group broke camp in the chilly dawn. The others waited until Zeyd's wife struck the chief's tent before pulling up their stakes and collapsing their tents. The men sat to one side, warming their hands over the embers of a fire, while the women toiled. To have helped their wives would have been "an indignity even in the women's eyes." The women stored the household effects in wool sacks of their own weaving. Hirfa strained to lift the heavy bags onto the backs of the camels and then called upon Zeyd for help. He did so grudgingly. "Is a sheik a porter to bear burdens?" he complained to his wife. Doughty was sympathetic, later writing: "Zeyd was a lordling in no contemptible tribe. Such a sheik should not in men's sight put his hand to any drudgery."

The men rode ahead, their swords and matchlocks hanging from the saddletrees behind them, their lances in their hands, while the women with the pack camels brought up the rear. They marched for ten miles and then pitched camp. The women spread out the black wool tent cloths, pounded in stakes with rocks, and then clumsily heaved the tents into place. The men sat silently around a fire, roasting locusts or drubbing sticks aimlessly upon the sand. There was little small talk because, as Doughty observed, "everything has been uttered a hundred times already." Soon afterward the women reappeared with bowls of buttermilk and dates. The men ate. The women sat within their tents, rocking upon their knees, making butter. Doughty was to learn that this was the eternal routine of Bedouin life in northern Arabia.

In that part of the desert most of the wells were polluted, the water reeking of camel urine and swarming with worms. Doughty learned to drink it and be grateful for anything wet. Each morning Hirfa on Zeyd's orders poured Doughty two ounces of precious water to wash himself, "as the townspeople do." Hirfa did as she was told but grumbled to Doughty that she thought it a terrible waste of the water, especially when the men went thirsty most of the day. Often, in their wanderings between wells, Zeyd had less than a pint of water in his tent, not even enough to make the obligatory coffee for his guest. He himself often went without water, giving his ration to his mare. "The horse," Doughty noted, "is of all the animals of the desert the most impatient of thirst."

Doughty settled into the routine of nomad life, his "long holiday, wedded to a divine simplicity." The desert was in its winter bloom, carpeted with sweetly scented wild rape, pimpernel, and sorrel, a veritable "fairy garden of blossoms." The tribe's camels gorged themselves on the pasture, building in their humps the fat that would see them through the lean summer months.

Hirfa was Zeyd's second wife. His first wife had fled from him, a common occurrence among Bedouins, and returned to her mother's tribe. When Zeyd learned they were camped in a nearby pasture, he rode over and wooed her back to his encampment, where she erected her tent near his. Zeyd's marriage with Hirfa, "whose golden youth was faded almost into autumn in her childish face," had become tenuous. She was a sheik's orphan whom he had married when she was eighteen, partly for a few camels she had inherited from her father. She sighed for motherhood. But after two years of marriage she had yet to get pregnant and blamed her husband. Eventually she ran off. "The fugitive Bedouin wife has good leave to run whithersoever she would," Doughty observed. "She is free as the desert; there is none that can detain her." Zeyd sent Doughty to persuade her to return, a sign the Englishman at that point had been accepted as one of the Bedouin family.

The months Doughty spent in the desert with Zeyd's tribe were the happiest of his long stay in Arabia. "Pleasant is the sojourn in the wandering village, in this purest earth and air with the human fellowship, which is all day met at leisure about the cheerful coffee-fire," he wrote in his *Travels*. "Lying to rest amidst wild basalt stones under the clear skies in a land of enemies, I found more refreshment than upon beds and pillows in our close [bed] chambers."

Although Doughty had been fully accepted by the band of Fukara Bedouins, his presence in the desert always puzzled them. Was he a spy come among them? they wanted to know. A seeker after hidden treasure? Or perhaps he had been banished among them for some great crime? They questioned Doughty at length about England.

"Have your people any great towns, Khalil?"

"Great indeed, so that all the Bedouin gathered out of your deserts would hardly fill one of our great cities," he told them.

"God is great," they exclaimed. "But are not the English uncles of the Sultan on his mother's side?"

Doughty told them about the Crimea War in which British soldiers had fought alongside Turkish forces against the Russians.

"Were your dead two or three hundred, or not so many?" the Bedouins wanted to know.

"We had 60,000 dead," he told them.

"Ah Lord God! Is not that more than all the men together in these parts?" one exclaimed.

When Doughty told them that England was a land without palm trees, the Bedouins were aghast. "There are no dates! How then do your people live, or what sweetness do they taste?"

Once when the Bedouins taunted Doughty for eating the flesh of pork, he lost his temper. "I see you eat crows and kites, and the lesser carrion eagle," he shouted at them. "Some of you eat owls, some eat serpents. The great lizard you all eat. . . . Many eat the hedgehog; in some villages they eat rats. You cannot deny it! You eat the wolf, too, and the fox and the foul hyena. In a word, there is nothing so vile that some of you will not eat it."

Over the weeks the small band of Bedouins frequently changed their camp. Each evening the men congregated in Zeyd's tent. Those were times of festive raillery and good-natured banter. To pass the time, the Bedouins asked Doughty to teach them some words of English. Zeyd was much pleased with himself when he could shout in English over the tent curtain to Hirfa, "Girl, bring me the milk!"

Doughty never ceased to be amazed at the Bedouin code of hospitality. Once he visited a camp of Moahib Bedouins in the midst of the rugged Harra plateau, "a sandstone platform mountain . . . overlaid, two thousand square miles, to the brink by a general effusion of lavas." The host prepared a traditional banquet of welcome, serving up a great tray of steamed rice and a pan of melted butter. Doughty and the others pressed small handfuls of the rice into balls and dipped them into the butter. Their host kindly urged them on: "Though it be a poor meal, yet take you in good worth as Allah sends." At the end of the meal the guests turned to their host to intone the Muslim blessing "May Allah multiply thy virtuous bounty."

Later Doughty learned that their host for that day's guest banquet had given in hospitality all the food remaining to him, leaving his family only a small amount of camel's milk. "The Bedouin can live for long months so slenderly nourished that it seems to us they endure without food," the Englishman observed in wonder. "Startling is this occasional magnanimity of the Bedouin in the religious sacrifice of hospitality, men who in their other dealings are commonly of so merely vile, fraudulent, self-serving mind and envious misanthropy. The most honour of a man's life is the people's praise of his bounty."

The winter became spring and was quickly followed by the scorching heat of summer. Life in the desert became a long nightmare. Feeling the accumulated effects of months of meager Bedouin food rations, Doughty languished in the tent in temperatures that often reached 105° F at noon. "The summer's night at end, the sun stands up as a crown of hostile flames from the huge covert of inhospitable sandstone bergs," he remembered later. "The sun, entering as a tyrant upon the waste landscape, darts upon us a torment of fiery beams, not to be remitted until the far-off evening. . . . Grave is the giddy heat upon the crown of the head; the ears tingle with a flickering shrillness. Mountains, looming like dry bones through the thin air, stand far around us."

Every aspect of Bedouin life unfolded before Doughty's eyes, from the sacrifice of a ewe at the birth of a male child through the circumcision ceremony to the funeral ritual. Once he helped bury a dead warrior, washing the corpse, wrapping it in a cloth, and then laying the man in a shallow grave with his feet pointing toward Mecca. Stones were piled on top to keep the wolves away. And a ewe was sacrificed. ("These sacrifices eaten in fellowship in the desert allay a little these nomads' almost incessant famine.") On another occasion, when a woman died, her body was sprinkled with perfume and buried with her comb, and the grave was marked with a tent stake.

Doughty spent most of the summer of 1877 on the Harra lava plateau with the Moahib Bedouins under a chief named Tollog. His health deteriorated. Much of the time he suffered from severe intestinal cramps and outbreaks of boils. Doughty's reception among these Bedouins was less friendly and often hostile. He had outworn his welcome as a guest and not yet established himself as an associate. Famine gripped the tribe, and the Bedouins increasingly resented Doughty's presence. Tempers often flared. "This man is a *Nasrany*," one Bedouin shouted. "I say cut his head off. There is none who will require his blood at our hand." Doughty took to wearing his pistol on a cord around his neck inside his shirt. But he believed that passivity and patience were his best defense and placed his faith in the Bedouin reverence for guests no matter how unwelcome they may have become. The sheik was forced to extend his hospitality to his English guest by stealth. On August 3 Doughty noted in his diary that after a daily fare of an ounce of milk and a small crust of bread he was "almost dead with hunger in this place."

Finally, on August 28, Doughty joined a small group of Bedouins for a march to the oasis town of Taima. He had visited there some months before with Zeyd. After his departure the walls of the well pit had collapsed, brought down, the townspeople believed, because of the *Nasrany's* evil eye. Three attempts to rebuild the sides had failed. Doughty was told that if he entered Taima, the people would cut his throat.

An official in town was convinced that if Doughty had the power to destroy the wall, he could just as easily raise it back up. Too feeble to travel farther, Doughty agreed to remain in Taima and supervise the construction. As he walked toward the well pit alongside the official, he heard the town Arabs talking among themselves as he passed. "Look, here he comes. Look. Look. It is the [infidel]. Will the sheiks kill him?"

Doughty spent a month in Taima, recovering his strength and working out a plan for the restoration of the well. Although the townspeople remained hostile toward him, they never threatened him with any physical violence. At the end of September Doughty was suddenly stricken with a painful ophthalmia that nearly blinded him. He was in Taima when Ramadan ended and with it the long season of fasting. The villagers invited Doughty to join in their festivities, feasting and singing. After a group of Arab women had finished dancing, they asked their English guest to give them a display of his "holiday dance." Doughty put on a solo display of ballroom dancing, much to the amazement of the gathered Bedouins: "Oh! what was that outlandish skipping and casting of the shanks, and this footing to and fro!" But when he explained that in England the men danced "bosom to bosom" with the women, the Bedouins were scandalized.

On October 10 Doughty set out for Hail with a group of Bishr Bedouins, who proved fanatical and intolerant of Christians, treating him with menacing rudeness the entire journey. The Bedouins traveled swiftly, one day covering fifty miles. The ill Doughty on his aged camel could hardly keep pace and often lagged far behind. Finally, on the morning of October 22, he saw in the distance the tall clay-brick towers of Hail.

Doughty arrived in the capital of northern Arabia dirty and in rags. The emir Muhammad ibn Rashid quickly learned of his presence. An official met him in the town square and showed him to a guesthouse opposite the emir's palace. That same afternoon Doughty had his first audience with Ibn Rashid. He found the emir propped up on pillows near a roaring fire. Doughty greeted him with the traditional Arab blessing "Peace be with you." The emir returned no answer. Some Arabs, Doughty noted, refused to give the traditional greeting to a Christian. Ibn Rashid questioned the Englishman at length about the purpose of his visit and his trip thus far. Afterward he showed his guest to a garden where he kept a pair of Arabian oryxes. Doughty believed himself the first European to see these rare antelopes.

Doughty spent the next several weeks recovering his health and exploring the city. Like the Blunts after him, he was impressed by Ibn Rashid's daily *mejlis,* the informal court where the emir dispensed Bedouin justice. Doughty's presence in the city provoked enormous interest, and he attracted crowds of curious spectators whenever he ventured into the streets. Sheiks and wealthy merchants sought him out in his room, eager to converse with the *Nasrany* who had come among them. One of Doughty's visitors was a Baghdad Jew who asked him in a whisper if he had smuggled any forbidden brandy into Hail. And his practice of medicine—there were no doctors in the city—also opened doors that otherwise would have been closed.

Hail was full of surprises. Doughty found in the bazaar a merchant selling imported silk folded into newspapers. Suddenly he realized that he was reading English, that the papers were issues of the *Bombay Gazette.* Doughty started examining more closely the wares for sale and discovered bolts of cloth, ingots of lead, boxes of gunpowder, crowbars, shovels, and other items carrying the British stamp of origin, all come into Arabia through the lively commerce in the Persian Gulf. The money was also European. Spanish reals, British sovereigns, French twenty-franc pieces, Maria Theresa dollars, and Turkish crowns all circulated together in Hail.

One day the Baghdad hajj arrived on its way to Mecca. The

pilgrims pitched camp just outside the Gofar gate and rested for two days. Doughty went out to watch their departure in the early morning. While he stood to one side, a Baghdad merchant with a chestnut-colored beard approached him.

"What do you seek?" Doughty asked him. He expected the man to ask him for some medicine.

Instead, he answered softly with a question. "If I speak in the French language, will you understand me?"

"Yes," a surprised Doughty assured him. "What's your country?"

"My name is Francesco Ferrari. I am an Italian from Turin."

"My God, man," Doughty gasped. "These people will cut your throat if they discover you."

The two talked quietly in French. Ferrari told Doughty how he had come to the Middle East eight years before, when he was a youth of sixteen. He had spent the past three years studying in an Islamic college in Baghdad, where he'd had himself circumcised. He planned to see Mecca and Medina and then explore the headwaters of the Jordan River. Afterward he would return to Italy, "wipe off all this rust of the Mohammedan life," and publish an account of his adventures. The caravan slowly moved off. The Italian mounted his camel, bade Doughty farewell, and followed after them.

Months later, when Doughty returned to Damascus, he left word about Ferrari with the Italian consul there and later inquired about him in Italy. But the man had not turned up. Doughty feared he had been murdered on the hajj. "I thought it my duty, for how dire is the incertitude which hangs over the head of any aliens that will adventure themselves to Mecca," Doughty noted sadly. "I have heard from credible Muslims that nearly no *hajj* passes in which some unhappy persons are not put to death as intruded Christians."

Doughty was eager to be on his way to Khaibar. The people of Hail had satiated their curiosity about the *Nasrany*. Imbarak, the captain of the palace guard, insisted upon his immediate departure and arranged for him to accompany a group of Bedouins to Khaibar. The two had an argument when the officer tried rudely to evict Doughty prematurely from his room. Imbarak manhandled him and spit in his face. Several soldiers began to beat Doughty savagely. He had his pistol hidden inside his shirt. But he never thought of using it. Instead, he put his trust in the desert's code of hospitality, crying "Dakhil-ak"—a Bedouin plea for sanctuary. Immediately Imbarak snatched up a camel stick and beat back his own men.

Doughty refused to leave Hail until Ibn Rashid gave him a passport of safe conduct. That afternoon, when the emir appeared in the square for his *mejlis*, Doughty was in the crowd of petitioners. Ibn Rashid was obviously surprised by the Englishman's appearance.

"What do you wish?" he asked.

"I am about to depart, but I would it were with assurance," Doughty said. "Today I was mishandled in this place, in a way that has made me afraid. Your slaves drew me hither and thither and have rent my clothing. Imbarak, who stands here, set them on. He also threatened me and spat in my face. "

Ibn Rashid conferred briefly with Imbarak. Then he turned back to Doughty.

"Fear not," he said emphatically, striking his breast. "We will give you a passport."

The emir's secretary wrote on a small slip of paper and then read aloud the passport: "That unto whose hands this bill may come, who owe obedience to Ibn Rashid, know it is the will of the emir that no one should do any offense to this *Nasrany.*" Ibn Rashid daubed his Arabic copper seal in the ink and sealed the paper with the print of his name.

On November 21 Doughty left Hail for Khaibar, 100 miles to the southwest through the Harra plateau, in the company of three Hutaim Bedouins. On the way out of the oasis he met with an example of the natural Arab courtesy that often eased the pain of the insults and indignities he experienced. The group stopped to buy dates from an impoverished family who treated Doughty with great kindness. "These poor folk, disinherited of the world, spoke to me with human kindness," he remembered later. "There was not a word in their talk of the Mohammedan fanaticism. The women, of their own thought, took from my shoulders and mended my mantle which had been rent yesterday in Hail."

But Doughty's situation was still precarious. He had little money, no tent, no camel, and precious little of value to barter. His companions were Bedouins of the lowest caste, outcasts from their tribes. Doughty knew they would be utterly unreliable on his desert journey. And within a few days they had deserted him. Doughty arranged for a guide from a Hutaim Bedouin sheik who was eager to be rid of him.

Everything about his trip from Hail thus far—the unfaithful guides and the foreboding Harra landscape of eroded lava flows—suggested an ill-fated journey. "We looked out from every height . . . over an iron desolation; what an uncouth blackness and lifeless cumber of volcanic matter!—an hard-set face of nature without a smile forever, a wilderness of burning and rusty horror of unformed matter," Doughty noted with a growing sense of disquietude. "We mounted in the morrow twilight; but long after daybreak the heavens seemed to shut over us, as a tomb, with gloomy clouds."

The sudden appearance of flies announced Khaibar long before Doughty could see the drab mud walls of the village. The town was under direct Turkish administration, unlike the other places which he had visited. Khaibar, where Guarmani had briefly stayed almost thirteen years earlier, was a curious phenomenon in the barren sands of inner Arabia: an all-black community ruled by a black Turkish governor. "Khaibar is an African village in the Hejaz," Doughty observed. Later he thought of it as an island: "It is hard to come hither, it is not easy to depart." Khaibar was to become Doughty's nightmare, his descent into the "heart of darkness."

As Doughty rode through the palm groves on the floor of the valley, he sensed immediately that he had come upon a place of evil: "Foul was the abandoned soil upon either hand, with only a few awry and undergrown stems of palms. The squalid ground is whitish with crusts of bitter salt-warp and stained with filthy rust. . . . How strange are these dank Khaibar valleys in the waterless Arabia! A heavy presentiment of evil lay upon my heart as we rode into this deadly drowned atmosphere."

Doughty's sense of nightmare deepened as he explored the village. He found the water in the town's well "tepid and sulphurous." A garden at a distance appeared a sanctuary, but upon closer inspection he saw it was infested with giant rats. A cemetery lay in the midst of black volcanic ash, the squalid grave mounds marked with black basalt headstones. "That funeral earth is chapped and ghastly, bulging over her enwombed corpses, like a garden soil in springtime, which is pushed by the new-aspiring plants," Doughty observed. "All is horror at Khaibar! There is nothing there which does not fill a stranger's eye with discomfort."

The people of Khaibar practiced magic and witchcraft and were slaves to bizarre African superstitions. They believed that naked witches, seeking satisfaction of their unnatural sexual desires, stalked the streets at night. Men who succumbed to the seductive wiles of these witches went mad. The village was almost empty of children. "I daily wondered to see almost no young children in Khaibar! The villagers answered me, 'The children die in this air! It is the will of Allah.' " Sickness was everywhere. A black man dying of tuberculosis told Doughty, "Khaibar is the whole world's sepulchre."

Ruling over this corruption was Abdullah el Siruan, an Ethiopian-born Turkish governor and "a hateful tyrant," and Sirur, his villainous lieutenant. Doughty identified himself as a Christian Englishman and was immediately arrested and brought before Abdullah. He was stunned. "In what land, I thought, am I now arrived! And who are these who take me (because of Christ's sweet name!) for an enemy of mankind?"

"What is this!" Doughty demanded. "I am an *Engleysy*, and being of a friendly nation why am I dealt with thus?"

He produced the passport of safe conduct from Ibn Rashid and a second document from a Turkish authority in Syria. But Abdullah could not read and simply confiscated the papers. He accused the Englishman of being a spy for the Russians and ordered a thorough search of his saddlebags. In their ignorance, everything unfamiliar was suspect. One man held up Doughty's comb and insisted that it must be a clever device to harm Muslims. Abdullah seized his notes and journal and said he would send them to the pasha at Medina for study. Doughty was forced to yield to the Turk his last small reserves of money for "better keeping." When he protested, Sirur bellowed savagely at him, "We will send to the Pasha, and if the Pasha's word is 'Cut off his head,' we will chop off thy head, *Nasrany*."

From that day on Doughty was a virtual prisoner. He was lodged with one of the Turkish soldiers. Abdullah waited three weeks before forwarding his papers to Medina. Doughty connived with the help of a friendly merchant to send with the messenger a private letter to the pasha deploring Abdullah's arbitrary abuse of his authority.

Although Doughty was allowed limited liberty to visit the village, he was Abdullah's prisoner and kept under constant supervision. Twice a day he was forced to report to the governor's office and endure his insults and contempt.

His only consolation was Muhammad el Nejumy, his one friend and protector in the village. "He was of a mild and cheerful temper, confident, tolerant, kind, inwardly God-fearing, lightly moved," Doughty remembered in later years. "His heart was full of a pleasant humour of humanity." But even Nejumy was cursed with the evil of Khaibar. He had syphilis, although dormant, and had infected his brother with the disease. The Englishman accompanied Nejumy to the lava fields of the plateau to see ancient Arabic inscriptions and near Khaibar to the ruins of a Jewish settlement, including a pair of antique clay pyramids.

In spite of Nejumy's kindness, Doughty hated Khaibar and genuinely feared that the Turkish pasha in Medina might order his execution. "These were days for me sooner of dying than of life; and the felonious Abdullah made no speed to deliver me." With the exception of his friend Nejumy, the superstitious blacks feared Doughty as "a warlock come to bewitch their village." Once, while he walked the streets, a terrified villager shot at him, but the bullet passed harmlessly over his head. Escape from the town was impossible without a guide to lead him through the bleak desert beyond.

Doughty languished for three and a half months in Khaibar. The weeks dragged on, and still no word came from the pasha in Medina. Doughty suspected the worst as he waited "in this darkness that is Khaibar." He was deeply moved by one of Nejumy's stories about a "Christian Martyr" murdered because of his religion the year before. The man (apparently a Sicilian) arrived in Medina, thinking he had come to Khaibar, and identified himself as a *Nasrany*. He was ordered to convert to Islam and say, "Allah is the only God, and his messenger is Muhammad." The visitor refused, pleading, "I may not say as you ask because I am a Christian." He was cast in prison. Worried about possible political repercussions from Constantinople if a European Christian was murdered, the Turkish pasha ordered the man's expulsion under armed guards to Yenbo on the coast. But as the small group marched through the desert, the officer in charge turned on his prisoner and demanded he convert immediately or be executed.

"You have heard the Pasha's orders," the man pleaded. "Take me peaceably to Yenbo."

"Who shall I obey?" the officer shouted. "In killing you I will obey Allah. Swear to Allah, and I will spare your life."

"You have your religion, and I have mine. You serve your God and I serve my God. Live in your religion and let me live in mine."

"*You* have no religion," the soldier shouted, and shoved his musket into the Christian's breast. "Once more—convert or die."

The Christian stood silent. A moment later the officer shot him dead.

One morning Abdullah summoned Doughty to his quarters and handed him a letter from the pasha in Medina, written in execrable French and dated January 11, 1878. He wrote to say that he understood the Englishman was traveling through Arabia for the purpose of gaining a greater understanding of Arabs and their way of life. He told Doughty that he was free to leave Khaibar and advised him to return to Hail and the security of Ibn Rashid's protection.

Doughty demanded both his money and his possessions back from Abdullah. The Turk refused. Doughty insisted. Then Abdullah attacked him savagely, striking him brutally in the face and threatening to put him in prison. Days passed. Finally Doughty wrote another letter to the pasha, explaining his dilemma: Without his money or possessions, he would never be able to buy the services of a guide and camel and so could never leave Khaibar. Two weeks later the pasha ordered Abdullah to "beware how he behaved himself toward the Englishman and to restore all his possessions and send him without delay to Ibn Rashid."

Doughty hired the services of two guides. In mid-March 1878, his long captivity finally at an end, he rode out of "pestilent" Khaibar into the "blissful free air" of the plateau beyond. Once again he found himself traveling through a landscape of "guttered and naked cinder-hills of craters in the horrid black lava."

Sixteen days later Doughty reached Hail to find Ibn Rashid away in the desert on a raid. Without the emir's protection he was subjected to numerous attacks by the local Muslims. People stared at him with "implacable eyes of fanaticism" and demanded of his guides, "Why do you bring him again?"

Several of the castle servants called out as he passed, "Now may it please Allah that you be put to death."

Ibn Rashid's steward showed Doughty to his old room for the night. But whenever he ventured into the streets, he quickly found himself surrounded by a jeering crowd. Once a one-eyed stranger whispered some advice into his ear: "Only say thou wilt be a Muslim and quit thyself of them. Do not die for a word."

Then the man called out to the crowd. "Khalil is a Muslim."

A coarse palace porter shouted back, "Let us make this man a Muslim and circumcise him. Fetch me a knife."

Once again the one-eyed man pleaded with Doughty to renounce his faith. "Just say the word and we will be friends with you. Say, 'There is no God but Allah and His apostle is Mohammed.' We will make you rich."

"Though you give me this castle and the sacks of hoarded silver which you say to be therein, I would not change my faith," Doughty shouted indignantly.

The mob jeered Doughty, cursed him, and threatened violence. But it never came. He may have been Christian, but all the people of Hail understood that he traveled under the passport of Ibn Rashid. Still, the court official in authority during the emir's absence ordered him out of Hail.

Once again Doughty found him in the hands of the two Bedouins who had accompanied him from Khaibar. In the first week of April he left Hail and rode aimlessly in a southwesterly direction. His companions were eager to be rid of their Christian charge. They rode camels while forcing Doughty to stumble by foot across burning wastes. "The gravel stones were sharp," he recalled later. "The soil in the sun glowed as an hearth under my bare feet. The naked pistol (hidden beneath my tunic) hanged heavily upon my panting chest. The air was breathless, and we had nothing to drink."

Doughty's ophthalmia worsened, and he feared his heart would burst from the exertion. Suddenly, blood spurted out of his nostrils. Doughty desperately pleaded with his guides to let him rest. Instead, they spurred their camels forward. Later he overheard them making plans to kill him. Doughty's situation was desperate. He appeared to have no options. Even the revolver was worthless. "Showing myself armed, I might compel them to deliver the dromedary, but who would not afterwards be afraid to become my guide?" he reasoned. "If I provoked them, they (supposing me unarmed) might come upon me with their weapons; and then I must take their poor lives! But [would that be] just? I thought that a man should forsake life rather than justice, and pollute his soul with outrage."

The image of Arabia that emerges from Doughty's book is one stripped bare of all picturesque, exotic, and romantic elements. "The sun made me an Arab, but never warped me to Orientalism," he later said with sadness. Except for the early months of Doughty's travel, his stay in Arabia had been one long ordeal. The unending suspicion coupled with sullen hospitality tore away at his spirits. Doughty's power lay finally in his acceptance of his weakness and his role as a victim. His response to insult and physical threat was always the assertion of Christian passivity. He suffered humiliation and courted martyrdom. Doughty's heroism was thus of a very different nature from that of the other British travelers who ventured into the Arabian Peninsula.

(This aspect of Doughty's *Travels in Arabia Deserta* deeply disturbed Richard Burton when he reviewed the book for a British publication. "Doughty is bullied, threatened, and reviled; he is stoned by the children and hustled by the very slaves," Burton protested in disgust. "His beard is plucked. He is pommelled with fist and stick. His life is everywhere in danger. He must go armed, not with the manly sword and dagger, but with a pen-knife and a secret revolver. . . . I cannot, for the life of me, see how the honoured name of England can gain aught by the travel of an Englishman who at all times and in all places is compelled to stand the buffet from knaves who smell of sweat."

(Yet in 1897 Wilfrid Blunt credited Doughty's "excellent counsel" of passivity in the face of potential Arab violence with saving his life during a visit to an Egyptian village. Convinced Blunt was a spy for the English, the villagers threatened to kill him. "I took the passive line," he wrote in his journal. "Any other would have cost me my life.")

Soon afterward Doughty's guides abandoned him. He gradually made his way from one Bedouin camp to another. Without a camel he decided to travel as lightly as possible. One day he took his precious library of books into the desert and gave them "an honourable burial" in a lizard's hole. Arab hospitality was given only grudgingly. Doughty was the first Christian ever to travel in these regions without disguising his religion, and everywhere he met with "heavy-hearted fanatics."

Doughty's spirits soared when he saw in the distance Buraydah, an oasis village of some 5,000 people: "a dream-like spectacle!—a great clay town built in this waste sand with enclosing walls and towers and streets and houses and a great square minaret!—a Jerusalem in the desert!" But it proved to be a false Jerusalem. Doughty alighted at the emir's guesthouse and asked for hospitality. He had a frugal meal. A court official advised Doughty to hide his Christian faith and pretend to be Muslim during his stay in Buraydah. That evening a group of men attacked him in his room. They struck Doughty with their fists, ransacked his pockets for money, and plundered his bags. Doughty shouted, "Thieves," in desperation. The emir's official quickly ordered the men to return everything or have their hands cut off, the traditional Islamic punishment for theft.

A much-shaken Doughty was led to an audience with the emir. "Is it a custom here that strangers are robbed in the midst of your town?" he demanded angrily. "I have eaten of your bread and salt. And yet your servants set upon me in your yard."

"They were Bedouins who robbed you," the emir insisted.

"But I have lived with Bedouins and was never robbed," Doughty protested. "I have never lost anything in a host's tent."

The emir demanded Doughty leave Buraydah the next day. That afternoon an angry mob stormed the guesthouse where the Englishman lodged. Two women barred the doors. But the crowds demanded the death of the *Nasrany* and attempted to smash down the door. A court official finally appeared and ordered the mob away. Early the next morning a man visited Doughty's room, collected his bag, and escorted him through back alleys to a waiting camel. They left town quietly for Anaiza, one day's ride away.

In Anaiza, a Wahhabi stronghold, Doughty practiced his medicine to make a little money. One of the first men to approach him was a kindly merchant named Abdullah el Kenneyny, who befriended the Englishman. When Doughty told him that he was English, the man was shocked. "Why tell people so in this wild fanatical country?" Abdullah protested. "I have spent many years in foreign lands. I have lived in Bombay, which is under the government of the English. You can tell me this. But say it not to the foolish and ignorant people. For we are in the land of the [Wahhabis], where the name of Christian is an execration."

Abdullah el Kenneyny arranged for Doughty to travel to Jiddah and even cashed Doughty's personal check for a few rials. (A year later Doughty had his canceled check back. It had cleared through a bank in Beirut.) At the end of June he departed Anaiza with a caravan of 170 camels carrying thirty tons of butter to Mecca some 450 miles away. He assumed that Abdullah el Kenneyny had made arrangements for a guide to take him from Mecca to Jiddah. To his horror, he learned this was not the case. "I was now to pass a circuit in whose pretended divine law there is no refuge for the alien . . . and where any felon of theirs is, in comparison with a *Nasrany*, one of the people of Allah," Doughty wrote in despair. "The aspect of this country is direful. We were descending to Mecca—now not far off—and I knew not by what adventure I should live or might die on the morrow."

The caravan traveled through the high desert country, where the temperatures went well above 100° F each day. Water holes were few and far between. At one well Doughty discovered the water heavily polluted with the droppings of cattle, but he drank it anyway. "Who will not drink in the desert, the water of the desert, must perish," he noted laconically. At another oasis, as he watched, a man drawing water slipped and fell into a well, breaking his back.

Doughty's journey reached a terrible climax on the seventeenth day at a rest station near Mecca. He had ridden more than 400 miles. His health was poor, and his spirits sagged under the constant humiliation he had endured. His money almost gone, Doughty was reduced to begging food from his companions. Tempers were short in the extreme heat. News that a Christian was approaching the holy city had traveled ahead. At no other time in his travels had he been so conspicuous. Everyone else in the caravan had stripped to the traditional loincloth that all pilgrims wear upon approaching Mecca. Only Doughty continued to dress in his desert robes.

Suddenly one of the camel drivers attacked Doughty, knife in hand, shouting "I will kill him." The Englishman spurred his camel forward, but the exhausted beast was on the edge of collapse. Slowly Doughty dismounted to face his attacker.

"Kill the *Nasrany*," the man screamed. "Kill him."

"Remember the bread and salt we have eaten together, Salem," Doughty urged softly. No one in the caravan came to his assistance.

"Let us hack him to pieces," several in the crowd shouted.

For the first time in his travels Doughty drew out the revolver from inside his robe. The crowd of camel drivers, armed only with sticks, closed slowly around him. Fheyd, the camel master, approached Doughty. The moment of decision had finally arrived: "I must slay him or render him the weapon, my only defense."

There was a long moment of silence. Finally, Doughty reacted in character. He handed the loaded revolver, butt first, to the evil Fheyd, who quickly snatched it, violently breaking the cord that still hung around Doughty's neck. Fheyd and Salem quickly set about robbing the Englishman of his money and possessions. Then Fheyd examined the pistol, turning it over in his hands, and snapped it open to count the six bullets in the chambers.

"Look at the pistol the *Nasrany* carries to kill Muslims," he shouted out.

"My friends, for two years I have traveled in the land of Arabs and never once fired my pistol," Doughty protested.

"Cut him to pieces," the crowd demanded.

"Remember the bread and salt," Doughty pleaded.

Fheyd lifted the pistol into the air and exuberantly squeezed off five shots, each one reverberating in the stillness of the desert.

"Leave one shot for the *Nasrany*," Salem ordered.

Salem glared at Doughty for a long time and then took the gun from Fheyd. "You were safe in your own country, but you chose to come to the land of the Muslims," he hissed, slowly bringing the pistol to bear on Doughty. "Allah has delivered thee into our hands to die."

"There is bread and salt between us," Doughty continued to protest. "I might have shot you when I had the pistol, but I spared you."

Suddenly, at the last possible second, Salem's hand was pushed aside. Doughty looked into the face of a stranger, Maabub, a respected black servant of the governor of Mecca. The crisis was over. Doughty's life had been spared.

On July 29 Doughty, accompanied by an armed escort, started for Jiddah. The governor of Mecca had ordered them to proceed slowly because of the Englishman's weakened condition. And so they stretched the 100-mile journey over five days. By his own admission, Doughty presented a dreadful sight: "The tunic was rent on my back, my mantle was old and torn; the hair was grown down under my kerchief to the shoulders, and the beard fallen and unkempt. I had bloodshot eyes, half blinded, and the scorched skin was cracked to the quick upon my face."

On the last day Doughty topped a ridge and looked down upon the city of Jiddah with the sea beyond. The party stopped at a roadside inn for some refreshment. Doughty changed into his new clothes, a gift from the governor of Mecca. The landlord was shocked to discover that Doughty was European. Then he quickly recovered himself. "Be no more afraid," he told the Englishman kindly. "Here all peril is past."

A few hours later, after twenty-one months of travel in the Arabian deserts, Doughty rode into Jiddah and the welcomed hospitality of the British Consulate.

As his ship sailed from Jiddah, Khalil became once again Charles Doughty. A cousin in England remembered his appearance and behavior when he first arrived home: "Charles was in bad health and terribly thin and had great difficulty in eating and digesting European food, complaining then and for a long time afterwards that meat burnt his mouth. . . . He wore whitish cotton cloths of some soft Eastern material, and a green band often twisted round his waist; sockless feet thrust into heelless sandals, and using when he went out a green umbrella. He spoke seldom and when he first returned with some hesitation, as if his native language did not come quite easily to him."

Doughty's later life was uneventful. He married and became a recluse, devoting his days to writing poetry in "a continuation of Chaucer and Spenser." *The Dawn in Britain*, which he published in 1906, ran three times the length of Milton's epic *Paradise Lost* and mixed patriotism with religion.

Doughty spent almost ten years on the writing of his *Travels in Arabia Deserta*. The final version ran 600,000 words or more than 1,200 pages in the two-volume set finally published by the Cambridge University Press. One of Doughty's chief purposes was to restore his language to its original purity. To this end he sought an archaic style suggestive of pre-Shakespearean English. Wilfrid Blunt called Doughty's *Travels* "certainly the best prose written in the last two centuries." But most reviewers were perplexed, and the book fell almost immediately into obscurity.

During the Arab campaign of the First World War, Doughty's *Travels in Arabia Deserta* was regarded as the bible of Arabian studies. The Arab Bureau in Cairo kept several copies on hand, and they were in almost constant use. No one read the book with keener enthusiasm than T. E. Lawrence. When Lawrence spent his two years in the Arabian desert, he had before him in the figure of Charles Doughty an example of another modern man who had submerged himself in the language and life of the desert Arabs and had also measured himself against the pitiless Bedouin standard of endurance.

When Doughty died on January 20, 1926, the brief service was attended by only a handful of family and close friends—and one unidentified man in the uniform of the RAF. He gave his name as "Shaw." That "Shaw," of course, was none other than T. E. Lawrence. When he wrote the long introduction to a new edition of *Travels in Arabia Deserta,* Lawrence summed up the central irony of Doughty's travels into Arabia. He had gone into Arabia without money or official sanction and traveled through the peninsula as little more than a beggar. Of all the nineteenth-century explorers who sought out Arabia, none was so reviled and mistreated as Doughty. Yet in the end it was Doughty who most impressed himself upon the imaginations of the Arab people. Long after the other European visitors had been forgotten, they remembered Khalil. Lawrence wrote:

> I spent nine months in Western Arabia, much of it in districts through which Doughty had passed, and I found that he had become history in the desert. It was more than forty years ago, and that space of time would even in our country cause much to be forgotten. In the desert it is relatively longer, for the hardships of life leave little chance for the body to recruit itself, and so men are short-lived and their memories of strangers and events outside the family tree, soon fail. Doughty's visit was to their fathers or grandfathers, and yet they have all learned of him. They tell tales of him, making something of a legend of the tall and impressive figure, very wise and gentle, who came to them like a herald of the outside world. His aloofness from the common vexations of their humanity coloured their imagination. . . . They say that he seemed proud only of being a Christian, and yet never crossed

their faith. He was book-learned, but simple in the arts of living, ignorant of camels, trustful of every man, very silent. He was the first Englishman they had met. He predisposed them to give a chance to other men of his race because they had found him honourable and good. So he broke a road for his religion.

The Arabs had made a saint out of Charles Doughty.

CHAPTER VIII

T. E. Lawrence:
Knight Errant, Bar Sinister

*H*is adoring public knew him simply as Lawrence of Arabia. Even today, more than fifty years after his death, he continues to loom larger than life in the popular imagination—a heroic figure of epic proportions dressed in white Bedouin robes astride his camel and set against the burning blue skies of the Arabian desert, an army of desert warriors at his back. His mobilization of the Arabs against vastly superior Turkish forces marked the highpoint of British involvement in Arabia.

"I deem [Lawrence] one of the greatest beings alive in our time," Winston Churchill stated after his death in a motorcycle accident in 1935. "I do not see his like elsewhere. I fear whatever our need we shall never see his like again."

Lawrence was the last of the Byronic adventurers to seek their destinies in the Middle East. (Let us not forget that Byron died in the war for Greek independence from the Turks.) Lawrence the man blended into Lawrence the myth, embodying in his person all the nostalgia the English people felt for the purity of the desert, the nobility of its people, and an earlier period of chivalric warfare. "It is [Lawrence] who stands, perhaps for all time, as the epitome of the Arabian traveler, the paradigm of the brave warrior who combines in himself all the honour of the Bedouin and all the high purpose of an Englishman," writes one British biographer.

Lawrence's complex personality was a bundle of contradictions. He mixed courage with vulnerability, a hunger for fame with a desperate craving for privacy, and a bookish learning with actions on an epic scale. An incurable solitary, he savored the Bedouins' isolated world of sand and stars and saw in their lives a mirror of the many agonies that racked his own soul. Like Keats in "Ode to a Nightingale," he was "half in love with easeful Death." (An ancient Bedouin woman once recoiled from his white face and "horrible" blue eyes, which looked, she said, "like the sky shining through the eye-sockets of an empty skull.")

For Terence Rattigan in his popular play *Ross*, Lawrence was "a modern Hamlet—the guilt-haunted man of action who despises the springs of action and questions whether the action is necessary or worthwhile." Sam Spiegel, who produced the David Lean film biography, *Lawrence of Arabia*, contrasted Lawrence with Gandhi, another larger-than-life figure of liberation, and concluded: "Gandhi had no chink in his armor. He was a saint, a man in complete harmony with his destiny, and that's dull. There's no tragedy in it. But Lawrence—there was a man in conflict with his destiny."

Thomas Edward Lawrence was born in the Welsh village of Tremadoc on August 16, 1888, the same year Charles Doughty published his *Travels in Arabia Deserta*. He was the illegitimate second son of Sir Thomas Robert Chapman, the seventh baronet of Westmeath in Ireland, who had earlier deserted his wife and four daughters to elope with a Scottish governess, Sara Maden. Chapman changed his name to Lawrence and had five sons by Maden. The two never married and eventually settled in Oxford.

In later years Lawrence treated his bastard status lightly, remarking that "bars sinister are rather jolly ornaments." In fact, the bar sinister was a tall hurdle to have to overcome in the highly stratified Edwardian society. Lawrence may well have compensated for his lack of "legitimacy" by developing into an over-achiever who put super-human demands upon his mind and body.

Lawrence's mother remembered her son in later years as "a big, strong, active child, constantly on the move." He was a precocious boy, learning the alphabet on his own and reading Macaulay's *Introduction to the History of England* when he was five. E. F. Hall, a childhood chum, recalled three things in particular about the young Lawrence: "the intensity of those piercing blue eyes, the curiously nervous smile, and the voice of singular charm."

Lawrence early developed a passion for medieval romance and knightly chivalry. He became an avid brass rubber and made bicycle trips around England to rub famous brasses of knights. "He covered the walls of his bedroom with them," his mother recalled later. "They made a wonderful show, especially by firelight. Some of them were over life-size." As a student he read heavily in the Arthurian legends of France and England, memorized lengthy sections of Tennyson's *Idylls of the King,* and worshiped the memory of King Richard I. His brother Arnold called Lawrence's medieval researches "a dream way of escape from Bourgeois England."

This interest eventually proved a determining factor in Lawrence's life. The research for his thesis on Crusader castles for Jesus College, Oxford, took him on a lengthy walking tour of Syria in 1909. At one level the Arab Revolt allowed Lawrence the opportunity to act out on an epic scale the chivalric fantasies of his childhood, while the same fantasies accounted in part for his intense empathy with the Bedouin warrior culture. (Throughout his Arabian campaign he carried a copy of Sir Thomas Malory's *Morte d'Arthur* in his saddlebags.) Years later his friend E. M. Forster observed of Lawrence's love of chivalry: "The notion of a Crusade, or a body of men leaving one country to do noble deeds in another, possessed him, and I think, never left him, though the locality of the country varied. At one time it was Arabia." (Churchill once summed Lawrence up perceptively as a schoolboy who never quite managed to grow up.)

The most important figure for Lawrence at Oxford was David Hogarth, the keeper of the Ashmolean Museum, where Lawrence worked part time. Very much a man of the world, Hogarth was a major figure in archaeology in his day, having directed important excavations in Greece and Turkey. In 1904 he published *The Penetration of Arabia,* the first important history of the exploration of the Arabian Peninsula, and toward the end of his life he authored a definitive biography of Charles Doughty.

Hogarth took the young student under his wing in 1908 and shortly became the major influence upon his life, sending him to spend three years on an archaeological dig in Syria and then in the early months of the First World War bringing him into the British intelligence bureau in Cairo. Later Lawrence recalled Hogarth as "the parent I could trust, without qualification, to understand what bothered me" and "the only man I never had to let into my confidence; he would get there naturally."

From the summer of 1909 to the outbreak of the First World War in June 1914, Lawrence made a series of trips to Syria, spending more time in the Middle East than in England. On his first trip he walked from Beirut to Haifa and from Acre to Aleppo, gathering material and shooting photographs for his thesis on Crusader castles. Everywhere he observed "sure signs of the decay of Imperial Turkey." It was a rugged, dangerous, and exhilarating trip. "This is a glorious country for wandering in, for hospitality is something more than a name," he wrote home to his parents. "Setting aside the American and English missionaries, who take care of me in the most fatherly (or motherly) way . . . there are the common people, each one ready to receive me for a night and allow me to share in their meals without any thought of payment. It is so pleasant, for they have a very attractive kind of native dignity."

The trip was not without its risks. Lawrence suffered four bouts of malaria. For protection against bandits he carried a German Mauser pistol in his pack. On one occasion he had to use it when "an ass with an old gun" ambushed him at a distance of 200 yards. Lawrence returned the fire, causing the man's horse to bolt. In a letter to his mother he passed the incident off as "a joke." But he complained to the local authorities, who chased unsuccessfully after the man.

In the summer of 1910 Lawrence with two brothers went on a long tour by bicycle through France. He took advantage of the occasion to do additional research on medieval castles. But he longed to return to the Middle East. That opportunity came late in the year, when Hogarth asked him to take over the supervision of a major new excavation at the ancient Hittite city of Carchemish in Syria. There Lawrence was to spend the next three years, collecting and classifying the pottery, dealing with the Kurdish and Arab workmen, and on the side gathering intelligence on German activities in the area. Lawrence first spent time at the American mission in Jebail, Lebanon, learning Arabic. In the summer of 1911, when the work at Carchemish ended because of the heat, he went on another lengthy walking tour through Syria.

Lawrence was finally in his element, for the first time able to indulge both his love of theatrics and his passion for digging up old civilizations. He decorated the floor of his hut with a Roman mosaic and dressed for dinner in a white and gold embroidered Arab waistcoat. "I'm with Ned [the family name for Lawrence] now, he's very well and a great lord in this place," his younger brother Will wrote home during a visit in September 1913. "Ned is known by everyone, and their enthusiasm over him is quite amusing."

After a year Lawrence wrote home: "It is very good. We sleep by the ropes of the camp, and we rise with the dawn and we tramp with the sun and the moon for our lamp, and the spray of the wind in our hair." In later years Lawrence remembered his time at Carchemish as "a perfect life."

The asceticism long inherent in Lawrence's character found strong reinforcement in the Arab culture. "The Arabs appealed to my imagination" he wrote soon afterward. "It is the old, old civilization, which has refined itself clear of household gods, and half the trappings which ours hastens to assume. The gospel of bareness in materials is a good one. . . . They think for a moment, and endeavour to slip through life without turning corners or climbing hills."

At Carchemish, too, Lawrence came to appreciate the magnificent emptiness of the desert. One day his assistant, Dahoum, guided him to a ruin from the Roman period in the desert between Aleppo and Hama. The Arabs believed that a Bedouin prince had originally built it as a palace for his queen and ordered the clay of the building kneaded with precious oils of flowers rather than water. Lawrence recalled that day later in *Seven Pillars of Wisdom*: "We went into the main lodging, to the gaping window sockets of its eastern face, and there drank with open mouths of the effortless, empty, eddyless wind of the desert, throbbing past."

Lawrence's years in Syria before the First World War were important for toughening him physically and psychologically and giving him an intimate familiarity with Arab culture. He developed a fluency in Arabic. Much of his leisure time was spent studying Saxe, Clausewitz, Napier, Mahan, Foch, and other military strategists. Professor John E. Mack in *A Prince of Our Disorder*, the finest biography of Lawrence to date, writes of Lawrence's years at Carchemish:

> By the time he returned to England, Lawrence had become highly skilled and resourceful, with an extraordinary capacity to adapt himself to a great range of situations and challenges. Though not yet twenty-six he had demonstrated his abilities as a leader of other men through his capacity to do most things better than they could; by his courage and his willingness to do almost anything first before he expected someone else to do it; by his readiness to take responsibility even for matters that were only his concern because he made them so; and above all through his capacity to understand a problem as it was perceived by other people. He was especially effective in leading Arab peoples, whose language he spoke, and they were awed by his knowledge of their ways and by his apparent fearlessness.

On June 28, 1914, Archduke Franz Ferdinand, heir to the Austrian throne, was assassinated in Sarajevo, Yugoslavia, precipitating the Great War, as it was then called. One nation after another quickly entered the conflict. It soon became apparent that the most powerful military forces belonged to the politically aggressive German kaiser, Wilhelm II, whose imperial ambitions were well known. "Germans must never weary in the work of civilization," he once proclaimed. "Germany, like the spirit of Imperial Rome, must expand and impose itself." To this end he developed a three-pronged strategy to acquire overseas colonies, achieve naval supremacy, and cut Britain's links to its world markets.

Early in the century the kaiser turned his imperial eye toward the Middle East. German money and engineers built the Berlin–Baghdad Railway, while German advisers flooded the Turkish Army. The ultimate prize was, of course, the Suez Canal. In 1911 a German adviser in Mesopotamia advised the kaiser on the long-term implications of railways for the geopolitical situation developing in the Middle East:

England can be attacked and mortally wounded by land from Europe only in one place—Egypt. The loss of Egypt would mean not only the end of her domination over the Suez Canal and of her communications with India and the Far East, but would probably entail also the loss of her possessions in Central and East Africa. The conquest of Egypt by a Mohammedan Power, like Turkey, would also imperil England's hold over her sixty million Mohammedan subjects in India. . . . Turkey, however, can never dream of recovering Egypt until she is mistress of a developed railway system in Asia Minor and Syria, and until, through the progress of the Anatolian railway to Baghdad, she is in a position to withstand an attack by England upon Mesopotamia. The stronger Turkey becomes, the greater will be the danger for England, if, in a German-English war, Turkey should be on the side of Germay.

As historian John Pudney has noted, this was, in fact, "a blueprint of the Germany strategy in this area in the First World War—an allegiance with Turkey and a German-sponsored occupation of the Suez Isthmus and Egypt." (This later became a major strategy of Adolf Hitler. He, too, sent German military forces marching on Egypt, but this time in the company of Italian, not Turkish, allies.)

Turkey greeted the outbreak of war with a proclamation of neutrality. The Ottoman Empire in 1914 included the present countries of Turkey, Syria, Israel, Lebanon, Jordan, Iraq, Kuwait, United Arab Emirates, and lengthy strips of coastal Saudi Arabia. But this was an empire tenuously held. In 1884 Denis de Rivoyre, a French traveler through the Turkish Empire, reported widespread unrest against the Turks: "Everywhere I came upon the same abiding and universal sentiment: hatred of the Turks."

In 1908 a group of revolutionaries calling themselves the Young Turks had seized power in Constantinople and reduced the sultan to a mere figurehead. Real power lay with the pasha Enver. Pro-German and anti-British, he had worked to develop close relations with the kaiser at a time of shifting alliances. When war broke out, Turkey's traditional allies, Britain and France, had entered into an alliance with Russia, Turkey's hereditary enemy, against Germany. For the first three months of the war Turkey had remained neutral. Britain and France negotiated furiously to keep Turkey neutral, while Germany sought to entice it into the war on the kaiser's side. In August Winston Churchill transferred to the Royal Navy two battleships constructed in British dockyards for Turkey and already paid for by public subscription. The kaiser immediately ordered two cruisers to Constantinople, where to public acclaim the crews exchanged their German sailor hats for red Turkish fezzes. In late October Turkey entered the Great War as an ally of Germany. Lord Kitchener, the secretary for war, complained bitterly: "Germany has now bought the Turkish government with gold, notwithstanding that England, France, and Russia guaranteed the integrity of the Ottoman Empire if Turkey remained neutral in the War."

England immediately put Egypt under martial law. In January 1915 Turkish forces massed along the eastern bank of the Suez Canal and exchanged fire with British soldiers. In February they mounted a major attack. The Turkish strategy depended for success upon a popular uprising in Egypt taking place against the British forces. It never came. And British lines along the Suez Canal held. The Turkish Army retreated into the desert.

World War I mixed nationalism and imperialism with oil for the first time. In 1908 large reserves of oil had been discovered in southern Persia. British interests had quickly formed the Anglo-Persian Oil Company, which eventually became British Petroleum. Persia was not a part of the Ottoman Empire. But in fairly short order European commercial interests scrambled for concessions to develop the oil reserves suspected to lie within Mesopotamia. From 1904 onward the Royal Navy had systematically converted its fleet from coal to oil. And in 1913 Winston Churchill, taking a page out of Disraeli's Suez book, had paid £2.2 million for a controlling interest in the Anglo-Persian Oil Company to ensure a steady supply of fuel oil for the British fleet. By then the company had more than 200 producing wells, a 150-mile-long pipeline, and a large refinery at Abadan at the head of the Persian Gulf.

That was how matters stood in early 1915. It was one of the ironies of the time that Germany had hoped to stir up nationalist uprisings against the British in Ireland and France in Algeria. Both efforts came to naught. If the plans had prospered, the Allied effort on the European front would have been seriously weakened. But with the help of T. E. Lawrence, England managed to foment against the Turks in Arabia a nationalist rebellion that eventually undermined the German strategy in the Middle East.

When the war broke out, Lawrence sought immediately to enlist but was turned down as too short. The recruiting office "was glutted with men, and [they] were only taking six-footers," he complained in a letter to a friend. However, his mentor Hogarth, already involved in setting up a British intelligence operation in Egypt, recommended Lawrence. In December 1914 he arrived in Cairo, where he would serve two years before assuming an active role in the Arab Revolt. Lawrence soon found himself engaged in drawing maps, interrogating captured Turkish soldiers, and editing the top secret *Arab Bulletin*, which provided an overview of intelligence efforts for certain high government officials. (Lawrence's lengthy contributions on his participation in the Arab Revolt provided him with much of the raw material for his later book on the subject, *Seven Pillars of Wisdom*.) Ronald Storrs, who worked with Lawrence in Cairo, left us a vivid description of him at the time: "Lawrence was of lesser medium stature and, though slight, strongly built. . . . His yellow hair was . . . parted and brushed sideways; not worn immensely long and plastered backwards under a pall of grease. He had a straight nose, piercing gentian-blue eyes, a firm and very full mouth, a strong square chin and fine, careful and accomplished hands. As a Captain in the Intelligence Branch of the Egyptian Expeditionary Force Lawrence was elusive and utterly careless of his dress. As a colleague, his quickness and instantaneous grasp of essentials were astonishing."

In 1915 Lawrence lost two brothers in action in France. His brother Frank died leading a charge against German positions. "Frank's death was, as you say, a shock, because it was so unexpected," he wrote to Will, his favorite brother. "I don't think one can regret it overmuch because it is a very good way to [go] after all." A few months later Will, an observer with the Royal Flying Corps, was shot down and killed shortly after arriving in France. The news stunned Lawrence.

In June 1916, there occurred an event that was to alter profoundly Lawrence's life. The sherif of Mecca and his sons led an uprising against the Turks. The Arab Revolt had begun. After several initial successes—the Bedouins captured Mecca and the small ports of Yenbo and Rabigh—the Arabs suffered painful losses at Medina. The attack there was a disaster. The Bedouins carried ancient muzzle-loading rifles and were short on ammunition. They went up against a well-disciplined, recently reinforced Turkish force equipped with modern artillery and machine guns. The terrified Bedouins were quickly routed with heavy losses. Soon afterward Fakhri, the Turkish commander, opened negotiations with the Arabs while secretly ordering his soldiers to surround an outlying suburb. The assault, when it finally came, was swift and deadly. Most of the Arab men were killed in the first rush. The women were raped and then crowded into houses with the children and burned alive. The massacre sent a shock wave throughout western Arabia. The Turks had violated every concept of Bedouin warfare, murdering women and children too young to fight and wantonly destroying property they could not carry off. The slaughter at Medina was the Bedouins' brutal introduction to the modern concept of total war. Soon afterward the British Army in Cairo received a desperate message for assistance from Abdullah, the second son of Husayn ibn Ali, the sherif of Mecca.

Fearful that the Arab Revolt might collapse, the British quickly dispatched to Jiddah Ronald Storrs, the secretary to the high commissioner and the second-ranking civilian in Cairo, to meet with

Abdullah. Storrs obtained permission from his superiors to take "little Lawrence, my super-cerebral companion," who was due two weeks of leave and had asked to tag along. The two departed on the ship *Lama* on October 13, 1916. This was Lawrence's first trip into Arabia and signaled the start of his involvement in the desert campaigns.

"We had the accustomed calm run to Jiddah, in the delightful Red Sea climate, never too hot while the ship was moving," he recalled later in *Seven Pillars of Wisdom*. "By day we lay in shadow; and for great part of the glorious nights we would tramp up and down the wet decks under the stars in the steaming breath of the southern wind. But when at last we anchored in the outer harbour, off the white town hung between the blazing sky and its reflection in the mirage which swept and rolled over the wide lagoon, then the heat of Arabia came out like a drawn sword and struck us speechless."

The English officers rode ashore in a launch belonging to the British consul and plunged into the jumble of buildings. Jiddah was an ancient Arab city of four- and five-story buildings, each with a profusion of wooden lattices and solid teak doors with ring knockers of heavy iron. "The style of architecture was like crazy Elizabethan half-timber work," Lawrence observed. "The atmosphere was oppressive, deadly. There seemed no life in it. . . . One would say that for years Jiddah had not been swept through by a firm breeze: that its streets kept their air from year's end to year's end, from the day they were built for so long as the houses should endure."

Lawrence had come to Jiddah without official sanction to act on behalf of the British government. However, he had private plans for what should be done. He had watched the revolt sputter along for several months and was convinced the problem lay in its lack of effective leadership. "My visit was mainly to find the yet unknown master-spirit of the affair and measure his capacity to carry the revolt to the goal I had conceived for it," he wrote later. Lawrence sought an Arab chief who possessed that "flame of enthusiasm that would set the desert on fire." He was convinced that for maximum prestige among the various Bedouin tribes the leader, if at all possible, should come from the family of Husayn, the sherif of Mecca, who could claim descent from the Prophet Muhammad.

At the British Consulate Storrs and Lawrence met Abdullah astride a white mare and surrounded by a crowd of heavily armed slaves. From their first meeting Lawrence was convinced that Abdullah with "his constant cheerfulness" was not the leader the Arab Revolt needed. He met and dismissed two other sons of Husayn—Ali ("too conscious of his high heritage to be ambitious") and Zeid ("a shy, white, beardless lad of perhaps nineteen . . . no zealot for the revolt").

Lawrence pinned his hopes on Husayn's fourth son, Faisal. He left Storrs in Jiddah and traveled by ship to Rabigh and then by camel to Faisal's camp at the oasis of Wadi Safra, where he arrived on October 23. Lawrence and his guide forded a shallow stream and traveled down a walled path between the date palm trees to a low house. They passed a slave guarding the doorway, a silver-hilted sword at the ready, and entered a cool courtyard. Faisal, dressed in white robes and surrounded by his advisers, waited in the shadows.

"I felt at first glance that this was the man I had come to Arabia to seek—the leader who would bring the Arab Revolt to full glory," Lawrence wrote in *Seven Pillars of Wisdom*. "Faisal looked very tall and pillar-like, very slender, in his long white silk robes and his brown head-cloth bound with a brilliant scarlet and gold cord. His eyelids were dropped; and his black beard and colourless face were like a mask against the strange, still watchfulness of his body. His hands were crossed in front of him on his dagger." (Later, in his official report published in the *Arab Bulletin*, Lawrence likened Faisal to "the monument of Richard I at Fontevrault.")

Faisal welcomed Lawrence and inquired politely about his journey. "And how do you like our place in Wadi Safra?" he asked.

Lawrence waited for a moment before replying. "Well, it is far from Damascus."

The word dropped "like a sword in their midst." The Bedouin chiefs sucked in their breath. No one said a word, not knowing whether Lawrence intended his comment as a prophecy of future Arab victories or a criticism of recent failures. At last Faisal lifted his eyes to Lawrence, smiled, and said: "Praise be to Allah, there are Turks nearer to us than that."

Lawrence found Faisal discouraged by recent events, driven by the Turks into the desert and forced to depend upon his native resources. His men were exhausted. Many had been killed in futile camel charges against secured Turkish positions. Most of his Bedouins carried ancient muzzle-loading rifles almost a century old. Faisal had asked the British for artillery and had received only four twenty-year-old Krupp cannons with a range of 3,000 yards, utterly worthless against the modern Turkish guns.

The long hours Lawrence spent in conversation with Faisal served only to confirm his original estimation of the man as England's best chance to rally the Arab Revolt. In his official report printed in the *Arab Bulletin,* Lawrence gave the following appraisal of Faisal: "Aged thirty-one. Very quick and restless in movement. Far more imposing personally than any of his brothers, knows it, and trades on it. . . . He is hot tempered, proud, and impatient, sometimes unreasonable, and runs off easily at tangents. Possesses far more personal magnetism and life than his brothers, but less prudence. Obviously very clever, perhaps not overly scrupulous. A popular idol and ambitious."

One evening Faisal asked Lawrence to exchange his British uniform for Arab robes when the Englishman was in his camp. He explained there would be two benefits. First, Lawrence would be more comfortable, the Bedouin robes being better suited to the extreme heat of the desert and the hardships of camel riding than his khaki army uniform. And secondly, Faisal suggested, the robes would give him greater credibility with the desert warriors. Lawrence agreed.

Lawrence's Bedouin garb became part of his carefully executed plan to gain complete mastery over the Arabs. He never saw himself as being in disguise. Lawrence always took his identity as a British officer and a Christian. For instance, he never grew a beard as the Bedouins did. "My burnt red face, clean shaven and startling with my blue eyes against white headcloth and robes, became notorious in the desert," he said later. "Tribesmen or peasants who had never set eyes on me before would instantly know me. So my Arab disguise was actually an advertisement. It gave me away instantly, as myself, to all the desert. And to be instantly known was safety, in 99 cases out of the 100."

Later Lawrence urged in the *Arab Bulletin* the advantages of Bedouin robes over the traditional khaki uniform for the British liaison officers. "If you can wear Arab kit when with the tribes, you will acquire trust and intimacy to a degree impossible in uniform. It is, however, dangerous and difficult. They make no special allowances for you when you dress like them. Breaches of etiquette not charged against a foreigner are not condoned to you in Arab clothes. You will be like an actor in a foreign theatre, playing a part day and night for months, without rest, and for an anxious stake." He added as an important afterthought: "If you wear Arab things, wear the best. Clothes are significant among the tribes. Dress like a Sherif, if they agree to it."

Lawrence returned to Cairo. Storrs had approved his trip to Faisal's camp. But he still needed the approval of his military superiors to continue his involvement with the Arab Revolt. Lawrence, recently promoted to captain, sought out Reginald Wingate, then the governor-general of the Sudan. He reported in person regarding his trip to Faisal's camp and the Arab's intention to mount a fresh assault on Medina. Wingate's first thought was to send a strong force of British troops into the desert to assist Faisal. Lawrence insisted that such a move would effectively kill the Arab Revolt, for the Bedouins would simply fade away into the desert before fighting alongside European troops. He urged Wingate to assist Faisal by supplying Faisal's army of 8,000 Bedouin warriors with desperately needed modern rifles, ammunition, artillery, and machine guns plus a small number of British officers to advise on the proper use of modern weapons.

Wingate vacillated and after a month ordered a large contingent of Allied troops to Arabia. A desperate Lawrence went over Wingate's head to plead his case to Sir Archibald Murray, the British commander in chief in Egypt. To his surprise, Murray was sympathetic. He canceled Wingate's orders, appointed Lawrence the British emissary to the Arabs, and agreed to ship them whatever supplies they needed. He also went along with Lawrence's request that the British recognize Faisal as the leader of the Arab Revolt.

Lawrence immediately returned to Yenbo, where he found the

Arab forces reeling from another defeat by Turkish forces. Many of Faisal's soldiers had deserted. Two British warships arrived in the harbor and started unloading much-needed rifles, machine guns, artillery, and the first group of British advisers. New Year's Day found Lawrence in Faisal's desert camp, planning their strategy for the next offensive. The first stage appeared obvious. The Arabs had to consolidate their hold on the western coast of Arabia. Lawrence understood that if the Turks regained control of the ports, they could easily crush the revolt. He decided to ignore the large Turkish force at Medina and concentrate instead upon harrying their supply lines. ("We must not take Medina. The Turk was harmless there. In prison in Egypt he would cost us food and guards.") The British Army in Cairo sent Lawrence at his request a group of experts on munitions who established a school for sabotage at the new Arab camp in the coastal town of Wejh. Lawrence planned to use the munitions to cut the railway between Medina and Damascus and prevent an orderly evacuation of the Turkish garrison at Medina.

Next Lawrence made some momentous decisions about the kind of warfare the Bedouins under Faisal could most effectively wage against the vastly superior Turkish forces. Clearly the previous policy of launching cavalry charges against Turkish machine guns and artillery had been a disaster. Lawrence recognized that he must evolve a strategy that took into account the tactics and strengths of the Bedouin fighting forces—their toughness, mobility, knowledge of the desert, intelligence, and courage. He quickly appreciated that there was no discipline in a Bedouin army, at least in the traditional sense understood by European officers. Each man served of his own free choice and could at any time take his rifle and depart without incurring the slightest rebuke. Centuries of tribal warfare meant that tribes could not be haphazardly mixed together when raiding parties were planned. Bedouins were hopeless in offensive attacks on entrenched positions but highly effective in hit-and-run desert raids, which took advantage of their mobility and intimate knowledge of the desert terrain. "Their acquisitive recklessness made them keen on booty, and whetted them to tear up railways, plunder caravans, and steal camels," Lawrence concluded.

He decided upon a strategy of guerrilla warfare against the Turks. "The Arabs hate the Turks but don't want to obey anyone's orders, and in consequence they turn out only as a mob of snipers or guerilla fighters," he wrote later. "In their smallness of number . . . lies a good deal of their strength, for they are perhaps the most elusive enemy an army ever had."

Confined to a tent for several days because of a fever and an attack of boils, Lawrence pondered the implications of such thoughts. What could the Turks do, he asked himself, if the Arabs refused to act like a traditional army, assaulting defensive positions with their banners flying, and became instead "a thing intangible, invulnerable, without front or back, drifting about like a gas? . . . The Turks were stupid; the Germans behind them dogmatical. They would believe that rebellion was absolute like war and deal with it on the analogy of war. [But] war upon rebellion was messy and slow, like eating soup with a knife."

To the Turks, Lawrence reasoned, the equipment of war was more precious and less easily replaced than their soldiers. Therefore, the destruction of a bridge, railway tracks and rolling stock, heavy guns, and trucks would hurt the Turkish war effort in Arabia more than the loss of soldiers. Precisely the opposite situation existed among the Bedouin forces. For them equipment could be replaced more readily than a dead warrior, whose death was "like a pebble dropped in water, [causing] rings of sorrow to widen out."

"Most wars were wars of contact, both forces striving into touch to avoid tactical surprise," Lawrence realized. "Ours should be a war of detachment. We were to contain the enemy by the silent threat of a vast, unknown desert, not disclosing ourselves till we attacked." He would keep the fighting units under 200 men, the size of the traditional raiding parties. Gazelle hunting had made many Bedouins excellent sharpshooters; therefore, he would use them as snipers. And because Bedouins "attacked like fiends when booty was involved," he would give them plenty of situations in which there was an excellent chance of plunder.

In 1937 Captain Basil Liddell Hart, a military historian who wrote extensively on Lawrence, appraised his contribution as a military strategist: "He turned the weakness of the Arabs into an asset, and the very strength of the Turks into a debit—forcing them to spread as widely as possible, in vain attempt to check the flame of the revolt—a flame which, like the will-o'-the-wisp, was always dancing in places where they were not. By this strategy, the Arabs inflicted the maximum damage with the minimum of loss. . . . But he did more than paralyze the Turks. He foreshadowed what I believe will be the trend of the future—a super-guerilla kind of warfare." (One of Lawrence's most successful admirers in this area was Mao Tse-tung.)

Modern biographers and historians have confirmed Lawrence's brilliance as a military strategist. In the popular imagination there has always been the temptation to see the victorious Arab armies as little more than an appendage to his Bedouin robes. Lawrence would have been the first to object to such a distortion. He always served in Arabia in the capacity of a British liaison officer. His place among the Arabs was to advise, not to command. His genius lay in his ability to insinuate his concepts into the counsels of war in such a way that the Arab leaders often took them as their own. However, on many occasions the Arabs ignored Lawrence's advice and followed their own instincts, often with excellent results. In *Seven Pillars of Wisdom* Lawrence often diminished his own part in the Arab Revolt and gave much of the credit for its military successes to its Bedouin leaders, especially Faisal. "The Arab leaders showed a completeness of instinct, a reliance upon intuition, the unperceived foreknown, which left our centrifugal minds gasping," Lawrence observed in admiration.

The infusion of British arms and gold sovereigns breathed new life into the Arab Revolt. Defeats gave way to victories. Lawrence was ecstatic. "This show is splendid," he wrote to a colleague back in Cairo. "You cannot imagine greater fun for us, greater vexation and fury for the Turks. We will win hands down if we keep the Arabs simple. To add to them heavy luxuries will only wreck this show. . . . After all it's an Arab war, and we are only contributing materials. And the Arabs have the right to go their own way and run things as they please. We are only their guests."

The Arab successes forced the Turks to abandon their plans to capture Mecca and fall back upon a passive defense of Medina and its railway. German advisers urged an immediate evacuation of all Turkish troops on the peninsula. The British shipped the Arabs two Rolls-Royce armored cars with British drivers. And Lawrence threw his formidable energies into harassing the Turkish lines of communication and supply.

In the meantime, Faisal joined forces with Auda abu Tayi, the sheik of the Howeitat Bedouins and widely regarded as the greatest warrior in northern Arabia. Auda was more than fifty years old. His hair was streaked with white, but his body was still straight and strong. He sported "large eloquent eyes, like black velvet in richness," and a beard and mustaches trimmed to a point in the style of the Howeitats. Overflowing with poems of old raids and epic tales of long-ago battles, the aging warrior captured Lawrence's imagination as the personification of desert chivalry. Auda's exploits had already become the stuff of legends.

"His generosity kept him always poor, despite the profits of a hundred raids," Lawrence wrote in awe. "He had married twenty-eight times, had been wounded thirteen times; whilst the battles he had provoked had seen all his tribesmen hurt and most of his relations killed. He himself had slain seventy-five men, Arabs, with his own hand in battle; and never a man except in battle. Of the number of dead Turks he could give no account. They did not even enter the register."

One day Lawrence rode out from Wejh with a group of his followers toward the camp of Abdullah, who had done nothing for more than two months on behalf of the Arab Revolt. Lawrence suffered from dysentery, exhaustion, and boils. On the third day they made their way across a wild confusion of granite shards, piled haphazardly into low mounds, and camped in a pasture near a spring. His body racked with pain, Lawrence collapsed among some rocks. He dozed fitfully. Through the haze of his fatigue he heard first the sounds of a quarrel, then a single shot. A few minutes later Lawrence felt a hand shaking his shoulder and heard an urgent plea to come quickly. Soon he was standing over the body of a dead

Bedouin, a bullet hole through his temples. Lawrence confronted the murderer, a Moroccan named Hamed, who confessed to having killed the man in a fit of passion. The dead man's relatives demanded blood for blood, and the other Bedouins were in agreement. Lawrence had no choice. Failure to exact the traditional desert justice would fracture the unity of his army. He also understood that he, not the Bedouins, would have to be the executioner, in order to avoid the start of a divisive blood feud. Pistol in hand, Lawrence informed Hamed that he must die.

"I made him enter a narrow gully of the spur, a dank twilight place overgrown with weeds," Lawrence recalled later. "I stood in the entrance and gave him a few moments' delay which he spent crying on the ground. Then I made him rise, and shot him through the chest. He fell down on the weeds shrieking, with the blood coming out in spurts over his clothes, and jerked about. . . . I fired again, but was shaking so that I only broke his wrist. He went on calling out, less loudly lying on his back with his feet toward me, and I leant forward and shot him for the last time in the thick of his neck under the jaw."

Within a few weeks Lawrence had recovered and was back in the desert, this time indulging himself in "train-bashing." Ambushes, exploding mines, camel charges—Lawrence was in his element and took to train bashing like an exuberant schoolboy. He wrote enthusiastically to a friend in Cairo:

The last stunt was the hold up of a train. It had two locomotives, and we gutted one with an electric mine. This rather jumbled up the [coaches,] which were full of Turks, shooting at us. We had a Lewis [machine gun] and flung bullets through the side. . . .

The Turks lost 70 killed, 30 wounded, 80 prisoners, and about 25 got away. Of my hundred Howeitat and two British NCO's, there was one (Arab) killed and four (Arab) wounded. The Turks nearly cut us off as we looted the train, and I lost some baggage, and nearly myself. My loot is a superfine red Baluch prayer-rug. I hope this sounds [like] the fun it is.

On one ride to ambush a train, Lawrence experienced his first sandstorm. The heat that day was oppressive and steadily increased as the sun set in the sky. Thunder rolled across the desert. Strange blue and yellow clouds hung over a range of nearby hills. A wind began to blow. Suddenly Lawrence saw ahead an enormous yellow cloud drop two funnel-shaped spouts as it advanced on the Bedouin raiding party, blotting out the sun. There was no time to seek shelter. "The brown wall of cloud from the hills was now very near, rushing changelessly upon us with a loud grinding sound," Lawrence wrote later. "Three minutes later it struck, wrapping about us a blanket of dust and stinging grains of sand, twisting and turning in violent eddies, and yet advancing eastward at the speed of a strong gale." The storm's vortex passed over them, crashing men and camels together helplessly, robbing them of all sense of direction. It lasted eighteen minutes and then passed on, leaving the men and camels smothered in sand.

Lawrence developed a sure sense of "camel instinct," praising the animal as "that intricate, prodigious piece of nature, [which] in expert hands yielded a remarkable return." (In *Seven Pillars of Wisdom* he noted that "there was nothing female in the Arab movement but the camels.") The animals were crucial to the Arabs' successes against the Turks. Lawrence developed many of his strategies to take advantage of the camel's extraordinary capabilities. In 1920 he published an article, "The Evolution of a Revolt," in the *Army Quarterly*, in which he wrote at length about the logistics of desert raiding.

> We had no system of supply. Each man was self-contained and carried on the saddle, from the sea base at which the raid started, six weeks' food for himself. [This] was a half-bag of flour, forty-five pounds in weight. Each man baked for himself, kneading his own flour into unleavened cakes, and warming it in the ashes of a fire. We carried about a pint of drinking water each, since the camels required to come to water on average every three days, and there was no advantage to our being richer than our mounts. . . . In the heat of summer Arabian camels will do about two hundred and fifty miles comfortably between drinks; and this represented three

days' vigorous marching. Wells are seldom more than one hundred miles apart. An easy day's march was fifty miles; an emergency march might be up to one hundred and ten miles in the day.

Lawrence quickly developed an enormous affection and respect for his Bedouin followers. "The Arabs made a chivalrous appeal to my young instinct," he freely admitted at the end of *Seven Pillars of Wisdom*. They also appealed to his longing for a way of life characterized by asceticism, renunciation, and self-denial. The Bedouins were free from "doubt, our modern crown of thorns." They took the "gift of life" unquestioningly and embraced the harshness of their existence as a means of achieving individual freedom amid the uncluttered world of the desert. The Bedouins accepted pain without suffering and endured stoically all the tribulations of desert life. This appealed powerfully to Lawrence, himself a firm believer in the Nietzschean doctrines of the supremacy of the will and an acceptance of endurance and pain as a means to self-knowledge. Once at Wadi Ais he saw a Bedouin youth whose broken arm had set crookedly. He watched the boy dig into his flesh with his dagger, expose the bone, break it again, and then set it straight. "And there he lay, philosophically enduring the flies, with his left forearm huge under healing mosses and clay, waiting for it to be well," Lawrence later wrote admiringly.

(Years later in England Lawrence helped a stranded motorist start his stalled automobile. As he turned the crank, the driver advanced the spark, the car backfired, and Lawrence broke his wrist. But he never mentioned it to the other man, who thanked him and drove away, unaware that his carelessness had shattered Lawrence's wrist. The accident cost him months of pain, which he endured without complaint.)

By the spring of 1917 British attention in Cairo was focused on the last Turkish port in Arabia, Aqaba in the Sinai Peninsula. The Turkish forces there threatened both the right flank of the British Army and the Suez Canal. One plan called for a naval bombardment of the port's heavy fortifications followed by a troop landing. Lawrence strongly opposed such a policy. He urged instead a march across the

600 miles of difficult desert east of Aqaba to the spring pastures of the Howeitat Bedouins, there to raise a mobile camel force and then storm Aqaba from the rear. The port's heavy guns all pointed seaward. Aqaba was undefended on the east, the Turkish commanders assuming no army could ever cross such a formidable desert.

The battle for Aqaba proved to be the critical engagement in the Arabian war, radically altering the balance of military power in Arabia. Its success put the Turks on the defensive and thrust Lawrence into a major role in the Middle Eastern conflict. In later years, Lawrence, Faisal, and Auda all claimed credit for the conception of the daring raid on Aqaba. After careful study of the conflicting claims, biographer John Mack determined that Lawrence first raised the issue to his superiors in Cairo in the early months of his involvement in the Arabian campaign and that "for reasons of diplomacy that are understandable the official command was left in the hands of the Arab chieftains."

On May 9, 1917, Lawrence left Wejh in the company of Sherif Nasir of Medina, Auda, and thirty-five Ageyl Bedouins. They carried £20,000 in gold sovereigns in their saddlebags, fifty-nine pounds of flour per man, extra ammunition and rifles, and six camels loaded with blasting gelatin. They quickly settled into a routine of six-hour morning marches, four-hour rests during the noonday heat, and then long rides until the early evening. "We had learned to sleep with nothing overhead but moon and stars, and nothing on either side to keep distant the winds and noises of the night," Lawrence wrote later. They traveled across a landscape empty of all signs of people, for after each crossing "the wind swept like a great brush over the sand surface," obliterating all footprints. Soon the sand gave way to a foreboding landscape of eroded black lava flows and small craters connected by spines of high, broken basalt. "Nothing in the march was normal or reassuring," Lawrence remembered. "We felt we were in an ominous land, incapable of life, hostile even to the passing of life. . . . We were forced into a single file of weary camels, picking a hesitant way step by step through the boulders for hour after hour."

Other problems plagued the small expedition. The health of the camels began to deteriorate rapidly. Lawrence's animal developed a severe case of mange on its face. The camels grew weaker with each passing day. Nasir feared many would break down under the severe stress of the desert crossing and leave their riders stranded in the sand and facing certain death. Late one afternoon they came upon the Turkish telegraph line and railway. Lawrence set dynamite under the rails, while the Arabs cut the three telegraph wires, tied the ends to six Howeitat camels, and dragged over the poles.

The next day the group started across a desolate rocky plain devoid of all signs of life—no gazelle tracks, no burrows of rats, no lizards, not even a solitary bird. "We, ourselves, felt tiny on it, and our urgent progress across its immensity was a stillness or immobility of futile effort," Lawrence wrote later. "The only sounds were the hollow echoes . . . of rotten stone slab on stone slab when they tilted under our camels' feet; and the low but piercing rustle of the sand, as it crept slowly westward before the hot wind along the worn sandstone." By noon a *simoom* had overtaken them. The dry wind reached near-gale force, splitting their lips and forcing them to draw their headclothes down over their faces like visors, leaving only narrow eye slits. Lawrence took a kind of perverse pleasure in the *simoom:* "Its torment seemed to fight against mankind with an ordered conscious malevolence, and it was pleasant to outface it so directly, challenging its strength, and conquering its extremity."

One day flowed into another, each bringing the burning wind, dust blizzards, and blown sand that stung their inflamed faces. They reached an ancient well and drank gratefully of the brackish water. They continued their slow, monotonous march across the scorched wastes, each man knowing the odds had now turned against his reaching a safe haven.

A Howeitat Bedouin rode up, leading a riderless camel belonging to Gasim, one of Lawrence's Ageyl Arabs. They soon realized that Gasim was lost and on foot somewhere in the desert behind them with no chance of survival away from the caravan. (Lawrence later learned the man had dismounted to catch a quick nap and had missed the departure of the caravan.) Lawrence was furious. "Gasim was a gap-tooth, grumbling fellow, bad-tempered, suspicious, brutal, a man whose engagement I regretted, and of whom I had promised to rid myself as soon as we reached a discharging place," he wrote later, but he was Lawrence's man and therefore his responsibility. As a foreigner he could waive the duty. "But that was precisely the plea I dare not set up, while I yet presumed to help these Arabs in their own revolt," Lawrence complained bitterly later. "It was hard, anyway, for a stranger to influence another people's national movement, and doubly hard for a Christian and a sedentary person to sway Moslem nomads. I should make it impossible for myself if I claimed, simultaneously, the privilege of both societies."

So an angry Lawrence turned his exhausted camel about and headed alone back into the desert, retracing their tracks. Within twenty minutes the caravan had disappeared. After riding ninety minutes through the desolate wilderness, Lawrence saw something black in the distant mirage. Was it a bush or a man? He took a chance and headed in that direction to find Gasim, babbling incoherently, nearly blinded, his black mouth gaping, arms outstretched. Without a word Lawrence reached down and swung the spent man up onto his camel and started back toward the caravan. An hour later he saw a black bubble coming at him out of the heat waves on the horizon. It split into three bubbles and grew in size to become three riders. Lawrence wondered if they were enemy. It was Auda with two of Nasir's men. They camped in the late afternoon in the midst of a flat, featureless desert. Having no water, they ate nothing.

The group lit signal fires in the darkness. Another man was missing, and they hoped the flames would guide him to their camp. He never appeared. Several months later a group of Bedouins discovered his dried and shriveled body lying beside his camel far out in the desert. "He must have lost himself in the sand-haze and wandered till his camel broke down and there died of thirst and heat," Lawrence noted. "Not a long death . . . but very painful, for thirst was an active malady; a fear and panic which tore at the brain and reduced the bravest man to a stumbling babbling maniac in an hour or two; and then the sun killed him."

At eight o'clock the next morning the small caravan finally reached the wells of Arfaja. They climbed down the unlined walls eighteen feet to water "creamy to the touch with a powerful smell and brackish taste." The next day, May 27, they rode into the camp of Ali abu Fitna, the chief of one of Auda's clans. Their long, dangerous march across the desert had finally come to an end.

The Howeitat Bedouins gave Auda and his companions a tumultuous welcome. That evening they sat down to a feast of boiled mutton piled high on an enormous platter of white rice and surrounded by the upturned heads of several sheep, their jaws open to expose the pink tongues still clinging to the lower teeth.

After three days the Howeitat Bedouins broke camp and moved to fresh pastures. Lawrence's party rode along with them. The desert there presented new, unexpected danger—a plague of poisonous snakes. The ground seemed alive with puff adders, cobras, and blacksnakes. Walking at night was extremely dangerous and drawing water from the wells impossible, for the snakes clustered in clumps around the edges. They slipped into the tents and curled up under the blankets alongside the sleeping men, probably drawn by the warmth of their bodies. Three of Lawrence's men died of snakebites, and four recovered after much pain. "Howeitat treatment was to bind up the [injured] part with snake-skin plaster and read chapters of the Koran to the sufferer until he died," Lawrence noted. "Our party of fifty men killed perhaps twenty snakes daily. At last they got so on our nerves that the boldest of us feared to touch ground; while those who, like myself, had a shuddering horror of all reptiles longed that our stay in Sirhan might end."

Using the £20,000 in gold sovereigns, Nasir and Auda recruited a force of 500 Bedouins for the assault on Aqaba. The Howeitats provided them with fresh camels. In the late morning of June 19 they departed for Aqaba. The first wells they reached had been dynamited after the Turks had somehow learned of the presence of an Arab army in the desert. A few days later the Bedouins attacked a Turkish outpost but were beaten back. Underestimating the strength of the Arab force, the Turkish commander sallied forth into the desert and fell upon the first Bedouin encampment he found, killing one old man, six women, and seven children. The outraged Arabs ambushed the Turkish patrol on its way back to the fort, killing all its members, and then stormed the fort, its numbers now depleted, and slaughtered the Turks there. At Ghadir Lawrence blew up ten railway bridges and lengthy stretches of rails.

After the Arab force had started for Aqaba, they discovered that a battalion of Turks held the only pass through the hills. Bedouin snipers took to the hills above the sleeping Turks and opened fire on the camp. The skirmish continued through the morning. Just before noon Auda, Lawrence, and a group of Bedouins on camels charged the Turkish position at full gallop, shooting from the saddle. It was a wild, exhilarating moment. The Turks wavered and then broke into flight. Lawrence fired his pistol at several Turkish soldiers. Suddenly his camel tripped and sprawled forward, pitching him violently onto the hard ground. Lawrence lay there, stunned, convinced he would be trampled to death by the rushing camels. But the body of his own mount divided the stream in half, and he emerged unscathed. Later Lawrence learned that he had brought himself down, having mistakenly fired his pistol into the back of his camel's head. Auda rode up, his field glasses shattered, his pistol holster pierced, and his robes riddled with six bullet holes. He had narrowly escaped with his life when the Turks had fired a volley at him from point-blank range. The tally at the end of the day was more than 300 Turks dead and 160 captured. The Arabs lost two men and twenty camels.

The Arabs plundered the Turkish camp and baggage train, even stripping the uniforms off the dead soldiers. That night under a full moon Lawrence walked alone across the battlefield. "The dead men looked wonderfully beautiful," he wrote in one of the most celebrated set pieces of *Seven Pillars of Wisdom*. "The night was shining gently down, softening them into new ivory. Turks were white-skinned on their clothed parts, much whiter than the Arabs; and these soldiers had been very young. . . . The corpses seemed flung so pitifully on the ground, huddled anyhow in low heaps. Surely if straightened, they would be comfortable at last. So I put them all in order, one by one, very wearied myself, and longing to be one of those quiet ones, not of the restless, noisy, aching mob up the valley, quarrelling over the plunder."

The Bedouins hurried toward Aqaba. The earlier successes against Turkish troops drew other Arabs to the cause. They found one Turkish outpost after another abandoned. The troops had panicked and withdrawn into fortifications above Aqaba. They had never imagined an attack from the desert and had no defense against one. On July 5 Nasir urged the surrounded Turks to lay down their arms. The next morning some 7,000 Turkish troops surrendered. Lawrence and the exuberant Bedouins raced across the remaining four miles of desert through a driving sandstorm to Aqaba and splashed into the sea, just two months after setting out from Wejh.

The Arab victory at Aqaba changed many things. Lawrence's fame now spread the length and breadth of Arabia. The British promoted him to major. The Turks posted a reward of £20,000 for Lawrence alive, £10,000 for him dead. With Aqaba firmly in Arab hands, the Hejaz war came to an end. The Sinai Peninsula was firmly in friendly hands for the first time in the war. And the British forces in Cairo gained a vital seaport through which they could supply their forces fighting the Turks in Palestine. Psychologically, the victory at Aqaba could not have come at a better time. British morale was reeling under two disastrous defeats in Gaza and the loss of 10,000 men. The Arab victory coincided with the arrival in Cairo of General Edmund Allenby, sent there to relieve General Archibald Murray.

The action at Aqaba illustrates perfectly why Lawrence's exploits later became the stuff of legends and the man himself more a creature of myth than history in the popular imagination. The Arab Revolt was, in the words of novelist E. M. Forster, the "last of the picturesque wars." As such, it stood in stark contrast with the horrors of the European front, where enormous armies faced one another across zigzag lines of trenches running hundreds of miles from the Swiss border northward and fought for control of a no-man's-land of barbed-wire entanglements, shell craters, rotting corpses, and minefields. That was a war of mass attacks that were no better than mass suicides, clouds of poisonous gas, and endless rain that turned battlefields into vast mud holes. On July 1, 1916, the first day of the Battle of the Somme, British forces alone suffered 60,000 casualties, with 20,000 dead. (To put that figure into perspective, 20,000 represents 40 percent of the American death toll for the entire Vietnam War.) By mid-November, when the battle finally played itself out in the mud, the British had suffered

420,000 casualties, the French 200,000, and the Germans about 450,000. The Somme front stretched for twelve miles. Never was more than eight miles of enemy territory gained.

The European war quickly degenerated into a conflict in which individual action and heroism finally counted for nothing. The grim reality of trench warfare overwhelmed everything. Robert Graves recalled in the account of his experiences in the trenches in *Goodbye to All That*:

> From the morning of September 24th to the night of October 3rd, I had in all eight hours of sleep. . . . We had no blankets, greatcoats, or waterproof sheets, nor any time or material to build new shelters. The rain poured down. Every night we went out to fetch in the dead of other battalions. . . . After the first day or two, the corpses swelled and stank. I vomited more than once while superintending the carrying. Those we could not get in from the German wire continued to swell until the wall of the stomach collapsed, either naturally or when punctuated by a bullet; a disgusting smell would float across.

Lawrence's campaign in Arabia stood in stark contrast with the grueling horrors of the European front: mobility against stagnation, desert sunshine against driving rain, clean sand against oozing mud, feudal chivalry against modern barbarism, and decisive heroic action against the utter futility of all action. In the popular imagination Lawrence was the last great warrior to be cut from the same cloth as Achilles, Alexander the Great, Richard I, and Roland.

Professor Paul Zweig in his study *The Adventurer* seeks to account for the adulation accorded such men as Lawrence and Charles Lindbergh in the 1930s and concludes:

> The course of the war had been so vast and machinelike, and its results so paltry, that a certain conception of national life became suspect. One was eager to admire the heightened figure of heroes, but war, the traditional field for heroic endeavor, inspired horror.

One wanted destiny scaled to the will of individuals, not cataclysms which made a joke of individuality, however brave or reckless. . . . World War I had wounded the very notion of bravery. Death in such vast, faceless numbers could no longer be an adversary; it became a plague, a dissemination of poisons. Lawrence himself understood the problem, when he called the strategies of the European theater "murder war" and defined his own aims in terms which we have seen come to identify as guerrilla warfare: an extended, minimally organized version of individual combat, on the model of medieval romance. By his own account, Lawrence stood in the shadow of Saladin, not Napoleon; his measure was legendary, not military. . . . Against the backdrop of trench warfare, Lawrence's desert tactics, as he describes them in *Seven Pillars of Wisdom*, represent a sort of adventure war.

Lawrence returned to Cairo, where he was accorded a hero's welcome and recommended for the Order of the Bath. He had spent the previous four months in Arabia constantly on the move and had ridden more than 1,500 miles by camel. In Cairo he savored his first bath and iced drink in months. Then, still wearing his Arab robes, Lawrence met Allenby, his new commander in chief.

"It was a comic interview," Lawrence remembered. "He sat in his chair looking at me—not straight, as his custom was, but sideways, puzzled. He was newly from France, where for years he had been a tooth of the great machine grinding the enemy. . . . [H]e was hardly prepared for anything so odd as myself—a little bare-footed silk-shirted man offering to hobble the enemy by his preaching if given stores and arms and a fund of two hundred thousand sovereigns to convince and control his converts."

Lawrence set about, with his maps, to explain his strategy. Allenby listened patiently. At the end of the presentation he tilted up his chin, looked hard at Lawrence, and said, "Well, I will do for you what I can." And so the interview ended.

Lawrence returned to Aqaba, now the major Arab base, and resumed his raids against the Turks. In four months his people destroyed seventeen trains, bringing chaos to the Turkish transportation system. "Travelling became an uncertain terror for the enemy," he gloated later. "At Damascus people scrambled for the back seats in trains, even paid extra for them. The engine-drivers struck." The Arab raids made a Turkish evacuation of Medina impossible.

Once again Lawrence was in his element and making a grand adventure of it. His private letters from this period show a remarkable detachment from his role as Lawrence of Arabia and a constant awareness of the extent to which it was a pose serving useful ends in the campaign. "My bodyguard of fifty Arab tribesmen, picked riders from the young men of the deserts, are more splendid than a tulip garden," Lawrence wrote Vivian Richards, a close friend from his Oxford days. "We ride like lunatics and with our Bedouins pounce on unsuspecting Turks and destroy them in heaps; and it is all very gory and nasty after we close grips. . . . Disguises, and prices on one's head, and fancy exploits are all part of the pose. How to reconcile it with the Oxford pose I know not. Were we flamboyant there?"

In November 1917 the major news from Europe concerned Russia. The Bolsheviks had overthrown the czar and consolidated their power. Meanwhile, in Egypt Allenby prepared to attack the Turkish defenses between Beersheba and Gaza. Lawrence, eager to be in on the action, suggested that he and his Bedouins cut the strategically important railway bridge across the Yarmuk River, east of Haifa, thus isolating the Turkish Army. He was joined by the emir Abd el Kader, grandson of the chivalrous protector of Christians during the terrible massacre in Damascus in 1860. Lawrence found him an Islamic fanatic, half-mad with religious enthusiasm and possibly very dangerous. Faisal advised him: "I know he is mad. I think he is honest. Guard your heads and use him." A few weeks later Abd el Kader betrayed them, going over to the Turks with information on the Arab plans and strength.

The assault on the railway viaduct over the Yarmuk River promised to be a difficult operation, involving a hazardous march of some 400 miles behind Turkish lines. Lawrence's party included a dozen handpicked Bedouins from his private troop, several Indian machine gunners, a British explosives expert, Sheik Ali ibn el Hussein, Abd el Kader, and some Beni Sakhr Bedouins, whom they recruited in the area. Everything went wrong. At the bridge one of the Arabs dropped his rifle, alerting the sentries. The Turks suddenly spotted the Indians lugging their machine guns up a nearby hill and opened fire. The porters panicked, tossed their packs of explosive gelatin into the gorge, and fled. The raid was a fiasco.

Later the same morning Lawrence set the remaining explosives under a small bridge and took out a Turkish train. Even that went badly. The charge failed to detonate when a troop train came along. Lawrence found himself trapped in the open alongside the passing coaches under the eyes of scores of Turkish soldiers, who thought him just another desert Bedouin. He corrected the charge and waited for a second train to come along. The mine exploded under the driving wheel of the first locomotive, showering Lawrence with metal fragments and bloody pieces of torn flesh. The scalded, smoking, legless torso of the engineer's body landed nearby. A dazed Lawrence tried to run, only to discover a sharp pain in his right foot. A group of Beni Sakhr Bedouins rushed to his aid. Turkish soldiers fired several volleys at them. Seven of his men were killed immediately. Lawrence scrambled desperately over a nearby ridge to safety. He checked himself for injuries and discovered that he had a broken toe and five bullet wounds, none serious. The explosion had shredded his robes and blackened his face.

Lawrence next decided to reconnoiter Deraa, the importance of which as the junction for the railways leading to Haifa, Damascus, Amman, Jerusalem, and Medina made the town the "navel of the Turkish armies in Syria." Sometime between November 12 and 22, 1917, Lawrence, wearing his Bedouin robes, entered Deraa with Feris, an old man sympathetic to the Arab Revolt, and scouted out the railway station and town. What started as a fairly routine spying operation ended as the most shattering emotional experience in Lawrence's entire life, a confrontation with an evil so horrible that it nearly destroyed him.

The pair strolled casually through Deraa. Lawrence limped painfully on his broken foot. They walked past the train station. Lawrence noted that there was too much open ground to take it in a surprise attack. They plodded on toward the Turkish defenses on the town's outskirts, Lawrence carefully making mental notes regarding the placement of barbed wire, trenches, and supply depots. At the airport he counted the number of planes and inventoried the types. Suddenly a Syrian soldier, suspecting Lawrence to be a deserter, started questioning him. The Englishman brushed him off and continued on his way. A sergeant hurried after him and roughly grabbed his arm. "The Bey wants you," he told Lawrence.

The Turk led Lawrence inside a nearby compound, where a fat Turkish officer, sitting on a platform, interrogated him.

"Who are you?" the Turk demanded.

"Ahmed ibn Bagr," Lawrence answered. "I am a Circassian from Kuneitra."

"A deserter?"

"We Circassians are not required to serve in the army."

The officer stared at Lawrence for a long moment. When he finally spoke, it was very slowly.

"You are a liar."

Lawrence spent the day in the guardroom with a dozen Turkish soldiers. They confiscated his belt and knife and made him wash. "Don't worry," one of the soldiers told him. "A soldier's life is not bad."

That evening three soldiers escorted him through Deraa to a two-story house and upstairs to the governor's bedroom. Hajim Bey sat on the edge of his bed in his nightgown, trembling and sweating as though feverish. He motioned the guard out, grabbed Lawrence, and threw him onto the bed. The two wrestled. The Turk began to fawn over Lawrence, praising his fair skin and insisting that he would make life easy in the army for him and even give him money if only he would cooperate as his lover. He ordered his captive to take off his drawers. Lawrence pushed him back. The bey started fondling him. Lawrence stood it as long as he could. Then he brought his knee suddenly up into the Turk's testicles.

Three guards rushed in and held Lawrence still. The outraged Turk beat him about the face with his slipper, then bit him savagely on the throat until his blood ran. Afterward he took a bayonet from a soldier, pinched up a fold of flesh over Lawrence's ribs, and worked the point of the blade through, slowly rubbing the blood over the Englishman's stomach. There was a lengthy silence before Hajim Bey finally spoke: "You must understand that I know. It will be easier if you do as I wish."

Lawrence was dumbfounded. (In his official report on the incident he stated that Hajim Bey told him that Abd el Kader had betrayed his identity.)

The guards dragged Lawrence downstairs and stretched him naked across a bench. A corporal began beating him with a long black whip. "To keep my mind in control I numbered the blows, but after twenty lost count, and could feel only the shapeless weight of pain, not tearing claws, for which I had prepared, but a gradual cracking apart of my whole being by some too-great force whose waves rolled up my spine till they were pent within my brain, to clash terribly together," a horrified Lawrence recalled. "Somewhere in the place a cheap clock ticked loudly, and it distressed me that their beating was not in its time. I writhed and twisted, but was held so tightly that my struggles were useless."

Afterward Lawrence lay on the floor, his body bloody and his spirit "completely broken." The Turkish corporal kicked him methodically with his nailed boot and cracked several ribs. He heard a soldier giggling, seemingly at a great distance. Then he passed out.

Lawrence recovered consciousness on a pile of dusty quilts in the infirmary. He struggled painfully to his feet. He was alone. He found some clothes—a dark broadcloth, a red fez, and slippers. He slipped out a window and disappeared into the night. Soon he was back among his Bedouin companions. A few hours later they rode away into the desert.

In his official report Lawrence wrote: "Hajim sent me to the hospital, and I escaped before dawn, being not as hurt as he thought. He was so ashamed of the muddle he had made that he hushed the whole thing up and never reported my capture and escape." But in *Seven Pillars of Wisdom* Lawrence hinted at a deeper truth about the experience: "In Deraa that night the citadel of my integrity had been irrevocably lost."

Lawrence in his published writings was vague about exactly what he meant by that. But on at least two occasions he confided the full truth of Deraa. In a letter dated March 26, 1926, to Charlotte Shaw, the wife of the playwright George Bernard Shaw, and discovered in the British Musuem collection by Professor Jeffrey Meyers, an agonized Lawrence wrote: "For fear of being hurt, or rather to earn five minutes' respite from a pain which drove me mad, I gave away the only possession we are born into the world with—our bodily integrity." And Colonel Richard Meinertzhagen, Lawrence's colleague and close friend in Cairo, insisted in his memoirs that Lawrence told him that he "was sodomized by the Governor of Deraa, followed by similar treatment by the Governor's servants."

In *Goodbye to All That* Robert Graves wrote of Lawrence's "morbid terror of being touched." And in a passage of extraordinary honesty in *Seven Pillars of Wisdom*, Lawrence admitted that his revulsion against being touched extended to a fear of hand-to-hand combat: "[If] combats came to the physical, bare hand against bare hand, I was finished. The disgust of being touched revolted me more than the thought of death and defeat."

Lawrence admitted later to his friend Graves that the encounter at Deraa had shattered his nerve, coming, as it did, on the heels of his failure to destroy the bridge over the Yarmuk River and the debacle of the attack on the train. The experience obsessed him in later years. He rewrote nine times the chapter in *Seven Pillars of Wisdom* depicting the events of that night. From 1923 on Lawrence paid a soldier to flagellate him regularly, an obvious attempt psychologically both to repeat the horrors of Deraa and to exorcise them. After exhaustive study of this aspect of Lawrence's behavior, psychologist/biographer John Mack concludes that Lawrence did not engage in flagellation for masochistic-sexual reasons but rather for "personal penance." He sets the beatings in the tradition of self-flagellation often practiced by medieval churchmen to mortify the flesh and subdue sexual cravings.

(Mack dismisses the persistent charges that Lawrence was a homosexual: "I have found no evidence that Lawrence ever as an adult entered voluntarily into a sexual relationship for the purpose of achieving intimacy or pleasure. This applies equally to the hetero-sexual and homosexual relationships. There are a few passages in his letters and notes which indicate a longing for sexual experience, but no evidence that he could act on these longings, and much evidence that he could not.")

When Lawrence reported back to Allenby in Gaza, he was no longer the bouncy, cocky victor of Aqaba. The general was so ec-static over recent British victories against the Turkish forces that he hardly heard Lawrence's brief report about his failure to destroy the Yarmuk bridge. While the two conferred, Allenby received word that Jerusalem had fallen. On December 11 Lawrence in the uniform of a major in the British Army triumphantly entered Jerusalem along-side Allenby. Yet he had taken no part in the capture of the impor-tant city, in fact had failed in his mission, which might have given greater significance to the victory. However, Allenby was still full of enthusiasm for the Arab Revolt and ordered Faisal's army north from Aqaba toward the Dead Sea to participate in the Allied assault on Jericho. Lawrence rejoined his Bedouins, who rode furiously around him, firing their rifles into the air and shouting, "Aurens! Aurens!"

Allenby assigned Lawrence numerous Rolls-Royce armored cars, which gave him a new mobility and brought out his mania for speed. On January 16, 1918, the Turkish stronghold at Tafileh fell to the Arab army under Nasir and Auda abu Tayi. The Turks counterat-tacked furiously. Lawrence led the defense. By the time the battle was over, more than 1,000 Turks had died. It was an impressive victory and lifted Lawrence's spirits. The war in Syria ground on through the spring and summer with no decisive battles taking place. On August 16 Lawrence passed his thirtieth birthday at a conference of Arab chiefs. Sergeant Tom Beaumont, one of Lawrence's armored car drivers, later recalled his performance that day: "bare feet tucked under him, swathed as the others, with gold dagger, girdle round his waist, gesticulating from one to the other, forcing his points home one by one."

On September 24 news reached the Arab army that Turkish forces had retreated from Amman. Lawrence urged they go on the offensive and attack the retreating Turks. The next day Faisal's Arabs headed north toward Deraa and Damascus, while to the west Allenby's considerably larger force of British, French, and Australian soldiers rolled over the last remnants of Turkish resistance there. At this time, as the Arab forces marched against Deraa, Lawrence's personality underwent a sudden transformation. In the words of one biographer, he changed from "an indifferent spectator . . . into a frenzied partisan, who for the next two weeks fought and killed like a man in the throes of some diabolical delirium." This was partly an explosion of suppressed rage over the horrors of his torture and rape almost a year before. But the immediate trigger was a string of Turkish atrocities that profoundly shocked all those in the Arab army.

While the Arab force moved upon Deraa, great clouds of dense smoke rose from burning buildings, planes, and supply depots, as the 3,000 Turkish, German, and Austrian soldiers prepared to abandon the town. The Arab forces, about 4,000 strong, rode into a nearby village of Tafas less than one hour after the Turkish soldiers had withdrawn, having massacred virtually the entire population. The bodies of old men, women, and children lay in heaps everywhere. Lawrence spotted the corpse of a pregnant woman slumped against a wall, a saw-bayonet buried between her naked legs. The Arabs sat on their mounts in stunned silence, unable at first to comprehend the extent of the carnage. A wounded child came toward them.

"It was a child, three or four years old, whose dirty smock was stained red over one shoulder and side, with blood from a large half-fibrous wound, perhaps a lance thrust, just where the neck and body joined," Lawrence wrote in Seven Pillars of Wisdom. "The child ran a few steps, then stood and cried to us in a tone of astonishing strength (all else being very silent), 'Don't hit me, Baba.' " She took a few hesitant steps toward them and then fell to the ground, dead.

Tafas was home to many of the Arabs riding with Faisal, including Tallal, the village's sheik and a magnificent warrior who had fought at Lawrence's side for several months. Tallal rode slowly through the remnants of his village. The retreating Turkish Army was in the distance. Slowly he pulled his headdress down over his face. Then he jabbed his heels into his horse's side and charged alone toward the main body of Turkish soldiers. Lawrence wrote later:

It was a long ride down a gentle slope and across a hollow. We sat there like stone while he rushed forward, the drumming of his hoofs unnaturally loud in our ears, for we had stopped shooting, and the Turks had stopped. Both armies waited for him; and he rocked on in the hushed evening till only a few lengths from the enemy. Then he sat up in the saddle and cried his war-cry, "Tallal, Tallal," twice in a tremendous shout. Instantly their rifles and machine-guns crashed out, and he and his mare, riddled through and through with bullets, fell dead among the lance points. Auda looked very cold and grim: "Allah give him mercy; we will take his price."

Auda assumed the command for the attack, skillfully driving the Turks onto poor ground and then splitting their formation into three parts. The fighting raged for more than two hours. For the only time in the entire war Lawrence ordered that no Turkish soldiers be taken prisoner. They were shot down as they attempted to surrender. When one group of Arabs appeared with 200 captured Turks, Lawrence ordered them executed on the spot. "The Arabs were fighting like devils, the sweat blurring their eyes, dust parching their throats; while the flame of cruelty and revenge which was burning in their bodies so twisted them, that their hands could hardly shoot," he wrote later. "In a madness born of the horror of Tafas we killed and killed, even blowing in the heads of the fallen and of the animals, as though their death and running blood could slake our agony." It was a sorry conclusion to Lawrence's carefree war of chivalrous adventure begun two years before in the Hejaz.

On September 30 Faisal's army advanced on Damascus. Lawrence rode in a Rolls armored car. Along the way they met Nasir and his men escorting several hundred prisoners, all that remained of the 7,000 men in the Turkish Fourth Army. The main column of British forces was nearby. The next day Lawrence rode into the ancient city of Damascus in the company of a group of British officers. People mobbed the streets. "Many were crying, a few cheered faintly, some bolder ones cried our names," Lawrence noted. "But mostly they looked and looked, joy shining in their eyes. A [sound] like a long sigh from the gate to the heart of the city marked our course."

The war in the Middle East ended in a wild carnival atmosphere. Ecstatic Arabs fired their rifles into the air and danced through the streets. S. C. Rolls, one of the armored car drivers, remembered in later years Lawrence's coming up to him, gripping his hand, and saying, "Goodbye, old fellow, I shall not be wanted any more. My job is done. We have had great fun together."

The fall of Damascus was a momentous historical event in the Middle East. It marked the thunderous collapse of the Ottoman Empire and brought into prominence the two nationalisms—Arab and Jewish—whose rival claims to Palestine were to shape the politics of the region for decades to come, turning the region after 1948 into a potential flashpoint for World War III. The fall of Damascus also signaled the start of a new era of British expansion into the region. Sinai, Palestine, and Mesopotamia fell under British control and supplied territorial compensation for the catastrophic loss of life the country had suffered on its European front. Henceforth, Britain was the dominant power in the Middle East and the Persian Gulf. Well might David Lloyd George, the prime minister, exclaim: "Side show? The British Empire has done very well out of side shows!" (So, too, one might add, has the modern Russian Empire.)

The Arab Revolt played a critical role in the war against the Turks, being, in effect, a second front that immobilized more than 30,000 Turkish troops along the railway from Amman to Medina. Had the Turks enjoyed free access through Medina to their garrison in Yemen, they might well have linked up with German forces in East Africa and closed the Red Sea to Allied shipping. In 1961 military historian Basil Liddell Hart summarized in the *Times Literary Supplement* the importance of the Arab Revolt:

On the eve of Allenby's offensive in September, 1918, his troops totalled 250,000 and the Turks had an equal number in that theatre of war. But he was able to attack with a five to one superiority of force because close on 50,000 troops were pinned down by the Arab force of 3,000 east of Jordan, operating under Lawrence's immediate direction, while a further 150,000 Turks were spread over the region in a vain attempt to stem the tide of the Arab Revolt so that little more than 50,000 were left to meet Allenby's assault. If it is unlikely that the Arab forces could ever have overwhelmed the Turks without the punch provided by Allenby's forces, the figures make it much clearer that Allenby could not have defeated the Turks without Lawrence.

As a youth Lawrence had dreamed of freeing the Arabs from their bondage to the Turks and establishing an independent Arab state. However, a postwar Lawrence quickly became disillusioned over his role in the Arab Revolt, concluding that he had betrayed the Arab cause. An angry Lawrence wrote later in a long-suppressed introduction to *Seven Pillars of Wisdom:* "We were casting them by thousands into the fire to the worst of deaths, not to win the war but that the corn and rice and oil of Mesopotamia might be ours."

Lawrence did not betray the Arab cause. Britain did. To gain support for the Allied effort against the Turks, officials of the British government made contradictory promises to the Arabs, the Jews, and the French. They offered the Arabs self-government throughout much of what had been the Ottoman Empire. To the Jews, they gave the Balfour Declaration of November 2, 1917, which called for the establishment of Palestine as "a national home for the Jewish people." (In 1917 there were more than 700,000 Arabs and fewer than 55,000 Jews living in Palestine.) And to France, England pledged that portion of Syria now known as Lebanon.

Lawrence realized soon after his involvement in the Arab Revolt that his government did not intend to honor its commitments. "Had I been an honest adviser of the Arabs I would have advised them to go home and not risk their lives fighting for [the British promises of a free Arab state]," he wrote after the war. "But I salved myself with the hope, by leading these Arabs madly in the final victory I would establish them, with arms in their hands, in a position so assured (if not dominant) that expediency would counsel to the Great Powers a fair settlement of their claims. In other words, I presumed . . . that I would survive the campaigns and be able to defeat not merely the Turks on the battlefield, but my own country and its allies in the council-chamber." After the war Lawrence for a time became the unsuccessful champion of the Arab cause for an independent state in the arena of British opinion.

After the armistice in 1918 Lawrence's exploits on behalf of the Arab Revolt were known only in official and military circles. Few in the general public had ever heard of the name T. E. Lawrence. His friend the Arabist Gertrude Bell was far better known. He did not appear in the British *Who's Who* until 1920. Yet within the span of a few months of 1919 Lawrence had become the most celebrated war hero of this century, a man known to millions as the "Uncrowned King of Arabia" and the "Modern Arabian Knight."

The myth of Lawrence of Arabia was entirely the creation of Lowell Thomas, a brash, young American journalist, who had traveled to the Middle Eastern theater in a search for a major story to lift the war-weary spirits of the people on the home front. In December 1917 in Jerusalem he met Lawrence and immediately realized the sensational possibilities of this blue-eyed British leader of the desert Arabs. On March 9, 1919, in the Century Theater, New York City, Thomas offered for the first time his illustrated lecture "With Lawrence in Arabia." The show was such a popular success that he moved it to Madison Square Garden. Soon afterward Thomas took his lecture on the road throughout the United States and England, playing to packed auditoriums at each stop. The myth of Lawrence of Arabia, the epic war hero who single-handedly led the Arab armies to victory over the Turks, was born out of Thomas's lecture (delivered more than 2,000 times) and his book (which sold more than 200,000 copies).

Thomas made Lawrence into a popular matinee idol and in the process established his own successful career. The legend gained additional impetus in 1922 when Paramount Studios released the enormously popular film *The Sheik*. Rudolph Valentino fixed in every woman's imagination the irresistible fantasy of the desert sheik as the noble, virile figure dressed in a burnoose and fancy robes with a bejeweled dagger in his belt, set against a background of a well-cushioned couch in a luxurious tent among the dunes.

Lawrence's own contribution was, of course, *Seven Pillars of Wisdom*, his account of his participation in the Arab Revolt, which he published privately in 1926. He rewrote the manuscript after an earlier draft was lost. Commercially the book was destined for major sales, and eager publishers in Britain and America offered Lawrence enormous advances. He rejected them all.

"Lawrence made up his mind to lose money by it," his good friend George Bernard Shaw recollected later. "He set able painters to work to make portraits of his Arab comrades-in-arms, and imaginative draughtsmen to let their fancy play on illustrations in black-and-white. He had the portraits reproduced in color. He had paper specially made, and directed the printing himself in the manner of Morris or Caxton. Finally he produced a private subscription edition after bringing the cost per copy up to £90 or so, the subscription price being £30. It was scarcely out when advertisements appeared in *The Times* offering £5 a week for the loan of a copy."

Seven Pillars of Wisdom took the critics by storm. Churchill wrote enthusiastically, "It ranks with the greatest books ever written in the English language." Forster insisted in *Abinger Harvest* that Lawrence "was so modest that he never grasped its greatness, or admitted that he had given something unique to our literature." And no less a figure than the poet William Butler Yeats wrote Lawrence's letter of election to the Irish Academy of Letters.

Seven Pillars of Wisdom is an intensely private and frank look into both the man and his experiences. Lawrence revealed his motives and emotions with an honesty rarely matched by other major historical personages in their memoirs. He joined his historical narrative of the progress of the Arab Revolt to a highly personal account of his spiritual odyssey toward self-knowledge. Professor Stephen E. Tabachnick sets

Seven Pillars of Wisdom in a literary tradition which includes Joseph Conrad's *Heart of Darkness*, E. M. Forster's *A Passage to India*, and George Orwell's *Burmese Days*, all books depicting Englishmen cast adrift between two cultures. He sums up the book's major movement: "The division between two political and cultural consciousnesses tears at his mind until he loses his belief in English methods and honor and finally in his own capacity to control body and mind. He struggles to retain his Western, British ego in the vast ocean of the Muslim desert, loses that battle, and awakens at the end of the adventure to find himself a stranger to English and Arab alike."

Lawrence refused to authorize an edition of his book for the general public. The public did not get its edition until after his death in 1935. However, in 1927 Lawrence did permit the publication of *Revolt in the Desert*, a severely abridged version which trimmed most of the passages of self-analysis. He refused to profit from the book and donated all his royalties to service charities.

Lawrence's years after his war service were marked by erratic behavior and great eccentricity. He refused all honors and offers of high government posts and important archaeological projects. He chose never again to exercise his enormous talent for leadership. Instead, he stepped off the stage and shed his old identity. In August 1922 Colonel T. E. Lawrence, a.k.a. Lawrence of Arabia, disappeared. In his place stood John Hume Ross, a private in the Royal Air Force. Within a few months the press had breached his new identity and published the sensational story that the great war hero was now serving as an ordinary soldier in the RAF. An embarrassed high command forced Lawrence to resign. On March 12, 1923, he enlisted in the tanks corps under the name of T. E. Shaw. But he loathed the army and petitioned unsuccessfully to return to the RAF. He fell into a deep depression and advised his friends that he planned to commit suicide. An anxious Bernard Shaw appealed to the prime minister. In July 1925 Lawrence was finally allowed to enlist in the RAF. In December 1926 he went to India to work in Karachi as a maintenance engineer in the engine repair section. In August 1927, back in England, he officially changed his name to T. E. Shaw.

(There is some evidence that he regarded the Bernard Shaws as surrogate parents.) Lawrence spent several happy years as a mechanic in the flying boats section and fantasized about organizing a flying boat cruise circumnavigating the world which would give him the material for another book. He actively involved himself in the development of high-speed motor launches, translated Homer's *Odyssey*, and wrote *The Mint*, a novel about life in the RAF. On February 25, 1935, he was discharged at his own request and resumed his identity as a civilian. Three months later Lawrence died in the crash of his motorcycle.

Lawrence's actions in the final fifteen years of his life appear a muddle only when viewed from the outside. From his perspective they made perfect sense. He told several close friends that he had enlisted in the RAF because it was "the nearest thing in the modern world to a life in a medieval monastery." He sought sanctuary and solace in the ordered routine of a common soldier, free from all anxieties about food, money, clothing, and shelter. "All that Lawrence asked from life after the War was peace and that he found in his own way," said Sergeant W. H. Brook, who had served under him in Arabia as a Stokes gunner.

But there were deeper motives. Turning his back on the persona of T. E. Lawrence and everything he represented became his way of dealing with the shame of the events of Deraa and the subsequent betrayal by the British government of its pledges to the Arabs. The Turks had raped his body, while the British had raped his sense of honor. It was finally too much for him to bear.

In 1926 in a painful letter to Charlotte Shaw Lawrence talked about the rape at Deraa and its consequences: "It's an unforgivable matter, an irrecoverable position. And it's that which made me forswear decent living and the exercise of my not-contemptible wits and talents. You may call this morbid. But think of the offense and the intensity of my brooding over it for these years. It will hang about me while I live, and afterwards if our personality survives. [Imagine me] wandering among the decent ghosts, hereafter crying, 'Unclean, unclean!' "

• • •

Lawrence's years of humdrum service in the Royal Air Force were years of healing and restoration. "It was a healthier man, physically and mentally, who took his discharge in 1935," his friend Liddell Hart remembered after his death. He came out "a man who looked much less than his forty-six years and radiated an air of contentment."

On May 13, 1935, Lawrence mounted his Brough motorcycle, a gift from his good friend Bernard Shaw, and rode to Bovington Camp. He was a careful motorcyclist and rarely took risks. (George Brough, the manufacturer of his machine, described him later as "one of the finest riders I ever met.")

In Bovington Camp Lawrence sent a telegram to a friend and then started home. He was not wearing a crash helmet. Lawrence revved his machine to fifty or sixty miles an hour. He crossed over the crest of a small hill and suddenly overtook two young errand boys on bicycles. Lawrence swerved, threw himself into a skid, lost control of his motorcycle, and crashed. Corporal Ernest Catchpole of the Royal Army Ordnance Corps was out walking his dog when he witnessed the accident. "I saw the bike twisting and turning over and over along the road," he stated at the inquest. "I saw nothing of the driver. I ran to the scene and found the motorcyclist on the road. His face was covered with blood which I tried to wipe away with my handkerchief."

Lawrence suffered severe head injuries. The brain surgeon who attended him stated later that had he lived, Lawrence would have suffered complete paralysis as well as the loss of both his memory and his ability to speak. He lingered in a coma for five days and died on May 19.

His good friend Gertrude Bell said of Lawrence after his death: "He lit so many fires in cold rooms."

Perhaps the modest and self-effacing Lawrence would have preferred for his epitaph the simple summary of his life from an omitted chapter to Seven Pillars of Wisdom:

"I did my best."

A Ford
Outside Every Tent:
The Death of
the Bedouin Culture

One evening in 1877 Charles Doughty met with Emir Muhammad ibn Rashid in Hail, Arabia. The two conversed in low tones in the emir's private apartments among clay walls stained with ochre. The powerful Arab chief quizzed his guest at length about the wonders of the modern world.

"What is the telegraph?" Ibn Rashid asked Doughty. "How does it work?"

Doughty thought for a moment. Then he tried to explain the telegraph by means of an image.

"If we may suppose a man laid head and heels betwen Hail and Constantinople, of such stature that he touched both," Doughty told Ibn Rashid, "then if one burned his feet at Hail, should he not feel it at the instant in his head, which is in Constantinople?"

The emir thought about this for a while. Then he asked Doughty about petroleum (did it have any use in Europe?) and America, the "new Continent" on the other side of the ocean. The pair talked until late in the evening. Ibn Rashid asked Doughty if the achievements of his court were frequent topics of conversation in Europe.

The Englishman replied truthfully that few Europeans had any knowledge of Arabia and almost none knew of the great emir Muhammad ibn Rashid. The Arab chief was disappointed. "It is time to shut the doors," he announced suddenly. A slave ushered Doughty out.

Within sixty years of Doughty's visit to Hail the Arabian Peninsula found itself a major focus of world attention. On February 14, 1945, King Abdul Aziz ibn Saud of Saudia Arabia, who had conquered the heirs of Ibn Rashid, met with President Franklin Roosevelt aboard the USS *Quincy* in the Suez Canal. They discussed the plight of the Jewish survivors in Europe and the various options for relocating them. By 1945 the vast oil reserves of the Arabian Peninsula were already under development, and Roosevelt understood that this would soon give the backward nation of Saudi Arabia major economic and political leverage in the Middle East.

Enormous changes swept through the Middle East after World War I. The vast expanses of open space which had nourished the Bedouin culture for thousands of years closed off. Lawrence's *Seven Pillars of Wisdom* had presaged the death of the desert Arabs, with its depiction of the violent intrusion into Arabia of the technology, communications, and weapons of the modern world, all of which threatened the independence of the Bedouins. The new governments in the region showed little tolerance for the near-anarchic life-style of the desert Arabs, who respected only their own set of laws. The great Saudi king Ibn Saud, himself a Bedouin, understood that effective consolidation of Arabia could occur only if the various Bedouin tribes were tamed through resettlement on farmlands near the major towns and cities. There and elsewhere in the Middle East the proud desert Arabs gradually went the way of the American Plains Indian, the cowboy, and the Mongol horseman.

There were other factors, of course. Geologists in trucks and helicopters scoured the deserts in a constant search for new oil reserves. In their wake they left oil fields, pipelines, and vast storage depots. The bus, truck, and car replaced the camel, horse, and donkey. Shortly before his death Harry Bridges St. John Philby, the last of the great British explorers of Arabia, predicted that within thirty years camels would have disappeared from the peninsula, and with them, their parasites the Bedouins. In 1960 that seemed preposterous. But Philby was correct. Today's Bedouin children are reared on powdered milk, not fresh camel's milk. And Arabia has ceased to be a happy hunting ground for the Western imagination.

In their book *Passing Brave*, William Polk and William Mares, both veterans of lengthy stays in Arabia, recount their return to Hail in the early 1970s. They were determined to recapture some of the old ways and cross the great Nafud by camel. But they quickly learned that the local Bedouins had long since lost all interest in their desert. None traveled there any longer or knew anything about its wells and routes. The vast migrations were a thing of the distant past, as modern Bedouins trucked fodder and 100 gallon drums of water to their herds.

At the end of two weeks Polk and Mares had found just six camels for their adventure, this in a town where hundreds of the animals once had been sold every day in the marketplace. A local Bedouin sheik told them: "There is something about you Westerners that make you love the desert. We who were born here will never understand it. For us, the desert is a place where we go because we must. The grazing is good for animals after the rains but it is miserable, hot, and hard on man and beast. No, there is nothing about the desert that is romantic or beautiful. I have my garden, where water flows bountifully from my well. I have electricity which gives me a radio and an air conditioner. I can sit at my ease and drink Coca-Cola. You are mad to go into the desert."

In the tent of another sheik Polk sat drinking coffee and talking about world politics.

"Do you still have a *rawi*, or teacher, to recite the great Bedouin poetry?" Polk asked.

"No," the old sheik replied. "But we have a transistor radio. Would you like to listen to the Voice of America, the Voice of the Arabs, or Radio Moscow?"

Polk saw a bicycle leaning against a tent pole.

"O Bedouin, what has happened to you and your people?" Polk wailed mockingly. "You have no poetry, only the radio. You have no camels, only the truck. And now I see in the place of the Arab stallion you have a bicycle tethered to your tent pole."

The old sheik shook his head sadly.

"Bicycles don't eat," he muttered.

But if the Bedouins, as a traditional culture, have largely disappeared from the Middle Eastern landscape, they continue to loom large in the Arab imagination as an ideal against which, in theory at least, a modern generation often takes its measure. It was not so many years ago that wealthy families sometimes sent their sons into the desert for a year or more to expose them to the experiences, ideals, and manners of the Bedouin life, much as the British upper classes send their children to Eton and the aristocratic Japanese place their sons in Zen monasteries for several weeks each year. Many important Arab leaders of the past thirty years have proudly claimed Bedouin origin. They include Colonel Moammar Khadafy, who was sleeping in a sprawling desert tent set up in a courtyard of the Bab el Azizia barracks when American bombers attacked Libya on April 14, 1986. Historian Raphael Patnai wrote in *The Arab Mind:*

> The fact is that Bedouins are looked upon, not only by the Arab cities, but by the entire Arab world with the exception of its Westernized elements, as images and figures from the past, as living ancestors, as latter-day heirs and witnesses to the ancient glory of the heroic age. Hence the importance of the Bedouin ethos, and of the Bedouins' aristocratic moral code, for the Arab world in general. . . . While the desert and its Bedouins are very far removed from the great majority of the Arabs, who are either town dwellers or villagers and have been for many generations, in ideology and scale of values both still loom large; in fact, they still hold the undisputed first place.

NAPOLEON IN EGYPT

Two fine books on Napoleon's Egyptian campaign are Christopher Lloyd's *The Nile Campaign*, which effectively uses original documents to tell the story, and J. Christopher Herold's *Bonaparte in Egypt*, a thorough history of all aspects of the French invasion. For additional reading on the Ottoman Empire, Noel Barber's *The Sultans* is a colorful and lively history of the empire as seen through the occupants of the Grand Seraglio. The major American scholar in modern times interpreting the Muslim world to the West has been Bernard Lewis. His books, *Islam and the Arab World* and *Istanbul and the Civilization of the Ottoman Empire*, are excellent introductions for the general reader. His more recent history, *The Muslim Discovery of Europe*, is a brilliant, engrossing, and sympathetic study of the interaction of Muslims and Europeans over the past 1,300 years.

LADY HESTER STANHOPE

Dr. Charles Meryon's two lengthy memoirs on his travels with Lady Hester Stanhope—*The Memoirs of Lady Hester Stanhope* and *Travels of Lady Hester Stanhope*—are indispensable. The Duchess of Cleveland, Lady Hester's niece, also produced an excellent biography, *The Life and Letters of Lady Hester Stanhope*, which prints many letters not included in the Meryon books. Ian Bruce's *The Nun of Lebanon: The Love Affair of Lady Hester Stanhope and Michael Bruce* is invaluable for the extensive correspondence between Lady Hester and the Bruce family, which is here printed for the first time. Of the several modern biographies on Lady Hester, John Watney's *Travels in Arabia of Lady Hester Stanhope* is the most useful. Agnes Carr Vaughan's *Zenobia of Palmyra* is good for separating fact from legend in the life of that remarkable woman from classical times. Iain Browning's *Palmyra* is an excellent history and appreciation.

THE PIRATE COAST

The most detailed history of piracy in the Persian Gulf is Sir Charles Belgrave's *The Pirate Coast*, which also has a chapter on the exploits of Rahmah ibn Jabr. J. B. Kelly's exhaustive *Britain and the Persian Gulf, 1795–1880* is definitive on England's role in the region in the nineteenth century.

ALEXANDER KINGLAKE AND THE GRAND TOUR

A. W. Kinglake's *Eothen* with a useful appreciation by Jonathan Raban is available in a paperback edition from the Century Publishing Company. The best biography is Gerald de Gaury's *Travelling Gent: The Life of Alexander Kinglake*. Two fine books on the development of Orientalist art are Philippe Jullian's *The Orientalists* and the National Gallery of Art's catalog to its splendid 1984 exhibition

The Orientalists: Delacroix to Matisse, both of which contain a wealth of information about early-nineteenth-century travel to the Middle East and the impact of the region upon the European imagination. Brian M. Fagan's *The Rape of the Nile* details the history of tourism and archaeology in Egypt, while Neil Silberman's *Digging for God and Country* does the same thing for the Holy Land. *Flaubert in Egypt: A Sensibility on Tour*, stylishly translated and edited by Francis Steegmuller, brings together all of the French novelist's letters and journal entries from his Egyptian trip.

LEBANON: THE ROOTS OF THE CIVIL WAR

The most reliable contemporary account of the nineteenth-century civil wars between Lebanese Christians and Muslims can be found in Colonel Charles Churchill's *The Druzes and the Maronites Under Turkish Rule, from 1840 to 1860*. The best of the modern histories is Kamal S. Salibi's *The Modern History of Lebanon*. A useful account of the most recent civil war which makes passing but insightful remarks on its nineteenth-century origins is David Gilmour's *Lebanon: The Fractured Country*.

SIR RICHARD BURTON AND WILLIAM PALGRAVE, SJ

The major account of Richard Burton's expedition to Mecca is, of course, his own book, *Personal Narrative of a Pilgrimage to al-Madinah & Meccah*, available in a Dover paperback edition. A great many anecdotes regarding his years in India can be found in his three books: *Goa and the Blue Mountains* (which contains a full account of his frustrated elopement with the nun, although he ascribes the adventure to another Englishman); *Scinde; or, The Unhappy Valley*; and *Sindh, and the Races That Inhabit the Valley of the Indus*. Most of the material in Burton's report for Napier on the Indian brothels ended up in the lengthy "Terminal Essay" he affixed to the end of his translation of the *Arabian Nights*. Of the many biographies on Burton, the best two are Fawn M. Brodie's *The Devil Drives: A Life of Sir Richard Burton* and Byron Farwell's *Burton: A Biography*. Robert Goldston's *The Sword of the Prophet* (Fawcett paperback), an excellent introduction to the history of the Arab world, has useful chapters on Muhammad and the Arab conquest.

William Palgrave's lengthy *Narrative of a Year's Journey Through Central and Eastern Arabia* is the chief source for his travels. The only biography of the man is Mea Allan's *Palgrave of Arabia: The Life of William Gifford Palgrave*.

SUEZ CANAL

As one might expect, an enormous body of literature has grown up about the Suez Canal. A good place to start is Ferdinand de Lesseps's own books: *The History of the Suez Canal: A Personal Narrative* and *Recollections of Forty Years*, both translations from the original French. Of the several histories of the actual construction, I found useful John Pudney's *Suez: De Lesseps's Canal* and John Marlowe's *World Ditch: The Making of the Suez Canal*. The most authoritative and definitive history continues to be D. A. Farnie's brilliant *East and West of Suez: The Suez Canal in History, 1854–1956*. Of the many books on the Suez crisis of 1956, two of the best are Hugh Thomas's *Suez* and Chester L. Cooper's *The Lion's Last Roar: Suez, 1956*.

LADY JANE DIGBY EL MESRAB

The most complete biography is Margaret Fox Schmidt's *Passion's Child: The Extraordinary Life of Jane Digby*. Schmidt drew upon hitherto-unexamined notebooks, sketches, letters, and legal documents in the possession of the Digby family as well as a large cache of Lady Jane's letters to King Ludwig I in the state archives in

Munich. E. M. Oddie's older biography, *The Odyssey of a Loving Woman*, is still useful, for Oddie had access to personal papers and journals from Lady Jane's years in the Middle East which have since been lost. There are chapters on both Lady Jane Digby and Isabel Burton in Lesley Blanch's *The Wilder Shores of Love*.

For the Burtons' stay in Damascus, the principal books are Richard Burton's *Unexplored Syria* and Isabel Burton's *The Inner Life of Syria, Palestine, and the Holy Land*. Fawn M. Brodie has an excellent chapter on this period of Burton's career in her biography *The Devil Drives*. The Isabel Arundell–Richard Burton romance is one of the most thoroughly documented of the century. The fullest accounts of the courtship can be found in Isabel Burton's *Life of Captain Sir Richard F. Burton* and W. H. Wilkins's *The Romance of Isabel Lady Burton*.

The best reference work on the life-style of the Syrian Bedouins is Alois Musil's encyclopedic *The Manners and Customs of the Rwala Bedouins*. John MacGregor wrote a lengthy account of his adventures in the Middle East, *The Rob Roy: A Canoe Cruise in Palestine and Egypt and the Waters of Damascus*.

CARLO GUARMANI AND THE HORSE OF THE DESERT

Carlo Guarmani's own account of his trip, *Northern Nejd: Journey from Jerusalem to Anaiza in Kasim*, was published in 1938 in an English translation. A full account of Guarmani's experiences can also be found in Zahra Freeth and H.V.F. Winstone's book, *Explorers of Arabia from the Renaissance to the End of the Victorian Era*. Of the many books on the Arabian horse, two of the most useful are General E. Daumas, *The Horses of the Sahara* (originally published in 1850, it includes a lengthy commentary by the emir Abd el Kader) and Judith Wentworth's *The Authentic Arabian Horse and His Descendants* (Wentworth was the daughter of Wilfrid and Anne Blunt).

SIR WILFRID BLUNT AND LADY ANNE BLUNT

The primary accounts of the Blunts' travels through Arabia are Lady Anne's books, *Bedouin Tribes of the Euphrates* and *A Pilgrimage to Nejd*. (*Pilgrimage* is available in a paperback edition from the Century Publishing Company.) Elizabeth Longford's excellent biography *A Pilgrim of Passion: The Life of Wilfrid Scawen Blunt* is definitive. No biography of Lady Anne Blunt exists. A handy source for Blunt's political opinions is his book *Secret History of the English Occupation of Egypt*; he included many additional details about his travels in the Muslim world. Excellent chapters on Wilfrid Blunt may be found in Albert Hourani's *Europe and the Middle East* and Kathryn Tidrick's *Heart-Beguiling Araby*. Mark Girouard has new information on Blunt's many love affairs in his enormously interesting book *The Return to Camelot: Chivalry and the English Gentleman*. For a superb discussion of the roots of the Shi'ite anger toward the Western powers in the 1980s, see Robin Wright's book, *Sacred Rage: The Wrath of Militant Islam*.

CHARLES DOUGHTY

Charles Doughty's *Travels in the Arabia Deserta* is the major source of information on his journey. Although published almost sixty years ago, David G. Hogarth's *The Life of Charles Doughty* is still the only biography available. Stephen E. Tabachnick's *Charles Doughty* is a fine scholarly appreciation of the literary dimensions of Doughty's works.

T. E. LAWRENCE

"People read themselves into Lawrence, and everybody sees him differently," the film director David Lean once observed perceptively. This undoubtedly accounts in part for Lawrence's enduring popularity. The reader who wishes to learn more about this extraordinary man should start with *Seven Pillars of Wisdom*, which is both the greatest war memoir of the century and a major literary accomplishment. Avoid *Revolt of the Desert,* the abridged version with all of Lawrence's interesting personal reflections edited out. Also important is *T. E. Lawrence by His Friends,* a fascinating collection of reminiscences on Lawrence by his family, friends, and associates after his death, edited by his brother A. W. Lawrence.

Of the dozen or so biographies, the most brilliant, thorough, and balanced is John E. Mack's *A Prince of Our Disorder: The Life of T. E. Lawrence.* Thirty years ago, when Lawrence bashing was in vogue, two hostile biographies caused considerable controversy. These were Richard Aldington's *Lawrence of Arabia* ("*Seven Pillars of Wisdom* is a monstrous lie") and Suleiman Mousa's *T. E. Lawrence: An Arab View* ("Deep within himself, Lawrence knew that the greater part of his fame was based on fraud"). Later scholarship has thoroughly discredited both writers' negative views of Lawrence's character and achievements. However, the Aldington book has an excellent chapter on Lowell Thomas's lecture tour.

Lawrence's *Seven Pillars of Wisdom* is great literature and deserves to be studied as such. Fortunately two scholars have written fine appreciations of the book: Jeffrey Meyers's *The Wounded Spirit: A Study of Seven Pillars of Wisdom* and Stephen E. Tabachnick's *T. E. Lawrence.*

A SELECTED BIBLIOGRAPHY

Addison, Charles. *Damascus and Palmyra: A Journey to the East.* 2 vols. Philadelphia: E. L. Carey & A. Hart, 1838.

Ahmed, Leila. *Edward W. Lane.* London: Longman, 1978.

Aldington, Richard. *Lawrence of Arabia.* Chicago: Henry Regnery, 1955.

Allan, Mea. *Palgrave of Arabia: The Life of William Gifford Palgrave, 1826–88.* London: Macmillan, 1972.

Anderson, M. S. *The Great Powers and the Near East, 1774–1923.* London: Edward Arnold, 1970.

Assad, Thomas J. *Three Victorian Travellers: Burton, Blunt, Doughty.* London: Routledge & Kegan Paul, 1964.

Barber, Noel. *The Sultans.* New York: Simon & Schuster, 1973.

Beaufort, Emily A. *Egyptian Sepulchres and Syrian Shrines.* 2 vols. London: Longman, Green, Longman, and Roberts, 1861.

Belgrave, Sir Charles. *The Pirate Coast.* New York: Roy, 1966.

Bevis, Richard. "Spiritual Geology: C. M. Doughty and the Land of the Arabs." *Victorian Studies,* vol. 16 (December 1972), pp. 163–81.

Bidwell, Robin. *Travellers in Arabia.* London: Hamlyn, 1976.

Bishop, Jonathan. "The Heroic Ideal in Doughty's *Arabia Deserta.*" *Modern Language Quarterly,* vol. 21 (March 1960), pp. 59–68.

Blanch, Lesley. *The Wilder Shores of Love.* New York: Simon & Schuster, 1954.

Blunt, Lady Anne. *Bedouin Tribes of the Euphrates.* New York: Harper & Brothers, 1879.

———. *A Pilgrimage to Nejd.* London: Century, 1985.

Blunt, Wilfrid Scawen. *My Diaries: Being a Personal Narrative of Events, 1888–1914.* 2 vols. New York: Alfred A. Knopf, 1921.

———. *The Poetical Works: A Complete Edition.* 2 vols. London: Macmillan, 1914.

———. *Secret History of the English Occupation of Egypt.* New York: Howard Hertig, 1967.

Brent, Peter. *Far Arabia: Explorers of the Myth.* London: Weidenfeld and Nicolson, 1977.

Browning, Iain. *Palmyra.* New Jersey: Noyes, 1979.

Bruce, Ian. *The Nun of Lebanon.* London: Collins, 1951. On Lady Hester Stanhope.

Buckingham, J. S. *Travels in Mesopotamia.* London: Henry Colburn, 1827.

Bull, Deborah, and Donald Lorimer. *Up the Nile: A Photographic Excursion.* New York: Clarkson N. Potter, 1979.

Burckhardt, John Lewis. *Notes on the Bedouins and Wahabys.* 2 vols. London: Henry Colburn, 1831.

———. *Travels in Arabia.* London: Henry Colburn, 1829.

———. *Travels in Syria and the Holy Land.* London: John Murray, 1822.

Burton, Isabel. *The Inner Life of Syria, Palestine, and the Holy Land.* 2 vols. London: Henry S. King, 1875.

Burton, Richard. *The Erotic Traveler.* Edited by Edward Leigh. New York: Berkeley Medallion Paperback, 1966.

———. *Love, War, and Fancy: The Social and Sexual Customs of the East.* Edited by Dr. Kenneth Walker. London: Kimber Paperback, 1964.

———. *Personal Narrative of a Pilgrimage to al-Madinah & Meccah.* 2 vols. New York: Dover, 1964.

———, and Charles F. Tyrwhitt. *Unexplored Syria.* 2 vols. London: Tinsley Brothers, 1872.

Carmichael, Joel. *The Shaping of the Arabs: A Study in Ethnic Identity*. New York: Macmillan, 1967.

Casey, Robert J. *Baghdad and Points East*. New York: Robert McBridge, 1931.

Churchill, Charles H. *The Druzes and the Maronites*. London: Bernard Quaritch, 1862.

Cleveland, Duchess of. *The Life and Letters of Lady Hester Stanhope*. London: John Murray, 1914.

Colledge, Malcolm. *The Art of Palmyra*. London: Westview, 1976.

Conant, Martha Pike. *The Oriental Tale in the Eighteenth Century*. New York: Columbia University Press, 1908.

Coon, Carleton S. *Caravan: The Story of the Middle East*. New York: Holt, Rinehart & Winston, 1958.

Cooper, Chester L. *The Lion's Last Roar: Suez, 1956*. New York: Harper & Row, 1978.

Cottrell, Alvin J., ed. *The Persian Gulf States: A General Survey*. Baltimore: Johns Hopkins University Press, 1980.

Curzon, Robert. *Visits to the Monasteries in Levant*. [1849.] Ithaca, N.Y.: Cornell University Press, 1955.

Da Cruz, Daniel. "The Camel in Retrospect. *Aramco World Magazine* (March/April 1981), pp. 42–49.

Daniel, Norman. *Islam and the West: The Making of an Image*. Edinburgh: University Press, 1960.

———. *Islam, Europe, and Empire*. Edinburgh: University Press, 1966.

Daumas, General E. *The Horses of the Sahara*, translated by Sheila M. Ohlendorf. Austin: University of Texas Press, 1968.

De Gaury, Gerald. *Arabia Phoenix*. London: George Harrap, 1946.

———. *Arabian Journey and Other Desert Travels*. London: George Harrap, 1950.

———. *Travelling Gent: The Life of Alexander Kinglake (1809–1891)*. London: Routledge & Kegan Paul, 1972.

Dickson, H. R. P. *The Arab of the Desert*. London: George Allen & Unwin, 1983.

Doughty, Charles M. *Travels in Arabia Deserta*. 2 vols. London: Jonathan Cape, 1930.

Duffy, John Dennis. "*Arabia Literaria*: Four Visions of the East." Ph.D. dissertation, University of Toronto, 1964.

Egremont, Max. *The Cousins: The Friendship, Opinions, and Activities of Wilfrid Scawen Blunt and George Wyndham*. London: Collins, 1977.

Fagan, Brian M. *The Rape of the Nile: Tombs, Tourists, and Archaeologists in Egypt*. New York: Charles Scribner's, 1975.

Farnie, D. A. *East and West of Suez: The Suez Canal in History, 1854–1956*. Oxford: Clarendon Press, 1969.

Farwell, Byron. *Burton: A Biography*. New York: Holt, Rinehart, & Winston, 1963.

Fedden, Robin. *Syria: An Historical Appreciation*. London: Readers Union, 1955.

Fernau, F. W. *Moslems on the March: People and Politics in the World of Islam*. New York: Alfred A. Knopf, 1954.

Finch, Edith. *Wilfrid Scawen Blunt, 1840–1922*. London: Jonathan Cape, 1938.

Fisher, Sydney N. *The Middle East: A History*. New York: Alfred A. Knopf, 1968.

Fisher, W. B. *The Middle East: A Physical, Social, and Regional Geography*. London: Methuen, 1978.

Flaubert, Gustave. *Flaubert in Egypt: A Sensibililty on Tour*. Translated and edited by Francis Steegmuller. Chicago: Academy Chicago Limited, 1979.

Freeth, Zahra, and H. V. F. Winstone. *Explorers of Arabia: From the Renaissance to the End of the Victorian Era*. New York: Holmes & Meier, 1978.

Georges-Picot, Jacques. *The Real Suez Crisis*. New York: Harcourt Brace Jovanovich, 1978.

Gervasi, Frank. *Thunder over the Mediterranean*. New York: David McKay, 1975.

Gilmour, David. *Lebanon: The Fractured Country*. New York: St. Martin's Press, 1983.

Girouard, Mark. *The Return to Camelot: Chivalry and the English Gentleman*. New Haven: Yale University Press, 1981.

Goldston, Robert. *The Sword of the Prophet*. New York: Fawcett, 1979.

Graves, Richard P. *Lawrence of Arabia and His World*. London: Thames and Hudson, 1976.

Graves, Robert. *Lawrence and the Arabs*. London: Jonathan Cape, 1927.

Guarmani, Carlo. *Northern Nejd: Journey from Jerusalem to Anaiza*. Translated by Lady Capel-Cure. London: Argonaut Press, 1938.

Hamel, Frank. *Lady Hester Stanhope*. London: Cassell, 1913.

Hamidullah, Muhammad. *Introduction to Islam*. Paris: Centre Culturel Islamique, 1969.

Harik, Iliya F. *Politics and Change in a Traditional Society: Lebanon, 1711–1845*. Princeton: Princeton University Press, 1968.

Haslip, Joan. *Lady Hester Stanhope*. New York: Frederick Stokes, 1936.

Hastings, Michael. *Sir Richard Burton: A Biography*. London: Hodder and Stoughton, 1978.

Herold, J. Christopher. *Bonaparte in Egypt*. New York: Harper & Row, 1962.

Hogarth, D. G. *Arabia*. Oxford: Clarendon Press, 1922.

——. *The Life of Charles M. Doughty*. New York: Doubleday, 1929.

——. *The Penetration of Arabia*. New York: Frederick Stokes, 1904.

Hopwood, Derek. *The Russian Presence in Syria and Palestine, 1843–1914*. Oxford: Clarendon Press, 1969.

Houghton, Walter E. *The Victorian Frame of Mind, 1830–1870*. New Haven: Yale University Press, 1957.

Hourani, Albert. *Europe and the Middle East*. Berkeley: University of California Press, 1980.

Hughes, Jean Gordon. *Queen of the Desert: The Story of Lady Hester Stanhope*. London: Macmillan, 1967.

Hunt, William Holman. *Pre-Raphaelitism and the Pre-Raphaelite Brotherhood*. 2 vols. London: Macmillan, 1905.

Ingram, Edward. *The Beginning of the Great Game in Asia, 1828–1834*. Oxford: Clarendon Press, 1979.

Izzard, Molly. *The Gulf: Arabia's Western Approaches*. London: John Murray, 1979.

Jewett, Iran Banu Hassani. *Alexander W. Kinglake*. Boston: Twayne, 1981.

Jullian, Philippe. "Baubles, Bangles, and Blood." *Réalités* (April 1979), pp. 75–79.

——. *The Orientalists*. Oxford: Phaidon, 1977.

Kelly, J. B. *Britain and the Persian Gulf, 1795–1880*. Oxford: Clarendon Press, 1968.

Kieran, R. H. *The Unveiling of Arabia*. London: Harrap, 1937.

Kinglake, A. W. *Eothen*. London: Century, 1982.

Kinross, Lord. *Between Two Seas: The Creation of the Suez Canal*. New York: William Morrow, 1969.

Klengel, Horst. *The Art of Ancient Syria*. New York: A. B. Barnes, 1972.

Lacey, Robert. *The Kingdom: Arabia & the House of Sa'ud.* New York: Harcourt Brace Jovanovich, 1981.

Landes, David S. *Bankers and Pashas: International Finance and Economic Imperialism in Egypt.* Cambridge: Harvard University Press, 1958.

Lane, E. W. *Manners and Customs of the Modern Egyptians.* London: J. M. Dent & Sons, 1954.

Lawrence, A. W., ed. *T. E. Lawrence by His Friends.* Garden City, N.Y.: Doubleday, 1937.

Lawrence, T. E. *The Essential T. E. Lawrence.* Edited by David Garnett. London: Jonathan Cape, 1951.

————. *Selected Letters.* Edited by David Garnett. London: Jonathan Cape, 1952.

————. *Seven Pillars of Wisdom.* Garden City, N.Y.: Doubleday, 1936.

Leslie, Shane. *Men Were Different: Five Studies in Late Victorian Biography.* Freeport, N.Y.: Books for Libraries Press, 1967. Chapter on Wilfrid Blunt.

Lesseps, Ferdinand de. *The History of the Suez Canal: A Personal Narrative.* Edinburgh: Blackwood, 1876.

————. *Recollections of Forty Years.* London: Blackwood, 1887.

Lewis, Bernard. *The Arabs in History.* New York: Harper & Row, 1958.

————. *The Assassins: A Radical Sect in Islam.* London: Weidenfeld and Nicolson, 1967.

————. *The Emergence of Modern Turkey.* London: Oxford University Press, 1961.

————. *Islam and the Arab World.* New York: Alfred A. Knopf, 1976.

————. *Islam in History.* New York: Library Press, 1973.

————. *Istanbul and the Civilization of the Ottoman Empire.* Norman: University of Oklahoma Press, 1963.

————. *The Muslim Discovery of Europe.* New York: W. W. Norton, 1982.

Lloyd, Christopher. *The Nile Campaign.* New York: Barnes & Noble, 1973.

Longford, Elizabeth. *A Pilgrimage of Passion: The Life of Wilfrid Scawen Blunt.* London: Weidenfeld and Nicolson, 1979.

Lunde, Paul. "Caravans to Mecca." *Aramco World Magazine* (November/December 1974), pp. 8–11.

Lytton, Earl of. *Wilfrid Scawen Blunt: A Memoir by His Grandson.* London: Macdonald, 1961.

MacGregor, John. *The Rob Roy on the Jordan, Nile, Red Sea, and Gennasareth:*

A Canoe Cruise in Palestine and Egypt and the Waters of Damascus. London: John Murray, 1869.

Mack, John E. *A Prince of Our Disorder: The Life of T. E. Lawrence.* Boston: Little, Brown, 1976.

Mansfield, Peter. *The Arab World: A Comprehensive History.* New York: Thomas Y. Crowell, 1976.

Ma'oz, Moshe. *Ottoman Reform in Syria and Palestine, 1840–1861.* Oxford: Clarendon Press, 1968.

Marlowe, John. *A History of Modern Egypt and Anglo-Egyptian Relations, 1800–1956.* Hamden, Conn.: Archon Books, 1965.

———. *Perfidious Albion: The Origins of Anglo-French Rivalry in the Levant.* London: Elek Books, 1971.

———. *World Ditch: The Making of the Suez Canal.* New York: Macmillan, 1964.

Meryon, Dr. Charles. *The Memoirs of Lady Hester Stanhope.* 3 vols. London: Henry Colburn, 1845.

———. *Travels of Lady Hester Stanhope.* 3 vols. London: Henry Colburn, 1846.

Meyers, Jeffrey. *The Wounded Spirit: A Study of Seven Pillars of Wisdom.* London: Martin Brian & O'Keeffe, 1973.

Michalowski, Kazimierz. *Palmyra.* New York: Praeger, 1968.

Miller, William. *The Ottoman Empire and Its Successors, 1801–1927.* Cambridge: University Press, 1936.

Montagu, Lady Mary Wortley. *Letters from the Levant During the Embassy to Constantinople, 1716–18.* London: Joseph Rickerby, 1838.

Montgomery, James A. *Arabia and the Bible.* Philadelphia: University of Pennsylvania Press, 1934.

Morris, Jan. "A Sardonic Grand Tour." *Connoisseur* (May 1983), pp. 136–38. On Kinglake's *Eothen*.

Mousa, Suleiman. *T. E. Lawrence: An Arab View.* London: Oxford University Press, 1966.

Musil, Alois. *The Manners and Customs of the Rwala Bedouins.* New York: Czech Academy of Sciences and Arts, 1928.

Nasir, Sari J. *The Arabs and the English.* London: Longman, 1979.

National Art Gallery. *The Orientalists, Delacroix to Matisse: The Allure of North Africa and the Near East.* Edited by Mary Anne Stevens. Washington, D.C.: National Art Gallery, 1984.

Nutting, Anthony. *Lawrence of Arabia: The Man and the Motive*. New York: Clarkson N. Potter, 1961.

———. *No End of a Lesson: The Story of Suez*. London: Constable, 1967.

Oddie, E. M. *The Odyssey of a Loving Woman*. New York: Harper, 1936. Biography of Lady Jane Digby.

Palgrave, William Gifford. *Essays on Eastern Questions*. London: Macmillan, 1872.

———. *Narrative of a Year's Journey Through Central and Eastern Arabia (1862–63)*. 2 vols. London: Macmillan, 1865.

Palmer, Edward Henry. *The Desert of the Exodus*. 2 vols. London: Bell and Daldy, 1871.

Paston, George. "Lady Hester Stanhope." *Little Memoirs of the Nineteenth Century*. London: Grant Richards, 1902.

Patai, Raphael. *The Arab Mind*. New York: Charles Scribner's, 1983.

Patent, Dorothy Hinshaw. *Arabian Horses*. New York: Holiday House, 1982.

Pears, Sir Edwin. *Forty Years in Constantinople*. New York: D. Appleton, 1916.

Phillips, Wendell. *Qataban and Sheba: Exploring the Ancient Kingdoms on the Biblical Spice Routes of Arabia*. New York: Harcourt, Brace, 1955.

Polk, William, and William Mares. *Passing Brave*. New York: Alfred A. Knopf, 1973.

Pudney, John. *Suez: De Lesseps's Canal*. London: J. M. Dent, 1968.

Raban, Jonathan. *Arabia: A Journey Through the Labyrinth*. New York: Simon & Schuster, 1980.

Ralli, Augustus. *Christians at Mecca*. Port Washington, N.Y.: Kennikat Press, 1971.

Raswan, Carl. *Black Tents of Arabia: My Life Among the Bedouins*. New York: Creative Age Press, 1947.

Redesdale, Lord. *Memories*. 2 vols. New York: E. P. Dutton, 1916.

Rodgers, William. "Arabian Involvement: A Study of Five Victorian Travel Narratives." Ph.D. dissertation, University of California at Berkeley, 1971.

———. "Lady Anne Blunt and Wilfrid Scawen Blunt: Aristocrats as Arabian Travellers." *Explorations* (December 1974), pp. 24–35.

———. "Romance, Science, and W. G. Palgrave's Central and Eastern Arabia." *Explorations* (July 1978), pp. 9–32.

Ross, Alexander M. *William Henry Bartlett: Artist, Author, and Traveller.* Toronto: University of Toronto Press, 1973.

Rostovtzeff, M. *Caravan Cities.* New York: AMS Press, 1971.

Ruthven, Malise. *Islam in the World.* London: Penguin Books, 1984.

Said, Edward W. *Orientalism.* New York: Pantheon Books, 1978.

Salibi, Kamal S. *The Modern History of Lebanon.* London: Weidenfeld and Nicholson, 1965.

Schmidt, Margaret Fox. *Passion's Child: The Extraordinary Life of Jane Digby.* New York: Harper & Row, 1976.

Schonfield, Hugh J. *The Suez Canal in Peace and War, 1869–1969.* Coral Gables, Fla.: University of Miami Press, 1952.

Searight, Sarah. *The British in the Middle East.* New York: Atheneum, 1970.

Silberman, Neil. *Digging for God and Country: Exploration, Archaeology, and the Secret Struggle for the Holy Land, 1799–1917.* New York, Alfred A. Knopf, 1982.

Sim, Katherine. *Desert Traveller: The Life of Jean Louis Burckhardt.* London: Victor Gollancz, 1969.

Stark, Freya. *Beyond Euphrates.* London: John Murray, 1951.

Stewart, Desmond. *T. E. Lawrence.* London: Hamish Hamilton, 1977.

Tabachnick, Stephen Ely. *Charles Doughty.* Boston: Twayne, 1981.

———. *T. E. Lawrence.* Boston: Twayne, 1978.

Thackeray, William M. *Notes of a Journey from Cornhill to Grand Cairo.* London: Chapman and Hall, 1846.

Thomas, Bertram. *The Arabs.* London: Thornton Butterworth, 1937.

Thomas, Hugh. *Suez.* New York: Harper & Row, 1967.

Thomas, Lowell. *With Lawrence in Arabia.* New York: Century, 1924.

Thornton, A. P. *The Imperial Ideal and Its Enemies.* London: Macmillan, 1959.

Tidrick, Kathryn. *Heart-Beguiling Araby.* Cambridge: University Press, 1981.

Tuckwell, Reverend W. A. *W. Kinglake: A Biographical and Literary Study.* London: George Bell and Sons, 1902.

Vaczek, Louis, and Gail Buckland. *Travelers in Ancient Lands: A Portrait of the Middle East, 1839–1919.* Boston: New York Graphic Society, 1981.

Varthema, Ludovico di. *Travels.* Translated by John J. Jones. London: Hakluyt Society, 1863.

Vaughan, Agnes. *Zenobia of Palmyra.* New York: Doubleday, 1976.

Vernon, Arthur. *The History and Romance of the Horse.* New York: Dover Publications, 1946.

Walker, Franklin. *Irreverent Pilgrims: Melville, Browne, and Mark Twain in the Holy Land.* Seattle: University of Washington Press, 1974.

Warburton, Eliot. *The Crescent and the Cross; or, Romance and Realities of Eastern Travel.* 2 vols. London: Henry Colburn, 1847.

Watney, John. *Travels in Arabia of Lady Hester Stanhope.* London: Gordon Cremonesi, 1975.

Weber, Shirley H. *Voyages and Travels in the Near East During the XIX Century.* Princeton: American School of Classical Studies at Athens, 1952.

Wellsted, James R. *Travels in Arabia.* 2 vols. London: John Murray, 1838.

———. *Travels to the City of Caliphs.* 2 vols. London: Henry Colburn, 1840.

Wentworth, Judith. *The Authentic Arabian Horse and His Descendants.* Canaan, N.Y.: Sporting Book Center, 1979.

Wilkins, W. H. *The Romance of Isabel Lady Burton: The Story of Her Life.* New York: Dodd, Mead, 1916.

Will, George. "The Lessons of the Somme: July 1, 1916." Selected newspapers, July 1, 1986.

Winder, Richard B. *Saudi Arabia in the Nineteenth Century.* New York: St. Martin's Press, 1965.

Wright, Robin. *Sacred Rage: The Wrath of Militant Islam.* New York: Simon & Schuster, 1985.

Zinsser, William K. "In Search of Lawrence of Arabia." *Esquire* (June 1961), pp. 101–104.

Zweig, Paul. *The Adventurer.* New York: Basic Books, 1974.

INDEX